Exploring England's Heritage

LONDON

Elain Harwood and Andrew Saint

Published in association with

English ☷ Heritage

London: HMSO

Elain Harwood and **Andrew Saint** are
historians with the London Division of
English Heritage, and members of the
Victorian Society's buildings committee.
Andrew Saint is also the author of
Richard Norman Shaw (1976), *The
Image of the Architect* (1983) and
Towards a Social Architecture (1987); as
well as the editor of *Politics and the
People of London* (1990), a collection of
essays on the work of the London
County Council.

© Elain Harwood and Andrew Saint 1991
First published 1991
ISBN 0 11 300032 4

British Library Cataloguing in Publication Data
A CIP catalogue record for this book
is available from the British Library

The following abbreviations appear in
captions to illustrations, as
acknowledgement of copyright:

AA	Architectural Association
AP	Architectural Press
BL	British Library
CI	Courtauld Institute
CL	*Country Life*
EH	English Heritage
GLRO	Greater London Record Office
NT	National Trust
PSA	Property Services Agency
RCHME	Royal Commission on the Historical Monuments of England
RIBA	Royal Institute of British Architects
V&A	Victoria & Albert Museum
WI	Warburg Institute

*Front cover: Westminster Bridge, the Houses
of Parliament and Westminster Abbey seen
from the river*, 1872 (detail), by John
Anderson. © Museum of London
Back cover: Trellick Tower, Golborne Road.
Photo: Nigel Corrie, EH.

HMSO publications are available from:

HMSO Publications Centre
(Mail and telephone orders only)
PO Box 276, London, SW8 5DT
Telephone orders 071-873 9090
General enquiries 071-873 0011
(queuing system in operation for both
numbers)

HMSO Bookshops
49 High Holborn, London, WC1V 6HB
071-873 0011 (counter service only)
258 Broad Street, Birmingham, B1 2HE
021-643 3740
Southey House, 33 Wine Street, Bristol,
BS1 2BQ
0272-264306
9–21 Princess Street, Manchester, M60 8AS
061-834 7201
80 Chichester Street, Belfast, BT1 4JY
0232-238451
71 Lothian Road, Edinburgh, EH3 9AZ
031-228 4181

HMSO's Accredited Agents
(see Yellow Pages)

and through good booksellers

Printed in the UK for HMSO
Dd 294205   C10'   11/91

Contents

Foreword

Today as midsummer approaches, Oxford is crammed with tourists. The roads near my office are choked with open-topped buses, their multilingual commentaries extolling the virtues of the city, while the pavements are impassable with crocodiles of visitors, eyes glued on the coloured umbrellas of determined guides. Dons wearing full academic dress attempt to make their way to and from the Examination Schools, to the delight of foreign photographers, and might as well be extras employed by the Tourist Board.

Oxford, Stratford-on-Avon and London together make up the golden triangle – golden, that is, to the tour operators – and millions of tourists are led through their crowded streets each year. The great majority of those who visit Oxford come for only a few hours, then move on to Stratford to stay overnight before returning to familiar London. It is London that takes the brunt. Westminster Abbey will be host to over 3 million, more than 2 million will visit the Tower of London, and then of course there are the museums and art galleries welcoming their annual tidal wave. Tourism, as governments are pleased to remind us, is one of Britain's biggest industries.

Looking at the tired, bewildered faces of the tourists off-loaded and scooped up again outside Oxford's St Giles, I long to grab them and say, 'It's all right – this is *not* what it's about. England is a beautiful, gentle country full of fascinating corners, breathtaking sights – an eclectic mix of insurpassable quality. All you need is someone with vision to show you how to start looking.'

Well, people with vision, as well as the knowledge of our cultural heritage and the ability to communicate, are not in ample supply, but the members of the team assembled to write the eleven volumes of *Exploring England's Heritage* share these qualities in abundance. Each author has a detailed and expert involvement, not only with the region they are writing about, but also with the buildings, the earthworks, the streets and the landscapes they have chosen to introduce us to. These guides are no mere compilations of well-worn facts, but original accounts coloured by the enthusiasm of people who know what makes a particular site so special.

Each volume introduces more than 100 places. Some are well known (who would dare to omit Stonehenge or Hadrian's Wall?); others are small-scale and obscure but no less interesting for that. We are led down alley-ways to admire hidden gems of architecture, into churchyards to search for inscribed stones and along canals to wonder at the skills of our early engineers. And of course there are the castles, the great houses and their gardens and the churches and cathedrals that give England its very particular character.

Exploring England's Heritage does not swamp you in facts. What each author does is to say, 'Let me show you something you might not have seen and tell you why I find it so particularly interesting.' What more could the discerning traveller want?

Barry Cunliffe

Preface

This is a new kind of architectural guidebook to London. It is arranged not by district, period, or style, but by type of building. We have made a personal selection of just over two hundred outstanding or engaging buildings in both Inner and Outer London of all scales and dates and kinds, ranging from the Houses of Parliament to a Dalston eel, pie and mash shop. We have then distributed them among seventeen separate headings, each prefaced by a short essay.

Diversity is the keynote of London's life and culture. Our hope is that readers will be stimulated to look at the miraculous diversity of its fabric afresh, from the standpoint of history and urban life as well as of architecture. We have chosen buildings, groups of buildings and buildings in the landscape (ranging from the square to the planned estate, park, cemetery or suburb), which we feel have enriched the city by their evolving presence. Many books, above all the incomparable London volumes of *The Buildings of England*, instituted by Sir Nikolaus Pevsner and revised by Bridget Cherry, now give minute information about the capital's architecture and architects. What sometimes gets lost is interpretation. In each of our short entries we attempt an interpretation of the building or buildings – a way of thinking or at least of seeing – that is personal, yet based on accurate history. The user is free to think and see differently. So long as he or she has engaged with the architecture, we will have fulfilled our aim.

Our grouping of buildings by type and use raises many questions about tradition and context in London's history and architecture. We answer these as best we can in the short introductions to each section. These introductions will tantalise as much as they satisfy, but we think the effort worth making. To understand and enjoy a building, it helps to think about why it takes the form it does and what it can be compared with. Sometimes a building type is familiar. Most readers will have a grasp of what is special about the London terrace house, or how a Georgian church is likely to be arranged. But few will be so clear on the way in which factories or offices evolved in London. By juxtaposing the general with the particular, we hope that the one will illuminate the other.

Often, a building belongs in more than one of our seventeen categories, or crosses a borderline between two of them. In such cases, we have had to make a choice. Crosby Hall, for example, was a City merchant's house which became a warehouse, then an early restaurant, before it was shifted to Chelsea to cheer up a university hall of residence. This qualifies it for a place in perhaps six of our sections; we have chosen 'Schools and Colleges' in order to illustrate our particular view of the building (p. 165). The Charterhouse (pp. 150–1) has a history almost as chequered. We have tried to apply common sense together with a measure of deliberate interpretation. There remain difficulties. Is a pub a place of entertainment, or merely somewhere to drink in? Reductively, we opted for the second category. Should St Pancras Station be separated from the hotel in front of it? We decided not. Is the Temple a seat of education, a professional institution or, again, just a place for eating and drinking? Here we respected the dignified self-image of the legal profession. Cross-references are provided to ease these problems. Now and then, we use an entry to discuss a pair or even a batch of buildings of the same type, for example, board schools (p. 164). Again, the principle is that one thing helps to understand another. Urban architecture should not be thought of as a set of monuments in isolation.

This is a book chiefly to read and think about in the leisure of the home or the hotel. But for the reader who wants to use it 'on the ground', maps and map references are provided to locate each entry, together with a full address, the name of the borough in which it is to be found and an indication of how to get there via the nearest station on the London underground, British Rail or Docklands Light Railway. Bus numbers are not given, on the grounds that the services have changed too often in recent years for any information given here to be reliable for long. We assume that the architectural tourist in London comes equipped with two valuable commodities: a full 'A-Z' or other street guide to Greater London in his or her pocket, and an English-speaking tongue in his or her head. With enterprise and energy, even the most distant of our entries can be reached from Charing Cross in less than an hour.

Accessibility is a complex matter. Most buildings in this book can be seen readily enough from the street. Many are open by virtue of use, some (railway stations) for most of the time, others (churches and museums) at stated times. Others again are specifically open for public view, either regularly or by appointment. Where we felt an option was available, we selected the building more regularly open to the public; hence, for instance, the inclusion of Apsley House rather than Lancaster House. But some buildings never open were too special to omit. Many entries are accompanied by an access code, giving the reader an indication of how easy it is to see more than the building's exterior:

A Buildings regularly accessible, with opening hours widely advertised.

B Buildings with irregular opening hours, or open by appointment.

C Buildings open by virtue of their use.

The omission of a code does not imply that there is not an interior worth seeing, should an opportunity arise. In some cases, particularly where opening hours are spasmodic or an appointment needs to be made in order to see the interior, we have tried to give extra guidance. But we do not give opening hours because they change too often. Another problem peculiar to London is the frequency of changes in use or ownership of many of its most interesting buildings.

For those with a particular interest in country houses and palaces, reference to one of the annual guides commonly available from bookstalls is essential. Weekday lunchtimes are the best occasion to tour churches in the West End and especially the City. Residents or those with more time in London may find it profitable to join a local society or one of the national amenity groups with special concern for historic buildings. The Georgian Group, the Victorian Society and the Thirties Society all have regular programmes which include visits to London's more unusual and inaccessible buildings.

For reasons of space, this book has to be a guide about buildings and their environment, not their contents. So we have taken an exclusively architectural line about interiors, mentioning fixtures and interior decoration in the broader sense, but not furnishings or paintings. The splendid collections of Ham, Hampton Court, Kensington Palace and Kenwood, for instance, as well as those of the gallery and museum buildings covered, receive regrettably short shrift.

Our selection of buildings, we emphasise, is a personal one. Limiting the choice to some two hundred has been very hard. We have included some 'minor' buildings, in other words buildings of lesser purely architectural significance, and left out some 'major' ones which we felt lacked 'character' or some other pleasurable quality. The expert will quickly detect omissions, the only apology for which can be the fabulous wealth of London's architecture. Many of our less familiar choices are there simply because we felt they ought to be better known or understood, not because they are 'minor' at all. Though the great majority of our individual buildings enjoy statutory protection, several are not 'listed', while a few at the time of writing face the prospect of major alteration or even, like Greenwich and Bankside Power Stations, total demolition. We have tried to keep a balance between the likely interests of the tourist, the historian, the conservationist and the architect. If there is a bias towards the 19th and 20th centuries, that reflects not only our enthusiasms but also the proportion of the London building stock that belongs to these centuries. That, too, is why we have come down to the present day in our choices.

Elain Harwood
Andrew Saint

Acknowledgements

Of the debts we have incurred in writing this guide, the greatest is to our colleagues, past and present, in the Historians' Section of the London Division of English Heritage, formerly the Historic Buildings Division of the Greater London Council. This book embodies a tithe of the expertise accumulated by that team in over twenty years' applied research on London's architecture. A high proportion of the buildings chosen have at some stage passed through the hands of the 'London Historians' as cases – not out of the mere desire for knowledge, but because there was some practical problem about the building and its future which could only be tackled and solved by first elucidating its past. We have freely and profitably plundered the files created by these cases. We are also grateful to other colleagues in English Heritage for help and support, above all to Nigel Corrie of the Photographic Unit for his patient and enthusiastic contribution to the illustrations. We are indebted to him for over one quarter of the illustrations, specially taken for this book. We would also like to thank all those who gave us special access to their buildings in the course of our research, and to Maureen Harwood who helped to assemble the final text.

Places of Worship

London has no special international reputation for its churches. Great trading cities encourage neither piety nor a settled, parochial way of life. Metropolitan church-going has lagged behind attendance in the provinces for as long as figures have been known. Yet cultures consistently pour their aspirations and their genius into religious art, and London is no exception. That is why places of worship come first in this book, and why more churches and chapels are included than any other building type. You may or may not enjoy church-crawling, but you cannot know London's architecture properly without knowing its religious dimension. For in this seemingly profane city the number, the variety of denomination, type and style, and the richness of its places of worship cannot fail to astound.

Medieval London, indeed, could boast proportionately more parish churches than any other great European city – more than a hundred by the 15th century. They reflected the persistent localism of London life. They were not for the most part St Bartholomew the Greats. Many came nearer to the scale of little St Ethelburga's, Bishopsgate: without tower, without visible facades, without significant enrichment. Fire, bombing and the exodus of population have put paid to most of them. Yet the proximity of surviving City churches to one another is still astonishing.

The impact of the Reformation caused most of London's great monastic buildings to be destroyed, most of its parish churches to be pillaged. The reformed Church of England at first adopted an indifferent policy towards new places of worship. For over a century little concerted church-building took place, a small blip in the 1630s apart. Anglican churches in London were built in spasms: the first forced upon the city by the Great Fire of 1666, the second a short but glorious, government-inspired campaign decreed by the Fifty New Churches Act of 1711

due to a gross lack of suburban accommodation. This was followed, after a dribble of privately financed chapels and churches, by the copious products of the post-Waterloo era – the last government-funded campaign of English church-building.

With official religious tolerance from the 1820s onwards came a reversion to private enterprise and a proliferation of churches. It was based not just on intense competition between the different confessions and within the Anglican church itself, but also on an acceptance of the parochial system by almost all denominations, for social and religious reasons alike. People might travel long distances to work, yet every district, rich or poor, had to have its accessible churches and chapels: High Anglican, Low Anglican, Baptist, Presbyterian and so on. Only smaller sects like the Methodists (never very successful in London) and the Jews (always factious) ever broke much from the parochial system.

By 1890 the attempt to civilise the 'great wen' through organised religion had run out of steam, leaving many new urban places of worship under-embellished, under-endowed and under-attended, with consequences that the London clergy are still reaping.. In the new suburbs, though the will to build worthy churches lasted till the Second World War, there was rarely enough money to provide more than a bare hulk.

The churches of London are a prime source for the study of that elusive phenomenon, Anglicanism. From the time that Sir Christopher Wren shadow-boxed with the Dean and Chapter of St Paul's over the right shape for the world's first new-built Protestant cathedral, there has rarely been agreement about what an Anglican church should look like or how it should be arranged. So London's churches reflect not just many denominations but many Anglicanisms. In planning terms, their history boils down to a dialectic between the priestly and the civic ideal

Coronation of Elizabeth II in Westminster Abbey, 1953. STAMP PRESS AGENCY

1

of religion, between the altar and the pulpit, or between the orientated and the square model of box.

The pre-Reformation belief in a distinguishable nave, chancel, sanctuary and pre-eminent altar was confirmed by William Laud's St Katharine Cree in the 1630s and respected by Wren's team in the post-fire rebuilding of the City churches. It survived the secularising 18th century to burst out anew with the Oxford Movement. In between come some tentative experiments with auditorial form. Three of the Wren, Hawksmoor and Archer churches included below (St James Garlickhythe, Christ Church Spitalfields and St Paul's, Deptford) make some play with a cross-axis as well as a long one. In most Georgian churches the building turns into a galleried box with an apologetic bit added on the end for a chancel (later often extended). Low Anglican churches of the Victorian period, dependent still upon preaching and pew rents for their congregations, go through a new series of contortions to blend auditorial form and visibility with the separation of parts insisted upon by ecclesiology. Queer St Martin's, Gospel Oak is an excellent example of this. Only outside the Church of England does the auditorium find free play, at Islington's Union Chapel, for instance, or Methodist Central Hall. But in the end, with the desperate post-war search for Anglican congregations and community in London, the auditorium comes back in cosier guise – as at St Paul's, Bow Common.

London's history of religious toleration is a chequered one. The first non-Anglican place of worship we select, Bevis Marks Synagogue of 1700, stands for a guarded acceptance of Jews after centuries of intolerance. But for its fittings, it could well be an early non-conformist chapel. Caution and a lack of external show typify the architecture of newly tolerated sects. It was to be nearly a hundred years after Bevis Marks before Catholics, for instance, dared to build openly, and not till some years after formal emancipation in 1828 did they do so distinctively. The great Catholic churches included here, Brompton Oratory and Westminster Cathedral,

date from the later Victorian period and acquired much of their embellishment only after 1900. Once London's Catholics started to build seriously, they did so with as much confidence as Anglicans. It would not be hard to make a selection of thirty noble Catholic churches in London alone, and another thirty contributed by lesser sects – Catholic Apostolic, Christian Scientist, French Protestant, Agapemonite, and so on.

Status and site determine the architecture of a church every bit as much as liturgy, in some respects more so. For all their differences of date, style, function and tradition, the two great Catholic and Anglican churches at Westminster have more in common than they do with the parish church of a former Middlesex village. More than a hundred one-time village churches now come within the London area, but most have been over-restored. If you are looking for village churches, you will do better outside Greater London. We have included just one picturesque example: box-pewed Petersham. Most of the churches and chapels below were built for urban and suburban settings.

The setting of London's urban churches is an under-studied subject. Most ancient City churches were hemmed in. Many had only one visible front and a tower, or not even that. Even such an open-seeming church as St Helen's, Bishopsgate was once much less open to view. In these conditions everything depends on the interior, and the way it is lit. It is always worth savouring the way in which the site and the limited options for lighting determine the architecture of the Wren City churches, for instance. The cramped, inner-city site and what can be made of it never fail to stimulate the better church architects. This contrast between tight exterior and the space, height and glory carved out within it is paramount, for instance, at Butterfield's All Saints', Margaret Street, or at James Brooks's St Columba's, Haggerston.

In reaction to this, the 1711 churches were built with churchyards and fine, visible architecture all round. They set an ideal for the suburban London church which lasted for a

century and a half, their scale, style and stonework in contrast to the stock brick houses all around. To build a Georgian church or chapel in brick, as was often enough done, was tantamount to admitting it was not a major building. Inigo Jones had signalled exactly that with his St Paul's, Covent Garden. In doing likewise at St John-at-Hackney, James Spiller was no doubt reluctant; when the opportunity came to add a tower, it was done in stone. In due course the style became Gothic, not Classic, and the stone became Kentish rag or Bath instead of Portland, while the surrounding houses slipped into stucco. But the ideal of contrasting material remained in most Victorian churches built to go with estate development. Only in the 1860s did a belief in the inherent nobility of brickwork, pioneered at All Saints', Margaret Street, begin to penetrate the middle-class suburb. Norman Shaw's St Michael's, Bedford Park (pp. 113–15) is a good early example of a church built to blend in, not contrast with, its surroundings. Most architects from then until the 1930s accepted brick as the natural material for a London church. With the facing of Westminster Cathedral in that material, brick was deemed dignified enough for anything.

Fine church architecture costs money – which, taken as a whole, London has never lacked. Much of the glory of its churches stems from the expenditure lavished upon them. The English are not always meaner than other nations; the extravagance of Henry III's Westminster Abbey makes most French cathedrals look bare. Not only the Abbey, but the lesser churches of London too were packed with costly monuments, as St Helen's Bishopsgate reminds us. If the Reformation plus the puritan temper of 17th-century London put a check upon the embellishment of religious buildings, it was a temporary one. What do most people enjoy about the Wren City churches? Not the arrangement of space and the manipulation of the orders, but the quaint, workmanlike craftsmanship of their pulpits, testers, reredoses, fonts, coats-of-arms and organs. The spirit of Restoration religion and society seems better incarnated in these accoutrements than in the actual architecture. Fittings, too, are what turn the plain box of Bevis Marks Synagogue into a theatre redolent of Sephardic observances.

The 1711 churches by Hawksmoor and others were very costly affairs – which was why in the end there were few of them. This time, the money went on the architecture, not extravagant fittings. They cost so much that the tower usually had to be delayed – a common enough circumstance in church-building. The wonder is that those undertaken were all finished. But the State learnt its lesson. When it again felt impelled to involve itself in church-building, in 1818, its subsidies were stingier and the architectural quality of the churches fell. The finest London churches of that era were those in which parochial dignity and identity were at stake, and the parish authorities were prepared to match the government subsidy, as at New St Pancras Church.

Thereafter, the Victorians had to dig into their own pockets. As always with private enterprise, where it worked it was marvellous, but the results were profoundly uneven. The richer Victorian church interiors depended either on patronage (as at All Saints', Margaret Street and St James the Less) or on a charismatic clergyman nagging his middle-class congregation to give their money and sometimes their skills to an intensive, short-lived campaign of embellishment. That is what St Cuthbert's, Philbeach Gardens is all about and why, though its architecture is no finer than that of perhaps fifty other Victorian churches in London, it is included in our selection. By contrast, the patient, Catholic tradition of adornment over the centuries, adopted at Westminster Cathedral and to some extent at the Brompton Oratory, has never found favour in London's Anglican churches. But the appeal of the unadorned church, represented here by Holy Redeemer, Clerkenwell, St Saviour's, Eltham and St Paul's, Bow Common, has much to be said for it too. For when a church is cheap or bare, nothing can disguise the underlying quality of its architecture.

St Bartholomew the Great. West front. RCHME

1

St Bartholomew the Great
West Smithfield, City of London

2/J3   Underground to Barbican or St Paul's

[C]

By virtue of its antiquity, size and grandeur, St Bartholomew the Great is the senior parish church of the City. Having escaped the Great Fire of 1666, it testifies to the splendour of medieval churches which London might boast today but for that fell event. Even so, it is only a fragment of what was here before the Reformation.

The story of St Bartholomew's foundation is simple in outline but obscure in detail. In Norman times Smithfield was a seedy, open, suburban district of London used for horse-trading. Rahere, Henry I's 'court jester', having taken religious vows, founded a

hospital at Smithfield in thanksgiving for recovery from malaria. This became St Bartholomew's Hospital, still there on the opposite side of Little Britain, with a Georgian quadrangle by Gibbs and a pretty entrance gate of 1702. To go with his hospital, Rahere established a priory of Augustinian canons. The knightly monument to the founder which survives in the church today is late medieval, not Norman, so his original status is hard to assess.

What we have today are the choir and ambulatory of the priory church finished in the 1120s, together with later transepts, an eastern Lady Chapel and southern cloister of early 15th-century date, a tower of the 1620s and an internal arrangement deriving from a patient, creative restoration of the 1880s and 1890s masterminded by Aston Webb. (A nicely lettered tablet in the porch records the chronology of the works then carried out to bring the church back into condition.) The nave of the church was demolished following

St Bartholomew the Great. Nave and ambulatory. GLRO

the Dissolution of the Monasteries, when speculators cashed in on the religious houses' valuable city properties. Tudor development was squeezed in all over the priory site. St Bartholomew's is now approached from under a pretty timber-framed gatehouse which was one fruit of this campaign. It was built in 1595 by a parishioner who almost certainly reused wood from the church nave. Though heavily restored, it is one of the oldest surviving timber fronts in central London. Below it the arch of the gateway itself is the chief remnant of the 13th-century nave, which faced the open space of Smithfield Market.

The exterior of St Bartholomew's is a British jumble. It is largely in a flint and chequerboard style of Gothic which we associate today with East Anglia and Kent but was once common in London. Much of it has to do with Aston Webb, who rebuilt the transepts, supplied the west porch in a late Perpendicular style and heavily restored the outlying Lady Chapel. The plain brick tower and wooden lantern make a comforting contrast. The bowed clerestory added to the choir in the 15th century is a fine feature but can be seen from few angles. There is also the remnant of a cloister.

Inside, the sense of muddle dissolves in face of the Norman austerity of the choir with its ponderous piers, thickly moulded capitals and four-light

openings to the gallery. The walls have a patched, almost mouldy feeling that imparts humility to the august architecture. The squeezed-up east end is to a degree a scholarly reinvention of Webb's. The later, lighter clerestory affords relief, as does a sweet internal oriel put in on the south side at gallery level to make an oratory for one of the last priors before the Dissolution. The ambulatory is vaulted, as the choir would once have been. Of its radiating chapels there is one vestigial survivor. The Lady Chapel beyond was rescued from industrial use in 1897 by Aston Webb, who was obliged to recreate it fairly completely.

2

Westminster Abbey
Broad Sanctuary, Westminster

2/G6   Underground to Westminster or St James's Park

[C]

What could be more English than the setting of Westminster Abbey? No place is more central to London's or the nation's history, no building a nobler embodiment of English medieval architecture and kingship. Yet the Abbey sits off-stage from the grand theatre of Westminster, all but outside Parliament Square and at an angle to the axis of the route through to Victoria Station. There is no high central tower to inspire, while the prominent northern transept is in great measure a shaky recreation of 1875–92. Moving round to the west facade, which ought to be the climax of the exterior, you find two cheerful but scarcely sublime towers of 1735–45 by Nicholas Hawksmoor, a banal little bookshop in the Gothick Georgian taste of 1954–6, and an undefined space in front at the side of the road.

The best thing to do is go inside and take stock. Choose, if you can, an unpopular hour, sit first in the nave and look. The arcades and vaults drive forward for twelve glorious bays before they encounter the crossing and march on to the apse. Here at last is architecture, and of a rare harmony and richness. What will immediately strike the British visitor is the height of the vault (104 ft), its consistency, the

Westminster Abbey, from Dean's Yard. GLRO

sharpness of the arches and the narrowness of the aisles. All these are marks of the French methodology of Gothic. What by contrast should leave a Frenchman agape is the complexity of the rib-mouldings, the grave colour of the costly Purbeck marble shafts and capitals, and the all-over diapering of flat surfaces in the nave's eastern portion – patterning once gaily, even gaudily coloured like the bosses far above. These are signs of native English enrichment and pride. French rationality elaborated by English romanticism: this is what the spirit of the Abbey is about.

The first abbey at Westminster was probably 7th-century in foundation, corresponding with the Saxon shift of gravity west of London's walled centre. Edward the Confessor, resident nearby, began to rebuild the church on an enlarged scale in the Norman style, but died before finishing it and was buried here in 1065. A year later, William I confirmed its royal status by taking the Crown at Westminster and helping the monks to complete the building. But not until the mid-13th century did the Abbey assume its present size. That great builder Henry III, pious, absolutist and supranationalist, wanted a symbol to rival the growing power and cultural achievements of France's Capetian kings. Under the guise of venerating Edward the Confessor, he set about a lavish reconstruction which would, in Christopher Wilson's words, 'combine in a single building the functions of Reims, St-Denis and the Sainte-Chapelle' – coronation church, burial church and private chapel. Rheims was the main model, as the name of the royal architect Henry of Reyns (thought now to be an Englishman who had worked at Rheims rather than a Frenchman) attests. But Westminster is too sophisticated to have a single exemplar. Amiens and the Sainte Chapelle, the latter built just as the Abbey was getting under way, were also taken into account. King and architect must have consciously decided to marry the best of French and English Gothic traditions. Building proceeded from east to west from 1245 under Henry of Reyns and his successors. It had got five bays into the nave, where the diapering ends and the gilded screen

Westminster Abbey. Detail of cloister. GLRO

(mostly now 18th- and 19th-century) interposes, when the king died in 1272. The nave was not taken up again for a century when, unusually for England, the old style was adhered to, slightly simplified. It ground slowly westwards, but the west front was still unfinished at the Reformation. Wren's successors in the Office of Works were left to clean up and finish off the outside after two centuries' delay and much decay of the original Reigate stone – a hapless choice of material. The rest of the story is mostly about restoration, embellishment and monuments – with one great exception, Henry VII's Chapel at the east end.

Before venturing further east, it is worth going out to the cloister. This runs the gamut from the reign of Henry III to that of Edward III and has what may be very early reticulated tracery (of c.1300) at the south end of the east walk. From the south walk you can look back and get a dramatic view of the Gothic wall, window and buttress system, here seemingly divided into four vertical layers – cloister, aisle, tribune and clerestory – because of the way cloister engages with aisle. The hefty, plainish buttresses, whence three 'flyers' spring to the aisle, two to the nave above, are of a complexity unparalleled in British architecture. Here, and in the queer convex-sided triangles lighting the tribune, the church seems slavishly French. But turn off the east cloister,

walk into the eight-sided chapter house, and you stumble upon a manifestation of Gothic uniquely English in type, though one of the earliest portions of Henry III's abbey. Westminster was never a cathedral and so had no diocesan canons. But its royal status meant it needed an imposing meeting place; indeed the King's Great Council met here for more than a century. Beverley and Lincoln were the models, but the Abbey's chapter house outdoes them in its lucid expression of the glass cage, the way in which the thin, central Purbeck pillar soars up and spreads out into a great vaulted umbrella, and the survival of its encaustic tiling and medieval painting. Much of the chapter house we owe to that abused restorer, Sir Gilbert Scott. He found it in 1866 with the vault gone, the entrance arch fragmentary and the exterior in tatters. Even medievalists have something to say for the care with which he undertook its reparation.

To enter the transepts, chancel and ambulatory you must pay – except on a Wednesday evening. Of the transepts, broader and longer than in any French cathedral, the better preserved is the narrower southern one, which still has its original rose and some exquisite medieval sculpture on the end wall. The crossing is where the public element of coronations takes place and so is like a theatre, visible from galleries, transepts, choir and sanctuary, though hidden from the common people herded in the nave. As in so many great churches, the choir area bites into the nave; its stalls (1848) are the work of Edward Blore, first of the respectful Victorian restorers, repairing Georgian outrage. On the other side of the crossing, the sanctuary boasts the most exotic of the Abbey's treasures, the Cosmati cosmographical pavement in mosaic, dated 1268. Medieval sedilia, altar screen and painted retable all miraculously survive, though the screen has a mosaic altarpiece by Scott and Clayton set in it. Behind the high altar, the Cosmati work carries on more simply on the floor of the Confessor's Chapel (now covered) and on the base of Henry III's tomb. Here was the centre of medieval veneration.

When the visitor reaches this point it becomes impossible to ignore the church's wealth of tombs. The Abbey is a national sculpture gallery, and its memorials must mostly be left aside here. Pamela Tudor-Craig's chapters in the New Bell's Cathedral Guide to Westminster Abbey (1986) give an excellent account of the monuments and furnishings, should the reader want more. Those who find the monuments an obstacle to liturgy or architecture may care to remember that the Abbey was conceived of as a shrine, a burial place and a place of sightseeing or pilgrimage. The great Gothic church was a framework within which all kinds of impediments to clarity were admitted. All that has happened since the Reformation is that the Catholic stress on proximity to Edward the Confessor's shrine has been dissipated, so that national worthies (and un-worthies) are now dotted about the Abbey without regard for status. Fortunately the clustering-up of the royal tombs close to England's only canonized king safeguards the original effect. It would be absurd not to pluck out the plums, seven bronze effigies of outstanding international quality and preciousness: Henry III by William Torel (1291); Eleanor of Castile, of the same date and by the same hand; Richard II and Anne of Bohemia, by Nicholas Broker and Godfrey Prest (c.1395); and, in Henry VII's Chapel, the two tombs by Pietro Torrigiano, to Lady Margaret Beaufort (c.1510) and to her son and daughter-in-law, Henry VII and Elizabeth of York (c.1512–18).

The four radiating chapels of the apse originally flanked a Lady Chapel, whose commencement by the monks in about 1220 seems to have spurred Henry III to lay his great plans for rebuilding. Between 1503 and 1512 it was replaced by the consummate achievement of Late Perpendicular architecture, Henry VII's Chapel. That monarch intended it to enshrine his predecessor Henry VI, and thus legitimize his own questionable title to kingship. Today it seems a sturdy affirmation of the new dynasty's confidence – an abbey in early-Tudor miniature, with its own tiny chapels clustering round a fan vault of unique

structure and ornateness. Surely its architect, probably Robert Janyns, looked at the glass cage and ponderous buttressing of the nearby chapter house and determined to outdo them? There is something provocative about the vault, as though Janyns wanted the beholder to enquire how the great pendants can possibly hold up. To be told that they depend upon the threading of masonry behind and above the barely visible transverse arches makes the effect no less breathtaking. Outside, the sense of commentary upon the rest of the abbey is, if anything, more marked. The

restless, corrugated wall-and-window surface, refusing any truck with plainness or flatness, the proud ogee capping to the high buttresses and the almost comical wheel-shapes sliding down the flyers proclaim a festive, new phase of Gothic creativity and English culture under the Tudors. How profound an influence Henry VII's Chapel had upon English architecture may be judged by casting a glance across the road where the Palace of Westminster, more than three centuries later, takes its motifs as a magnificent point of departure.

Southwark Cathedral. East end and central tower. RCHME

3

Southwark Cathedral
London Bridge Approach, Southwark

2/K5   Underground to London Bridge

[C]

The 19th century assaulted the church of St Mary Overie, as Southwark Cathedral then was, with an awesome battery of destructiveness. First the approaches to the new London Bridge hacked off a fine chapel foolish enough to project too far to the east, in 1830. Nasty rebuilding of the ruinous nave and heavy restoration of the transepts ensued. The Victorian muddle of potato market to the south and grim Thames-side warehouses to the north and west compounded the church's problems. Then in an environmental *coup de grâce*, the railway smashed past the tower in the 1860s, covering the building with soot and making the anguish of rolling stock grinding over Borough Junction the counterpoint of sacred liturgy and song. Sir Arthur Blomfield tried to undo the damage by reconstructing the nave again in the 1890s. In 1905 St Mary's was given cathedral status in compensation for its injuries. But as it is at the northern extremity of its diocese, local clergy tend still to curse its position.

And yet the medieval church survives with dignity down in its odd, inaccessible hollow. Those with a taste for the harsher side of the urban aesthetic may even regret the sprucing-up that has now taken place around it, chiefly to the north, where a new chapter house and other buildings have clawed back space long lost to commerce and opened the church up towards the river.

The church started out as a priory of Augustinian canons which, by common English practice, acquired its own parish. The site, close to London's only bridgehead, was superb. The priory's heyday seems to have been the 13th century, when St Mary Overie was reconstructed to cruciform plan following a bad fire of *c*.1212. The choir

Southwark Cathedral. Austin monument by Nicholas Stone. GLRO

and retrochoir are the main remnants of this church, and are in their fragmentary way as remarkable as anything Gothic left in London. The choir consists of arcade, triforium and clerestory and shows touches of French taste, notably the way that the colonnettes carrying the ribs of the vaults come down to the ground and unite with the piers of the arcade. The retrochoir, on the other hand, is utterly English: a low, squared-off space of twelve ribbed bays terminating the east end abruptly. Is it contemporary with the choir, as Pevsner believes, or earlier, following straight on from the date of

the fire? Most of what one sees of these parts from the outside are in flint and of the 19th century, but for a change the restorer (George Gwilt) wrought his work respectfully here. The crossing tower and south transept are 14th-century ashlarwork (Henry Yevele's hand is suspected in the tower), while the north transept is vestigially earlier. Last of the major pre-Reformation features is the high stone screen separating choir and retrochoir, given by Bishop Fox early in Henry VIII's reign but with figures and features almost all restored. The rest of the fabric derives largely from the respectable interventions of Sir Arthur Blomfield and his sons.

The solution of recent administrations to Southwark Cathedral's scruffy image problem, egged on by the architect George Pace, has been to brighten up the interior with splodges of colour. Conspicuous among the features to have been given the treatment is a good set of monuments. These commemorate a ragbag of the famous, notorious (the quack physician Lockyer) and obscure. John Gower, contemporary of Chaucer and author of the rarely read *Confessio Amantis*, has become especially gaudy. So has the great Jacobean divine Lancelot Andrewes, last of the bishops of Winchester to live locally and enjoy a special relationship with the church. He lies beneath a canopy which turns out to be a clever 20th-century sham by Ninian Comper. The Shakespeare Memorial of 1911, described in the *Buildings of England* as of 'gelatinous brown alabaster', has defied coloration. Finer than any of these is an allegorical wall monument of 1633 by Nicholas Stone in the north transept. Among other fittings, note the font by Bodley, organ case by one of the Blomfields and tabernacle in the north transept's Harvard Chapel by A W N Pugin – a recent acquisition. Here too is perhaps the only English example of the American glass-painter John La Farge's work. But it does not show him at his best.

4

St Helen's, Bishopsgate
Great St Helen's, City of London

2/L3   Underground or British Rail to Liverpool Street

[C]

It is rare to find an English medieval church with two even naves, rarer still for one to survive in the heart of London within an ample, discernible enclave. Over and over these two distinctions, St Helen's, Bishopsgate boasts the best collection of monuments in any City church.

Like many of London's early parish churches, St Helen's was connected with a religious house. In this case the church, a 12th-century one of which fragments subsist in the main south wall, came first. Then in about 1210 the Benedictines built a convent in the grounds to its north. The shape of the conventual buildings, destroyed at the Reformation, is well established. There was a square cloister with a hall on the west which would have flanked the church and, on the east, a dorter and small chapter house. The south side consisted of a new aisle or 'nun's choir' which has survived as the north aisle of the parish church. This was made of equal length with the nave to its south and, by a curious arrangement, separated from it by some sort of arcade and a screen. The screen proved inadequate for keeping secular and religious worshippers apart. Whether for that reason or because of dilapidation, a new Perpendicular arcade was built between the two naves in about 1475 and this, much renewed in the 1630s, is what divides them today. Other 14th- and 15th-century features are a reminder of how much late Gothic work was once to be found in City churches.

But St Helen's did not get the tower which many of them acquired during this period. The square wooden bellcote perched between the naves is of late 17th-century date. Rather earlier are two remarkable doorways on the south side. The external stone frame of the main south door, dated 1633, is a *locus classicus* for the quirky, inventive style that has been clumsily dubbed 'artisan mannerism'. Of the same period are the finest of the fittings, a full-blown pulpit with sounding board, and the more modest font. Among later restorations the most important was J L Pearson's. He it was who in 1892–3 set out the chancel as it now is, with orthodox wooden screens all round, choir stalls, a reredos and a pleasing floor mixing marble and encaustic tiling.

Many of the older surviving City churches have become repositories for memorials formerly to be found in others which succumbed to demolition. Thus the most beautiful of St Helen's monuments, tucked away amidst a muddle of organs and oddments in the south-east corner, comes from St Martin Outwich. It commemorates the late 15th-century John and Mary de Oteswich, whose stylised recumbent effigies in alabaster. This is one of a set of five remarkable tombs which line up in parallel across the church close to the east wall. Next to the Oteswiches lies their contemporary Sir John Crosby, the wool merchant and builder of Crosby Hall (formerly nearby but rebuilt in 1908–10 on the Chelsea Embankment; see p. 165). Across the chancel is the large, railed-in Pickering tomb of 1574, with a recumbent military effigy under a double canopy. Round in the north aisle comes Nicholas Stone's table tomb of the delightfully named lawyer Sir Julius Caesar Adelmare (d. 1636); his death is whimsically symbolised by a document with a break in the threads linking the seal to the text. Last but not least, that great Elizabethan Sir Thomas Gresham, father of the modern City of London, is allotted a more modest table tomb near the north wall.

5

St Katharine Cree
Leadenhall St, City of London

2/L4   Underground to Aldgate

[C]

The lacuna in English church-building between the Dissolution of the Monasteries and the Restoration can be exaggerated. On the outskirts of London alone, churches were built or rebuilt in the 1620s and 1630s at Charlton, Malden, Morden and Stanmore. Inner London would have more to show – Inigo Jones's recasing of St Paul's Cathedral, for instance – were it not for the Great Fire. Happily St Katharine Cree stood far enough east. It escaped devastation in both 1666 and 1940–1 to bear intriguing witness to the mood of Anglican church-building and fitting during the brief 'Laudian' period.

The church had been a medieval one. It originated as an adjunct of one of

St Helen's Bishopsgate. Tomb of John de Oteswich from south chapel. EH

London's priories of Augustinian canons, Holy Trinity, Aldgate. The tower, though scraped of its Gothic features and topped by a trim wooden cupola of 1776, is of late pre-Reformation date, 1504. So it escaped the rebuilding of the dilapidated 14th-century church that took place in 1628–30. This seems to have had much to do with William Laud, the tactless, energetic anti-Puritan who alienated the citizenry while Bishop of London, only to make more enemies when translated by Charles I to the see of Canterbury. Laud reconsecrated St Katharine's in 1631. Its arrangement embodies his policy of cleansing and reordering churches in such a way as to emphasise the sacramental side of Anglican worship.

As far as architectural style was concerned, the Laudian movement pointed back towards the Gothic tradition. In the remote countryside 'Gothic Survival' would have been natural enough. But by the 1620s London had seen enough of the new classicism to make Gothic Revivalism a self-conscious business. So there is nothing naive about the fresh, Tuscan-looking arcade of the nave, with its Corinthian capitals carrying a

Perpendicular clerestory and pretty plaster vaulting of the lierne variety, centred on bosses with the arms of the livery companies, nor about the Catherine-wheel symbolism of the east window, with its cusped tracery within a rectangular frame. The unknown designer must have been exploring the reconciliation of religious traditions on which Laud and the High Church party were bent. The lack of a chancel arch, the clean and visible simplicity of arrangements round the altar (with the altar rail which was one of Laud's postulates) and the lightness of the church testify to a hankering for Anglican reasonableness and compromise which, alas, was far from being in the immediate religious offing.

There are few original fittings, though there is a macabre cadaver monument of 1631 over a blocked-up gateway in the burial ground behind the church. The font is of 1646, the fine organ case of the 1680s, while the pulpit and communion table are Georgian. The reredos is an importation from a demolished Wren church, St James's, Duke's Place. It is a pity that the side aisles have been boxed in for offices. This was just the kind of secularisation Laud strove to avoid.

6
St Paul's Cathedral
City of London

2/J4   Underground to St Paul's
[C]

Perhaps because there is something forced about a great classical cathedral in a commercial context, Sir Christopher Wren's masterpiece has never quite naturalised itself. Its dome has become one of London's symbols – above all through the famous, fabricated image of 1941 which purported to show it rising unimpaired against the smoky backdrop of the Blitz. But in contrast to the Wren city churches, it remains a building respected rather than loved – a monument to intellect in a setting of architectural unreason.

The site is a very ancient one. Some scholars still suspect there was a temple here, on the more westerly of the two hilltops contained within Roman London's walls. The first cathedral is supposed to have been built in 604. Old St Paul's, the predecessor of the present building, had a Norman nave, a Gothic chancel and a proto-Perpendicular chapter house. It was the sorest architectural loss in the Great Fire of London. But its fabric was in decay before the fire: its steeple had been removed, Inigo Jones had partly recased it and added a giant classical portico at the west end, and Wren (with others) had just been asked what to do about the state of the tower. Already he had in mind a cupola or dome, 'a forme of Church-building, not as yet known in England, but of wonderful grace'. Five years after the fire, in 1671, Wren started seriously to contemplate the design of the rebuilt cathedral, always with his thoughts centred on a dome. The process proved frustrating. Faced with the challenge of designing the world's first great Protestant cathedral, Wren opted for the centralised cross plan under a dome – exemplified in his 'Great Model' of 1673. But the clergy prevaricated, as clergy will. Wren was forced on liturgical grounds to go back to the drawing board and produce the feebler 'Warrant Design', with a

St Katharine Cree. RCHME

St Paul's Cathedral. EH

conventional nave and chancel. This formed the basis of the plan as built from 1675, though he transformed the elevations over the long course of building. The interior was fitted out in the late 1690s, but the dome and west towers were not added till 1704–10.

Wren had a deft feeling for urban context, which makes it a double shame that the environs of St Paul's have suffered so grievously. The surrounding architecture is not so much low in quality or wrong in style as mistakenly open and uneven in scale. The specially created post-war vista of the south transept and the open view of the east end were never intended. The high, horizontally divided Portland stone sides of the cathedral had two functions. They screened the lean-to roofs of the aisles, which were constructed in old-style Gothic fashion, and they were geared to the scale of the houses that pressed around, so that the upper half of the elevations shouldered up above the rooftops and gave the dome visible

support. This effect can still be savoured in old photographs. Wren also gave his fronts sufficient movement and sculptural detail so that they could give pleasure from close, oblique angles. Even the show facade to the west was only half revealed up Ludgate Hill. Here the centrepiece with its fluted pairs of columns (showing the influence of Mansart and Perrault) and the flagrantly baroque western towers (in which the hand of Hawksmoor is to be suspected) are unsurpassed. Less happy than its chief Bramantesque rivals in Rome and Paris is the profile of the dome itself. Might it have looked better if it had been sheathed in copper, as Wren wanted, than in the lead which the prelates preferred? But the ingenuity with which Wren combined an inner and outer dome and supported the lantern on an invisible brick cone between them is a brilliant structural stroke.

The interior is ponderous and scarcely devotional in feeling. The place to start is under the vast dome – a

reverberant, Corinthian space blurred at ground level by the system of double arches Wren employed in the corners. With the equal and opposite nave and chancel stretching either way, the residual centralism of Wren's conception is clearest here. The nave and its aisles are plain enough, having whitewashed saucer domes. The crossing and chancel have been more elaborated. Original are Jean Tijou's iron screens in front of the chancel aisles, Grinling Gibbons's choir stalls and organ case (which formerly surmounted the chancel screen but was later divided in half and set on either side over the stalls), and Thornhill's frescoes of 1715–19 on the underside of the dome. The Victorians added the controversial mosaics of the crossing and chancel, well worth study, by Alfred Stevens, Sir William Blake Richmond and others, and further fine iron screens between chancel and chancel aisles. The baldacchino, by Stephen Dykes Bower and Godfrey Allen, is post-war and equally questionable, as is the sham baroque pulpit, replacing a splendid marble affair of 1860–1 by F C Penrose (designer of the old choir school in Ave Maria Lane nearby), now relegated to the cleaned-up crypt.

The crypt indeed, glimpsed now and again deep below through pierced bronze plates in the cathedral floor, is well worth the entrance fee. Besides Penrose's pulpit, it includes a very good audio-visual presentation on the history of St Paul's, the enormous Great Model of 1673, and a plethora of worthwhile monuments and tablets. Pride of place under the crossing goes to the black marble urn that now commemorates Nelson but was made by Benedetto da Rovezzano for Cardinal Wolsey in the 1520s. But why has Gottfried Semper's bombastic funeral carriage for the Duke of Wellington, long beloved of young visitors to the crypt, been given away to the Duke's home at Stratfield Saye? Up above, among the acreage of military monuments in the frigid 'Peninsular style' that afflicted English sculpture for forty years after 1815, the lofty Wellington monument on the north side of the nave stands up to closest scrutiny. It was designed and largely made by

St Paul's Cathedral. Interior looking east. A F KERSTING

7

St James Garlickhythe
Upper Thames St, City of London

2/K4   Underground to Mansion House

[C]

The spacious feeling of this Wren church, built in 1676–83, contains just a hint of Hawksmoor to come. Its pretty steeple, added as late as 1714–17, may even have been designed by the great Hawksmoor himself.

The architecture of the Wren City churches was much influenced by the position of their sites. Drastic changes in context have occurred to almost all that survive, making their arrangement harder to understand. St James Garlickhythe was formerly hemmed in except at the west; Upper Thames Street, to the south, was only recently broadened to its present width and unpleasant character. The body of the church was therefore built of brick (now cemented over at the east end), while the more visible west end and tower were faced in Kentish ragstone. (The refacing of the upper stages of the tower in Portland stone is post-war and inauthentic; the recent facade to Upper Thames Street is even more regrettable.) Inside, the auditorium was made wide and high, with a flat ceiling over a cove, and lit from a run of upper windows. Notable is the rare string of seven windows round the east end, reduced to six in 1815 when Alexander Geddes's painting of the Ascension was installed over the altar. The effect, following the clearing-out of Victorian stained glass in an exemplary restoration completed in 1962–3, vividly conveys the blend of Italian Renaissance architecture and Dutch Protestant ethos that marked the churches rebuilt after the Great Fire. Broadly spaced columns break up the simple box into nave and passage aisles – a contrivance used to get better clerestory lighting. But the entablature above the columns is broken back in the centre of the building, allowing a suggestion of the kind of cross axis and transept to be exploited in the London

Alfred Stevens but not completed till after the sculptor's death. Its one rival in quality is John Donne's arresting, upstanding shroud by Nicholas Stone (1631), rescued from Old St Paul's and now in the south chancel aisle.

Outside again, the splendid cast-iron railings of 1714 round the north side of the churchyard are a technical curiosity. At that date elaborate casting was a new technique. The railings were made in the Weald of Kent, in the dying days of charcoal-smelting iron production there, not in the coke-smelting Midlands which were to become the centre of the English cast-iron industry.

churches built by Wren's disciples in the reign of Queen Anne.

The interior is fitted out in the homely, semi-secular spirit of the City churches. The aisles and high column bases (which would look less strange if the pews rose still to their original height) are panelled in painted deal rather than oak. Most remaining City churches have gained from the demolitions of others, and so it is that St James's has inherited the best pieces of its fine woodwork, the high pulpit with tester and the choir stalls with their tall backs, from St Michael Queenhithe. But the unusually well preserved Father Smith organ of 1697 in the west gallery has always belonged to the church. Original too are the communion table and the reredos, though the latter was cut down when the Geddes painting was put in above it.

St Mary Abchurch. East end and reredos. RCHME

8

St Mary Abchurch
Abchurch Lane, City of London

2/K4   Underground to Bank

[C]

Hitler's bombs grazed but never gravely damaged St Mary Abchurch, which is why it must come high on any list of Wren City churches to visit, for authenticity and atmosphere alike.

St Mary's was not among the churches scheduled for immediate post-fire rebuilding, and had to put up for fifteen years with a temporary structure. But in 1681 the parish supplied the Lord Mayor, Sir Patience Ward, through whose influence and an inducement to Wren of twenty guineas on the part of the Vestry matters were put on a fresh footing. By dint of pushing, shoving and further inducements at critical stages to the Surveyor-General and the workmen, the new St Mary Abchurch was finally ready in 1686. Sir Patience earned a wall

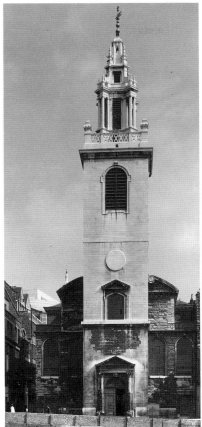

St James Garlickhythe. A F KERSTING

13

tablet in the church as his reward.

The result from the outside is a simple brick box amply lit from the south and east, with a tower and spire – once surmounted by the pelican in her piety – comfortably tucked into an angle of Sherborne Lane. The interior is simple too, at any rate in architectural form: just a square, or nearly so, with a great dish-lid of a painted dome on top, pierced by four oculi to supplement the south and east lighting. The base of the dome is ringed by a heavy cornice, beneath which come shallow plastic pendentive vaults springing from rather arbitrary Corinthian-capped corbels without pilasters against the walls. At the west end the arches descend on to proper supports so as to make room for a gallery and organ loft; only here, jiggery-pokery with the position of the tower means that one support is a proper column, the other an engaged pier. There is a homely room with a little dome of its own beneath the tower, formerly the inner porch but now used as a kitchen.

A survey of the rich, dark woodwork which is St Mary Abchurch's glory may begin with the high and narrow pierced-fronted pews which line the walls. Almost all Wren-period church seating has been cut down, with a consequent loss in the sense of tight privacy and civic pride that was so marked a feature of post-Restoration church attendance. There used even to be dog kennels in the base of some of the pews here. But that is to stress history at the expense of art, when in its reredos St Mary Abchurch boasts one of the very few authenticated pieces of carving in a City church by Grinling Gibbons. It is a huge thing with a great broken pediment in its centre, notable less as a piece of design than for the delicacy of its limewood garlands. In the centre is a gilded pelican. Almost as elaborate is the pulpit with its tester, the work of William Grey. The font too has a finely carved cover, attached by a bizarre arrangement to the underside of the gallery stairs. The organ case is one of the few features which comes from elsewhere; it is of 1717 and once belonged to All Hallows' Bread Street. Of the dome painting of the Heavenly Choir, painstakingly executed in 1708–9

by parishioner William Snow, the best that can be said is that its faded, smoky range of browns harmonises well with the woodwork.

The current condition of the various City churches has much to do not only with their fate during the Second World War but also with the variable quality of the restoration work undertaken in them thereafter. No account of St Mary Abchurch should omit reference to the exemplary restoration performed in the 1950s by Godfrey Allen, after a lifetime's experience of and love for the church architecture of Wren and his time. His main alteration was to drop the floor by more than a foot to its old level.

9

Spanish and Portuguese Synagogue, Bevis Marks
City of London

2/L3   Underground to Aldgate or Underground/British Rail to Liverpool Street

[C]

Few religious buildings in London can have changed as little as this one. There are more sumptuous and dramatic synagogue interiors of Victorian and Edwardian date in London – the New West End in St Petersburgh Place, Bayswater, the New London in Abbey Road, St John's Wood and the New Synagogue in Egerton Road, Stamford Hill are all worth visiting – but enchanting and venerable Bevis Marks must take precedence.

Toleration and freedom of worship for Jews in England goes back to a 'Humble Petition of the Hebrews at Present Residing in this citty of London', presented by Menasseh ben Israel and others to Lord Protector Cromwell in 1655. Cromwell eventually gave this small group of Spanish and Portuguese Jews, mostly merchants, a guarantee of security. Their first place of worship was in Creechurch Lane. By 1699 the congregation had sufficiently grown for it to contract with Joseph Avis to build a new synagogue in Bevis Marks nearby. Tradition has it that Avis was a Quaker

and erected the fabric at cost price. It was completed in 1701.

Historic synagogues were usually plain buildings externally, as Jews in European cities did not like to be needlessly ostentatious. Outside and in, Bevis Marks is just like a dissenting chapel of the day – square and friendly, with unpretending brick walls and a flood of light coming through two storeys of windows. The interior manages to be dignified without any show of ornament. Its arrangement was probably based on the large synagogue built in Amsterdam in 1675. There are galleries on three sides, supported on round wooden pillars which were formerly marbled. The seating is made up of prim benches, some of them original. The ark, much in the form of a Wrenian reredos and enclosed by a low railing, and the elevated reading desk at the other end of the synagogue are the points of incident. Such changes as have occurred, like the introduction of choir stalls in about 1830 and the installation of modern heating and lighting, have been delicately managed. Until 1929 the building was lit solely by the seven brass candelabra, six candlesticks in front of the ark and the various wall sconces.

Bevis Marks has a 'branch' synagogue in Maida Vale, the Spanish and Portuguese Synagogue, Lauderdale Road (Davis and Emanuel, architects). This too is a small and handsome building, though in a quite different, Byzantinising style.

10

Christ Church Spitalfields
Commercial St, Tower Hamlets

2/L3   Underground to Aldgate East or underground/British Rail to Liverpool Street

[C]

Nicholas Hawksmoor took his church-building responsibilities seriously. The six incomparable churches which he designed under the Act of 1711

Bevis Marks Synagogue, interior. RCHME

Christ Church Spitalfields. East end, with vicarage (2 Fournier Street) to left. EH

providing for new Anglican places of worship in London, far from being products of architectural whim, were geared in an exact, scholarly manner to the politics and theology of the age.

The City churches rebuilt by Wren and his team after 1666 were the fruits of the first sizeable bout of church-building in Anglican history. They provided architects and liturgists with experience, but they had to be built in a hurry on old sites and for existing congregations with their own traditions and prejudices. 1711 was different. Churches were particularly needed in the spreading East End suburbs, to combat dissent. The authors of the Act wanted conspicuous monuments upholding the civil and religious order, large churchyards for burials and enough room for baptism by total immersion, should anyone want it. The Church of England was supposed by the Tory apologists of the time to have inherited the values of the early Christian church before it had been corrupted by Romanism. Like his master Wren, Hawksmoor had a scholarly bent and was keen on the use and

reinterpretation of history. A sketch-layout for a 'Basilica after the Primitive Christians' in the East End represents an early attempt on his part to give form to these ideas. Christ Church Spitalfields and his other East End churches (St George in the East, Wapping, and St Anne's, Limehouse) are their partial embodiment.

The silk-weaving suburb of Spitalfields was prospering in the early 18th century, as the delightful houses of Fournier Street and Princelet Street in the church's shadow attest. Huguenot weavers driven out of the dominions of Louis XIV after France revoked toleration of Protestants in 1683 flocked to the district, spreading dissent. A powerful demonstration of Anglican loyalism was needed, and Hawksmoor supplied it. The body of the church was built between about 1714 and 1720, to be followed by the tower and steeple called for by the Act. But such a fantastic, imperious pile of Portland stonework as Hawksmoor raised to stop the vista down Brushfield Street can hardly have been anticipated. Pevsner was so flabbergasted by it that he calls it

a 'Baroque contraption'. Can it be doubted that by putting a Gothic spire (originally with little lucarne windows in three tiers on all four sides) on a classic body Hawksmoor wanted to symbolise the continuities in Anglican tradition? Or that by playing so forcefully with the Venetian arch in the great portico and again in the belfry stage above, he was keeping a step ahead of the increasingly influential Palladian theorists, who set much store by this feature? No less extraordinary than the flat face of the tower are the scooped-out sides of the belfry. The whole creation is the nearest that English architecture approaches to the spirit of Borromini. After this the body of the church seems quite tame, however nobly Roman. It has a series of niches along the sides with portholes above and, at the east end, a more orthodox Venetian window under a gable.

Inside, Hawksmoor had to grapple with an ambivalence in contemporary Anglicanism. He was obliged both to provide an auditorial preaching box so that as many people as possible could be near the pulpit and reading desk, and to face the church eastwards and give traditional, sacramental emphasis to the altar. As he did elsewhere, Hawksmoor resolved the problem by planning the church on intersecting axes with a centralized space in the middle. This is defined by a screen of columns on high bases – arched at the sides and so providing a hint of the traditional nave arcade, but with a flat entablature surmounted by the royal arms at the east end as a kind of ultra-classical interpretation of the chancel arch. There is a hint of early Italian Renaissance churches about the arrangement, augmented by the flat panelled ceiling of the nave. The loss of the side galleries (one day soon, let us hope, to be put back), obliteration of the north–south axis and cutting-down of fittings make it hard to imagine the church as it once was. But the fine organ case in the west gallery is redolent of former stateliness. Restored now to dual use as church and concert hall after years of neglect and near-demolition, Christ Church is today in better shape than it has been since the 18th century.

11

St Mary Woolnoth
King William St, City of London

2/K4   Underground to Bank
[C]

The tangle of streets that intersect at the heart of the City erupts in a plethora of architectural incident: the Mansion House, the Bank of England, the Royal Exchange and big banks by Edwin Lutyens and Edwin Cooper, not to mention the impending James Stirling building on the Mappin and Webb site and other clamorous contenders. With all this competition the most extraordinary building of all, St Mary Woolnoth, is in danger of being overlooked. It stands a little apart from the hubbub at the angle of Lombard Street and King William Street, looking small now in view of the scale of everything around it.

It is Nicholas Hawksmoor's one City church and a miniature of his architectural mastery. From one point of view it should never have existed at all. The Fifty New Churches Act of 1711 was supposed to be for fresh, suburban churches. Under a supplementary Act of 1712, however, one existing parish was able to muscle in on the generous funding provided. This was St Mary Woolnoth, whose congregation had seen their church patched up rather than rebuilt after the Great Fire but now found it too dilapidated to go on with. Hawksmoor was appointed architect and undertook the job between 1716 and 1724. Despite the constricted site and lack of a churchyard, he produced a scaled-down version of the plan he had used for other, more open sites: a strong external statement at the west end and a small, well-lit, central auditorium interrupting the traditional east–west axis.

The west tower is almost as astonishing as its counterpart at Spitalfields and every bit as powerful. Such insistent rustication as grips the base, hooking even round the attached Tuscan columns in the corners, had never been seen in an English church

before. (It became a favourite source, second only to Newgate Gaol, for architects of the Edwardian Baroque.) The temple front of the belfry stage might be orthodox, were it not 'skied' like some great Roman funerary monument. Above it are the queerest features of all, little twin turrets almost of a Victorian Italianate nature, huddling together for support. There are no proper elevations for the south and east walls, as they are virtually blind. Instead, Hawksmoor keeps his remaining fireworks for the north front towards Lombard Street, where a series of swaggering niches worthy of Giulio Romano punctuate the blank stonework of the wall.

Being so small, the interior has to be simple. It is dominated by Hawksmoor's fine formation of a higher square within the blank square of the walls. The inner square is defined by groups of three splendid fluted Corinthian columns in each of the corners. Above their entablature in the attic come large Diocletian windows, grander versions of the one which appears over the entrance door. The original reredos, pulpit and organ case are still there, but as at Spitalfields the side galleries have gone. The culprit in this case was William Butterfield, in 1875. The combination of Hawksmoor and Butterfield might be

St Mary Woolnoth. West front. GLRO

thought to be that of the proverbial irresistible force meeting the immovable object. In fact Butterfield behaved with more respect than many Victorian restorers would have done. He raised the chancel and lowered the pulpit, but he condescended to keep the gallery fronts, sticking them rather oddly against the walls. Enthusiasts for hymn-singing will appreciate the monument on the north side to John Newton, anti-slavery vicar of St Mary Woolnoth and author of 'Amazing Grace'.

12

St Paul's, Deptford
Deptford High St, Lewisham

1/H5   British Rail to Deptford
[C]

St Paul's, Deptford, is the better preserved of the two London churches designed by the shadowy figure of Thomas Archer (the other, four-towered St John's, Smith Square near the Houses of Parliament, was gutted during the Second World War and is now well known as a concert hall). Archer, a gentleman with money enough to have spent time in Rome, was for four years a commissioner under the Fifty New Churches Act of 1711. He and Nicholas Hawksmoor appear to have spent much effort interpreting the theological and liturgical ideas of the Anglican Church of Queen Anne's reign into coherent plan form and style.

Deptford, impoverished now, was then a prosperous ship-building, victualling and fishing village dependent on the naval yard founded by Henry VIII. Enough sea-captains and gentry lived there to make it among the wealthiest of London's outer suburbs. The medieval village church being too small, the parishioners fastened upon the 1711 Act to carve out a fresh parish and get themselves a spacious new church, which was built between about 1713 and 1720, though not completely finished till 1730.

The brief of the architects who worked under the Act was to build dignified, stone-faced churches, correctly oriented within their own

churchyards and possessing porticoes, towers and steeples. To this Hawksmoor and Archer added a preoccupation with planning around two axes and with arranging the galleries so that they did not interfere with the central space. St Paul's exemplifies all this. Its churchyard is lavish, in expectation of many burials to come. In the centre is the church, with full architectural expression on all four sides. The approaches are grand indeed, with great sets of steps on north and south sides leading in under the galleries to circular staircases in the corners. The main west entrance is semi-circular with columns in the manner of Pietro da Cortona's Santa Maria della Pace, a model first imitated in Wren's transepts for St Paul's Cathedral. Over it, the tower and steeple were modified and perhaps toned down from Archer's first design. They are pretty enough but not as robustly baroque as the body of the church.

The interior, though often altered and restored, is as palatial and as well preserved as that of any of the 1711 churches. Archer's auditorium is a Corinthian hall, with giant columns engaged at the ends and against the canted corners, free-standing in front of the main galleries. A hint of the theatre is given by the appearance of extra little galleries, like boxes, on columns in the corners flanking the steps up to the short, apsidal chancel. The cornices and flat ceiling, made by James Hands, are examples of the succulent English plasterwork of the period at its best. The grandeur of the architecture dwarfs the few original fittings that survive, among them a cut-down pulpit and pews.

13

St Mary-le-Strand
The Strand, Westminster

2/H4   Underground to Temple   [C]

The Scottish Catholic architect James Gibbs, not long back from Rome, pipped the English gentleman-amateur Thomas Archer to the post as architect of this

St Paul's, Deptford. South side. GLRO

St Mary-le-Strand. South side. GLRO

little church on its conspicuous island site. The happy result is London's only full-blooded essay in the Roman baroque style of the *seicento*. Sandwiched between the elegance of Somerset House on one side and the respectful bulk of Bush House on the other, its delicately tiered steeple is one of London's most effective landmarks. With the echoing steeple of St Clement Danes behind (added by Gibbs to Wren's church), it gives a stately and picturesque termination to the Strand.

St Mary-le-Strand had been a medieval church. It was pulled down by Protector Somerset for the sake of the short-lived Thames-side palace he built himself here. For the next 170 years its congregation had to make do with the Savoy Chapel; but they did not forget they were owed a church. In 1711 they managed to get themselves high on the list of parishes eligible for a new one under the generous London church-building Act of that year. In the early years of this legislation there was much boxing and coxing between the commissioners who administered it (Wren, Vanbrugh and Archer) and their surveyors (Hawksmoor, Dickinson and Gibbs). Vanbrugh, Hawksmoor, Archer and Gibbs were all interested in the site in the middle of the Strand, as much for the sake of putting up a column and

statue in honour of Queen Anne here as for the church itself. A church plan by Archer and a column by Gibbs had been approved and foundations started for both when the Queen suddenly died in 1714 and work stopped. Gibbs then deftly put in a new idea for the church, using Archer's dimensions, and it was this design (the boxwood model is in the RIBA Drawings Collection) which was built over the next seven years. The column was in due course forgotten. Even the Queen's statue, at one time intended to surmount the church portico, got left out too.

The free-standing but tight and traffic-plagued site suggested to Gibbs a rich and plastic treatment all round the church, and a rigid division into a blank lower storey and a well-windowed upper one to reduce the rumble of carts and coaches. That intention failed, for an 18th-century guide to London was soon bemoaning that street noise 'hinders the hearing of Divine Service plain enough therein'. This was one of many complaints – mostly architectural – voiced against the church from early days. Aficionados of the English school of baroque did not like it because of the petty and 'Popish' scale of its ornament. Palladians objected to its deviations from Vitruvian purity. We can afford to be less fastidious and admire the vim with which Gibbs adapted the style of the Roman architecture he admired – chiefly Carlo Fontana's rather than that of the more restless Borromini or Bernini – to an Anglican church-building context. By the time Gibbs had quietened down and moved on to St Martin-in-the-Fields nearby, he had lost the authentic Italian sense of movement and relief, rarely met with in English architecture but palpable at St Mary-le-Strand.

The exterior, with its compartments of aediculed niches and windows and its semi-circular portico and apse answering one another, is more imaginative than the interior. This is an aisle-less box, without the galleries which give most Georgian churches their intimacy. It is again articulated into storeys, and has an over-grand pediment bearing the royal arms over the chancel arch. In compensation there is an exuberance of plastic ornament in the vault and in the apse. The Commissioners of New Churches did not like this, probably on grounds of expense more than taste, and in 1718 ordered Gibbs to put a stop to the 'extravagt. carvings therein'.

Over the years, St Mary-le-Strand has survived several threats of demolition in the interest of road-widening. It has recently been restored and its ornament elegantly regilded.

14

St Peter's, Petersham
Church Lane, Petersham, Richmond

1/D6   Underground or British Rail to Richmond, then bus or river walk [C]

Petersham must stand in this guide for the many village churches that have been incorporated into London, many of them medieval but including among the western riverside suburbs a distinctive group partially rebuilt in the eighteenth century. Whilst Twickenham, with a nave of 1714–15 by John James, and Richmond make the grander display, only Petersham retains its high box pews

St Peter's, Petersham. A F KERSTING

and galleries intact.

The church is tiny and charming, Georgian architecture at its most humble and timeless. Traces of a medieval church survive in the chancel. Most of it, however, is 17th-century, though the octagonal lantern that gives light and grace to the tower was added only in 1796, the presumed date of many of the interior fittings. Strangest is the shape of the church. The nave is so wide as to resemble two transepts, its two ranks of box pews facing each other with a line of singularly uncomfortable benches being the only 'free seats' not available for hire. There are more box pews in the little galleries, supported on the slenderest of iron columns. The two-decker pulpit had to be raised high to see up to these pews as well as inside the tall-sided ones at ground level.

The body of the church was further widened in 1840: the very year in which the Cambridge Camden Society launched its attack on the appearance of church interiors being dictated by pew rents. The 1840 work can be detected by a change in brickwork on the exterior and by slightly thicker columns to the balconies. The fittings are completed by a 17th-century altar rail and monuments, and a hatchment. In general, however, it is the simplicity, cheapness and rare sense of the interior having been thrown thoughtlessly together that make the most lasting impression.

The scale of the church is in humble contrast to the imposing houses that surround it, a galaxy of William and Mary, Queen Anne and early Georgian styles that are difficult to appreciate amidst the heavy traffic storming round the bends of Petersham Road. The grandest is off Sudbrook Lane: James Gibbs's Sudbrook Park, built in 1726 for the Duke of Argyll and Greenwich, and now a golf club of uncommon grandeur.

15

St John-at-Hackney
Lower Clapton Rd, Hackney

1/H3   British Rail to Hackney Downs or Hackney Central [C]

Artists are allowed to be temperamental, but it does not do for architects to be so. If they cannot get on with clients and make compromises, they will build little. Among the casualties of that iron law seems to have been James Spiller, on the strength of this august and virile church one of the ablest London architects of the years around 1800. St John's is almost all there now is to show for Spiller's career (until 1941 there was also a fine synagogue in Aldgate). We must be thankful to the forbearing burghers of Hackney that they allowed him to complete what is surely the best church built in a London suburb during George III's long reign.

Hackney in the 1790s was not the shabby, under-serviced district it has now become. It was a prospering outer suburb, dotted with the villas of City merchants and other 'carriage folk', who wanted an ample parish church to replace old and outgrown St Augustine's (its tower survives nearby) and who could well stump up for Spiller to build them one. Their tombs line the shaded sides of the church, behind the war memorial garden that is the down-at-heel prelude to Spiller's architecture.

The body of the church is of brick, a pale brick handled with the unapologetic largeness of North Italian classicism – no fiddling, Adamesque detail here. Smirke is the architect it brings to mind, but Smirke was a youth in 1792–7. The entrance front, facing north, is unusually broad, with a blank pediment of Tuscan depth stretching right across it, blank arches to the sides, and a semi-circular Ionic porch (added by Spiller in 1812) below. It would be fine by itself, but what makes it magnificent is the tower above, also an addition of 1812, unexpectedly in stone, Ionic at the belfry stage, then topped by a queer feature with freely curving volutes at the corners. Its spare originality comes somewhere in between the styles of two other eccentric architects of the day, Spiller's friend John Soane and S P Cockerell.

The interior, correctly orientated so that you enter under the north gallery and turn left to face the altar, is the kind of vast hulk which gives modern inner-city incumbents a headache. In essence a plain, centralised auditorium, it has just enough shallow gallery-space at the sides and back and enough eastward projection to qualify as a Greek cross. But the central space, with its bare ribbed vault, is dominant. It could be as splendid as the exterior, but poverty, liturgical change and, worst of all, a disastrous fire of 1955 followed by a necessarily cheap restoration, have left the church too much of a shell. The parquet floor, plain rough stucco of the walls and ceiling, and wan, Comper-ish hues of Christopher Webb's east window are not right for Spiller's large-scale treatment, which cries out for rich, Regency colour. If someone were to give the vicar a fortune, something

St John-at-Hackney. Entrance front. EH

21

might be done. Meanwhile, St John's must soldier on, getting what decorative benefit it can from the remnants of Victorian fittings (pulpit and reredos) and some quaint monuments and brasses salvaged from the old church in 1797.

Around the churchyard are reminders of Hackney's palmier days: the pretty terrace of Sutton Place to the south-east and older Sutton House on the bend beyond, where Urswick Road turns into Homerton High Street, while to the north lies fragmentary Clapton Square. But the church's most curious and thought-provoking neighbour is another square, built directly behind the east end in the late 1980s on the site of a derelict factory. This is Sutton Square, an attempt on the part of developers Kentish Homes to bring yuppies into Hackney, and on the part of architects Campbell, Zogolovitch, Wilkinson and Gough to revive the tradition of the speculative London square. On either count, the success was partial. The cute, flattened Dutch gables, the carriage lamps and the meanness of the central space will displease the fastidious. But can it be said that all previous London squares were planned with taste as their top priority?

16

St Pancras Parish Church
Upper Woburn Place, Camden

2/F2   Underground or British Rail to Euston   [C]

For full-blooded Hellenism, New St Pancras Church brooks no rivals. There is something at once noble and naive about the building, as though some disjointed hunks of ancient Athens had come adrift and washed up together on the edge of the Euston Road.

In its day (1819–22) the church was one of the most extravagant ever built in London. Its cost of some £80,000 reflected the ambitions of the burgeoning suburban parish of St

New St Pancras Church, from the south-east. EH

Pancras, which had hitherto had to make do with the battered little church that still survives in the old burial ground north of St Pancras Station. The new church beside the 'New Road', as the broad artery of Euston Road was then called, offered a fresh civic image and a focus for development on Bedford and Southampton lands in northern Bloomsbury.

As architects, the vestry selected William and Henry Inwood, son and grandson of parish bigwig Lord Mansfield's bailiff. The Inwoods chose the Greek Revival style, just then (at the end of the Napoleonic Wars) in great vogue. Henry was promptly dispatched to Athens and came back with detailed drawings of the Erechtheum and Tower of the Winds wherewith to embellish the building. Hence the church's egregious features – the three-stage octagonal tower translating the Wrenian or Gibbsian steeple into terms of Grecian purity, and the bizarre northern and southern vestries flanking and overlapping the apsidal east end. The caryatids which support the entablature of these identical vestries are cribs from the Erechtheum, 'improved' in their features by the sculptor J C Rossi (you

can see one of the originals in the British Museum if you wish to compare) and cast in Coade's patent stone on an iron framework. Behind them are sarcophagi, signifying that the double doors lead down to burial vaults beneath the church. The vestries, tower and false pediment over the western portico all give the air of having been spatchcocked on to the simple body of the church. But this is made up for by the enthusiasm and consistency with which the Inwoods deployed their new-learnt scholarship all round the building, and by the sharp and luscious quality of their Portland stone detailing.

Entering, one passes through an octagonal vestibule beneath the tower into a flat-roofed hall flanked by galleries on Egyptianising columns with burnished capitals. The effect is long, horizontal and somewhat barrack-like, but offset by the magnificence of the elliptical apse, which has six polished Ionic columns raised above the level of the altar over a dado of veined marble. The ceiling, 60 ft wide but unsupported in the middle, is now divided into tame panels painted tame colours. Better details are to be found on the gallery fronts and on a variety of plaster cornices and friezes which run the decorative gamut of Greek key, acanthus and honeysuckle. The pride of the fittings is a superb pulpit in polished mahogany, octagonal on a square base of four Ionic columns. It is one of the finest of all pieces of Greek Revival furniture, ecclesiastical or secular.

17
All Saints'
Margaret St, Westminster

2/E3   Underground to Oxford
Circus   [C]

In 1849 the young William Butterfield took on the task of building a replacement for the former Margaret Chapel on the understanding that it was to be a model urban church for the burgeoning Tractarian Movement within the Church of England. The effective client was A J Beresford Hope, a man of large wealth and dogmatic views about the nature of Gothic church architecture. The result was a spatial, emotional and intellectual masterpiece, and the most influential town church of the Gothic Revival.

At that date, no British architect since Wren had grappled with the problem of designing a spatially imaginative church on a tight, inner-city piece of ground, blind on three sides. The brief for All Saints' was intimidating. The separate parts of the church had to be articulated and finished on Tractarian and Puginian lines. A choir school and clergy house had also to be got on to the site. Butterfield's brilliant response was to reduce the space further by creating a small court in the front, to range his buildings round it with a pointed entrance arch from the street, and then use sheer height to create architectural effect. The secular blocks which front the street are unremitting, functional stacks in red and black brick with small, randomly spaced windows, in defiance of the contemporary penchant for gault brick, contrived symmetry and redundant stucco mouldings. These buildings are heavily influenced by the

Bishop's House at Birmingham designed by Pugin shortly before. Over them looms the tower, rising from an invisible base over the porch until it changes over the belfry stage into a Teutonic steeple of inspirational crispness. Glimpses of this epoch-making spire are hard to get amidst the dense West End streets. Nor can much of the body of the church itself be seen. But the view from the court reveals originality enough: strong tracery forms to the aisle windows, a bellcote over the chancel arch, and a chancel itself higher than the nave. The disciplined use of fine brickwork throughout the exterior, derived from the Gothic town churches of Italy and northern Germany, was part of the

Butterfield–Beresford Hope programme. After All Saints', the best Victorian urban churches were to be faced in brick, instead of masquerading in a dress of ragstone or freestone.

The patterning Butterfield uses to relieve the austerity of his elevations gives only a hint of the shocking, un-English colourfulness within. This contrast is deliberate. The Tractarians believed that external show in a banal, urban context was unseemly; what Beresford Hope and Butterfield wanted to advocate was the idea of a plain and honest carcase, within which money might be lavished over the years on interior embellishment. Just as the church was begun, Ruskin published his

All Saints', Margaret Street. Tower and spire. MARTIN CHARLES

Seven Lamps of Architecture, to be followed by *The Stones of Venice*. Their first effect was to spur Butterfield and other church architects to use internal colour in a bolder, more Italian way, whether in the form of painting, veneer or 'structural polychromy'. All Saints', with its blank walls, its stunted length and its reliance upon clerestory lighting, offered a chance to show how colour could exalt a gloomy interior into a jewel-case for the kind of worship favoured by the Tractarians.

The vaulted interior, with its painted reredos by Dyce, stained glass by the Gerente brothers and O'Connor, tile pictures by Alexander Gibbs, monolithic piers in polished granite and obsessive patterning on floors and walls, reflects the excitement generated by this sense of mission. It is excessive for most tastes, and not always harmonious. In part this is because Butterfield's tastes in colour and design evolved over the years, leading to acrimonious arguments with Beresford Hope, who felt that the architect was spoiling their great venture. The hues of the tile patterning in the aisles, installed as late as the 1870s and 1880s, for instance, conflict with Ninian Comper's more fastidious chancel decoration. It was Comper who in 1909 supplied the copies of William Dyce's original reredos paintings, which had been executed in fast-decaying 'spirit fresco'. If these anomalies prevent All Saints' from attaining perfection, it remains (in the words of Butterfield's biographer Paul Thompson) 'unforgettable, as if suddenly an overwhelming and triumphant chorus of praise had broken the monotonous rumble of the streets'.

18

St James the Less
Vauxhall Bridge Rd, Pimlico, Westminster

2/F7   Underground to Pimlico
[C]

Ten years on and the polychromy of All Saints', Margaret Street had become the language of advanced Anglican church

architecture, following the assurance and direction given it by Ruskin's *Seven Lamps of Architecture*, of 1849, and *Stones of Venice*, of 1851–3. The style was further refined by G E Street, who saw the architecture of northern Italy, France and Spain at first hand and published his findings extensively. His style is more weighty and coherent than Butterfield's, and at St James's more clearly Italian in inspiration. In Street's buildings jagged dog-tooth mouldings, heavy marble shafts with blunt squared-off capitals and vigorous polychromy in red and black brick urbanely hang together where in other hands they have been dubbed 'muscular' or even 'roguish'. Philip Webb could not have had a better teacher.

St James the Less was sponsored in 1860–1 by the Misses Monk, the three daughters of a former Bishop of Gloucester and Bristol, to proselytise what was then a desperately poor area. Their high Tractarianism has gone, but the fittings glow lavishly in the evocative gloom. The building is made to seem larger than it really is by the massive tower stuck to the side as a porch

through which the body of the church is reached via a low arcade. It consists of a short nave and aisles, with a lower vaulted chancel, apsed in Street's typical fashion. The browns, reds and blacks of the walls and floor tiles are relieved only by the brilliant glass supplied by Clayton and Bell. Light is concentrated on the chancel arch, above which glints a mosaic by G F Watts, the only decoration Street did not have control over. The ironwork of the church is particularly resplendent, both inside around the massive font and outside in the railings, also designed by Street.

In the manner of All Saints', Margaret Street, the church gathers round it a parish hall and schoolrooms, the latter extended by Street's son. But the surroundings of St James the Less were transformed in the 1960s when the front was opened to Vauxhall Bridge Road and Lillington Gardens encircled it. This estate, built in many phases from the early 1960s to the late 1970s to the designs of Darbourne and Darke, ushered in a new form of planned housing: low, densely packed into seemingly informal squares and

St James the Less. Apse and tower, with school to the right. RCHME

alleyways, with varied levels and balconies dripping with carefully careless foliage. Most importantly, the facings were in rich red brick. Lillington Gardens, where Street's church gave both justification and *kudos* to the Darbourne and Darke technique, inspired developers and especially local authorities to produce a rash of high-density imitations all over Britain.

19

St Martin's
Vicar's Road, Gospel Oak, Camden

1/F3   Underground to Kentish Town or British Rail to Gospel Oak [C]

What can have been going on in Edward Buckton Lamb's mind when he designed this church? Was he in pursuit of sheer, personal originality at all costs, or is there some lost key to its construction and appearance?

St Martin's was put up in 1865–6 and paid for by a wealthy glovemaker, John Derby Allcroft. He was a partisan of the Low Church wing of Victorian Anglicanism and funded two other London churches, St Matthew's, Bayswater and St Jude's, Courtfield Gardens, South Kensington. In plan, all three were the Victorian urban equivalent of the Georgian preaching-box. As large a pew-renting congregation as possible was shoehorned into each building. But everyone had to have a sight of altar, pulpit and reading desk, and the basic Gothic Revival precepts of separate nave, aisles, chancel and tower had to be respected. All this indicated a plan with a short, wide chancel and aisles which bulged into something like transepts. At St Martin's and his other London church, St Mary Magdalene, Addiscombe, Croydon (1868–70), Lamb managed cleverly to fit in all the necessary seating without having recourse to galleries, which so rarely look right in Gothic churches.

The staggering thing is the style of architecture in which all this is dressed

St Martin's, Gospel Oak. Interior looking east. RCHME

up – restless, neurotic, yet, in its own terms, logical. Lamb was not a young man when he designed St Martin's. His architectural personality had been formed during the 1830s by J B Loudon, apostle of a rational approach to picturesque design. He was a thinker and a loner, alive to the ideas of Pugin and Ruskin but hostile to slavish imitation of Gothic precedent. More than Butterfield or the other Victorian Low Church architects like Teulon or Peacock who veered into eccentricity, Lamb sought a consistent style for modern church-building. He wanted to extend the gamut of 'pointed architecture' by exploring the structural expressiveness of its traditional materials, stone and wood.

Outside, St Martin's is one of the few Victorian churches in London to make anything of its stone walling. In most churches coursed in 'jumperwork', the patterning of the walls has nothing to do with the building's detailing. But Lamb uses it to stress his abrupt arrangement of tower, nave, transepts and chancel, his strange, elongated windows, and his unique vocabulary of intersecting mouldings, scooped out, corbelled, set off and chamfered with a kind of bony bravura. Inside, the masonry is dressed

and left bare round the walls – again a rarity in Victorian London – and the Lamb style of stonework is carried through, from a set of bizarre, pipe-like corbels and colonnettes into the font and other fittings. But it is the width, richness and dominance of the dark roof, daringly constructed of intersecting hammerbeams so as to cover the church's wide, auditorial spaces, that most astounds. The outcome has a savage quality, not to everyone's tastes and hardly devotional. The virtuosity of Lamb's detailing, too, must have provided amazement and relief during many a long Victorian sermon. His Gothic may have turned out to be a dead-end, but it is one of the most remarkable dead-ends in English architecture.

The north-west corner of the church, beyond the tower, is an addition by E B Lamb junior in a less ardent version of his father's style. It detracts from the artful massing of separate parts contrived by Lamb senior. Also perhaps by Lamb junior is the former church hall opposite. But the vicarage designed to go with the church has disappeared, and St Martin's is now a Victorian island in an ocean of post-war municipal housing.

St Augustine's, Kilburn. Nave, screen and chancel. RCHME

20

St Augustine's
Kilburn Park Rd, Westminster

2/A1   Underground to Kilburn Park
[C]

The humdrum terraces and semi-detached villas that once pressed close to the majestic bulk of St Augustine's, Kilburn have mostly gone now, leaving Pearson's masterpiece in proud, roadside isolation in this unfashionable corner of north-west London.

J L Pearson is an architect for the purist. Of the major church-building architects of the English Gothic Revival, he was closest to his medieval French predecessors in his search for harmony of proportions, clarity of conception and loftiness of ideal. Sometimes his architecture is a little dull, for want of incident or personal detail. At St Augustine's, Pearson's profound grasp of Gothic joins with his unique capacity for creating architectural space to make a church which comes as close to perfection as any of the 19th century.

St Augustine's was built for a Tractarian curate, Richard Kirkpatrick, who fell out with the vicar of Kilburn, decided to build a new church on his own account and lured part of the congregation away with him. An iron church was erected in 1870 while funds were raised and Pearson matured his plans. The chancel came first, in 1871–2, to be followed by the nave in 1876–8 and the upper stages of the tower and steeple in 1897. Little has changed since.

Though it looks like a cathedral, St Augustine's was quite a cheap and modest-sized church. On the outside, it is the magnificent tower and spire that create the illusion. Pearson in the years of his maturity built four great brick churches in the London area (St Michael's, Croydon, St John's, Upper Norwood, and the bombed St John's, Red Lion Square, Holborn were the other three). For each of them he designed a lofty tower which answered Ruskin's call in *The Lamp of Power* for sheer, unimpeded campaniles standing clear on their own foundations; but only at St Augustine's was Pearson able to build his design. How pleased he must have been to see it go up in his old age! With its elongated belfry stage and spare, stone tourelles (based, like other features of the front, on St Etienne at Caen) anchoring the spire, it is an aristocrat among towers. The complex, gradual recession of planes from the

front of the narthex to the face of the tower is brilliantly controlled.

The great rose window prepares one for a tough early French Gothic job inside, of the kind Pearson had enjoyed building as a young man. Instead there unfolds a serene and cool hall, rib-vaulted and groined in brick from end to end and pierced by lancet windows alone. At the sides are galleries over a low arcade, lit from a clerestory concealed behind a high upper arcade and related in level to the chancel screen which alone interrupts the nave. It all looks simple, natural and expansive, but is in reality complicated, scholarly, revolutionary – and modest in scale. Pearson's abolition of the chancel arch at St Augustine's, modelled on Albi Cathedral but transforming and elaborating the original, was seminal to the development of late Victorian church architecture. His double passage aisles round the nave, quietly and beautifully widened into hidden transepts to cast light on the screen and chancel, were entirely novel. And the gallery, which may seem a functionless piece of theatre, was destined for the reclusive young ladies of a nearby High Church home.

Drawings by Pearson show that he looked forward to the day when the whole of St Augustine's would be delicately decorated in a consistent, austere French-Gothic style of painting. Some of this was carried out over the years, and Clayton and Bell put in a good deal of their conventional, small-scale glass. But much of the brickwork remains bare and is none the worse for it. Any mature Pearson church relies for its majesty not on its accoutrements but upon its plan and the noble skeleton of its architecture.

21

Union Chapel
Compton Terrace, Islington

1/G4   Underground or British Rail to Highbury & Islington
[C]

'A society of opulent and respectable individuals' came together in 1805–6 to erect the first Union Chapel, a modest building which formed the centrepiece of the new Compton Terrace, Canonbury. In 1839 it acquired a large classical portico and clock tower, tokens of opulence and respectability indeed. But the great epoch for the Union Chapel was yet to come. Between 1844 and 1892 under the pastorate of Henry Allom, the regular Sunday flock grew to over a thousand, sometimes reputedly fifteen hundred. Intellectual sermons (Allom was joint editor of the *Quarterly Review*) coupled with a flourishing tradition of choral music seem to have been the secret. So an adjoining house was acquired, a building committee formed and an architectural competition for a new chapel and school decreed in the early 1870s, with Alfred Waterhouse as assessor. The upshot was the grandest Victorian non-conformist chapel in London.

James Cubitt, the winner of the competition, had previously been in partnership with Henry Fuller, with whom or for whom he designed the notable Congregational Chapel in Lower Clapton. In 1870 he had published *Church Designs for Congregations*, the thrust of which was that Congregationalists should abandon the hackneyed long church plan in favour of centralised arrangements – equally hallowed by medieval precedent and better suited to congregational traditions of worship. In conformity with this theory, he based his winning design for the Union Chapel on the plan of the octagonal 11th-century church of Santa Fosca at Torcello, but enlarged and translated into the strong-minded early Gothic style of James Brooks, whom Cubitt admired.

The body of the new chapel was built in 1876–7, the virile tower which so dwarfs the flanking houses of Compton Terrace following on in 1889. It sets the scale for the interior, which was made gigantic enough to hold 1,600, all within close sight and sound of Pastor Allom's focal pulpit. Cubitt's noble auditorium consists of an irregular octagon inscribed within two rectangles. Outside the octagon are the first-floor galleries, the remotest benches of which are hardly more than 50 ft from the pulpit. The central space, high and light, rises to an arched, decorated and top-lit ceiling in wood in which Cubitt cleverly resolves the irregularity of his octagon. Outside and inside alike are in red brick and stone, with a quality of Gothic detail rare in British non-conformist architecture; Cubitt knew his mouldings well, and applied them with confidence and precision. If there is something of Waterhouse as well as of Brooks about the interior (particularly the ceiling and the pulpit), this may be more because Waterhouse admired Cubitt's design for the chapel than because Cubitt was trying to please the competition assessor. Both Waterhouse's Congregational buildings in London, Lyndhurst Road Chapel, Hampstead (1883) and the King's Weighhouse Chapel, Mayfair (1889–90), were designed after the Union Chapel and seem to show the influence of Cubitt's planning and detailing.

After Henry Allom's ministry, the Union Chapel found it increasingly hard to attract the vast congregations which Cubitt's auditorium anticipated and deserved. But, by the skin of its teeth, it has so far survived.

22

Brompton Oratory
Brompton Rd, Kensington and Chelsea

2/C6   Underground to Knightsbridge or South Kensington [C]

Herbert Gribble, architect of this most chic of London's Catholic churches, was candid about the ultra-Italian style of his creation. It was made so, he said, 'so that those who had no opportunity of going to Italy to see an Italian church had only to come here to see the model of one'. Behind this architectural logic lay ecclesiastical policy. The church was and is the London headquarters of the Oratorian order founded by the Italian Renaissance saint Filippo Neri, and the desire of the order, when they built the

Union Chapel. Front. EH

church in 1880–96, was to refer to their headquarters in Rome, the baroque Chiesa Nuova.

The Oratorians were the most successful of the Catholic orders to establish themselves in Victorian England. Among their early adherents were Frederick Faber and John Henry Newman, to whom a memorial (designed by Bodley and Garner with a statue by L J Chavalliaud) stands to the west of the church. Newman and the other Oratorian intellectuals rejected Pugin's view that the Roman church had declined since medieval days and that Gothic was the only justifiable style for revived Catholic architecture in England. So when the Oratorians set themselves up at Brompton in 1853, their buildings were Counter-Reformation in spirit and Italianate in style. First came the L-shaped Oratory House, a restrained composition by J J Scoles. In its west wing are the private 'Little Oratory' and a library – modest apartments lovingly embellished over the years. Scoles's barn-like temporary church had also acquired some internal dignity by the time that the present building replaced it.

Gribble, a young and unknown architect, appears to have gained the Oratorians' confidence through the favour of their patron, the 15th Duke of Norfolk. In 1876, aged twenty-eight, he produced a design for the permanent church much like the one built. An architectural competition followed, the controversial upshot of which was that Gribble was confirmed as designer in 1879. The core of the church was built, minus the entrance front and the outer dome, in 1880–4. These followed in 1892–3 and 1895–6 respectively. Gribble died prematurely in 1894. The dome and lantern, raised to a higher curve than he had intended, were the work of another architect, George Sherrin. The baroque profile of the lantern is attributable to Sherrin's assistant E A Rickards, later architect of such flamboyant buildings as Deptford Town Hall.

The completed church is a conspicuous South Kensington landmark. The front (not quite completely Italian – there is something of the Panthéon out of St Paul's

Brompton Oratory. Dome and choir. RCHME

Cathedral about the portico) looks splendid from the top of the Fulham Road, and there is an unexpected, un-English vignette of the dome from Cheval Place. At the back, its bulk deals a crushing blow to the impoverished Anglican church of Holy Trinity, Brompton, which cowers in a garden behind.

The oratory interior seen today follows the lines intended by Gribble but is largely the product of 20th-century adornment. The biggest campaign of decoration took place in 1927–32, when a certain Commendatore Formilli was entrusted with marbling and gilding the nave, adding mosaics beneath the dome, installing Stations of the Cross and various figures in high and low relief, and erecting the enormous, blowzy pulpit. All this was done in a defiantly Roman taste. But some of the Oratory's fittings are older than the church itself. Chief among these are the twelve figures of apostles in the nave, carved for Siena Cathedral in the 1680s by Giuseppe Mazzuoli, and the grand altar and reredos of the Lady Chapel, again of the late 17th century and made for the church of San Domenico, Brescia, by the Corbarelli family. By these acquisitions the Oratorians affirmed that they valued Italian baroque art in the late 19th century more than the church of their mother country did. The Chapel of St

Wilfrid also has notable fittings – an 18th-century altar and baldacchino originally in the Belgian church of St Rémy, at Rochefort, and a triptych of the 1930s by Rex Whistler. The high altar has second-rate paintings above it and to the side by B Pozzi, 1924–7.

23

St Cuthbert's
Philbeach Gardens, Kensington and Chelsea

1/F5   Underground to Earl's Court [C]

The financing of Victorian church-building in the inner city was precarious. Everything was done through private enterprise. Rival sects and different wings of the same church competed fiercely with one another. In middle-class districts like Kensington there were simply too many churches, each with a tiny parish. To attract flock and funds they depended on the charisma of their preachers, the solemnity of their services and – to a degree – on the elaboration of their architecture and fittings.

St Cuthbert's, Philbeach Gardens was one of the last products of the competitive church-building boom which infected Kensington from the 1850s to the 1880s. It was promoted by Henry Westall, the energetic yet pious High Church curate of the nearby St Matthias', Warwick Road. Following church-building custom, Westall in 1881 staked his claim to a separate parish cut out of the area already allotted to St Philip's, Earl's Court Road, whose poverty-stricken vicar, anxious about the loss of pew rents, opposed him. He then scraped enough cash together to buy a site and build a little iron church (christened the 'dust-bin' by parishioners) in 1882–3, meanwhile scouting about for more money to build something better. His architect was Hugh Roumieu Gough whose design, in a lofty, Cistercian style of Gothic with proportions based on Tintern Abbey, rose up slowly round the iron church in 1884–7. A presbytery for Westall was tacked on to the north-west corner, to be later supplemented with a hall.

What distinguished St Cuthbert's from other High Anglican churches of the age was Westall's skill in embellishing this austere skeleton with fine fixtures and fittings. The result, achieved by badgering the congregation and organising them into 'guilds' which gave and made objects for the building, transformed the church into London's most interesting repository of late Victorian ecclesiastical art. Its only rival, Sedding's Holy Trinity, Sloane Street, appears bare and cold in comparison with the rich gloom of St Cuthbert's. Gough had given the nave a certain opulence by specifying splendid monoliths of polished Torquay marble for the clustered columns of the arcade. The earliest fittings – font, pulpit and sedilia – are his, with fulsome carving by an obscure Polish 'baron', Felix de Sziemanowicz. Gough's too is the rood, of 1893. But from about 1887 the metal art-worker William Bainbridge Reynolds took the initiative. His are the hanging lamps, royal arms, clock, most of the candle standards, altar front, the superb set of metal screens and, above all, the Art Nouveau iron and copper lectern of 1897. The Guild of St Peter, consisting of supporters of the church under professional guidance, furnished a background for these fittings by lining the brick walls with carved stone diapering between 1890 and 1909. Other guilds contributed the choir stalls and a fine set of vestments. The climax is the elaborate Hispanic reredos against the blank east wall, designed by Ernest Geldart and executed by the carver Gilbert Boulton in 1913–14. The stained glass, by Kempe and others, is disappointing. Some of it was blown out during war damage of 1944. Afterwards, a new copper roof was put on instead of the original slated one, the west end lost its bellcote, the church hall was much rebuilt, and new windows by Hugh Easton were installed in the Lady Chapel.

The worship conducted by Westall at St Cuthbert's competed in ritualistic grandeur with the fittings. In 1898 the notorious ultra-Protestant John Kensit interrupted a Good Friday service by way of protest and was prosecuted for his

pains. He was acquitted on appeal, but in revenge was depicted on one of the chancel misericords with asses' ears. Today the passions aroused by St Cuthbert's have departed, as have most of the 'non-resident' middle-class families who travelled across London to make up Westall's High Church congregation. The church stands in its unfrequented sidestreet against the railway, noble but forlorn.

24

Holy Redeemer
*Exmouth Market,
Clerkenwell, Islington*

2/H2   Underground to Farringdon or Angel

[C]

This little-known church, designed by J D Sedding and built in 1887–8 with later additions, would hardly be remarked on in Latin countries. In the English context it is significant as the boldest acknowledgement in orthodox Anglicanism that the days of the Gothic Revival were numbered. Its *quattrocento* aestheticism is the architectural equivalent to Walter Pater's essays on the Renaissance; and indeed Pater admired the building.

Exmouth Market, not far from the

Holy Redeemer, Exmouth Market. Front.
RCHME

Dickensian slums of Saffron Hill, was a shabby district when this church was founded. Stalls still line the street most days, though the Cockney element in Clerkenwell is fading fast. Holy Redeemer was a modest mission church, in contrast to the opulent Holy Trinity, Sloane Street which was on Sedding's drawing-board at the same time. Though notable for the delicacy rather than the force of his designing, Sedding never wanted for courage or thoughtfulness. Cheap basilican churches had been built by the Victorians before, but no previous architect had dared to emulate the external plainness and internal purity of the early Tuscan Renaissance. So far had Sedding become disenchanted by orthodox Gothicism that in the great, projecting eaves of the roof all round there may even be a tongue-in-cheek reference to the 'handsomest barn in England', Inigo Jones's St Paul's, Covent Garden. But Sedding's brick barn is tall, striped and stately compared to Jones's squat performance. It rises from stock brick for the lower portion of the front to alternating Portland stone and red brick above. Round the sides the stripes continue, but in tones of brickwork alone.

Sedding's other model was Wren, as appears from the interior. The planning concept of a square elongated by a Corinthian arcade comes straight from the City churches, the element of Baroque extravagance deducted. The columns, raised in a Wren-like way above panelled bases, screen passage aisles that bulge out into semi-transepts. Above comes a simple plaster vault, currently washed blue in contrast to the white walls. The east end is blank, and in the centre is a big baldacchino. The frescos Sedding hoped for have never come. It is all very simple, of the kind one would expect to find in a poor urban parish in Italy. What adornment there is was due mainly to Sedding's faithful assistant and successor Harry Wilson, who lengthened the building with a Lady Chapel (1894–5) and raised the austere, tall campanile in 1901–6. Its earlier basilican style is at slight odds with the tone of the church, but does much for the mood of the street.

29

Westminster Cathedral from behind. RCHME

25

Westminster Cathedral
Howick Place, Westminster

2/E6   Underground or British Rail to Victoria

[C]

The slender, striped campanile and heaving saucer domes of Westminster Cathedral shed an exotic influence over the streets east of Victoria Station. Byzantine, Italian or Oriental: however you define the great church's style, its feeling is far from English. Its setting amid mansion blocks seems to belong not to London but to the bourgeois quarter of some other European capital altogether.

Built between 1895 and 1903 to the designs of J F Bentley, the Cathedral offered the Catholic Archdiocese of Westminster magnificent headquarters after years of makeshift accommodation and altered plans. There had been a scheme for a Gothic cathedral on the site, but during Cardinal Manning's archbishopric Catholics had had to make do with a 'Pro-Cathedral' in Kensington

High Street. Herbert Vaughan, who succeeded Manning in 1892, promptly commissioned Bentley, doyen of Catholic architects, to build the cathedral. By then Gothic was no longer *de rigueur* for thinking church architects; the aesthetic and devotional qualities of Early Christian architecture were beginning to excite them instead. In any case, Vaughan wanted to avoid competing with nearby Westminster Abbey. So in 1894 Bentley went off to Italy to observe, think and draw. He came back with the finest basilican design in British architecture.

Bentley had belonged to the advance guard of the English Gothic Revival. The hierarchy and use of materials on the outside of the cathedral complex reflect this. At the back, the Archbishop's House and associated buildings in Ambrosden Avenue and Francis Street are clever essays in the plain, asymmetrical style pioneered by Philip Webb and often used by Bentley for his secular buildings: red brick with sparing stone dressings and homely sash windows, often paired under arches. On the church the Portland stonework turns into stripes and pale granite is

wrapped round the base, making a colourful composition which owes something to Norman Shaw's New Scotland Yard. The stone intensifies on the west front, but only on the portal itself, carried out by J A Marshall after Bentley's death in 1902, does it take over completely. The fine red brickwork is backed by Flettons. Westminster Cathedral was the first major London building in which these bricks were used. Above, the vaults and domes are of mass concrete. All this is expressed in a style which owes something to Rome, Byzantium and medieval Italy but most to Bentley's powers of synthesis and invention. Very striking are the massive, recessed Diocletian windows that light the nave from high up, their heavy tracery buttressed and shaded as if from the Mediterranean sun.

The bulging and patterning of the elevations give way inside the building to a profoundly spiritual interior: a serene, lofty, echoing space, brick-vaulted over massive supporting piers. It is often counted a mercy that the all-over marble veneering envisaged by Bentley never made great progress. Lewis Mumford, for instance, found that the cathedral gave him a sense of the difference between the 'chaste straightforwardness of Roman engineering and the voluptuous appearance of the finished structures'. Certainly the looming bareness of the nave vaults and blank, apsidal east end allows one to concentrate on such distant points of decoration as the pulpit, baldacchino and hanging rood, all original fittings made under Bentley's supervision. Most of the rich marblework on the main piers and intermediary columns of the nave, which boast a delicate series of capitals, was completed quite quickly. In the side chapels behind the piers and aisles, mainly elaborated after 1903, there is more variety of decoration and much use of mosaic. The most rewarding are the Holy Souls' Chapel at the west end of the north aisle, fitted out in 1902–4 with mosaics and a reredos by Bentley's colleague W C Symons, and St Andrew's Chapel in the south aisle, contributed in 1910–15 by an Arts and Crafts team led by the architect R Weir Schultz which included the sculptor Stirling Lee and the woodcarver Ernest Gimson. Shortly thereafter Eric Gill's Stations of the Cross were installed – probably the most moving series of 20th-century reliefs in any British church.

26

Methodist Central Hall
Storey's Gate, Westminster

2/F6   Underground to Westminster or St James's Park

[C]

The *parvis*, as the French would call it, in front of Westminster Abbey, presents one of London's strange stylistic muddles. Though Victoria Street slams through it from one corner to the other, there is a square here in form if not in name. On one side stands the Abbey; flanking it, Gilbert Scott's neo-Gothic Broad Sanctuary Chambers, an escaped morsel of Oxbridge; opposite, Powell and Moya's Queen Elizabeth II Conference Centre, a mannered piece of 1980s architecture bristling with 1980s security devices; and on the fourth side the relentlessly patterned fronts and lead-covered dome of Lanchester and Rickards's Central Hall, making an unblushing stand for the lingua franca of international classicism in the years before the First World War.

That this protuberant affair should be the flagship for London's Methodists seems almost arbitrary; it might as well be a pleasure palace in Paris, a concert hall in Vienna or a valhalla for departed heroes in Munich. In building thus, the Wesleyans were trying to shed their traditional image. Methodists had not had much success in Victorian London. In the 1890s they decided to switch policy to more intensive pastoral, community, mission and administrative work, combined with a renewal of the preaching tradition by which forceful speakers would call forth souls to salvation by addressing the people *en masse*, in the manner of John Wesley. Out went parochial and pallid Gothic chapels; in came arresting, robust, centralised auditoria. The policy did not last for long, but long enough to see

Methodist Central Hall. Entrance. EH

Central Hall, Westminster – a bare-faced challenge to the Church of England in the heart of its territory – competed for, built and opened in 1912.

Lanchester and Rickards, avid competition enterers, were the kind of architects who enjoyed being showy and put most of their effort into the outsides of buildings. Their fronts, which cover an earlyish reinforced concrete frame,

certainly display discipline and scholarship. Cognoscenti can spot borrowings from Hawksmoor, Gabriel, Soufflot, Ledoux and Soane, and there is even a touch or two (which perhaps the Methodists missed) of Gribble's Brompton Oratory, where Rickards had helped complete the dome. But the real pleasure is to be gained from savouring Rickards's sculptural ornamentation on the Storey's Gate frontispiece – his *fasces* over and besides the door, his angels in high relief, his dipping swags, trophies, oxen and lion heads and so on. None of it has much to do with Methodism, but it hardly matters. The flanks and back in Matthew Parker Street, whence entrance is gained to the building's substantial office content (Edwardian Methodists were no bad businessmen) are sparer.

Inside, you come up into a swaggering entrance hall with overscaled classical detail, elliptical arches and a double-flight staircase which leads up to the auditorium on top. Once reached behind a screen of fine columns, the big hall is not so high as you might fancy from the outside and is ceiled with a saucer dome well below the level of the steel-framed, lead-clad topknot above. It is seated like a theatre with deep cantilevered balconies on three sides, of a type only possible with reinforced concrete construction. The organ is the focus of attention. As often with Lanchester and Rickards, the detailing lacks the brio of their external architecture and sculpture. The same is true of their other major London building, delectable little Deptford Town Hall of 1902–7.

27

St Saviour's, Eltham
Middle Park Avenue, Greenwich

1/H6   British Rail to Mottingham or Eltham

[C]

Seeing St Saviour's has the same shock as meeting with a faience-clad Odeon on a leafy street corner. Both were inspired by German expressionism, but since St Saviour's built in 1932–4, well before the Odeon cinemas, there was nothing vulgar-seeming at the time about the stumpy tower and strongly moulded bulk of its dark brick exterior. The interior is unexpectedly high and light, especially since more glass was put into the west end by Laurence King in the 1960s. The chancel is the full height of the tower, lit by long lancets filled

with richly coloured glass. The nave is by contrast very simple, with a gallery for the choir at the west end. The strongest feeling is that the walls and reinforced-concrete roof are paper-thin, a frailty in marked contrast to the solidity of the outside.

The architects were Welch, Cachemaille-Day and Lander, a young partnership formed in 1930. All three had trained within the garden city movement, Nugent Francis Cachemaille-Day and Felix Lander under Louis de Soissons at Welwyn Garden

City and Herbert Welch in Hampstead Garden Suburb. The practice built several housing estates in north London but are best known for the startlingly modern churches that enliven some of the duller 1930s suburbs, especially of Manchester and London.

The planning of St Saviour's is remarkably similar to that of another church of the same date, St Wilfred's in Brighton by H S Goodhart-Rendel. This has the same high chancel-cum-tower and choir gallery, but its round-arched Gothic seems antiquarian compared to

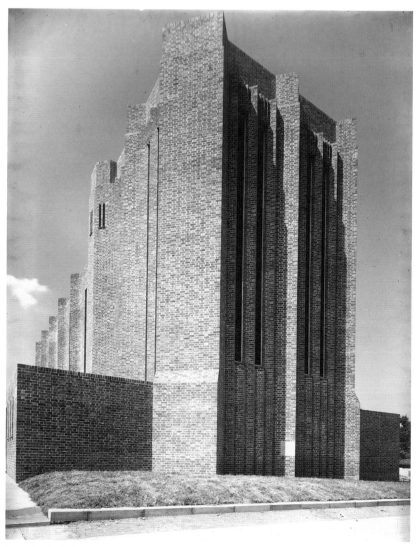

St Saviour's, Eltham. East end. RCHME

St Saviour's fresh approach to style. Cachemaille-Day was Goodhart-Rendel's chief assistant from 1926 to 1928 and he is credited with the office's church work. In 1935 he left Welch and Lander to form his own church practice.

St Saviour's solution of how to provide an appropriate sense of atmosphere and mystery within a cheaply built frame was much repeated, although rarely with such forcefulness. It anticipated the form of most churches built in the early 1950s, and Cachemaille-Day himself built variations on the idea into the early 1960s. In London his best later works are probably Sutton Baptist Church of 1935, with Welch and Lander, and All Hallows', Uxbridge Road, Hanworth, of 1951–7.

28

St Paul's, Bow Common
Burdett Rd, Tower Hamlets

1/H4   Underground to Mile End
[C]

The Diocese of London was not in good shape after the Second World War. Scores of destroyed and damaged churches, a diminishing population and lower attendances at Anglican churches – all these difficulties were greatest in the working-class districts of the East End. The boost given to organized religion by immigrant groups had yet to come. New church-building attracted little initiative or innovation. Buildings were patched up, rebuilt on a reduced, unambitious scale or simply left to rot. The grand but unendowed churches of the Georgians and Victorians became headaches to maintain instead of cause for pride.

St Paul's, Bow Common represents the dawn of a fresh attitude. Sited in what was in 1958 and (to London's shame) remains a specially forlorn patch of the urban wilderness, it seems ordinary enough now: a brick box with a 'helm' in glass on top, and some fussy, 1950s-style frills around the edges. At the time it was the first sign that anyone in London had taken on board the

St Paul's, Bow Common. Interior. EH

debates going on all over Europe, especially in Lutheran Germany, about liturgical arrangements for churches. Simplicity, centralism and visibility were the watchwords of the hour. The church's young architects, Robert Maguire and Robert Murray, expressed all this by adapting for their purposes and their scanty budget the compromise of styles worked out by Sir Basil Spence for his churches and cathedral at Coventry – the most talked-about English ecclesiastical buildings of the decade. Plain slabs of brickwork inside and out contrast with concrete columns

and construction, a mixture of flat and pitched roofs, and a few concentrated points for the display of modern craftsmanship. The altar beneath its canopy and steel 'corona' in the well-lit centre is surrounded by humble, moveable benches. The whole space can be cleared for community use. Extra room and a processional route are provided by a modest internal peristyle. On the outside, the peristyle, porch and vestries distract from the purity of the central core, but lessen the church's austerity. The scale of the lettering over the entrance was perhaps a mistake.

2

Public and Municipal

Until Victorian times, London's monuments of authority and administration derived chiefly from three bodies: the Crown, the Church and the City Corporation. 'Crown' and 'Church' are ambiguous terms. The fiction that the king or queen authorises government actions remains. But the Crown and the State had visibly begun to part administrative ways as long ago as the reign of Charles II, when the Office of Works was already building departmental buildings distinct from palaces. After Whitehall Palace burnt and became defunct as a home of monarchs in 1698, Georgian administrations began to litter its environs with purpose-built offices – first of them the Admiralty, the Treasury and Horse Guards (partly a War Office). These, then, are the nucleus of modern Whitehall – the nearest that evolutionary Britain has ever come to a 'government complex'. But the creation of a set of offices devoted to different departments of public business had to await the compact between Crown and State hammered out in the reign of George III. The upshot was Sir William Chambers's Somerset House, most magnificent of London's Georgian public buildings. Major government offices for the following century and a half continue to respond to the model it set, and some – notably Brydon's imposing, multi-functional offices at the corner of Parliament Street and Square (1898–1912) – pay precise homage to its style as well.

'Church' has a less obvious double meaning. The medieval church enjoyed both spiritual and legal powers, symbolically bound up in its architecture. But there is a simpler sense in which London's older churches stand for authority. Until as late as 1900, the basic unit of local administration was the parish, presided over by the 'Vestry'. Before the 1830s, civil and religious administration in the parish were technically one and the same. We have to imagine local affairs being announced, explained, debated and decreed upon in the body of the church. Important parishes had a special vestry room from the time of the Great Fire onwards, and improved provision for the growing business of local administration was a strong motive in the rebuilding of such churches as St Marylebone and St Pancras (p. 22). Only in the Victorian period do we begin to see secular Vestries detaching themselves from the bosom of mother church and building themselves first vestry halls, usually modest, and then, when the fairy wand of the 1899 Local Government Act turns them into boroughs, grandiose town halls fit for the tasks of the 20th century.

In comparison with Crown and Church, the Corporation of the City of London is a simple thing. Quasi-independent City government goes back to the time of the signing of Magna Carta, when King John was weak and had to cede power not only to barons but also to London's importunate citizens. As the business of the City Corporation multiplied, its organisation became more elaborate, though no less oligarchical. Of the two major buildings that it raised to its own glory and power, its ancient seat of administration, the Guildhall, has been too sorely impaired by bombs and rebuildings to be included in our selection. Instead we represent the Corporation's status with the Mansion House, residence of its august chief functionary, the Lord Mayor, and an example of a building conceived as combining residential and ceremonial use, so common in the past, so alien today.

The City Corporation is easy enough to define. Its historical relations to the rest of London are of impenetrable opacity. Operating from a jealously guarded territory, it stretches selective tentacles out to embrace matters like markets, shipping, bridges and housing, often far beyond its own tiny boundaries. It is left to governments to pick up the slack and cope with the rest of London's problems *ad hoc*. The setting-up of the

Members of the Kensington Fire Brigade outside their new station, 1906. GLRO

Metropolitan Board of Works in 1855, its transformation into the elected London County Council in 1889, the proud construction of County Hall as the seat of London government, the enlarging of the LCC into the Greater London Council in 1965 and the abolition of the GLC in 1986, are all symbols of this feckless toying with London's coherence and very identity.

So, as the manifold tasks of metropolitan administration widen in the 19th century to encompass such things as prisons, hospitals, schools, libraries, police stations, fire stations and an urban transport system, their creation falls to a medley of institutions, local, London-wide or central, elected, statutorily constituted or voluntary. When, as at Hammersmith, a fire station is built by the County Council, a library across the road is paid for by a private donor and then given to the local borough to administer, while the police station is in the hands of a non-elected, government-funded body, it is in vain to expect cohesion of architectural approach. More than that, the very category of 'public and municipal' becomes impossible to define. For simplicity's sake, we include below all services which do not have a special category of their own, as do schools, hospitals and transport buildings.

Until the 1840s, London's public and municipal buildings were generally classical. Classicism, the only style of architecture that had well-defined rules, stood by time-honoured European tradition for the authority of secular government or (as at the British Museum and National Gallery) for high culture. Things began to break up under the influence of the Palace of Westminster, where context and sentiment led to the choice of the Tudor-Gothic idiom (pp. 67–9). The Foreign Office competition and its aftermath made confusion worse confounded. London's one great planned group of public buildings, what is now known as the 'Museums Area of South Kensington', starts by trying to turn this confusion into a matter of eclectic principle and ends in incoherence. It has its moments, notably the court of the Victoria & Albert Museum. But the idea

was always too eccentric and un-English to command general acceptance. For a short while in the 1860s and 1870s – the era of the Law Courts and the Natural History Museum – it looked as though Gothic had triumphed. Then, with little fuss, it collapsed as a mode for public buildings and classicism made a comeback. This was a new, robust kind of classicism, which could be orderly and scholarly (County Hall, Hammersmith Police Station) or flagrantly eclectic (Croydon Town Hall). London's vestry and town halls of the period 1890–1914 are often memorable, flashy and fun, but, being largely products of the competition system, few of them involve serious thought or architectural principle.

To find that, one must seek out the best of the smaller kinds of building so assiduously built during that period: settlement houses like Mary Ward House (p. 175), the gallant run of fire stations designed by the LCC's architects, or Harrison Townsend's fascinating trio of the Bishopsgate Institute, the Whitechapel Gallery and the Horniman Museum. In their differing ways they all exemplify the attitudes, experimentalism and range of urban Arts and Crafts architecture. On a larger public scale, there is nothing quite of this kind except for Norman Shaw's puzzling New Scotland Yard. Many reasons have been hazarded for this: the conservatism of clients, the love affair between Edwardian imperialism and the new classicism, the failure of Arts and Crafts architects to agree upon a non-domestic idiom, English anti-urbanism, or sheer 'loss of nerve'. There is certainly something to be explained.

This sense of a void in London's public architecture has persisted. While there are some smart inter-war municipal town halls, like those at Hornsey and Greenwich, and while the LCC continued spasmodically to create worthy public buildings – chief among them the Royal Festival Hall (pp. 201–2) – government patronage of good architecture in London since 1918 has been all but non-existent. Once upon a time it was fashionable to praise a very plain inter-war Ministry of Pensions building in Acton, for want of anything

better. Nor can much be said in favour of the post-war buildings in which ministries carry out their functions. The lumpen Ministry of Defence in Whitehall stands at the fag-end of the older classical tradition; its outliers are no better, save perhaps the design-and-build blocks (much sneered at in the 1950s) in Theobalds Road. The blocks of offices which shelter the Department of the Environment in Marsham Street are a mockery of the trust imposed upon its occupants. And so one could go on, pointing the finger in turn at the Department of Education and Science, the Home Office and the Department of Health and Social Security. Two exceptions may be made. One is the Commonwealth Institute, cheap and imperfect, yet with a welcome air of bold inventiveness in the company of such dull competitors. The other is Sir Basil Spence's chunky Knightsbridge Barracks, a worthy descendant of London's long barrack-building tradition.

29

Mansion House
Queen Victoria St and Walbrook, City of London

2/K4   Underground or British Rail to Bank

The Mansion House is the residence and function centre of the Lord Mayor of London, elected annually but far from democratically. It also once housed courts and a prison, though the Guildhall remained the City Corporation's administrative centre. But, through depopulation, the Corporation's responsibilities have had to evolve relatively little from the 18th century and its ceremonial functions retain unusual importance.

The idea of a mayoral residence originated in about 1670 but little was done until a competition was held in 1737 for a clear site not rebuilt after the 1666 fire. The appointment of the City Surveyor, George Dance, as architect in the face of educated opposition such as James Gibbs and Giacomo Leoni represented the City's preference for

The Mansion House. A F KERSTING

efficient planning over a first-rate facade. For whilst lacking nothing in power, the main porticoed front facing the Bank of England is oddly proportioned, with a low rusticated base that does little to emphasise Dance's equally low *piano nobile*. Instead the drama is played up in the high attic, which originally rose even taller in two clerestories across the front and back of the building, dubbed the 'Mayor's Nest' and 'Noah's Ark'. Today the most exaggerated feature is the massive pediment enlivened by the young Robert Taylor, who began his career as a sculptor.

At York in 1730 Lord Burlington had adapted Palladio's concept of a colonnaded Egyptian Hall as a civic idiom for the York Assembly Rooms. Dance repeated the form on a massive scale, cunningly hidden along the rear of the building. The problem was its height, resulting in the 'Noah's Ark' clerestory at the back, its form repeated over the ballroom across the front. These were causing structural problems even as the building was finally completed in 1753. In the 1790s Dance's eponymous son lowered the Egyptian

Hall and installed a barrelled and coffered vault, leaving the massive Corinthian columns looking bereft of purpose and the space lit only from each end. The present side fenestration dates from the 1930s. The 'Mayor's Nest' was lowered in 1842. The attics may be imagined from the side elevations, especially by venturing down Walbrook. The importance of the Egyptian Hall and ballroom to the plan can still be appreciated from their massive arched sash windows that pierce the heavy cornice on either side.

The Mansion House is no longer entered under the portico but from a side entrance in Walbrook that leads to a basement hall inserted by J B Bunning in the 1840s. This has confused Dance's planning of the *piano nobile*. His vestibule, filled with sculpture bought at the Great Exhibition, is now only an office. Odder still, his central hall or *cortile* was open to the skies until 1795. Only its heavy Doric colonnade gives any suggestion that it was once an open court. To either side are mayoral parlours and the justice room, as well as two staircases that are survivors of an original four. All are quintessential City

pieces of the 1730s: heavily moulded, and richly and fruitily decorated in a baroque tradition that is still indebted to Wren. The quality of these details is infinitely more satisfying than the academic innovation of the Egyptian Hall.

30

Somerset House
Strand, Westminster

2/H4   Underground to Temple
[C]   (parts)

The architecture of Sir William Chambers grows on one. Repeated visits to Somerset House are recommended for the full savouring of this most august of Georgian public buildings.

The novel idea of gathering together as many government offices as possible into one capacious complex owed something to the statesman and philosopher Edmund Burke, more to the prime minister of the 1770s, Lord North. Departments were strung all along the river, from the Navy Office at the eastern edge of the City to the Treasury at Whitehall. The navy clerks were especially ill housed. An Act of 1775 provided for pulling down old Somerset House, technically the Queen's dower house but long given over to a medley of official uses. William Robinson was to design the new offices, but died in the same year. Into his shoes stepped Chambers, the 'Comptroller of the Works'. It was the chance of his life and Chambers took it, consecrating the rest of his career to the job and conceiving it as a showcase for advanced Palladian principles. Begun in 1776, Somerset House was finished only in 1801, five years after his death. The outer wings are later still, the eastern extension of 1830–5 incorporating King's College (by Smirke), and the fine western extension of 1851–6 facing Lancaster Place – a fresh invention added in Chambers's style by clever Sir James Pennethorne to house the Inland Revenue.

The layout adopted by Chambers took something from the collegiate and legal tradition of planning, something from the modern London square, and something from the Paris *hôtel*. His simple scheme was for a big, open, Portland-stone-clad court flanked behind by a pair of streets with a row each of brick-faced terraces for officials' houses. Of the streets, only the western one (well worth a look for the special beauty of its brickwork) was constructed. Like the Adam brothers' slap-happy Adelphi, built just previously, the back of all this had to be raised up above the Thames on a great substructure. In the name of the government, Chambers was determined to do magnificently what the Adams had

done speculatively and cheaply. He therefore allotted the Thames front to the main naval departments and projected out below them a long, hollow terrace of granite with the river lapping underneath. In the middle of the terrace below the central colonnade, pediment and rather puny dome is a Piranesian arch of broad robustness designed for the use of the King's Barge-Master, while under the open Palladian bridges at the end of the side streets come further fine water-gates. The whole river front, too long by the time all the additions had been finished, can be taken in from Waterloo Bridge. But the

effect of the terrace was irreparably damaged when the Thames was pushed back and the Victoria Embankment formed right in front of it in the 1860s.

The Strand front of the building was the first portion to be finished, in 1778. It is quite narrow, like the entrance to a Parisian *hôtel*. Indeed, when he designed it Chambers had a recent French 'office block' in mind, Antoine's Hôtel des Monnaies. With great suavity, it is blended with elements from the gallery of the former Somerset House, then attributed to Inigo Jones, which Chambers regretted having to destroy. The carving of this front, typical of the high sculptural standard of the building, was the work of three Englishmen, Wilton, Nollekens and Bacon, and two Italians, Carlini and Ceracchi. In honour of the Navy Office its theme is marine, with keystones of (from left to right) Severn, Tyne, Tweed, Medway, Ocean, Thames, Humber, Mersey and Dee. Justice, Prudence, Valour and Moderation ('qualities by which dominion alone can be maintained') front the raised attic. On the courtyard side of the block, note among more docile continents 'America armed and breathing defiance'. Poor Lord North!

A triple, vaulted entry, the most assured and Italian thing of its kind in Georgian architecture, takes you through into the court. Alternatively you can turn under the last bay of the entrance – left into the former premises of the Royal Society, or right into those of the Royal Academy, which shared the upper storeys of the front block. The Academy (of which Chambers was Treasurer) had been in old Somerset House and so was rehoused here. Its old apartments, including a double-height exhibition room lit from behind the attics, have been recently reclaimed and restored by the Courtauld Institute for showing its own art collection, with rather disappointing results for both building and pictures. But a visit does allow one to sample two of the fine staircases scattered throughout Somerset House; Chambers was incomparable with stairs.

The court beyond the entry opens out to greater breadth and ease than a *hôtel*. It is quiet, dignified, mostly English but

Somerset House. Looking into the courtyard. RCHME

Somerset House. The river front. RCHME

with a few French touches, and without the tiresome breaks and recessions that mar immature Palladian architecture. It has pediments and cupolaed centres to the sides, arches to the streets behind, and lively reliefs (mainly by Joseph Wilton) flanking the doors to the various offices. If the statue of George III by John Bacon in the middle of the court is a disappointment, so too is the sea of civil servants' cars which still surround it, despite years of protest about their presence.

If you wish to get a flavour of the old-style civil service, lineal descendants of the clerks of Sir William Chambers's day, you could take the opportunity to look up a relative's will, to get inside the Principal Probate Registry in the centre of the south front, formerly the waiting room of the Navy Office.

31

Royal Artillery Barracks
Grand Depot Rd and Repository Rd, Woolwich, Greenwich

1/J5   British Rail to Woolwich Arsenal

Woolwich is a hotchpotch of urban blight, open space and the formidable litter of armed might. Brumwell

Thomas's florid Edwardian town hall apart, its architectural interest is exclusively military and industrial. Central to both traditions and to the whole history of this part of London is the mouldering Royal Arsenal behind the Plumstead Road, with fascinating but inaccessible buildings by Vanbrugh, James Wyatt and others. Wyatt was Architect to the Ordnance, in which capacity he contributed to the army's two most visible older buildings to have survived Woolwich's wartime pounding. Wearing his threadbare Gothic hat, he built in 1805–8 the large Royal Military Academy in Academy Road near the Herbert Hospital, home now to the Royal Artillery Museum. In more respectable classical guise Wyatt added to the Royal Artillery Barracks, vaster still. This is one of the most astonishing sights of London – but for its extent alone, not for any architectural refinement.

'Leningrad,' exclaim all the commentators on contemplating the barracks stretching their staggering, symmetrical length along the breadth of Artillery Place at the top of Woolwich Common. It is a natural reaction, yet in many ways a misleading one, for the elements of the building are unmistakably British and banal. There are eighty-eight windows altogether in the front, which nowhere rises to more than three storeys altogether. Long brick ranges alternate with little white-

painted pavilions and culminate in a stuccoed triumphal arch embedded in the middle. The intermediate blocks with their trim pediments and cupolas look as though they had been lifted from the Midlands factory of some Georgian industrialist. There is not a great deal that is old now behind this front, though the complex formerly continued northwards to make an immense, camp-like square. It was begun in 1775, to whose design seems not to be known, and completed by Wyatt in about 1808. In front of the barracks John Bell's Crimean War Memorial of 1860, a gun or two and a helicopter enliven the tarmac.

For a refreshing bonne-bouche, a visit is counselled to the nearby Museum of Artillery in the Rotunda, an outlier of the main display in the old Military Academy. Off the beaten track in Green Hill, this miniature circular building topped by a tall copper roof looks like a cross between the Chalk Farm Roundhouse (p. 237) and some centralised church of the 1950s. Its true origins are odder still. It started life as a temporary tent in St James's Park, designed by John Nash for the calamitous victory celebrations there in 1814. Translated to Woolwich and into permanent materials in 1819–20, Nash's tent now houses a small museum about the history of the gun. A Thunderbird missile by the gate offers a premonitory hint of its aggressive content.

Royal Artillery Barracks, front. GLRO

39

British Museum. The round reading room. BL

32

British Museum
Great Russell St, Camden

2/G3   Underground to Tottenham
Court Road or Holborn

[A]

'Here at last is a proper public building,'
proclaim the forty-four serried columns
that fringe the front of Sir Robert
Smirke's British Museum. Stylophily, as
the building's monographer, Dr Joe
Crook, calls the extravagant practice of
obscuring the light from half a dozen
perfectly serviceable rooms with giant
Greek cylinders, enjoys no grander
moment in London than this facade. It
begs for a great axial avenue leading up
to it, but this is not the way the English
do these things. Architects as different
as Lethaby and Colin St John Wilson
have proposed destroying the Museum
Street quarter across Great Russell
Street for the sake of such a creation,
but have failed. So the museum has to
make do with a broad forecourt graced
with an ice cream kiosk, a lively set of

cast-iron railings designed by Smirke's
brother Sydney along the street and, at
the entrance, two comic lodges carved
out of blank granite pylons.

The national collections have been
here longer than the building itself. The
'curiosities' bequeathed to the nation by
Sir Hans Sloane, mainly natural history
specimens, together with the Old Royal
Library, were slung haphazardly into
Montagu House in 1759, and much
augmented over the next half century.
What made a new building inevitable
was not just that fast rate of acquisition
but the all-powerful romantic ideal of
Culture – the belief that a nation's
history, destiny and vigour were
reflected in the art and antiquities it
could boast. In the heady years after
Waterloo, with Napoleon's Egyptian
plunder and Elgin's Parthenon marbles
under their belt, even the slow-thinking
British were not immune. So Smirke,
one of the attached architects to the
Office of Works and a fervent Hellenist,
was called in and told to rebuild the
Montagu House site in worthy style.
Then that old Anglo-Saxon fault with
public buildings, short-sighted
parsimony, intervened. Smirke began

work in about 1821 and was given the
green light in 1823. But the House of
Commons never voted enough money,
so that the building dribbled on for over
twenty years in frustrating stages. When
it was completed in 1848, it was out of
date and too small. By then poor, patient
Smirke had handed over the
architectural torch to his brother, 'little
Sid'.

As a result, Smirke's front is a fine
thing, but has somehow missed the bus.
By the time it was put up in 1841–7
great museums by Schinkel in Berlin
and von Klenze in Munich were
complete, and the portentous temple
front as an architectural approach to
high culture was on its way to becoming
a cliché. Smirke uses the Ionic order
(from the Temple of Athena Polias at
Priene) with masterly precision. Yet
there is something elusively Victorian
about the thing, epitomized by
Westmacott's rigid and uninspired
'Progress of Civilisation' in the
pediment. A restoration of the original
blue background to the sculptures
might cheer things up.

Inside, the impression is the same.
Robust, romantic colours could do
much to save Smirke's acreage of eternal
trabeation from dullness, and on the
west side might pep up the marmoreal
booty in which this sector of the
museum abounds. The old Elgin
Marbles Room (where the Nereid
Monument from Xanthos is now
displayed) is an example. Though
mutilated, it is still a well-proportioned
space with excellent top-lighting and
fine Greek details between the grid of
beams. But its décor makes it flat and
pallid. The vast Duveen Gallery beyond,
added by the American architect John
Russell Pope in 1939 but not opened till
1962, is a grey, lithic space in which the
Parthenon frieze and pediment
fragments shrink into the background
and visitors start to feel their feet.

Three great zones of the building
stand exempt from criticism. The first is
the old King's Library, the earliest
portion of Smirke's museum to be
finished (1823–8) and the richest of the
original interiors. It runs the complete
length of the east wing, its high cream
and marmalade scagliola walls

stretching away into the distance. It is the Banqueting House reinterpreted in fastidious Greek idiom, lined with books, more than doubled in length and backed with cast-iron technology. Its 41 ft width, spanned by Ironbridge-made beams specified by the engineer John Rastrick, was seminal to the spread of concealed iron construction. Here Smirke the constructor shows at his surest.

Then there is the circular, domed reading room of the British Library, inserted by Sydney Smirke in 1854–7 (at the instigation of Panizzi, the museum's ferocious librarian) in place of his brother's useless quadrangle. It is a space as much to listen to as to look at, with a slow, soporific acoustic that takes every rustled page, every mumble, sniffle and cough, up to the iron ribs and back down to the reader in muffled parenthesis. It is not great architecture, but its diameter and atmosphere are unforgettable. In 1993 the readers will remove to Euston Road. What will then take place beneath the celebrated dome?

Last comes Sir John Burnet's Montagu Place extension of 1907–14, at the back. Though only part of what Burnet designed, it is enough to be going on with. An enfilade of engaged, three-quarter columns confronts the street in a clean, French manner, while fine sedentary lions (by George Frampton) flank the entrance. Inside, the hall is low, modest, and lit by an open ring from above. Hence you come to a staircase of unexpected breadth and sumptuousness, lined with light Greek marble; a pair of black columns with a gigantic Buddha between thrust up into the well, while a gilt bronze lift cage ascends to one side. The galleries are in the trabeated Smirke style, but with side compartments and stripped-classical details that reveal their true date. All this is neo-classical architecture of a high level. Its author, be it noted, was not an Englishman but a Glasgow Scot. Behind the stair is the North Library, entirely altered from Burnet's original mannerist concept. Stubby Egyptian columns slam down now between the desks and enforce a mood of grave concentration absent from the main reading room.

33
Foreign and Commonwealth Office
Parliament St, Westminster

2/G5   Underground to Westminster

The Foreign Office, with the former India Office to its rear facing St James's Park, began Whitehall's redevelopment with government offices worthy of the centre of Britain's expanding empire. Foreign affairs had since the 18th century been conducted from a terrace of Georgian houses, like Downing Street next door. But by the 1850s the Foreign Office houses were not only overcrowded, but unsafe.

In 1856 Lord Palmerston's government held competitions for new Foreign and War Offices, won by little-known architects with classical designs. Then one was found unworkable, just as Palmerston's government fell. The only

Foreign and Commonwealth Office. The former Durbar Court. RCHME

41

established architect placed in both competitions was also the only Gothicist, Sir Gilbert Scott. The new pro-Gothic First Commissioner of Public Works, Lord John Manners, gave him the job.

The War Office had meanwhile found accommodation on Pall Mall. Instead the East India Company, embarrassed by the Indian Mutiny of 1857 and reconstituted into a government office, needed a home in Whitehall. Scott was given this job also, to the consternation of the Company's architect, Matthew Digby Wyatt, an eclectic but a classicist. A compromise was hammered out whereby Wyatt did the interior of the India Office and Scott the rest. But in 1859 Lord Palmerston was returned to power. Considering Gothic wholly inappropriate for both the site and function of the building, he insisted on an Italianate scheme.

It is Wyatt's work that stands out as the most assured. Of the four courts in the building, that for the India Office (named the Durbar Court in 1902) is not only the most ornate part of the building but spatially the most imaginative, the court being unified with its surrounding offices by open loggias at each end and by a glazed roof added in 1867. All three storeys and four sides are given round-arched arcades, with a mounting sequence of statuary to past heroes of British India, plaques to towns and rivers, and tiled relief panels to give colour. The design is held together by a heavy cornice, whose brackets spell out: 'THIS COURT WAS BUILT AD 1866 BY M D WYATT ARCHITECT'. Equally magnificent are the ceremonial rooms, especially that of the Secretary of State. The scheme suggested the continuity of Indian government from the East Indian Company, as well as reflecting the influence of Wyatt's friend Owen Jones. The front of St James's Park meanwhile gave Scott scope for a picturesque stepped composition, dominated by an assymmetrical tower. Later commentators have exaggerated Wyatt's hand in the design, limited to a rough sketch.

For the main building, Scott was faced with the problem of accommodating not only the Foreign

Office but the Home and Colonial Offices also, and with greater financial stringencies. The result is a labyrinth of corridors and staircases, some impressive, some simple; any ceremonial sequence has largely been lost in subsequent reorganisations of the departments that use them. The principal rooms, finished in 1868, are built around the Grand Staircase, of gilded and marbled opulence. To the ground floor is an Ionic colonnade, to the first a Corinthian, and the space is topped by a dome filled with murals by Clayton and Bell of the zodiac and the principal nations arranged by continent. To one side were placed a sequence of opulent function rooms, to the other a suite of equal grandeur served the Secretary of State. The circular staircase to the Colonial Office, completed in 1875, is simpler but no less striking for its height and careful geometry.

The exterior owes much to earlier schemes for the site and especially to the Louvre extensions, which Scott saw in 1860. Originally intended to contain far more sculpture than was eventually allowed, the facade facing Whitehall is taut, but cold without its intended embellishment. Instead it is overshadowed by its more blowzy neighbour, built alongside between 1898 and 1912 to the design of John Brydon and now the Treasury. Only by venturing down King Charles Street can the public glimpse the cross-axis intended through these comparable yet contrasting buildings; this, though, was blocked long before mere voters were dismissed from the hallowed precincts of Downing Street.

34

The Royal Courts of Justice
The Strand, Westminster

2/H4   Underground to Temple or Aldwych (peak hours only)

[C]

H S Goodhart-Rendel described the Law Courts (as they are usually known) as the grave of Gothic Revival. They have

been charged too with the death of their architect, George Edmund Street, a year before they opened in 1882. Unlike Scott at the Foreign Office, Street persevered against a plethora of government ministers and officials to get the building he wanted, and he controlled every detail himself, giving little over to his assistants.

Nineteenth-century England inherited a system of justice that was obtuse and unwieldy, with no decent building in which to administer it. In 1824–5 Soane squeezed new courts around Westminster Hall, which became a communal entrance and gathering ground. This zonal arrangement around a *salle des pas perdus* was Street's prototype, at several removes. By 1840 courts were being held in makeshift buildings across London. The Law Society's campaign for better facilities dovetailed with one for the reform of the legal system itself, achieved only in 1873. Lincoln's Inn Fields were suggested as a site for a new building, handy for the Inns of Court, and Charles Barry prepared a symmetrical design around a central hall. An even more convenient option was an overcrowded rookery between Carey Street and the Strand, whose clearance was finally ordered in 1865. A competition was called the next year.

Following the débâcle of the open competition for the Foreign Office, only six architects were invited to compete for the Law Courts, increased under protest to eleven. But the brief was hazardously vague in its essentials and the jury amateur. The difference was that in 1866 a Gothic scheme had a good chance of winning, with a preponderance of the entries in that style. Most striking was William Burges's, a Gormenghast of towers and tourelles. By contrast E M Barry's thin Gothic trim was unconvincing but his scheme was the best planned. Alfred Waterhouse, with experience of court-building in Manchester, offered a picturesque compromise. Instead the jury made its own compromise, selecting Barry's plan and Street's elevation. When forced to choose by an angry Treasury, it plumped in 1868 for Street.

The Law Courts. Strand front. RCHME

and busy skyline, is the simplicity of the Portland stonework. Street's ornamentation always holds up to scrutiny, but it is the overall massing that impresses – especially of the great clock tower judiciously placed at the sole point where it can be seen behind St Clement Danes down the Strand. Inside, the Great Hall is more serenely English: its Purbeck marble shafts, paired lancets and stone vaulting are relieved from ecclesiastical remorselessness by stairways and little viewing points. Stairwells within stairwells and vaulted cross-corridors add to the impact. Street designed most of the furniture, completed after his death by his son and Arthur Blomfield. But the most pleasurable part of the building are the brick elevations facing Bell Yard, ending in a chequerboard brick and stone tower on Carey Street which looks its best from across Lincoln's Inn.

Street has two memorials in the building: the Strand clock, installed on the anniversary of his death, and a seated effigy in the hall by H H Armstead.

35

Natural History Museum
Cromwell Rd, Kensington and Chelsea

2/B6   Underground to South Kensington
[A]

So unsatisfactory a victory was only the start of Street's problems. He was charged with using elements of the other entries in revised designs, and indeed Burges's elevations may have prompted him to revert to his youthful taste for simple massing and French detailing. He was forced to make designs for an alternative site by the Thames before the government reverted to Carey Street. He had to argue for years over the cost of every detail, especially with Gladstone's parsimonious administration of 1868–74, and suffered inexperienced builders who overstretched themselves in undercutting the established firms.

Work on the superstructure only began in 1874. While the arrangement of courts around a great hall with separate corridors for the judges and spectators was common to most of the competitors, the brilliant device of setting the hall at right-angles to the Strand was Street's own inspiration, in 1870. It gave not only a ceremonial way from the Strand to Carey Street but allowed better use of the sharp difference in street levels. Most importantly, it gave meaning to the enriched entrances on the two main facades.

The abiding feature of the Strand frontage, despite the elegant arcading

Darwin published *The Origin of Species* in 1859. In the same year Richard Owen, forceful superintendent of the British Museum's natural history collections, first sketched out a separate building for them at South Kensington. The classification, display and explication of the natural sciences was a tremendous force in the mid-Victorian intellectual world. The introduction of natural science teaching at Oxford coincided with the creation of the epoch-making Oxford Museum (1855–60), which for the first time (at Ruskin's prompting) strove to make the fabric of a museum as instructive as its contents by representing fauna and flora accurately upon its Gothic capitals and other features. Owen's new, national museum followed on from the Oxford precedent but blended it with the 'South Kensington' concept of how a museum building could instruct, through the display of new materials and techniques. It fell to Alfred Waterhouse's genius to make a superb synthesis between these sometimes conflicting ideals.

The museum took long to realise. Owen was given the go-ahead in 1862, after the International Exhibition of that year had been cleared away from the site. A competition ensued, won by Francis Fowke, the right-hand man of Henry Cole, *éminence grise* of official South Kensington. Fowke was then erecting what is now the courtyard of the Victoria & Albert Museum in a mixed German and Italian style, with bold new forms of terracotta decoration exemplifying anti-Ruskinian principles of reduplicated pattern and ornament. His Natural History Museum would have been similar. But Fowke died, and was replaced in 1866 by Alfred Waterhouse, whose brief was to modify the design he had inherited. Waterhouse used the many changes that followed to make the project entirely his own, while adhering to Fowke's basic layout. Work started in 1873, staggered from one crisis to another, including the 'absolute ruin' of the contractors, George Baker and Son, and was completed in 1880.

What Waterhouse (an avid Goth and qualified Ruskinian) did was to translate Fowke's curious idiom into full-hearted Gothic or, more accurately, the Romanesque of Auvergne; and to frame the building largely in iron and then clad it for reasons of fireproofing, inside and out, with a luscious display of terracotta. The plan is a model of clarity, with lateral galleries on two storeys along the great front, a central hall of breathtaking magnificence behind the imposing twin towers and portal, and smaller single-storey galleries for study parallel with the hall. The principles of the layout were determined by Owen, a pioneer of palaeontological classification. He wanted the great hall to be open to the public for longer hours than the specialised side galleries, and to display in epitome the wealth and diversity of creation.

Owen's programme for the decoration also embodied the ideas of variety and classification: extinct species were to be shown on one side of the building, extant ones on the other. So, for instance, on the left of the front you see a sequence of figures including wolf, panther and lion; on its right a sequence of machaerodon, palaeotherium and mylodon. That is to pick out just one of a seemingly infinite variety of creatures beautifully sketched by Waterhouse himself, drawn out by his assistants, modelled by one Dujardin of the firm of Farmer and Brindley, fired in Gibbs and Canning's terracotta works at Tamworth and then put up on the building. They range through pterodactyls, dodos, fossil and living fish amid conventionalised waves on the delightful square piers of the long galleries, to the dogs and birds on the central hall's stairs and the rampant monkeys clambering up its arches. In reality there is much reduplication. If Waterhouse was trying to prove that mechanical reproduction of natural ornament was compatible with the variety and humanity of decoration which Ruskin advocated, he succeeded magnificently. But the wonderful terracotta which we enjoy today was a headache at the time. Never before had a complete building been clothed in the material. The technical problems involved (to get the blue blocks, for instance, expensive cobalt had to be injected) were greatly responsible for the bankruptcy of the unfortunate Bakers. The building came in vastly over cost and did Waterhouse's reputation for efficiency no good.

Of later additions to the building, the most significant is the inter-war Whale Hall, tucked away in the north-west sector. In its essentials, Waterhouse's museum is intact. But a protest must be entered against the persistent refusal of the museum's officials and trustees to work with the spirit of the masterpiece which they are so lucky to have, rather than against it. Over recent years more and more of the beautifully lit galleries have been cut up with one fashion of ephemeral display after another. The attitude seems to be that so long as the central hall is respected, anything should be allowed at the sides. A more enlightened attitude to the relation between architecture and exhibition display is urgently needed.

36
New Scotland Yard
Victoria Embankment, Westminster

2/G5   Underground to Westminster

New Scotland Yard – as the complex comprising the Norman Shaw Buildings, North and South, is still popularly known, although the police deserted it in the 1970s for a bleak new block of the same name off Victoria Street – is an enigmatic building by an enigmatic architect. Norman Shaw, the architectural cat with nine styles, first came near to being totally serious in this, his only complete public building. As there is nothing quite like it, it can be hard to grasp what he was up to.

The buildings come in two parts: a square, pink-grey-and-purple fortress to the north (1887–90) separated by a private roadway from a briefer building in the same style facing the embankment (1901–7) and from Cannon Row Police Station behind (1900–02). Only the northern portion was originally intended. The Metropolitan Police needed a proper headquarters, and in 1886 were promised this fine embankment site, long empty through a succession of mishaps. The original proposal was that the police surveyor, John Butler, should design the building, with an eminent architect as consultant. Shaw was nominated and soon took over the job. He adopted Butler's plan of a square building round an open court, but pulled the corridors out of the middle of the offices and placed them against the court to give them light and air. Otherwise the plan is not of special interest, unless you care for in details like the tracking of multiple flues to the four great stacks of the roofs.

The elevations are a different matter, and show Shaw striving to create a public architecture for the 1880s that would combine originality, appropriate expression and a feeling for texture. The difficulty was that he was trying to do so without any clear architectural theory. His main method was to take ideas from his own commercial and domestic architecture and dignify them. Thus the motif of a corner tourelle juxtaposed with a sharp gable comes from his Alliance Assurance Building at the bottom of St James's Street, with the riotous Flemish ornament stripped off; while in the generally symmetrical lines of the fronts there is the covert admiration of Wren often to be found in Shaw. The robust classical detail imposed upon the building to give it gravity is influenced by Belcher's Institute of Chartered Accountants, finished when New Scotland Yard was on site.

As usual, too, Shaw allowed himself to be inspired by circumstance. So when Sir Edward DuCane, Director of H M Prisons, made the grimly ironic offer of granite for the police building quarried by Dartmoor convicts, he closed with the suggestion. Hence the high granite plinth – one of New Scotland Yard's most influential features – rising to a mix of thin pink bricks and Portland stone strips. The colours are pretty, but at strange odds with the building's formidable bulk and outline, which hint at the custodial power of the police and the castle-keeps of Shaw's own native Scotland. The sophisticated eclecticism of the building puzzled contemporaries. But its masterly qualities were in the end sufficiently recognised for a

commemorative medallion of its architect (made by Hamo Thornycroft with help from W R Lethaby, Shaw's chief assistant when New Scotland Yard was built) to be set up on the front in 1913.

The extension buildings are a mistake in terms of the architecture of the original, diminishing its wonderful squareness and stoutness. But the police, expanding and specialising the whole time, wanted more accommodation, and Shaw was put in the common position of an architect who had to decide whether to let someone else tamper with his work or accept the job himself. The scheme was conceived in 1897 but not finished for a decade. This time Shaw, in nominal retirement, was on more equal terms with the police surveyor, John Butler's son John Dixon Butler. Shaw provided the fronts but Butler did a lot of the planning, especially for Cannon Row Police Station. Another style altogether might have been better for the extension, but the need to link old and new parts by a bridge prompted continuity of elevation. The bridge itself, the avenue – alas, no longer accessible to the public now that MPs have rooms in the two buildings – and the gates (not designed by Shaw but by Reginald Blomfield) are fine enough. But the manner in which the embankment front of the extension building stops abruptly with a weak gable not long after it gets started, shows Shaw below his best. The most remarkable feature of the extension is the way in which the back of it is carried by great girders slung over the underground by Sir John Wolfe Barry, the engineer of Tower Bridge.

37

Croydon Town Hall
Katharine St, Croydon

1/G7   British Rail to East or West Croydon

[C]

The clue to Croydon is its inferiority complex. A bustling town too near London, it refused to accept its commuting destiny gracefully, in the

New Scotland Yard. River front. GLRO

45

Croydon Town Hall, front and tower. CROYDON LIBRARIES

manner of Bromley or Barnet. Croydon always had to do things for itself. That, allied with a Protestant, *petit bourgeois* tradition going back to 16th-century Archbishop Whitgift (for Croydon has its archiepiscopal palace), does much to explain the unexpected rash of 1960s office blocks that assault the eye as you approach the town. None is worth a close look, and their erection – with attendant ring roads – proved fatal for the modest charms of Croydon's townscape. At least they show that the borough is adaptable and alive to the main chance. They also do something to set off the indeterminate acreage of small houses that is the lot of this region of suburban London.

One good thing that Croydon's will to be different achieved was to furnish the place with a fine town hall in the 1890s, the last decade when there was still some ring of truth to its ideal of independence. This is not, then, the headquarters of some minor metropolitan borough with arty aspirations, fostered after 1900 by central government as a counterweight to the radical London County Council. It is a show of civic identity on the part of an ancient town – 'incorporated 1883', as an inscription on the side elevation does not let us forget.

The architecture is to match: assertive, virile, pedantic, more than a

trifle coarse, but honest, exuberant stuff. It was designed, naturally, by a local man, Charles Henman junior, and built by the reputable local building firm of the then late W H Lascelles. There is plenty of movement to the composition, which takes up most of the south side of Katharine Street. First comes Union Bank Chambers of 1893. Then, set back, is the reference library, housed in the robust and generous Braithwaite Hall. After that we advance again with Henman's big tower, Tudorbethan in its lower stages but rising to something akin to the cupola of Wren's St Magnus the Martyr on top. Finally, back on the street line, we arrive at 'Corporation Chambers', symmetrical, with three more or less equal gables at the ends and in the centre.

The embellishments are particular fun. In front of the Braithwaite Hall on a high plinth is a full-size bronze of Queen Victoria, at her most sedentary and triangular (1903). As a foil Archbishop Whitgift, also seated but at a fittingly smaller scale, looks down from the angle of the Information Centre. Finer than either and indeed a cut above the architecture are the Arts and Crafts reliefs on the front of the Braithwaite Hall by E Roscoe Mullins. They incite Croydonians to the pursuit of Health, Study, Religion, Recreation (boys play cricket, girls just dance demurely) and Music. Above, the heads of fifteen British worthies adorn the cornice. Inside the hall, the Reference Library still functions in the good old way. There is a solid oak hammerbeam roof high up in the gloom, the galleries have solid oak Jacobean fronts, and you read still at solid oak tables – only the chairs have changed. More worthies are delineated in glass on the long side, and as if this were not enough, Reading, Thought, Writing, Science, Religion (again) and Art are allegorized in the end windows. If the diligent reader should need some other municipal service, he must first pass a front door decorated with the watchwords Education, Protection, Justice, Order, Sanitation and Recreation (again) and with shields representing State, Borough, Church and Education.

It would be fond to think that these

ideals are daily before the eyes of every Croydon council officer. In reality, most of those good people now inhabit motto-free Katharine House opposite or Taberner House behind, both fairly soulless representatives of the new Croydon. The town hall itself, with only two full storeys above ground, is capacious enough just for a large marble staircase, corridors to match (though they soon peter out into banality), a galleried council chamber, and rooms for the main dignitaries and a smattering of officials. The interiors are 'appropriate', no more, but have the remnants of some sturdy municipal furniture – made in Croydon. The back of the building, towards Mint Walk, is worth a glance, if only because Henman made no self-conscious effort with it. The Braithwaite Hall, blank with a green slate roof, rises sheer to the left of the tower, while to its right comes a medley of corporation chimneys, projections and gables.

38

Horniman Free Museum
London Rd, Forest Hill, Lewisham

1/G6   British Rail to Forest Hill, or bus

[A]

Of London's myriad museums, the Horniman is one of the most striking and strange, both in its architecture and collections. Building and contents were bequeathed to the London County Council in 1901 by F J Horniman, a successful tea merchant.

The architect, C Harrison Townsend, had a small but curious output. Most important are his three public buildings. The Bishopsgate Institute of 1895 and the Whitechapel Art Gallery of 1897–9 presumably led to his commission for the Horniman. Though the Whitechapel was never finished, they and his church at Great Warley, Essex, show how successfully Townsend could work with decorative artists. At the Horniman Museum the mosaic frieze of 'Humanity in the House of Circumstance' by Anning Bell feels truly part of the building. More interesting still are the rounded organic forms of the barrel-vaulted galleries and the round-cornered clock tower that rises to four turrets wreathed in vinery. They are too strong and regular to be dubbed *art nouveau*, but since they grow out of smooth ashlar they are less muscular than the forms of the great American H H Richardson, whose work Townsend certainly knew and admired. The tower gains further strength from its vastly over-scaled clockfaces.

The combination of nature and artifice in the facades is appropriate to the museum's collection. The upper gallery houses specimens of the natural world; the lower, more spectacularly, displays the works of man round the world. English folk customs are shown side by side in revealing comparison with those of New Guinea aboriginals and American Indians. It is this gallery whose blind end wall stands head-on to the road.

F J Horniman lived at Surrey House, on the site of the museum and where he first exhibited his collection to the public. But he also had a house at Coombe Cliff in Croydon, where in 1894 he built himself an elaborate iron conservatory. By the 1980s this was derelict, and in 1987–90 it was rebuilt in the gardens behind the museum.

always give a fillip to their scattered suburban locations. Gothic at first, Arts and Crafts after 1900, London's Victorian and Edwardian fire stations are a tribute to the talent within the municipal architect's department of the MBW and LCC. Too few of these stations, constricting for the fire brigade today, are still in service. Outstanding among these are Chiltern Street, Marylebone (1888–9), Euston Road, Euston (1902–3), Evelyn Street, Deptford (1903), Trinity Road, Tooting (1907), Shepherd's Bush Road, Hammersmith (1913) and Lancaster Grove, Belsize Park (1913). Among redundant examples, the ex-station at the corner between Tunnel Avenue and Woolwich Road, East Greenwich (1900–1) can stand comparison with the smartest architectural experimentalism from turn-of-the-century Vienna, Glasgow or Brussels.

West Hampstead is chosen here because it is a working fire station that has all the virtues of the genre, and because it is among the few for which a job-architect can be singled out. William Alphonsus Scott (1871–1921) was to become the premier architect of the Celtic Revival in Ireland and be labelled a 'drunken man of genius' by W B Yeats, for whom he restored an ancient tower-

house, Ballylee Castle, Co. Galway. At the time he designed this station (1901), Scott was one of a band of young men getting their first experience of carrying through something of their own within the overstretched LCC Architect's Department. Just after the building was finished he went back to Dublin.

The station presides demurely over the dip at the top of West End Lane. It is unusual in having roughcast elevations and a deeply hipped roof – a rarity for non-domestic buildings in London, but tried out also on one other contemporary fire station, Perry Vale in Lewisham. Perhaps Scott was thinking of his native Ireland; certainly he wanted to give his first building freshness and zip compared to the banal brick terraces round about. The architectural language comes from Voysey, whose refined variety of stone mullions embellishes the deep bay window to the watchroom, saving the facade from absolute symmetry. Another of these strong-minded, flat-topped bays adorns the back, where the change from roughcast to exposed brickwork forecast in front by the chimneys becomes general. Tucked away behind is a nicely capped thin tower. London fire stations had previously had towers from which firemen watched for signs of untoward

39

West Hampstead Fire Station
West End Lane, Camden

1/E3   Underground or British Rail to West Hampstead

Fire stations are fun the world over. London has some of the most delightful anywhere, dating from the days when firemen were obliged to live 'over the shop' and had to be ready to drop what they were doing and career off in quest of a blaze. From the days of its inauguration in 1866, London's fire brigade was image-conscious. Under the Metropolitan Board of Works and its successor, the London County Council, it contrived between 1870 and 1914 to get itself a series of new stations which

West Hampstead Fire Station. GLRO

smoke. With the advent of the telephone after 1900 this was deemed to be pointless and the towers were phased out, or used just for practice and drying hoses. West Hampstead is one of the last where it is an architectural feature integrated with the building.

Behind the station yard are four cottages in a short, sweet row, built as extra accommodation for firemen. Brick on the ground storey but roughcast under the eaves, they look like standard, Voysey-esque work. For their pre-garden-suburb date, they are early and excellent imitations of his style.

40

County Hall
Westminster Bridge Rd and Belvedere Rd, Lambeth

2/G5   Underground or British Rail to Waterloo

What is to become of County Hall? It is an eerie place at the time of writing: bluff and solid as ever from the outside, festive even towards the river, where the colonnade curls round in a swaggering crescent to give the South Bank of the Thames its supreme architectural incident. Inside, all is funereal. Shadowy creatures of the London Residuary Body, undertakers to metropolitan government, flit along the acreage of half-lit corridor now and again, but most of the rooms are void. The Greater London Council was ejected in 1986, the Inner London Education Authority in 1990. The best the government can think of is to turn the great building into a luxury hotel cum conference centre. But even that ignominious idea has faltered.

Turn back the clock to 1907 and a happier picture presents itself. An expansionist London County Council has been presiding over the capital for almost twenty years. It runs London's schools and its fire service and has built much housing. It controls most of the bridges and main roads, and has started a municipal tramway service. It wants to do more but is hampered, among other things, by inadequate headquarters.

Many sites have been canvassed before the splendid one at the southern foot of Westminster Bridge is secured. Then things go a little wrong. The ebullient Progressives are ousted at the LCC elections by economy-minded Municipal Reformers. Yet a grand, two-stage, open architectural competition for County Hall goes ahead in 1908; in the first stage, 'a single walk round the hanging represents a third of a mile'.

Out of it all emerged the unknown Ralph Knott, perhaps chosen in preference to luminaries such as Belcher, Lutyens and Rickards because his design was capable of being cut down for cheapness. Since Knott's friend and future partner, E Stone Collins, was working in the LCC Architect's Department, it is likely he was well briefed on changes in priority within the Council.

Knott was a capable architect, and after sundry interventions from Norman Shaw, one of the assessors, and Riley, the LCC's chief architect, his simplified – perhaps improved – design painfully rose from 1911. The Council's staff had not completely moved in when war broke out and the building was requisitioned, so the official opening had to be postponed till 1922. Even then the northern (downstream) end was unbuilt. It was added with a few revisions by Collins in 1931–3, Knott having prematurely died in 1929.

The great gesture of County Hall, seen too rarely even when the building was in full democratic function, was the

Members' Entrance and Courtyard on the Westminster Bridge side. Chauffeured motors would sweep through these rusticated caverns, every bit as august as the entrance to Somerset House, turn in a half circle and deposit their elected contents outside the Council Chamber, hidden in the middle of the building. No matter that the sides of the court were impaired by curtain glass in the 1960s; the architecture is worth penetrating yet. LCC white-collar staff had to use the Belvedere Road entrance, which has another fine giant order, but here the front is a trifle too long. There are faults also on the river front, if one wishes to be critical; the chimneys, pantiled roof and cupola are too weak for the mighty elevations. But the crescent, river wall and steps are nonpareil.

Inside, Knott concentrated his architectural effect upon the first or Members' floor, to which a processional stair leads from the Belvedere Road lobby. It is high-panelled and plaster-vaulted, and that is the style too of the former committee rooms, some of which are excellent. The octagonal, marble-lined Council Chamber in the centre, by contrast, is something of a disappointment, and was never an acoustical success. But the building is a minor treasure trove of the applied arts. Foremost are the brooding external figures hewn in an Epstein-ish manner by Ernest Cole, a very fine young sculptor whose working life was short. The interior craftsmanship and

County Hall. NIGEL CORRIE

materials are everywhere of high quality. A few of the first-floor rooms even boast beautiful Georgian fireplaces salvaged when Edwardian Kingsway was cut through.

The County Hall extensions (1936–74), strung eastward of the main building along York Road and scheduled for probable demolition, exemplify the gradual demise of the grand manner. Sir Giles Scott had a momentary consulting hand in them. 'North Block' came first, then 'South Block' and finally the Greater London Council's 'Island Block' in the middle of a roundabout, which in the immortal words of W S Gilbert, 'really won't be missed'.

41

Hornsey Town Hall
Crouch End Broadway, Haringey

1/G3   Underground or British Rail to Finsbury Park, then bus

[C]

Stylistically this is Britain's quintessential municipal building of the 1930s. It combines the massing, tower and clean brick lines of Dudok's Hilversum Town Hall with details from Stockholm Town Hall, features that came together to fulfil a need for a municipal style that was modern and monumental but not aggressive. In particular it allowed for the carved reliefs, etched glass, heraldic emblems and bronze fittings still thought necessary to a display of civic pride. The style – first adopted at Hornsey – was suitable for a prosperous Conservative borough that was mildly trying to shape an identity in the face of advancing London.

To add to the building's internationalism the architect was a New Zealander, Reginald Uren, who won a competition in 1933. The town hall today, at the rear of its little garden, flanked by buildings in a similar style, supplies a note of calm in jostling Edwardian, red-brick Crouch End. But the site was not originally so fortunate, since the council was unable to purchase the street frontage. This is why the

Hornsey Town Hall. GLRO

building is so far from the road, on the widest part of the site, and why it is planned so compactly. The flanking blocks were added in 1935 and 1937–9 as gas and electricity showrooms, the latter also by Uren. Like the town hall they carry reliefs by Arthur Ayres, the glories of gas vying with the 'Spirit of Electricity' across the forecourt.

Since the borough was incorporated into Haringey in 1965 Hornsey has not used its town hall. This has not preserved it from slow decay, but it has created a time capsule in which every piece of veneered panelling, every fitted bookcase, lampshade, piece of furniture and curtain has survived: a fragile, unique atmosphere. Richest of all is the mayor's parlour, occupying a pivotal position in the centre of the plan. To the left is a large assembly hall with a stage, reached through its own entrance; to the right, stairs lead to a ghostly council chamber whose cracked leather seats are resonant of the debates and in-fights of a past era.

42

Hammersmith Police Station
Shepherd's Bush Rd,
Hammersmith

1/E5 Underground to
Hammersmith

A clutch of classy municipal buildings gives a fillip to the traffic-ridden south end of the Shepherd's Bush Road. Nearest the roundabout, the Hammersmith Fire Station (1913) is one of the sprightliest efforts in the fire-fighting genre by the London County Council's Architect's Department, with quaint little pantiled projections showing early influence from Lutyens. Further north and across the road lies H T Hare's Hammersmith Central Library of 1904–5, dignified and cheerful, if not quite the best of the many London public libraries funded by philanthropists (here Andrew Carnegie) in the late Victorian and Edwardian years. Seated figures of Milton and Shakespeare look down from the upper storey, spurring locals on to studious endeavour.

The pearl of the group stands opposite the library and can easily be taken for granted. This is the

Hammersmith Police Station of 1939, a reminder that a few canny conservatives – much derided by 'progressive' architects – continued throughout the 1930s and indeed after the Second World War to explore the classical language of architecture with an adroitness that leaves our posing post-modernists flat-footed. The architect in question was Donald McMorran of Farquharson and McMorran, better known for his Wood Street Police Station in the City (a mannered exercise in 1950s classicism), the Old Bailey extension, and university work at Exeter and Nottingham.

As with the fire station, the basic vocabulary and texture come from Lutyens, here mediated through the example of McMorran's master, Vincent Harris. There is a sturdy granite base in the New Scotland Yard tradition, rising to a third of the elevation's height and ornamented with a comforting pair of blue lamps and the royal arms over the door. To help give the building proportion and presence, the ground-floor windows have little blank recesses beneath them, as if to hint at a basement that is not really there. Then comes a band of thin brickwork and above that two rows of upper windows. The larger of these have full granite architraves which look marvellous against the pink,

handmade bricks, while the smaller second-floor ones are fewer in number, sit boldly over the piers rather than the voids, and are surmounted by further recesses in playful answer to the ground floor. One big chimney dominates the pitched roof. To the side, the entrance to the station yard is enlivened by a curved niche. It is all exceedingly neat, graceful and a good deal superior in quality to the Victorian police stations to whose basic *parti* Farquharson and McMorran were still adhering. There were even stables for police horses rather than garages for squad cars behind.

43

Commonwealth Institute
Kensington High Street,
Kensington and Chelsea

1/F5 Underground to High Street
Kensington

[A]

The Commonwealth Institute belongs to the tradition of exhibition buildings rather than of museums proper. There is something still of the home-grown, Festival of Britain or 'Young Elizabethan' spirit about the great, tent-like hall, where youngsters flit from alcove to alcove finding out about Nigeria, the Gilbert Islands or other of the nations over which the Queen still exercises nominal dominion. The structure itself, however, has an involved international pedigree.

After the Second World War the Imperial Institute, then occupying Collcutt's fine building in South Kensington (only its tower survives today, amid the dog's dinner of Imperial College), was outmoded and unworkable. Under the directorship of Kenneth Bradley, there emerged instead the ideal of a Commonwealth Institute that would display and promote the cultures of the member countries (few in number in the 1950s) on an equal footing. Exhibitions would be lively, changeable and contributed by member states, but the mother-country would offer the womb in which they were shown. In 1958 a bite out of the edge of

Hammersmith Police Station. EH

Commonwealth Institute. Entrance front. AP

Holland Park and parsimonious funding were conceded by the government. Robert Matthew, Johnson-Marshall and Partners were appointed architects. Stirrat Johnson-Marshall, the senior London partner in the firm, came up with the idea of a 'tent in the park' – a kind of semi-permanent structure surrounded by water and grass. It fell to others to turn this vision into reality.

Great, open-vaulted halls without intermediate support were an architectural and engineering preoccupation the world over in the 1950s. They were made possible by advances in concrete and in cable-hung roof construction. Eero Saarinen's Ingalls Ice Hockey Rink at Yale, his Kresge Auditorium at the Massachusetts Institute of Technology, the CNIT Building which became the first element in La Défense at Paris, and Hugh Stubbins's Kongresshalle in Berlin (a building similar in form to the Commonwealth Institute) all contributed to their development. But what most excited British architects and engineers was the Mexican work of Felix Candela, who made a specialism of 'anticlastic shells' – thin concrete roofs of double curvature in the mathematical shape of hyperbolic paraboloids or 'hypars'. This was the starting point for the engineer, (Sir) Alan Harris of Harris and Sutherland, and the job-architects in RMJM, notably Peter Newnham and

Roger Cunliffe. Eventually the idea of using true 'hypars' for the outer warps was dropped, while Harris came up with the notion of prefabricating the roof in sections instead of casting it *in situ*. Time and budgetary difficulties put paid to this. The roof as finally redesigned by James Sutherland and constructed in 1960–2 is a compromise, with an *in situ* concrete shell in the centre and an ingenious system of radiating beams for the outer warps. The whole is covered with copper given by the Government of what was then Northern Rhodesia. The sweep of the roof is exhilarating, inside and out, but it has given endless maintenance problems – the common price of experimentalism.

The concept of the exhibition space remains, after thirty years, simple and convincing. You enter through a gradually darkening space, turn, rise up a ramp into the light, and find yourself on a round podium central in section as well as in plan. Hence you can see, above, below and all round, the whole variety of displays and you can choose as you wish between them. This is the great stroke. That apart, there is plenty to quibble about. The cheap patent external cladding is discouragingly dull, the roof is less visible than one would wish it to be, and the concrete stays or prows that project from the front and back angles are awkward. Nor are the administration buildings at the side of special merit. The approach from Kensington High Street, with flagpoles, water, grass and a covered walkway, is effective, but the building is cut off from the park, as the architects never meant it to be, by means of a wall on the north and east. At the time of writing major changes to the Commonwealth Institute are in the pipeline. Whatever is done, one prays that the wall may be got rid of.

3

Palaces

The definition of the palace offers food for thought. The Italians are generous in their concept of the *palazzo*, employing it (much as the French use the word *hôtel*) to mean any stately building, domestic by origin, which is arranged around courts. English usage is more niggardly. Burlington House and the other great West End mansions of the London aristocracy were never called palaces. Yet the proverbially inadequate accommodation of British monarchs meant that such houses seemed often to be more palatial than royal palaces proper – a predicament summed up in Queen Victoria's celebrated quip, on a visit to the Duke of Bridgewater, that she was going 'from my *house* to your *palace*'. There is, in fact, an element of pomposity and romantic revivalism about the term. Hampton Court remained plain Hampton Court throughout its years of royal occupation; the modern 'heritage' title, 'Hampton Court Palace', is to be deprecated. George III lived in 'Buckingham House' and his son in 'Carlton House'. Even now, few royal seats outside London incorporate 'palace' in their name.

The word is not quite confined to royalty. Prelates, too, have or had their palaces. London's outstanding example is Lambeth Palace. Scruffier, suburban examples of the episcopal palace at Fulham and at Bromley have been abandoned by their bishops; the latter, once the seat of the Bishops of Rochester, is now the offices of Bromley Borough Council. And the greatest palace of all, the Palace of Westminster, is colloquially known as the Houses of Parliament. Its function reminds us that government and Crown buildings are inextricable. Anciently, palaces were not just entertainment centres where kings and queens jousted, revelled, collected, received, slept and occasionally prayed – a 'Merrie England' concept of which we still find it hard to rid our minds. They were places where the complex business of ruling the realm was carried on. That is why the capital has so many of them.

If we see more of kitchens and paintings in them today than we do of studies, ledgers or law books, that is because of the nature of what survives, because of the itinerant habits of government down to the days of the Stuarts, and – it must be added – because of the way in which palaces are displayed to us by their modern caretakers. The government offices that surround Inigo Jones's Banqueting House, the one remnant of Whitehall Palace visible above ground, are as much heirs to that palace's ancient functions as the Banqueting House itself.

The gravity of the medieval palace is preserved for us in the Tower of London, whose grimness no horde of tourists can dispel. No question, here, of whether monarchs were well or poorly housed; the first function of the place was to defend, the second to incarcerate. Its later uses, including those of mint, zoo, archive and stable, were every bit as germane to the nature of palace life as the comfort of royalty. Even at Eltham, a suburban palace subsidiary to Greenwich and favoured for its hunting, there were by the 16th century offices a-plenty for the transaction of business. Yet it is Eltham's Great Hall, surviving almost but not quite alone, that catches the eye. This happy fragment forms an architectural link in the chain of open-roofed royal halls that runs from venerable Westminster Hall, 11th-century in origin, through Eltham to Hampton Court. Add private Crosby Hall, institutional Middle Temple Hall and episcopal Lambeth Palace, and you have the most splendid sequence of survivals in and around London of any secular-Gothic building type.

Henry VIII was London's greatest palace-builder, and indeed the last monarch to be an interested and effective architectural patron until George IV 300 years later (Charles I was interested, but not effective; William III effective but not interested). Henry's mania for bricks and mortar must not be exaggerated; his father, too, was a

Standing guard over Churchill's body, Westminster Hall, 1965. HULTON-DEUTSCH prolific builder, while many of his shorter-lived predecessors were no sluggards. Richmond, Whitehall, Bridewell, Greenwich, Nonsuch and Oatlands have all or mostly gone, but we still have large hunks of Henry's Hampton Court and St James's. A substantial amount of the structure at Hampton Court is Wolsey's; here and elsewhere, the king had a head-start. Nevertheless he did build a lot, and it is legitimate to ask why. One answer is that with the shift towards absolutism and destruction of Church power which Henry VIII initiated, room had to be found for the new secular bureaucracy. The expansion of Greenwich, for instance, was related to the formation of the navy and the making of new royal dockyards at Woolwich and Deptford nearby. The other reason is that elaborate building was one of the few ways open to a 16th-century monarch to stimulate national skills and trade, as Henry's French rival, François I, also knew. If great church projects were not to continue, royalty would have to supply builders with patronage instead. A similar motive inspired the Elizabethan and Jacobean 'prodigy houses' – only here the impetus came from the mercantile aristocracy, not from the monarch.

Stuart palaces, because of that dynasty's chequered history, are rather a matter of bits and pieces. Not that the pieces are to be sniffed at, since Inigo Jones's two supreme efforts for James I, the Banqueting House at Whitehall and the Queen's House at Greenwich, determined the mainstream of English classical architecture for the next two centuries. Despite intensive restorations, neither conveys the flavour of what a royal palace of the time was really like; for all their magnificence they are both puzzling buildings. The Queen's House is axially related to the rebuilt Greenwich (p. 153), the one courted and colonnaded royal palace of continental stringency ever to come off in London. Yet Greenwich ironically is not a palace at all, having been relinquished for use as a naval hospital long before completion. For genuine palace architecture by Wren and his successors – Vanbrugh, Hawksmoor and

the rest of the Office of Works team down to the time of Kent – one must choose between the charming insignificance of Kensington or the frustrated grandeur of Hampton Court, both conceived for William and Mary but finished under the first Hanoverians. Both are full of good things, but do not add up to a whole. The spectacular shade of Versailles remained unexorcised.

For a long period from the 1720s there is little royal architecture to report, or at least to survive – some nice follies littered about Kew Gardens apart. It was at this stage, as Parliament were increasingly permitted to get on with the business of ruling, that the idea of the palace as principally a *home* for the monarch began to take hold. That was the spirit in which George III, Buteish thoughts of renewed absolutism destroyed, acquired Buckingham House in the 1760s, and perhaps too the spirit in which his artistically prodigal heir rebuilt Carlton House. But the latter's thinking changed after he became Prince Regent. Carlton House was first extended, then after George IV's accession destroyed, and Nash was put to the ambiguous task of rebuilding Buckingham House.

The basic fault in that politically and architecturally abused project was the lack of a clear vision of what the monarchy was about in the 1820s. Ought Buckingham Palace to provide for government and administration once again, or was it to be merely Britain's pre-eminent country house, with a few ceremonial features thrown in? Nash never had a proper brief from his ambitious but confused client, and the palace soon got into all sort of difficulties. Once Victoria had come to the throne and acquired the clear-sighted Albert by her side, the concept of the modern monarchy which we have inherited began to take shape. Nash's ill-fated design was duly emended, alas by the desiccated hand of Edward Blore, and the open court facing the world and seeming to speak of business became a mere blank and private front. Offices once again proliferated, but this time they were devoted to dignifying the trappings of rule rather than to the business of rule itself. The same

motivation of enhancing royal dignity determined Aston Webb's wafer-thin facade to Buckingham Palace and his showy architectural apparatus in front, stretching right up to Trafalgar Square. Buckingham Palace, for all that, is a much better building than people will admit. It is a pity that most of us see only its facade. But then in today's monarchy, the facade is what matters.

44

Tower of London
Tower Hill, Tower Hamlets

2/L4   Underground or Docklands Light Railway to Tower Hill
[A]

'Julius Caesar's ill-erected tower', Shakespeare called it, and he was half right. Beefeaters, Crown Jewels and the trappings of international tourism cannot dispel the chill of the Tower of London. In its time it has been palace, fortress, factory, barracks, arms dump, stack for public records, muddle of government offices and home for royal pensioners. From the architectural standpoint, the Tower is a medieval fortification unparalleled for size and completeness in any European capital. But from the human angle it is memorable chiefly as a grim prison for VIPs. The sufferings of those incarcerated there are still to be read upon its walls.

The best approach has always been from the Thames, whence the White Tower stands up blithely behind the double circuit of enveloping stone. From landward the views are less crisp and close, as the outer line of defence is seen across the no man's land of the filled-in moat. You were meant to keep your distance; for this was a castle built chiefly against the enemy within, to ward off troublesome citizens rather than marauders coming up river. Grey Kentish rag – partly in ashlar, partly in rubble – is not the most winning of building materials, and the heavy restorations by Anthony Salvin round the perimeter in the 1850s give the outer walling a Victorian feeling at odds with the place's antiquity.

gallery and tunnel vault afford an austere display of Norman permanence. To the south was a Great Hall, a separate structure that has wholly disappeared.

Henry III gave the White Tower its name by whitewashing it inside and out in the 1240s. He too it was who, with his son Edward I, set about expanding the Tower of London by breaking out east beyond the old Roman wall and constructing the present circuit of defences between about 1220 and 1285. That is the period of Westminster Abbey, and the Tower fortifications are the military counterpart of Henry III's superlative Gothic church. Both buildings were influenced by French architecture: the river entrance through Traitor's Gate under St Thomas's Tower mimicked the former gateway to the Louvre from the Seine. But the new circumference was not built to a single consistent plan. Under Henry, work on the main ring of towers began on the river side, then moved round to the north and east. Edward completed the west side and added the elaborate new landward approach in the south-west corner, the original wharf on the Thames and the lower outer wall in front of the moat. Dug and flooded at fabulous expense in 1275–6 with the help of a hydraulics expert from Flanders, the moat was not drained until 1843.

The 13th-century works gave the Tower a broad Inner Ward and a poky, circuitous Outer Ward. Its later building history consists of makeshift additions within these wards, as monarchs found the stronghold less to their taste to live in and put it to whatever uses could be made of it. The towers of the inner ring were handy for the safekeeping of important prisoners, whose tribulations are sufficiently attested on the walls of the Beauchamp Tower. But there were many other activities, from royal mint to royal menagerie – a function going back to a short-lived elephant presented to Henry III. By the mid-19th century the wards were jammed with a jumble of buildings. Most have since been cleared by archaeological zeal. The Outer Ward is now completely purified. In the Inner Ward the oldest survival is the disappointing chapel of St Peter ad Vincula, dating in its present form from

The White Tower, Tower of London. RCHME

Julius Caesar never came here, but later Romans did. It was on Tower Hill that the inscription commemorating Julius Classicianus, the reforming procurator mentioned by Tacitus as sent to settle wrongs after Boudicca's sack of London, turned up; it is exhibited in replica there alongside fragments of the Roman city wall. The south-east end of that wall sliced through the Tower's later northern line of defences. William the Conqueror found its remnants to his purpose when he wanted to keep Londoners in check after 1066. First he had a temporary wooden fort built and then between about 1075 and 1095, within the protective shadow of the wall

to its east, the Caen-stone keep we know as the White Tower. Erected by William's aide-de-camp Gundulf of Bec, Bishop of Rochester, it is an astonishing survival. It has three full, quaintly irregular storeys upon a massive basement. The battlements and turrets are wrong (one must imagine some sort of wooden overhanging feature all round the top), while the little Norman windows were savaged in 1715–16 to make them look classical. The *pièce de résistance* is the noble chapel of St John, London's earliest intact place of worship. It cuts through the two top storeys, its apsidal end sticking out to the east. Its elephantine piers, capitals, about 1515 but heavily restored. To its east are the Waterloo Barracks of 1845. The buildings on the east side are mostly modern. In the south-west corner, facing the area called Tower Green and with something of the air of a cathedral close, is the so-called Queen's House, built as the Lieutenant's Lodgings. Its friendly Tudor timber-framing and rambling brick extensions are at welcome odds with the ramparts all about.

45

Westminster Hall
Palace of Westminster,
Westminster

2/G6   Underground to Westminster
[B]

In outline and structural core, Westminster Hall is almost as ancient as the White Tower at the Tower of London. There had been a royal palace at Westminster for less than a century and the Abbey opposite had been not long completed by Edward the Confessor, when, between about 1095 and 1100, William II built himself a great hall. At 240 ft long and 69 ft wide, it must have been much the longest and largest hall in Europe. It had a shingled roof, a run of Norman windows high up along the sides and was divided by internal columns (of timber probably) into nave and aisles.

Of all this only the mass and dimensions remain. For in 1394 Richard II gave his great architect Henry Yevele and master-carpenter Hugh Herland the go-ahead to reconstruct the hall on modern Gothic lines so as to bring it up to the standard of St Stephen's Chapel nearby. Yevele nobly reclothed the core in Yorkshire (Marre stone) ashlarwork, refenestrated the whole, pushed out stumpy flying buttresses to east and west, and created the sumptuous north entrance with towers, a nine-light window and niches for statuary which we see (in a form heavily restored by Soane) today. Yet it is not Yevele's work that commands most admiration but Herland's, to whom it fell to leap the

Westminster Hall with Oliver Cromwell. RCHME

69 ft span in one bound with a timber roof unparalleled in extent and magnificence, so as to avoid interrupting the king's business and pleasure with obstructive columns. A torch is needed to savour the intricacies of Herland's bold braced and hammerbeamed structure – 'the masterpiece of English medieval carpentry', as *The History of the King's Works* unequivocally puts it. It was made in pieces near Farnham, carried to the Thames and shipped down river to Westminster. The hall was nearly ready when Richard II seized absolute power in 1397 but not completed until 1400, after that ill-advised monarch's downfall.

The uses and abuses of Westminster Hall over the nearly 600 years since its reconstruction defy full itemization. It has functioned as council chamber, parliament house, banqueting house, venue for show trials, ceremonies, debates and lyings-in-state, *salle des pas perdus* and, at least in part, as pie shop. This last use is explained by the fact that for centuries the innocent-looking green sward in front was encumbered by the highest law courts of the land, courts not indeed removed to the Strand until the 1880s. Access to them was through a series of holes hacked along the west side of the hall, which was chiefly used for lawyers to foregather and (for a period) 'snack' in – hence the pie shop. J L Pearson was the architect called in to

tidy up the west front in 1888, tuck in an aisle (used as offices) under the buttresses, and reface the whole in Ketton stone. William Morris disliked this plausible sham and suggested an inscription which was to read: 'This building was built in such-and-such a year of the reign of Queen Victoria, and was done by such-and-such a gentleman, and it pretends to be old, and is not.' Earlier, Sir Charles Barry had been obliged to alter the hall's south end in the 1840s, so as to spatchcock it on to his new Palace of Westminster. This involved shifting Yevele's south window bodily southwards so as to make it visible from Old Palace Yard, and opening out a great vista down steps into the hall from the higher level of the St Stephen's Entrance. It was not exactly an archaeological thing to do, but it works marvellously. The pity is that this cavernous space, imbued with English history, looks so friendless and functionless today.

In front of Westminster Hall, an intriguing confrontation in statuary perpetuates the rancour of the English Civil War. On the site of the old courts, Hamo Thornycroft's stout figure of Oliver Cromwell (1899) now glowers across the street at a bust of 'King Charles the Martyr', placed above a door at the end of St Margaret's Church by angry, inveterate royalists unwilling to let the Lord Protector steal the show. This rare memorial to Britain's brief flirtation with republicanism stands plum before a building which is not only a venerable symbol of English law and kingship, but also the place in which Charles Stuart was tried and sentenced to death.

46

Eltham Palace
Court Yard, Eltham,
Greenwich

1/J6   British Rail to Eltham or Mottingham
[B]

A palace is the last thing to be looked for from placid, suburbanised Eltham. As it is, the remnants of one of Britain's foremost medieval royal seats contrive to tuck themselves in a private, semi-rural setting away from the public eye. Only the memorable bulk of its Great Hall is easy to reconcile with the pride and extent of Eltham Palace revealed by ancient plans.

Antony Bek, Bishop of Durham, presented the manor and house of Eltham in 1305 to the future Edward II. Over the next three centuries there were few monarchs who did not extend or embellish the place. From the reign of Richard II to that of Henry VIII it functioned as a favourite suburban pleasure palace, good for hunting and within easy reach of Greenwich, where state business came to be concentrated. By the time of James I there was a dense range of walled buildings within the circumference of the moat, outstanding among them Edward IV's hall of about 1475–80 and Henry VIII's chapel of 1528–30. Outside the moat was the U-shaped Green Court, entered through a vanished gatehouse and in the main made up of timber buildings. Its long sides ran roughly parallel, left and right,

with the present approach from the east.

The Stuarts neglected Eltham, and the Commonwealth saw most of it destroyed. In due course the hall became a barn, narrowly escaping demolition in the 1820s. The remains were finally put into a semblance of order with textile money by Stephen Courtauld, who built a new house within the moat in 1933–7 to designs by Seely and Paget and restored the hall. The Army Education Corps now has a lease of the palace, but the hall is regularly open to the public.

Approaching from Court Yard, it comes as a shock to discover that the long, very restored timber range of houses on the right, Nos 34–38, are the chief remains of the outer or Green Court – in fact, the tip of one of its long arms, with vestiges of a great chamber and hall for 'My Lord Chancellor' at the projecting end next to King John's Walk. The pretty Georgian front of No. 32 hides another fragment of the same court. But it is only when you come upon the medieval bridge, four sharp arches spanning a tidied-up moat, that you know something serious is going on

in the way of architecture. The bridge is probably Edward IV's, the restricted size of the moat and planting along its margins more certainly Stephen Courtauld's. Beyond the moat and retaining wall comes Courtauld's house, in a Frenchifying style hard to reconcile with the owner's antiquarian enthusiasms. It is mixed up with fragments of the palace and attached at an angle on to the Great Hall, making an open, L-shaped court that has nothing to do with the former plan of the palace. In front of these buildings are footings of Henry VIII's chapel and barely identifiable pieces of structures going back to Bishop Bek's manor house.

The hall is the main reason for making the pilgrimage to Eltham. Its likely architects were Thomas Jordan, royal mason, and Edmund Graveley, royal carpenter. Fifty-one masons and forty-eight carpenters were busy on it in 1479, when ironwork for 'spykyngg' and for 'bynddyng of the great principyles' of the roof was being procured. The exterior is a blank business today, all high windows with modest tracery over cleaned-up stone cladding concealing brickwork, and a squared-off pair of oriels projecting on either side at the western or dais end. To make a better impression it sorely needs its long-lost lantern and lead roof; the parapet, too, is not right. But all is forgiven when one sees the hammerbeamed roof inside, with its great four-centred arches, ornamental tracery above the collars and dipping pendants. Eltham stands midway in the sequence of English wide-span timber roofs running from Westminster Hall to Middle Temple Hall, at a point when structural clarity was beginning to be overlaid with decorative ambition. The bays to the oriels have delightful little stone vaults. But the bosses here and the roof pendants are clever copies of the originals. Magnificent though it is, the hall has lost much; the panelling behind the dais is modern, nor are the screen and gallery at the other end wholly authentic. The bare brickwork of the walls peeping over the top of the wall coverings should not surprise, however, as it was always intended to be covered with tapestry.

Eltham Palace. The court. CL

Lambeth Palace. The hall. RCHME

47

Lambeth Palace
Lambeth Palace Rd, Lambeth

2/G6   Underground to Westminster or Lambeth North

[B]

Broad and hearty in front, tall and stringy from behind, Archbishop John Morton's gateway stands as the illustrious preface to Lambeth Palace. It is London's earliest brick building of substance, having been raised in the 1480s by one of the wiliest prelates to climb to the top of England's episcopal tree. Its mellow patchwork of red, blue and black stands up against the ragstone tower of Lambeth's former parish church like some kind of orchestrated contrast in Gothic styles.

For all the knocks that it has taken, the palace to which Morton's Tower admits entrance is the one place where you can grasp how the houses of London's riparian magnificoes must have looked in medieval times. Water once lapped up almost to the gate, next to which there would have been a landing stage. Beyond it lies River Court, open towards the Thames and once often waterlogged (Lambeth was marshy). A great hall takes up most of the long side. Then at the north end is a squatter medieval tower behind which, away from public view, are the remoter setpieces, the chapel and the guard

room, where the primates conducted much of their business.

The archbishops of Canterbury acquired the manor house of Lambeth in the 1190s. It kept them out of the clutches of monks back in Canterbury and gave them a base nice and close to the king at Westminster. Given their importance, it is strange how small that base remained throughout the Middle Ages. No great collegiate quadrangles here; nothing on the scale of Wolsey's Hampton Court. The little palace survived the Reformation, only to come a severe cropper during the Commonwealth. Archbishop Laud had infuriated London's powerful puritans by decking out his chapel at Lambeth in a 'popish' fashion. After his execution, the regicide Colonel Scott got hold of the place, turned the chapel into a dancing hall and pulled down the great hall. It was left to Archbishop Juxon, in one of the most remarkable early gestures of Gothic Revivalism, to decree the rebuilding of the hall on the old lines from 1663.

After that symbolic making of amends, the palace shambled along till 1827. Then Archbishop Howley, finding it not up to snuff for a modern prelate,

brought in Edward Blore. Over the ensuing years that rather soulless architect turned the hall into the library, restored the chapel, all but reconstructed the guard room, and added a great residential wing in Bath stone – really an archiepiscopal country house, whose not unskilful Tudor-Gothic front dominates the wide-open back court. The palace was badly damaged by bombs in 1941, the chapel and the garden side of Blore's works suffering sorely. Seely and Paget set things right, eliminating some of Blore's stodgier features in the process.

Tours of Lambeth Palace, now the 'nerve-centre of the Anglican communion', are conceded by occasional appointment and guided by a cheerful nun. She shows you first the empty undercroft beneath the chapel, the earliest part of the palace. It is a cool, plain, vaulted Early English space, two bays by four, with Purbeck columns down the middle. Next comes the hall (1663–85), a wonderful affirmation of English traditionalism. Yet no one seems to know who designed it. Because it is still used, as part of the famous Lambeth Palace Library, it has a warmth too often missing in authentic medieval

Lambeth Palace. Pew ends in the chapel. EH

great halls. The walls are lined with tomes in Blore's big bookcases. Up above them is a spirited lantern, and the hammerbeams of the great roof are wittily intersected by an arc derived from classical geometry. Classic and Gothic details intertwine amiably throughout, in the best Anglican spirit of compromise.

Up a floor and round a much-recast cloister is the guard room, a second hall seemingly built in about 1385 to house those hired to protect the archbishops after Simon Sudbury lost his head and the palace was sacked during the Peasants' Revolt. Shutting the stable door in this way proved ineffective; the weapons that lined the guard room were in due course sold, and it became a reception room. In its present state it owes much to Blore, though the main elements of the waggon roof are genuine. Last in the sequence, and approached from the 'post room', an old 'solar' in Archbishop Chichele's Water Tower (c.1435), is the beautiful Lambeth Palace Chapel. Today the chapel is probably in better decorative shape than it has been since the Reformation. The bones of it are a chaste, lancet-windowed and Purbeck-shafted structure of the early 13th century, perhaps the conception of the famous ecclesiastic and architect Elias of Dereham. Stalls line the walls, and the recent reinstatement of Archbishop Laud's sumptuous screen, a miraculous survivor from the troubles of the 1640s, adds to the collegiate atmosphere. As the vault was destroyed by bombing, much of what you see is Seely and Paget's post-war handiwork, gradually embellished by modern craftsmanship. There is a complete scheme of 1950s glass, but what most draws the eye is the charming, almost satirical series of vault paintings by Leonard Rosoman on the history of Anglicanism.

On the way out, if you are in luck, your guide will shepherd you through the archbishop's domestic rooms in the big Blore wing. It has portly corridors, a fine series of portraits, and a vast drawing room looking north over the ample garden. As you descend Blore's grand stone stair note the footman's bell, still intact, by the front door.

Hampton Court. Entrance front. RCHME

48

Hampton Court
Hampton, Richmond

1/D7   British Rail to Hampton Court

[A]

Hampton Court began in about 1515 as an ecclesiastical rather than a royal palace for Henry VIII's overweening minister, Cardinal Wolsey. The earlier stages of its construction and the manner in which it passed to Henry are far from clear, but it was effectively already Henry's when Wolsey fell from power in 1529. The king then enlarged and enriched it in 1532–7 for himself and the second and third of his queens, Anne Boleyn and Jane Seymour. A large proportion of the Tudor structure the tourist sees today started out as Wolsey's rather than Henry's.

The main approach is from the north end of Lutyens' Hampton Court Bridge. England being England, it is neither axial nor focused upon the river, nor as grand as the Lion Gate on Hampton Court Road, planned by Wren for a new northern approach to the palace from Bushy Park that never came off. In compensation, tremendous trophies and a rampant lion and unicorn, put up for that military monarch William III, top the gate piers as you enter. To the left of the drive grace-and-favour residences, once lodging ranges for minor courtiers, disguise the car park. Then the semi-civil, semi-military jostle of turrets, pinnacles, chimneys and battlements that marks the spirit of Tudor ceremonial architecture commences. This martial but festive look was

formerly enhanced by a plethora of 'towers', 'banket houses' and 'arbours' littered all round the palace grounds. The present environs are too sedate.

The expansive, moated front is Wolsey's apart from the short side wings, and its brickwork, still a newish and costly material in the 1510s, sets the tone for the whole. The broad gatehouse, alas, was mutilated in the 1770s, cut down in height and refronted in too pink a hue. Set upon its side turrets are the first pair of eight famous terracotta roundels of Caesars ordered by Wolsey from Giovanni da Maiano in 1521 which now adorn the Hampton Court gateways. These Renaissance jewels, displaced within a Tudor-Gothic setting, give a clue to the rich 'antique' decoration that was the mark of the lost royal interiors. Within, one comes first to the Base Court, simplest and biggest of the palace's three main courts. Here lesser personages were lodged. It is much as Wolsey left it, though stupidly disfigured by a ticket office. In layout it is much like an Oxbridge quadrangle; not for another hundred years or so were the traditions of collegiate and domestic architecture to part company. But the separate apartments were formerly reached by corridors, not by individual staircases.

Clock Court beyond, entered through a better-preserved gatehouse, was formerly Conduit Court. It once had a 'splendid, high and massy fountain' in the middle, rebuilt in Elizabeth I's reign with a trick spray to drench innocent bystanders. At the back is a third gateway, a clever sham in the Tudor style by William Kent in 1732. On the right a colonnade by Wren, inserted as an approach to his new state

apartments, obscures a range which houses the best surviving small-scale early interiors, the so-called Wolsey Rooms and Closet. On the left of Clock Court, raised high above the beer cellar and buttery, is the Great Hall of 1532–4. This is the chief remaining portion of Henry VIII's Hampton Court to bespeak royal scale and pomp. Its interior offers an ornamental climax to a fine English building type. The spandrels and dropping pendants of the hefty, two-way hammerbeam roof graft Italianate enrichment upon the Gothic tradition. But the Willement stained glass, the loss of the central hearth and lantern above it, and the cleanliness and emptiness of the space detract from the Great Hall's robustness. The scale of activity and supply it generated are better conveyed by the width of the service stair and the warren of kitchens, pantries and cellars underneath.

East of the hall is the Great Watching Room, once the prelude to the king's and queen's lost private apartments, arranged in separate 'stacks'. Their climax was Henry VIII's 'Paradise Chamber', resplendent with gold, silver and jewels. East again, the Round Kitchen Court is the remnant of Wolsey's cloister, laid out in what we now think of as a collegiate manner and connected to a T-shaped chapel on the far side. The Chapel Royal was refitted in 1535–6 and again in 1711–12. Of the former period is the highly coloured, false timber vault, once more with swooping pendants, prefabricated at Sonning in Berkshire and brought to Hampton Court in segments by water. Of the later fittings, the finest is the full-height Grinling Gibbons reredos.

Hampton Court's second phase of building activity started in 1689, after the accession of William and Mary, and sputtered on from then until the 1730s. As a seat favoured by the late Stuarts and early Hanoverians but neglected after the death of George II's consort Caroline in 1737, Hampton Court has a history in common with Kensington Palace. But the architectural results were very different. At Kensington, Wren and his

successors in the Office of Works made piecemeal additions. At Hampton Court, the carcase of Fountain Court and the new south and east fronts was completed in 1689–94, to be fitted up in stages thereafter.

Wren's Hampton Court exteriors are a puzzle. William III, in a hurry, first wanted a palace to compete with his great foe Louis XIV. The Surveyor-General pulled out all the stops to oblige. Then the project was cut back from a complete new palace to a mere new court, leading to a cramped, tense feeling to the design, as though all the elements have been squeezed up. Fountain Court is the place to see this. It is almost Edwardian in its insistence on doing much in a small space. Storey is jammed upon storey, the edges of the pediments to the first-floor windows touch, and the difficulty of getting a well-proportioned open arcade beneath a *piano nobile* is solved only by the device of squashing arches down behind the level of the openings to the court. The explanation given in Wren's *Parentalia* is that the asthmatic king did not like stairs, and so insisted on keeping the *piano nobile* as low as possible. Even if this instruction came at a late stage, it was given before building started. Why then was the architect not able to adjust his design properly? But for the beautiful rubbed brickwork and the second-floor oculi with their luscious, carved lion's-skin surrounds, one might deem Fountain Court a botched job. On the garden fronts, where no arcade is called for and the first-floor windows are straight-headed, there is more repose. Yet the proportions and position of the Corinthian centrepiece to the east front are odd. Aspects of all this suggest the hand not of Wren but of a tetchier architect, William Talman, Comptroller of the King's Works. Talman certainly quarrelled with Wren about the standard of construction on the job, following an accident. Something of an interior specialist, he is known to have handled the fitting-out of the building for William III. Can he have had more to do with the exterior than is usually assumed?

Inside, the main floor of the Wren additions resolves itself into the king's

and queen's state apartments, facing south to the privy garden and east to the formal garden respectively. Both have grand painted staircases inserted behind Clock Court, with lavish iron balustrades by the great French smith Jean Tijou, who also furnished the florid gates in the privy garden. Verrio was the 'dauber' who painted the king's side staircase, while Kent did the later queen's side. Of the painted ceilings in the state apartments themselves, that in the Queen's State Bedchamber is outstanding. The king's side was finished first. Here Talman, with the help of woodwork by Grinling Gibbons, made his acknowledged mark. Here too restoration is proceeding, following a severe fire in 1986.

More extensive is the queen's side. Its more intimate private chambers are lit from Fountain Court, while the state rooms turn to face the radiating avenues and canals laid out in Charles II's day and elaborated under William III. The most individual rooms are those devised by Vanbrugh in 1715–17 for the Prince and Princess of Wales. His robust marble fireplaces and beefy coves, brackets and cornices are a world away from the nervousness of the exterior. The Queen's Guard Chamber has hefty brackets to the half-height cornice, while in the Presence Chamber a stone fireplace is flanked by gargantuan Yeomen of the Guard. Here the ritual of fitting out the royal apartments and allegorising royal achievement reaches the refreshing point of satire. Or was this an attempt on the romantic Vanbrugh's part to encapsulate the spirit of Henry VIII – the beginnings of a self-conscious concept of 'Merrie England'?

49

St James's Palace and Queen's Chapel
Marlborough Rd and Cleveland Row, Westminster

2/F5   Underground to Green Park
[C]   chapel only

What possessed Henry VIII, already engrossed in expanding Whitehall and

Hampton Court. Fountain Court. WI

St James's Palace, looking along Cleveland Row. EH

Hampton Court, to begin in 1531 yet another palace? The rebuilding of the ancient leper hospital that stood here may have been meant for his bastard son the Duke of Richmond, whom he was then considering at his heir. But the young Duke's death at St James's in 1536 – or perhaps that of Anne Boleyn, whose initials appear around the resplendent gatehouse closing the vista down St James's Street – seems to have curtailed Henry's building campaign. The crashing-up against the gatehouse of the Chapel Royal, fitted up in 1540 and bearing the cipher of Anne of Cleves, is the chief indication that Henry contracted his original scheme.

Still, as an atmospheric bit of townscape the range along Cleveland Row makes an impressive sequence. First comes the gatehouse, dressed up with a lantern in the 18th century, then the great uncusped window of the Chapel Royal, followed by a line of chimneys like domestic buttressing. If it were cleaned, the brickwork would reveal a mess of rebuilding and modernization. The eastern portion of the Tudor palace was destroyed by fire in

1809, so that whilst the elevation to Marlborough Road is enlivened by a real 16th-century tower and oriel, the picturesque arcading dates from the 1820s.

Thanks to the vigilance with which it is guarded, that is almost all of the palace proper that the public sees, though we are suffered down Stable Yard, where Hawksmoor's stables of 1716–17 have been tamely rebuilt. Tantalisingly invisible except from The Mall between the trees, is the run of state rooms along the southern side. They date from the only period when St James's functioned as a principal royal residence, between Whitehall's burning in 1698 and George IV's upgrading of Buckingham House. Wren started the sequence for Queen Anne, Vanbrugh and Hawksmoor kept going under George I, contributing *inter alia* a cavernous kitchen. The state rooms, red, gilded and ponderous, were refitted in about 1821–3, largely destroying additions for intermediate Georges but retaining excerpts of William Kent's work. It was however this recent and costly refurbishment that saved the palace

from demolition as part of Nash's Mall improvements. A pair of rooms redecorated by Morris, Marshall and Faulkner in 1866 afford a lively and surprising contrast. The instigator was probably William Cowper Temple, First Commissioner of Works, whose wife was a friend of Ruskin's. The Armour and Tapestry Rooms, taking their cue from Tudor fireplaces of which at least one is genuine, glow with stencilled patterning and delicious colouring redolent of 'Merrie England'. Apropos of this commission, Philip Webb reminded William Morris: 'Just remember we are embezzling the public money now – what business has any palace to be decorated at all?'

Four outliers of St James's Palace warrant special mention. To the south Clarence House, effervescent in pink and cream, was built by Nash for William IV in 1825–7 and raised a storey in the 1870s. More serious, sombre and refined is the contemporary Lancaster House closer to the palace, mostly built by Benjamin Dean Wyatt for George IV's other brother, the Duke of York, in Bath stone and a French neo-classical taste. At the end of Cleveland Row is Sir Charles Barry's Bridgewater House (1846–51), built for an earl grown rich on canal tolls and more presumptuous than the *palazzi* of the royal dukes.

Less ostentatious is the Queen's Chapel, now isolated on the east side of Marlborough Road. Once it was an integral part of the palace, to which it was attached by the low cloister of a Capuchin friary. For this was a Catholic chapel, built in 1625 for the use of Henrietta Maria when she married the future Charles I. Inigo Jones was the architect, but he took care not to make the building too prominent in puritan London. So it is a simple, stucco-covered vessel, with an 'implied' rather than 'applied' order at the west end. Only the generous east window, out of Scamozzi rather than Palladio, could be construed as ornate. A wing on the south side houses a stair leading up to the royal 'closet' or 'tribune', which eats into a third of the chapel's length. The interior can only be seen at the time of Sunday service – Low Anglican now, not Catholic. The coved and coffered ceiling is Jones's, but the handsome woodwork round the altar is due to craftsmen (one of them Grinling Gibbons) working under Wren, who refitted the chapel for Charles II's consort Catherine of Braganza in 1682–3. The current altarpiece is by Annibale Carracci.

50

Banqueting House
Whitehall, Westminster

2/G5   Underground to Westminster or Charing Cross

[A]

Ill-briefed tourists, distracted by larger and louder government buildings all along the shallow curve of Whitehall, can easily miss the Banqueting House. Even when you know it is the one remaining section of Whitehall Palace, the seminal work of English classical architecture and the recognised masterpiece of Inigo Jones, it can be hard to credit that it dates back to 1619–22.

The Banqueting House has always been anomalous. There had been a royal banqueting house here since 1581, when Elizabeth I added a temporary wooden building to Henry VIII's ramshackle Whitehall Palace. It was what is now called a 'function room', used to receive and feast dignitaries and, after James I's accession, for court masques. A second banqueting house, associated with the masques of Ben Jonson and Inigo Jones, burnt down early in 1619. This gave Jones, not long promoted to be Surveyor of the King's Works, his chance. On the same site and to a plan of similar dimensions he and his assistant Nicholas Stone built the drastically different Banqueting House we have today – the fruits of Jones's study of *cinquecento* Italian buildings and of his determination to drag English court architecture kicking and screaming into the 17th century. When finished, its suave stone elevations stuck out like a sore thumb amidst the brick and timber buildings all around.

Jones must have envisaged the Banqueting House as part of a larger

rebuilding of Whitehall Palace. Otherwise, the fact that the building never had a proper staircase or ground-floor entrance would be inexplicable. All it consists of is a vaulted basement (with brick walls of enormous thickness) and a vast room of double-cube proportions above. Functionally, the room is curious. Jones conceived it in terms of the basilica or Egyptian hall described in Vitruvius, but without the columns and aisles that had blemished the previous banqueting house. The entrance was always from the north, with the focus for royal receptions and masques on the south (Westminster) end. Yet the architecture was regular and undifferentiated all round, with nothing but a niche at the farther end. Even the present large south window seems to have been an afterthought, of 1625–6. Thrones and stages, therefore, were free-standing, temporary structures. Despite the hall's use and height, spectators must have been confined to floor level, as the timber galleries (originally round three sides only) are too shallow for anything but ornament. The ample fenestration is peculiar, too. From early

days it seems that the room was hung with tapestries, so that four of the great first-floor windows on each side had to be blocked. Their present subdivision is not authentic. To imagine the original effect, one must remove the present white-painted sashes and substitute mullions and transoms painted 'Tymber coullor'.

For Jones and King James, 'magnificence' came before practicality. The Banqueting House was built as a pure architectural statement, and is best enjoyed as such. Inside and out, it testifies to Jones's faith in the principles of Palladio and Scamozzi tempered, as Sir John Summerson puts it, by the 'phlegmatic Englishness of his mind'. The resolute regularity, symmetry and linearity of the building's dimensions, proportions, compartments and details are meant as a reproof to the licentiousness of Tudor and Jacobean architecture. Yet the Banqueting House is august and festive, not puritanical. Along its sides, the slight projection of the centre, the alternation of pediments over windows and the garlanded frieze were object-lessons for English builders

Banqueting House. Whitehall front. GLRO

Banqueting House. Detail of front. GLRO

on how to do more with less. The richness of the facades would be more palpable if we still had Jones's original colour scheme. Ashlarwork in warm Northamptonshire and Oxfordshire stones was formerly set off by detailing in the more crisply carvable Portland stone (for the transport of which Jones procured the construction of a special pier near the quarry). In 1829 Sir John Soane refaced the crumbling fronts throughout in Portland stone.

When Jones built the Banqueting House, there was no thought of the opulent Rubens panels that now adorn its ceiling. Commissioned by Charles I in honour of his father and installed in 1635–6, they give the interior welcome colour. To protect the paintings, the building was not used for masques thereafter. Then in 1649 the king stepped through one of its first-floor windows to his beheading on a scaffold constructed in Whitehall. During the Commonwealth and the later Stuart reigns, John Webb, Wren and others tinkered with schemes for rebuilding Whitehall Palace around the Banqueting House, but nothing came of them. In a constitutionally important ceremony, William III accepted the Crown here. But he disliked the palace and was not sorry when most of it burnt down in 1698. The Banqueting House escaped, only to be half-heartedly transformed by Wren into a Chapel Royal.

In about 1809 James Wyatt at last provided the building with a proper staircase at the north end, in place of the temporary erection which had served for so long; and in the 1830s the northern gallery was deepened. Eventually it became the museum of the Royal United Service Institution, for whom in 1893 the architects Aston Webb and Ingress Bell added the cleverly uncompetitive building attached to its south. They also put in the south gallery within the hall. In due course the museum in its turn was ousted. The present, rather barren arrangement of the interior dates back to a restoration and purification of the 1960s, when the Banqueting House became a 'function room' once more.

51

Queen's House
Romney Rd, Greenwich

1/H5   British Rail to Greenwich or Maze Hill

[A]

What to do with a palace little more than a hunting lodge, scarcely used by royalty, whose fitments had been stripped out during two centuries of other uses? When in 1933 the Queen's House became part of the new Maritime Museum, the Ministry of Works filled it with the portraits and seascapes that still give part of the ground floor its municipal character. But between 1984 and 1990 the *piano nobile* was revamped with new hangings and furnishings thought more worthy of its status. The

controversial result is a monument to modern scholarship, needlework and technology: clever, but an unreal and perhaps overly-precious recreation.

A problem is the reverence accorded by historians to the house because it is a rare survivor of Inigo Jones's accredited *oeuvre*. In the 16th century architects had adapted the new classical motifs filtered through from Italy into a style of imaginative verve and intelligence, coupled with masterful planning. Nearby Charlton House (pp. 73–4) is a good example. Enter the shadowy figure of a minor courtier who had been to Italy and given himself the rudiments of an architectural training, and thus began the Palladian-inspired classicism that forms the most continual thread in Britain's architecture.

The Queen's House was begun in 1616 as part of a larger building scheme at Greenwich for Anne of Denmark, James I's queen, but work ceased at ground-floor level shortly before her death in 1619. The walls were thatched over and left until in 1629 work began again for Charles I's queen, Henrietta Maria. How much Jones altered his design in the interim is a mystery, but the curious plan dates from 1616: an H-shaped block spanning the main road to Woolwich. Now that the earlier palace has gone it is hard to imagine the shortage of space that provoked this setting; however, the English royal family had perhaps grown accustomed to living over major routeways, for the palace of Whitehall also spanned a road. At Greenwich it meant that the north side faced the formal palace gardens,

The Queen's House, Greenwich, from the south. EH

whilst to the south was a clear vista over the park.

How Jones's rooms were used is unclear. At their centre is the entrance hall, a cube of virtuous Palladian simplicity with the original white paintwork to the gallery surviving as a gangrenous green. The ceiling was originally also white and gold, inset with paintings by Orazio Gentileschi that in 1710 were moved to Marlborough House. Their effect is hinted at by laser copies, their trabeated framework complemented by the pattern of the marble floor. This is one magnificent space in the house; the other is Britain's earliest cantilevered staircase, which leads to the gallery and is known as the Tulip Stair from the flat pattern of its iron balustrade, probably intended to represent *fleurs-de-lis*. It is the undercutting of each stone tread that makes it so dramatic as a piece of patternwork seen from below. The two most lavish rooms, now exhibited as presence chambers, face the river. To the east is a richly coffered room with heavily fruited pilasters in blue and gold, whilst on the opposite side of the hall the ceiling of what was probably a bedchamber is encrusted with symbols of fertility and heraldic devices. How then did the great loggia facing the park fit into a formal sequence?

The plan of the rest of the house is confused because in 1661–2 two more rooms were built over the road to make formal suites for Charles II and his queen. The architect was John Webb, and the rooms are distinguishable because their surviving ceiling decoration is so much more florid than Jones's. But their principal incumbent was Charles's mother, Henrietta Maria, who herself stayed only a few months. The recreation is based on an inventory made at her death in 1669, plus two drawings by Jones for fireplaces.

It is the exterior that shows Jones at his most refined. The *piano nobile* was once more prominent than now: the ground-floor windows have been lowered, and sashes have everywhere replaced casements. The original intention of a limewashed first floor contrasted with a stone ground-floor plinth has been lost under many coats of

Kensington Palace. South front. PSA

render. The setting of the Queen's House has also changed radically. In 1807–16 the house was made the centre of a new complex by Daniel Asher Alexander. He added the east and west wings, joined by an open colonnade on the line of the old road, to form a school for the children of seamen and pensioners.

52

Kensington Palace
Kensington Gardens, Kensington and Chelsea

2/A5   Underground to Queensway, Notting Hill Gate or High Street Kensington

[A]

Monarchs must always have second-string palaces wherein to house their children, siblings, cousins, mistresses, minor art-treasures and other appendages. Apart from some forty years in the sun after the Glorious Revolution, that is how Kensington Palace has always functioned. Its lack of grandeur is made up for by its cheerful aspect, homeliness and accessibility.

Of the Jacobean house built here by Sir George Coppin (one of several suburban estates created at that period on the sloping ground between the London to Oxford and London to Brentford highways) little remains. It

was in the ownership of the Earl of Nottingham when, shortly after their accession, William and Mary decided to live here in preference to Whitehall for the sake of their health. Sir Christopher Wren set to work, and got the royal pair into residence by Christmas 1689, moving the main entrance round from the south to the west. To its north Wren laid out the capacious Clock Court behind a big, rather rustic arch and cupola, while on Palace Green, now the site of smart Edwardian houses, a barracks was constructed, for William's position was far from secure. Large corner pavilions were added to the house itself – the first of a near-continuous set of remodellings and extensions by Wren and his successor architects in the Office of Works over the ensuing thirty-five years, culminating in a lavish scheme of decoration undertaken by William Kent for George I (1722–7). Nor were the gardens neglected (pp. 88–9).

Progress stopped abruptly after the death of George II's queen, Caroline, in 1737. The king 'has locked up half the palace since the queen's death,' reported Horace Walpole. Kensington was never lived in again by a monarch, unless one counts the first few days of Victoria's reign. She was born and brought up here, and always liked the palace. The state apartments were first opened to the public in 1899. Portions of the building were used for years by the London Museum, on the removal of which to the

Barbican in the 1970s a thorough restoration took place. The courts to the west and north and the sundry outlying buildings are apportioned, as they always have been, to royal relatives and connections, notably the Prince of Wales's family and offices. In this sector of the palace, a two-storey classical block facing north over Kensington Gardens and boldly dated 1989 broadcasts the Prince's architectural predilections.

What one sees of Kensington Palace today from the outside has the aura of the English country house: pleasant, civilised but lacking in ambition. The railed-in gardens to the south and east of the palace are banal and half-hearted, compared to the extent of Kensington Gardens beyond. Much the best front is that of the King's Gallery to the south (1695–6), attributable to the young Nicholas Hawksmoor. The texture of its brickwork, its slender windows and the simplicity of its central pilasters and attic, topped by exuberant stone vases, proclaim it an economical masterpiece of English baroque architecture. Other elevations are merely plain and decent. Most of the main east front is due to a campaign by William Benson and Colen Campbell in 1718–21, partly tidying up earlier work by Wren.

From the decorative standpoint, the chief interest of the first-floor royal apartments on show is their run of early interiors by Kent, the bumptious young artist who attracted Lord Burlington's patronage only to make his name as an architect and landscape gardener rather than as a painter. To Kent fell the task of embellishing the three northern rooms recast for George I by Benson and Campbell – Privy Chamber, Cupola Room and King's Drawing Room. He also redecorated the Presence Chamber, King's Staircase and King's Gallery. All this he undertook with gusto and eclecticism. Most fetching among the paintings are the 'Etruscan' ceiling of the Presence Chamber, in a homespun archaeological style foreshadowing Robert Adam, and the graphic *trompe l'oeil* walls and ceiling to the staircase, in a debased Veronese style. In the central Cupola Room, Kent's touch with *trompe l'oeil* proved less sure; its bogus coffers and trophies look like cheapjack

substitutes for plasterwork. In sentimental contrast to these heavy-handed interiors are the Duchess of Kent's Dressing Room and Queen Victoria's bedroom – largely recreations supervised by George V's consort, Queen Mary, of how these apartments might have looked during Victoria's girlhood in the 1830s.

53

Buckingham Palace
Westminster

2/E6   Underground to St James's Park or Victoria

Ever since John Nash turned Buckingham House into a palace for George IV, it has been the fashion to be rude about it. Yet if you take together the facade, the gates and piers in front encircling the Queen Victoria Memorial, the breadth of the Mall and the Admiralty Arch at its further end, the whole adds up to a very fair stab at summarising how Europeans for the past 300 years have thought royalty ought to be approached and represented. It is because that conception is French and prompts comparisons with France that English people find fault. But those with short patience and flagging feet have cause to be grateful that the Palace abbreviates the glories of Versailles and the Louvre.

Embedded in the back of the palace lie fragments of the large suburban house built by Captain William Winde for the first Duke of Buckingham in 1702–5, bought by George III in 1762 and enlarged for him by Sir William Chambers. The tourist sees nothing of this; nor does the Queen, unless she makes an archaeological effort. What royalty enjoys but John and Jane Bull cannot justly appreciate, short of gatecrashing garden parties, peering obliquely over walls or riding down Grosvenor Place on the top of a double-decker bus during winter, when the trees are less obstructive, is the work of Nash. For although Nash all but rebuilt the palace in 1825–30, his architecture

was so poorly received and the accommodation it offered proved so inadequate that the great U-shaped court he created in front was cut off from view by a solid east wing in 1847–50. This plodding affair, the creation of Edward Blore and Thomas Cubitt, remained until 1913, when its cheapjack stucco elevation was in turn deemed inharmonious with Sir Aston Webb's new Queen Victoria Memorial. So Webb just added to Blore's front the skin of Portland stone we see today, applying a respectable order *à la* Place de la Concorde in homage to the soon-to-be-tested Entente Cordiale.

Was Nash's palace so bad? To judge from the long garden elevation, unaltered except for the substitution of an attic and lower dome in the centre where Nash had stuck a dome quickly thought to be too large, the answer is no. It has the amplitude and articulation of the better Regent's Park terraces, but in Bath stone rather than raw stucco. It is a shame that it is so little seen. But the trouble, in so far as it was about aesthetics (it mostly concerned the slap-happy attitude of George IV and his architect towards spending public money) was with the front, not the back. Here Nash certainly made mistakes. One was the placing of the Marble Arch right in front of the palace. Nobody seems to have been sorry when that costly triumphal folly was moved from the forecourt, though a better second setting should have been found for it in 1851 than its haphazard site at the top of Park Lane. Further away there was a second extravagant gateway, Decimus Burton's arch at the top of Constitution Hill; this too has been shifted, but less radically.

To get a grasp of the palace's character it is first worth tracing the south side along Buckingham Palace Road, in the area of the Queen's Gallery. It starts with a Doric colonnade and a minor Bath-stone court with a neat Ionic frontispiece. This is mostly Nash's, but the higher block beyond, festively Corinthian and containing Queen Victoria's State Supper Room and Ball Room, was added by his successor James Pennethorne in 1852–6 to make a reasonable continuation of Nash's

Buckingham Palace. The gates. EH

54

Palace of Westminster
Parliament Square, Westminster

2/G6   Underground to Westminster
[B]

'C'est un rêve en pierre!' cried the Czar, presaging in diplomatic French what any parliamentarian, patriot or tourist with an ounce of sensibility is bound to feel. For once Britain and London pull it off and make an unblushing triumph of a great and prominent public building. Thanks to Barry's cool capacity and Pugin's verve, the largest and most symbolic building of them all, at the heart of the city's and the nation's history, is a cause for architectural pride instead of the muddle and embarrassment it might have become.

The outside of the monumental complex is as much as most of us normally get to see. Great George Street, Victoria Palace Gardens and the farther ends of Hungerford, Westminster and Lambeth Bridges are the best vantage points from which to savour the fairy silhouette and capture the advance and recession of its uneven towers, crests and pinnacles. That done, you can stand across the Thames in front of St Thomas's Hospital, confront the 800 ft symmetrical river front head-on and estimate Pugin's famous but flippant criticism: 'All Grecian, Sir; Tudor details on a classic body'. Even were the pliancy of the detail inadequate to banish monotony, there are always the eye-catching, off-centre turrets and lanterns behind.

Old Palace Yard, in front of Baron Marochetti's martial statue of Richard Coeur de Lion, is a good spot for a closer look. Here you can refer back to Henry VII's Chapel on the end of Westminster Abbey, the starting point for the undulation of the walling, the bulbous pinnacles and the mechanical, all-over rectilinear tracery. Even the brown stone seems to correspond. In effect Barry and Pugin in the 1830s were taking up Gothic at the point it had been left at Henry VII's death and stretching it for modern purposes. Had the old palace

garden front. After that a high wall conceals most things but not the Riding House of 1764, to the pediment of which William Theed added a powerful sculptural tableau showing Hercules engaged in a spot of horse-taming. It is the most visible of the many relief panels incorporated in the palace's facades.

After this it is time to readdress the front – really a backdrop to the Mall rather than part of Buckingham Palace proper, and a response to the Edwardian swagger of the Admiralty Arch at the other end. So the accent falls on Aston Webb's Beaux-Arts *rondpoint* and Queen Victoria Memorial (1901–3). Together with the circumferent gates, screens and

lamps, they take a great hunk out of St James's and Green Parks. As so often in British classicism, the craftsmanship is more absorbing than the architecture. The iron gates and railings, made by the Bromsgrove Guild, are specially magnificent. On the glistening groups of statuary provided by Thomas Brock for the memorial, Nikolaus Pevsner's verdict of 1957 remains true: 'better than experts nowadays are ready to admit, though of course originality and daring must not be expected'. The figure of the seated elderly queen staring with owlish rigidity down the Mall embodies an interest that few of us can feel for her allegorical companions.

burnt down even ten years later, when Tudor-Perpendicular was beginning to be despised in favour of earlier types of Gothic, their model would doubtless have been not Henry VII's Chapel but Westminster Hall. In the interests of a cheerful architecture, we may thank the workmen who overheated the stove with old tallies that fateful day in November 1834. As it is, the medieval hall provided Barry with a sturdy obstacle which he never quite managed to marry in function or style with the festive new palace. Yet had Westminster Hall not survived the fire, we would never have got so powerful and plastic a building.

Everyone except the Treasury must have been delighted when the old Palace of Westminster went up in flames. Kings had long abandoned it to Commons, Lords and Law Courts. The place was a shambles, and in the aftermath of the Reform Act of 1832, when MPs became semi-professional, almost unworkable. But it had a history so venerable that legislators shrank from destroying it. Additions since 1800 had nearly all been in the Tudor-Gothic style, increasingly identified with national roots and culture. The survival of Westminster Hall and rudiments of its equally

venerable neighbour, St Stephen's Chapel, made the stipulation of 'Gothic or Elizabethan' for the architectural competition of 1835 a certainty. It also meant that the competitors had to tackle a site with a bite taken out of it – namely Westminster Hall and New Palace Yard. Irregularity on the landward side was inevitable, and the older buildings had to be acknowledged. Most architects chose some asymmetrical manner or other of Gothic; Charles Barry won, to quote Michael Port, because of his 'skill and mastery in the handling of features common to many entries'.

From the time of Barry's victory through the commencement of works in 1839 to their completion in the 1860s, the history of the building is one of perpetual change and grind. No clients could be more arbitrary, demanding or ungrateful than legislators, whose unfocused requirements grew only with their insistence that the building be finished fast and cheaply. Barry kept his head throughout, bending when necessary, pushing ahead when he judged he could get away with it. Part of his wisdom was to bring in Pugin, the acknowledged expert on Gothic detailing, to help him. Their

collaboration was harmonious, though their families later crossed swords about it. In 1835–6 Pugin helped Barry with details of his competition designs and drawings for estimate. Then in 1844–52, when the carcase was rising and Barry was pressed, Pugin was brought back to do as much detailing as he could, particularly for the interior. Breathtakingly rapid and inventive, he designed mouldings, furniture, glass, tiles, wallpapers, escutcheons, locks, bookbindings and almost anything else you could care to name. But Barry never lost control, and kept a tight hold on the external architecture. 'Big Ben' is a case in point. The revered clock tower started as a thin little thing, no grander than a City steeple. Pugin seems to have introduced the idea of an overhanging clock stage. But the wondrous final topknot was designed after Pugin's premature death in 1852, showing that Barry and his office had learnt to absorb and refine ideas that came to them from the mercurial Goth. At the other extremity, the punchy Victoria Tower developed in the same way. Pugin provided the spark, Barry the concentration and courage to push revisions and embellishments through to completion.

After Barry in turn died in 1860, it was left to his able son Edward to tidy up and finish off. His is the stone arcade round the edge of New Palace Yard and the piers and railings along Bridge Street, easily identifiable because he used Portland instead of the by-then suspect Anston stone, and because of the tougher, 'High Victorian' character of his designs. E M Barry also contributed well to the interior, particularly the Queen's Robing Room.

The inexhaustible interest of the interior is best divided into three categories: technical, political and artistic.

Two famous Victorian structures vie for the title of 'the first modern building' – the Palace of Westminster and the Crystal Palace. On examination, the romantic, backward-looking building wins hands down over the sleek harbinger of high-tech architecture. Almost everything except the look of the place was new, and the process of

Palace of Westminster. Big Ben and Westminster Hall seen from the roof of Westminster Abbey. RCHME

Palace of Westminster. Crypt Chapel. RCHME

making it was revolutionary. It took
lessons and borrowed personnel from
the railway-building mania of the day. It
introduced the concept of the building
team, it established the profession of the
quantity surveyor and it led to a new
type of architectural partnership. Stone-
cutting and carving machinery,
travelling cranes and framed timber
scaffolding had never been used on so
concerted, productive and influential a
scale. The archaic floors and walls and
roofs hide a forest of iron girders, strewn
around with a liberality and assurance
hitherto unknown. And for the first
time, the provision of services helped to
shape a public building. Politicians
being politicians and the Victorian
Thames smelly in summer, ventilation
was the great preoccupation. A Scots
chemist, David Boswell Reid, was
appointed and threw his 'ventilating

whimsies' about. In due course he was
dismissed, but not before he had
influenced the design, conspicuously the
size and shape of the lantern over the
central lobby. Acoustics too were
studied, with little more success, the
science being in its infancy. On
completion, the House of Commons had
to have its roof lowered and changed in
shape because MPs claimed they could
not hear. The present chamber, Sir Giles
Scott's rather pallid reconstruction after
war damage, is therefore the third
version.

How far the layout and distinctive,
even oppressive, appearance of the
building affect the business carried on
within it is worth pondering. Few
initiates to these hallowed halls escape
their influences. As all visitors remark, it
feels like an august, palatial, rambling
and baffling club – a concretisation of

the labyrinthine British political
process. It takes experience even to sort
out the basic arrangement – Speaker's
and royal apartments at the north and
south ends respectively, Commons and
Lords between, divided by the central
lobby. After years of attendance,
habitués find that whole tracts remain a
mystery. The building induces gravity
and respect, but hardly that openness,
accessibility and accountability we hope
for from our politicians.

Of the artistic riches of the interior it
is possible only to give a glimpse. Bombs
damaged the Commons' side, leaving
the sleepier Lords, always more ornate,
the focus of magnificence. The ideal
route to take is through St Stephen's
Hall into the great lobby, then right into
the Lords and on beyond it to the Royal
Gallery and Queen's Robing Room. This
sequence is like going from the nave to
the chancel and then the sanctuary of a
great and colourful Gothic church.
Stonework, cold statuary, encaustic
tiling and vaulting give way first to the
woodwork, brass and leather of the
Lords and then to the more intimate
intricacy of the royal suite. Glass, light
fittings and carving all testify to the
manic dedication of Pugin and his
craftsmen. A few of the statues and
paintings, an uneven treasure-house of
mid-Victorian art, strike a discordant
note. Otherwise the harmony and poise
of the whole are remarkable. These
interiors come at a turning point in the
history of British design. If they look
back to the processional sequences of
the true, inhabited royal palaces of the
18th and earlier centuries, they look
forward too to the self-conscious
craftsmanship of the Arts and Crafts
Movement. For it was from Pugin's
patriotic efforts to embellish the Palace
of Westminster that the English Arts and
Crafts Movement first took wing.

4

Country Houses and Villas

If the town house is defined as one constrained by its site, then we take the country house to mean one detached in sufficiently ample grounds to have complete freedom of setting, planning and style. That is not to say that such houses here are larger or more lavish than many built in town. Indeed, few compare with aristocratic West End houses such as Burlington House (p. 174), Spencer House (pp. 136–7) or Home House (p. 137). For what we are largely dealing with here is the suburban villa.

The term 'villa' derives from Palladio, to whom, however, it meant a country estate. Its English use as a diminutive house seems to have begun with Pope's Villa in Twickenham and the writings of his architect, James Gibbs, who used the term in 1728. It caught on in the 1750s, when Horace Walpole so described the 'little plaything' at Strawberry Hill he was then engulfing in Gothick excrescences. As a building type its origins are usually taken to be Campbell's reworking of Palladian themes at Mereworth, Kent, and Stourhead, Wiltshire, both dating from about 1721–4. Marble Hill, in which he is thought to have had a hand, followed close after. But as small retirement homes for City businessmen something very similar can be traced back to the 16th century. Sutton House, built around 1525 and now swallowed into urban Hackney, may be the earliest survivor. Unlike the true country houses of the Midlands and North, even the largest houses of the London area, Syon and Osterley, were the centres of relatively small estates incapable of being financially self-sufficient. The difference may be established by comparing the holdings of the third Earl of Burlington: huge swathes of Yorkshire governed principally from a mansion at Londesborough, a London town house, now the Royal Academy, and a house at Chiswick set in grounds smaller than the present park that was used simply as a haven and for entertaining.

The villa had to be as impressive as possible within its small compass. It was generally compact in plan, with several showy facades and a far higher proportion of space devoted to big function rooms than usual in grand houses. The number of villas built to impress on all four sides made for some awkward service arrangements, with kitchens thrust into the basement (Asgill House), pushed into a wing and hidden by a shrubbery (Marble Hill, Kenwood), or kept in a separate house alongside (Chiswick). Such impracticalities are very much at odds with the Victorian houses included here.

The development of the suburban or weekend estate away from but accessible to the 'great wen' closely followed the available transport routes. Hence the high proportion of examples along the Thames, with aristocrats, businessmen and literati establishing Richmond as their cultural centre. In the 19th century new picturesque sites were opened up by the railways, so that whilst up to 1850 it is perfectly feasible, though erroneous, to discuss the villa without reference to surrounding counties, after that date it is impossible.

The earliest houses in this section, Syon and Osterley, are also the largest. In their original configuration, now mostly lost, they cannot be called villas, though the remodelling of the state rooms at Syon as an entertainment suite around the art of dining may come close. But their courtyard plan with corner turrets is peculiar to southern England. Syon, like Lacock in Wiltshire, may be influenced by some buried remnant of the medieval abbey it replaced, although Osterley, and also Cobham Hall in Kent, were constricted by no such earlier work yet are virtually identical in plan. Their similarity points up another feature rare outside the Home Counties until the 19th century: that houses of equal stature could be built by the aristocracy (Syon) and successful City men (Osterley).

Pageant time at Marble Hill. GLRO

The rationalisation of the courtyard plan into a single block can be seen at Ham, and most convincingly at Charlton House with its great hall running from front to back across the centre of the house. Although courtiers' houses, neither is large by Jacobean standards. The City merchants followed suit, in a building spree across Middlesex and Hertfordshire that is commensurate with their power in the period 1620–60. Whilst Inigo Jones was pushing the court towards Italian classical purity with the Queen's House (pp. 64–5), the City's architects and builders were evolving a domestic style that was an eclectic mix of Elizabethan and Jacobean frippery and more refined north European (Protestant) classical brick forms. The results are a miscellany that Summerson calls 'artisan mannerism': with curly Flemish gables and brick bonding, as at Kew (p. 89), and misapplied orders and busty caryatids doing sport with hipped roofs and pediments of unimpeachable and often puzzling correctness. Forty Hall and Boston Manor are the most puzzling examples within London. In planning, too, the artisan mannerists foreshadow the so called 'double-piles', with central spine walls, of the post-Restoration period. Synthesised into architecture of the first rank, the Restoration house is eptomised by Eltham Lodge, built in 1664 for John Shaw, revealingly both a successful banker and an important figure in Charles II's court. Its architect Hugh May had travelled widely in Holland, which state influenced the style of country houses as much as town ones for the rest of the century, as the post-fire City terraces and four-square brick boxes such as Fenton House in Hampstead equally reveal.

Baroque, so forceful in public works, lent itself little to any but the grandest domestic interiors, where murals could impart some sense of *trompe l'oeil* distortion of space. The early loss of the profligate Canons, broken up in 1747, has left Greater London with only one non-royal interior of top quality: Sudbrook Park, Petersham, like Canons, by James Gibbs. But whilst the cube room plays with pilasters and interpenetrating vaults in a way more

interesting than anything at Hampton Court (pp. 59–61) or Kensington Palace (pp. 65–6), it is – like the best bits of the latter – late in date and its planning is Palladian. For a baroque front one can do little better anywhere than Roehampton House, Wandsworth, now Queen Mary's Hospital, of 1710–12 by Thomas Archer. Meanwhile Vanbrugh preferred a conscious historicism when building for himself and his family on Maze Hill, Greenwich around 1718.

The Palladian insurgence that produced Marble Hill and Chiswick House is in its way also historicist, its model being the golden age of Inigo Jones. The chunky staircase at Marble Hill and heavy plasterwork of Chiswick are derivative of the early 17th century, owing much to Jones certainly, but also to the many contemporary houses then spuriously attributed to him. They bring us too to the perfection of the villa as a building type, and to the Thames around Richmond as its predominant location. But Robert Adam's Kenwood, in Highgate, fits the formula despite being a remodelling of an earlier house, and its greatest exponent, Sir Robert Taylor, put up villas all along the Thames from Harleyford in Buckinghamshire to Danson in Bexley, all for City contacts. His Asgill House is the perfect example, both in terms of location and diminution. Taylor's forte was the imaginative planning of the principal rooms: octagonal, apsed, rarely rectangular. His top-lit staircases also add architectural excitement within a minimum of space. These picturesque qualities were inherited by his pupil, John Nash, whose Grovelands is proudly, and unusually, rectangular externally but not without its spatial tricks inside.

No attempt can be made to trace the development of the larger Victorian villa within the London area. Since it was the richest who could commute furthest, so Devey, Shaw, Lutyens and the like exploited the styles and materials of Kent, Sussex and Surrey as these counties were discovered in turn. London can boast two major examples of such houses. The first is the inspiration of the whole genre: Philip Webb's Red House for William Morris, built in 1859

of local brick and tile, asymmetrical in form without being unnecessarily Gothic in detail. Webb's L-shaped plan was intended as part of a courtyard, Norman Shaw's typical L-plan was deliberate but taken from the same source as much of Red House, the vicarages of Butterfield and Street. Within the London area Shaw's only true country house is Grim's Dyke, built for the painter Frederick Goodall. Old English in style, with a lofty first floor painting room like a medieval great chamber, it is not only bigger but designed with more spatial freedom than his town houses for artists such as in Melbury Road (p. 142). Yet in character it is not so very different.

The change in favour of a suburbia of detached villas on pocket-handkerchief sites rather than a continuation of urban forms is perhaps the point where our definition begins to break down. Henceforward it is the mark of a good architect to make his detached town houses work as villas, with the same motifs, no matter how constrained by their setting. The best examples are no longer individual houses, but planned groups, such as those built by Shaw's pupil Ernest Newton in Chislehurst (p. 118). Even in the individual houses of the Modern Movement, setting places little constraint on style. There is no great conceptual difference, for example, between what Maxwell Fry produced at the Sun House, Hampstead (p. 146), with only one front, and on an open site as at Miramonte in Coombe Lane, Kingston, built in 1936–7.

55

Ham House
Ham Street, Richmond

1/D6   Underground or British Rail to Richmond, then bus

[A]   National Trust

'Vivat Rex 1610' proclaims the front door of Ham House. The loyal builder of this Thames-side mansion, off the beaten track and so less frequented than its striking interior deserves, was one Sir Thomas Vavassour. But Vavassour is hardly remembered now in comparison

Ham House. Entrance front. NT

with three later 17th-century owners who made Ham what it is today: the first Earl of Dysart, his daughter Elizabeth, Countess of Dysart, and her second husband, the Duke of Lauderdale. All were tough political taskmasters, who in a dangerous era demanded and displayed the magnificence they felt due to their rank. It is hard after three centuries to associate mellow Ham with ruthlessness, but its early owners were no complacent country squires.

The approach to the house, off the rural end of Ham Street and along a quiet avenue beside the river, is informal and amiable but modern. It is not altogether misleading, as sensible 17th-century travellers from London would have come by boat. Passing through a fine pair of gates and piers – a unique English example of the work of Scottish gentleman-architect Sir William Bruce, 1671 – you find yourself in a curving forecourt surrounded by lead busts in niches, confronting an H-shaped Jacobean house. The busts go back to the 1670s too, but the sixteen on the front of the house were stuck there in about 1800, when the forecourt walls were curtailed and the Coade stone river god in its centre was set up. Formerly this north front was quite different: there was a high frontispiece in the centre, the arcaded bays in the corners

were turreted and capped, and the ends of the wings have been much changed. But the little open arcades are original features.

Entering, one encounters an interior that bespeaks two main campaigns of reordering: the former by the Earl of Dysart, perhaps under the direction of the painter Franz Cleyn, in 1637–9; the latter under the Duke and Duchess of Lauderdale in 1672–4, along architectural lines suggested by Sir William Bruce but carried out by another gentleman-designer, William Samwell. The Lauderdales' changes were the larger. They involved infilling the open centre between the south wings of Vavassour's house with a new block, so giving that front a Restoration flavour. Renovations and redecoration by the National Trust and the Victoria & Albert Museum, which manage Ham jointly, have gone far – maybe a touch too far – to recreate the feeling of the house as it was in its political heyday under the Lauderdales. Some rare decorative survivals and the no-less precious preservation of detailed early inventories have aided in the scholarly endeavour of historicising Ham.

From the hall, Jacobean in shape but thoroughly gone over by the Lauderdales (who appear sculpted as Mars and Minerva over the fireplace),

you proceed to the long run of Lauderdale rooms along the south front. These are exceptional not only for their decoration but also in their sequence, which conveys graphically how 17th-century grandees received, lived and slept. After the plain chapel, at odds with the sumptuous Lauderdale apartments, comes the staircase, a rumbustious prelude to the works of 1637–9. All of wood, it has a rich gilded balustrade adorned with fetching trophies of war in a mix of modern and antique fashions, and abundant baskets of fruit on the newels. Hence you enter a gallery, beautifully opened up to the hall below in about 1690 and painted a sharp blue, and go on to a drawing room with paintings and a bizarre chimneypiece with fat barleysugar columns attributable to Franz Cleyn. The nearby Mortlake Tapestry Works, where Cleyn was artistic director, enjoyed Charles I's patronage in the 1630s, and the columns derive from one of the Raphael tapestries in royal ownership much copied there. It is odd, then, that Cleyn's columns seem rustic and mannered compared to the refined, Jonesian plaster ceilings in this sequence of rooms. Beyond are a long gallery and further fine Lauderdale interiors along the south front. The basements are open too, with domestic displays in the National Trust manner.

The main south garden has been restored in recent years to the open, formal layout of the 1670s, to the detriment of remains of a Repton arrangement. Those who like their gardens shadier can promenade among more mature elements to the sides.

56

Charlton House
The Village, Charlton, Greenwich

1/J5   British Rail to Charlton
[C]

Charlton House has the finest front of any surviving Jacobean house in the environs of London. It belongs to the rigorous, rectilinear tradition of Elizabethan H-shaped house, with flanking lantern turrets at the ends, curt, bayed wings and a centre raised just a fraction above the parapet. Most of the building is in austere brick with bands of stone, but the centre rises to a magnificent, all-stone frontispiece which mixes grotesqueness and an apotropaic face or two with hints of the more orderly classicism just coming into vogue. The date 1607 is inscribed above the door. The back, overlooking municipal Charlton Park, is more raw.

One would like to know more about this house. Its builder was Sir Adam Newton, tutor and intimate of James I's son Prince Henry, the heir to the throne at the time and a promising patron of the arts before his untimely death. Newton will have chosen the hamlet of Charlton – to which he left money to build the present parish church in the 1630s – because the early Stuarts, like the Tudors, preferred Greenwich as their place of residence. Charlton looks old-fashioned compared to the Queen's House of a decade later, but it was not so old-fashioned as all that. This becomes plain when you step through the door and find not the traditional hall with a screens passage, but a double-storeyed hall running from front to back. No one

knows who was responsible for this innovation.

The interior of Charlton House has been mauled over the centuries, and suffers today from local authority penury and hard use as a community centre. But there are still some impressive spaces, including a carved wooden staircase, a saloon above the hall and a long gallery taking up the top floor of the north wing. The fireplaces veer from sophistication in the Nicholas Stone style to a crude mannerism. Much of the panelling seems to be relatively recent. The main set of documented alterations was undertaken by Norman Shaw for Sir Spencer Maryon-Wilson in 1877–8. Shaw added a single-storey billiard room to the south, now the core of the branch library, but quite what he did by way of restoration inside the house is unclear.

South of the house are the contemporary stables, now converted into housing, while in a corner to its north-west next to the road is the only public lavatory ever attributed to Inigo Jones, a neat brick building which once functioned as Sir Adam Newton's summer house.

57
Forty Hall
Forty Hill, Enfield

1/G1   British Rail to Enfield Town or Enfield Chase, then bus; or British Rail to Turkey Street and longish walk

[A]

Forty Hall is an architectural puzzle that deserves to be better known. It is one of the group of early 17th-century houses built in Middlesex and Hertfordshire for London merchants, here haberdasher Nicholas Rainton. Building began in 1629. Since the City was at odds with the court throughout the 1630s we may be sure that the tradition that has ascribed the house to Inigo Jones since the 18th century is fallacious. Moreover, much that can be clearly attributed to the 17th century, the dramatic gateway to the stableyard and large parts of the interior, is very different from Jones's style. Instead it is in the artisan-mannerist tradition common to the merchants' houses of the area.

Though much of Forty Hall's decoration is gawkish and unsophisticated, elements of its architecture are surprisingly progressive. The hipped roof, with its modillion cornice resting unnervingly on the upper windows, has long been written off as one of many alterations of *c.*1700; however, recent investigation by Andor Gomme and Alison Maguire has confirmed that it is original. This refinement may be compared with the motley gables of Forty's contemporaries, Boston Manor in Brentford, built in 1622–3 and Swakeleys, Hillingdon, of 1630–5.

Enough remains internally at Forty Hall for us to guess at its original plan. The survival of the screen to the great hall left of the entrance suggests that the door was always in its present position, with kitchens and service rooms to the right. The present hall was created from one of these in the mid-18th century. A sale catalogue from 1773 comments that 'the singularity and boldness of the original Ornaments are ingeniously opposed to the petite neatness of the present', and nowhere is this contrast better seen than

Charlton House. Entrance front. RCHME

Forty Hall. East front. EH

in passing from the fruity plasterwork of the entrance hall into the former great hall. The massive classical mouldings and grotesque heads of the screen are particularly impressive; the delicate Gothick centre dates from the insertion of the door. One other room on the ground floor is completely of the 17th century, as is a simpler one on the first. Another ceiling there is dated 1629, though most of the panelling upstairs is early 18th century. The exterior was altered again about 1800, the date on two hopper heads on the entrance front, whilst the staircase was rebuilt in the 1890s.

The remains of a 17th-century lime avenue lead north to the New River. This was a canal that almost encircled Forty

Hall, built in 1609–13 to bring water from Hertfordshire to the City down a gentle gradient. Although it largely followed the Lea, the New River looped up and down subsidiary valleys until it was straightened in 1853–6. The remains of two loops survive in the grounds of Forty Hall and along Gentleman's Row in Enfield; these were the only sections not subsequently widened. Many of the large houses on Forty Hill were built with money from the New River, notably Myddelton House, where from the 1890s E A Bowles established a huge collection of exotic plants – a plantsman's garden rare in London.

58
Eltham Lodge
Court Rd, Eltham, Greenwich

1/J6   British Rail to Eltham or Mottingham

[C]

Close to Eltham Palace, behind a belt of trees at the end of an informal drive, lies the range of the Royal Blackheath Golf Club, whose pedigree goes back to that good Scotsman, James VI and I. The four-square brick club house, better known as Eltham Lodge and built in 1663–4, is one of the most gracious British houses of its date.

Eltham Lodge's builder was Sir John Shaw, a royalist banker who shot to court prominence at the time of the Restoration. Shaw had taken a lease of the Eltham manor, sorely damaged by 'Rich, the Rebel', but opted not to live in the palace. Instead he procured Hugh May, Paymaster of the Works, to build him a new house. May too was an ardent royalist who had spent time abroad, and what is more an original and practical architect of whose work regrettably little remains. It was most directly through May, who seems to have known Holland well, that the amiable brick forms of Dutch 17th-century classicism were so influentially assimilated into England.

The outside of the house is solid and demure, just two storeys with a hipped roof of slate rising to hidden valleys in the centre. A wooden balcony on top of the roof originally gave it more 'go'. The entrance front, with its giant pilasters, its modillioned pediment poking into the roof and its flight of steps leading to a modest front door with nothing in the way of a porch, is the one usually illustrated. It comes as a surprise to find the sides and back rather more enchanting. The eastern flank has been cut into by outbuildings, but its western counterpart is intact and displays shallow-arched blank niches alternating with thin twelve-light sashes (replacing the original transomed windows). The back towards the golf links has a yet more fetching and unusual rhythm of niches and white-painted windows. All this is carried out in a lovely rubbed brick, the diffusion of which may have been one of the fruits of May's Dutch

enthusiasms. There is almost no stonework, but the basement is in a coarser brick.

The front door opens into a spacious but altered hall. Beyond it on the right is the staircase compartment, containing a fine but badly overpainted wooden closed-string stair. Robust baskets of fruit top the newels, while cherubs wrestle with the overwhelming foliage within the balustrade. It is like an updated version of the staircase at Ham House, and very different from the restraint of the exterior. The deep plaster ceiling above has something of the density of a Restoration wig. There are good fireplaces and plasterwork in some of the rooms on both floors, again with the same exuberance of taste, as though May lost control of his craftsmen inside the building or simply enjoyed a certain amount of internal baroqueness of taste. The latter is the likelier explanation, given what is known of May's vanished interiors of the 1670s at Windsor Castle.

59

Marble Hill House
Richmond Rd, Twickenham, Richmond

1/D6   British Rail to St Margarets; or underground/British Rail to Richmond, then bus

[A]   English Heritage

In 1714 Henrietta Howard took a position in the court of the Prince and Princess of Wales to escape her

extravagant and dissolute husband. Six years later she became the mistress of the Prince, the future George II, who in 1723 settled on her about £11,500 of South Sea Stock. This seems to have prompted Mrs Howard to build her own house as an insurance for her future. She was assisted by members of the Prince's circle: in particular the Earl of Ilay, who had property at nearby Whitton, acquired the land on her behalf, and Henry Herbert, the 'architect Earl' of Pembroke, advised on the building.

Marble Hill is an exemplar of the Palladian villa, adapted as a real house rather than an architectural plaything like Chiswick. The result is more truly Jonesian in feeling. It was illustrated in volume III of Colen Campbell's *Vitruvius Britannicus* in 1725, and a surviving drawing at Wilton, seat of the earls of Pembroke in Wiltshire, suggests Campbell produced the first design for Marble Hill. Both Pembroke and Campbell seem to have made use of Roger Morris as a job-architect to execute their plans, and this is what happened at Marble Hill. Work began in 1724 and was completed, with a three-year interval during which Mrs Howard seems to have been starved of funds, in 1729.

The house has two main fronts, since at least as many visitors were expected to arrive by boat as by road. The north front is given added severity by means of Ionic pilasters and a rusticated base to the projecting centre bays, but their similarity suggests their equal status. As often in Palladian designs, the importance of the door is lost in the need to emphasise the *piano nobile*. The hall, facing the river, is based on Palladio's version of Vitruvius's design for an atrium. The status of the ground-floor rooms is confused by the conversion of a vaulted pantry into the dining room in 1751. The staircase, with its heavy balusters and fat handrail, is 17th-century in inspiration, and is presumably based on Coleshill, then misattributed to Inigo Jones.

In pride of place on the first floor is the Great Room, a single cube again of Jonesian inspiration, like the ones at the Queen's House (pp. 64–5) and Wilton.

Eltham Lodge. Garden front. GLRO

Marble Hill. Entrance front. GLRO

Where Wilton contained real Van Dycks, Mrs Howard had copies, but the plaster decoration is very similar. The overdoors contained imaginative landscapes by Giovanni Pannini, three of which have been restored to the house. To its east is Mrs Howard's bedchamber, denoted by its columned recess. The function of the other rooms is uncertain as they were changed late in her life when she shared the house with her great-niece. The secondary staircase, cantilevered and with a bulbous iron balustrade more dramatic than that of the Tulip Stair at the Queen's House, leads from the ground floor to a gallery and guest apartments on the second floor. A service wing added to the east of the house by Matthew Brettingham was demolished in 1909.

Alexander Pope, a friend and neighbour, advised on the garden layout in consultation with Charles Bridgeman, who carried out the work. It was the land, and its importance in the classic view of the Thames from Richmond Hill opposite, that was the salvation of Marble Hill. It was purchased by the London County Council in 1902 to save the park from redevelopment, though

the house was not restored until 1966. All Mrs Howard's furniture and movable fittings had been sold; the present contents, acquired by loan or purchase, are perhaps of higher quality.

60

Chiswick House
Burlington Lane, Chiswick, Hounslow

1/E5   Underground to Turnham Green, or British Rail to Chiswick
[A]   English Heritage

In 1704, Richard Boyle, at the age of ten, succeeded to the title of 3rd Earl of Burlington, and with it inherited land in Piccadilly, in Chiswick and large estates in northern England and Ireland. He came of age in 1715, and his interest in architecture dates from about this time. That year two books of seminal importance to English architecture were published: the first volume of Colen Campbell's *Vitruvius Britannicus* and the first English translation of Palladio's books on architecture. Burlington's

response was to employ Campbell to reface Burlington House in Piccadilly and to head himself (in 1719) for Vicenza to see Palladio's work. He returned with two collections of Palladio's drawings, a minor painter named William Kent and the composer Buononcini. Burlington showed his appreciation of Inigo Jones and Palladio by placing their statues to either side of his new building at Chiswick.

At Chiswick Burlington was his own architect. His possession of Palladio's drawings enabled him to be more adventurous in his motifs than the Jones-inspired Campbell. His principal source was Palladio's Villa Rotonda, but he cribbed elements from many other ancient and 16th-century Italian sources. The villa was built in about 1727–9 as an adjunct to a 17th-century house to the south-east, a link to which was added c.1732. A great part of the charm of the building is its jewel-like idiosyncrasy, with a shallow dome modelled on the Pantheon in Rome and obelisk chimneys.

The purpose of the new house is obscure. It had a wine cellar, but no kitchen, and it had long been supposed that it was a sort of private library or club for entertaining in. However, its use seems to have more closely resembled that of the state rooms of an average country house, with a

Chiswick House. Entrance portico. EH

bedchamber as well as entertainment rooms. The first floor forms a *piano nobile*, reached via imposing flights of steps on the entrance front and down a long passage. This leads directly to the central hall or Tribunal, originally gilded. Along the garden side runs the 'gallery': three interconnecting rooms, in plan a circle, a rectangle with apses and an octagon, an early example of dynamic room shapes in villas and taken from the Baths of Diocletian but with 16th century forebears also. The other rooms formed two apartments, and the eastern side followed the usual form of gallery, bedchamber and closet. The more richly decorated western side also has a picture gallery, but instead of a bedchamber the blue velvet room was probably intended as a connoisseur's room. The closet beyond this contained the most precious items of Burlington's collection.

There was one important room added to the old house, the Summer Parlour, fitted out in 1735 for Lady Burlington. The rest of the old house was pulled down in 1788 by the 5th Duke of Devonshire, to whom Chiswick had passed by marriage. He employed John White to add wings to either side of the villa to make it more convenient. These were demolished by the Ministry of Works in 1956, so that we see the house now in a purist's isolation it never had in its earlier history.

Burlington modelled his gardens on those of the ancient world as perceived by Roman architects of the 16th century, such as Bramante, Raphael and Vignola. His employment of sphinxes and terms derives from the same source, and the garden was pregnant with mythological and political imagery that would have been readily understood at the time. The earlier features are formal: a *patte d'oie* ending in eye-catching buildings and statuary, and the round Orange-Tree Garden centred on the Obelisk Pond with its temple. These date from before 1728. Lord Burlington then acquired Sutton Court, an estate west of a straight canal called the Bollo Brook. This latter was then given a more irregular form to become the first irregular-shaped piece of water in an English garden – anticipating lakes such

as the Serpentine. The cascade, added in 1738 by William Kent, was the first garden structure consciously designed as a ruin. The exedra is part of this later scheme, so that the garden was developed as a fascinating mixture of the formal and informal: a language at once reminiscent of ancient Rome but consciously transferring the elements of its culture to England. The debt to Jones was meanwhile acknowledged with the acquisition of one of his buildings: a gateway from Beaufort House in Chelsea.

61

Strawberry Hill (St Mary's College)
Waldegrave Rd, Twickenham, Richmond

1/D6   British Rail to Strawberry Hill

[B]   by written appointment

In 1747 the writer and *bon viveur* Horace Walpole leased a 'little plaything house' at Twickenham. He bought the freehold in 1749 and began making improvements and additions that occupied him until his death. The original house of 1698 survives, still symmetrical, at the south end of the complex, wrapped in the fanciful Gothick style already used by Kent at nearby Esher Place and Hampton Court.

But then Walpole demanded something more. The house was extended westwards, piecemeal and asymmetrical, to produce something at once rococo and romantic – suited equally to lunch parties and the writing of Britain's first Gothic novel, *The Castle of Otranto*. The plan was dictated in part by the proximity of the road, now set back, and by views towards the river, now blocked; these however are only partial excuses for the building's novelty. Walpole's innovation was to use real Gothic sources, usually designs from screens or tombs that he knew either from the original or from engravings of varying accuracy. These were then transposed into fireplaces, bookcases or plaster ceilings creating in

the house an ambiguity between serious antiquarianism and frivolousness, just as there was in its builder. Walpole employed a series of architects, who for a time formed a 'committee on taste': a mixture of country gentlemen and antiquarians who shared similar interests in architecture and suffered fairly evenly from his changing whims. Chief among them was John Chute, architect of his own house, The Vyne, Hampshire.

The first architect to work on the interior, however, was Richard Bentley. He it was who produced the staircase hall with a fretwork balustrade and wallpaper based loosely on a point of the tomb of Prince Arthur in Worcester Cathedral. Although much restored, most recently and carefully by Sir Albert Richardson in 1960, it is still delightful. The exterior of this first phase was the work of John Chute, who added the library block to the east in 1754. His also are the main features of the library interior, the elaborate Gothic bookcases copied from the side doors to the screen of Old St Paul's, the first serious medieval imitation.

The larger rooms to the west were added piecemeal between 1758 and Walpole's death in 1779. First was Bentley's Holbein Chamber, its huge Gothic screen and chimneypiece inspired by Rouen Cathedral, and furnished originally with drawings after Holbein. Below it is a little three-bay cloister, the first sign that the very structure of the house was taking on a pseudo-religious form. This theme was developed further after 1761, when Walpole quarrelled irreparably with Bentley and turned to Chute and Thomas Pitt. The result was a larger cloister with a gallery over that is the single grandest room. The vault was taken from Henry VII's Chapel in Westminster Abbey, the door from St Albans and the arrangement of niches from Archbishop Bourchier's tomb at Canterbury; yet the whole effect is both secular and frivolous. To one side is the tribune, most fantastic of all: a star-shaped room modelled very loosely on the chapter house at York (the falseness of its vault indicated by its termination in a star of yellow glass) with all the

Strawberry Hill. The gallery. CL

atmosphere of a chapel except consecration. The Round Tower that terminates the northward expansion of the house includes a ceiling designed by Robert Adam in 1760. The final touch of the Beauclerk turret, for greater romantic effect, was added by James Essex only in 1778.

Walpole also remodelled the grounds, of which only the Chapel in the Woods survives. Designed by Chute in 1772, it was built by Thomas Gayfere, no mere antiquarian but the master mason

at Westminster Abbey. It and the tribune have been converted into real chapels by the Catholic teacher-training college of St Mary. So the balance of sacred and profane has now shifted.

The house has been much expanded since Walpole's day. In 1860–2 Lady Frances Waldegrave added large reception rooms to the south, largely to her own designs, and remodelled Walpole's breakfast room as a Turkish boudoir. Even larger are the buildings added by the college, the best of which is

Sir Albert Richardson's chapel of 1962. It was his last important work, pale brick but gloomy, inspired by Albi Cathedral although barely Gothic in its details.

62

Asgill House
Old Palace Lane, Richmond

1/D6   Underground or British Rail to Richmond

[B]   by written appointment with the trustees

Asgill House is in many ways a smaller Marble Hill, forty years on. It too is a riverside villa, with one entrance to the rear for guests arriving by coach and one to the front for those coming by boat. Its facades have a simple but telling effect, showing how the Palladian style evolved into the 1760s. The architect, Sir Robert Taylor, developed the picturesque qualities of the style exploited by William Kent in his pavilion blocks and garden buildings to produce whole buildings, usually small villas, of which this has been described as the most perfect and consummately planned.

The house was built for Sir Charles Asgill, Lord Mayor of London in 1761–2 and one of Taylor's many City clients. The exterior is distinctively Taylor's: a ground floor treated as a rusticated basement with vermiculated quoins, whilst the upper storeys are completely without mouldings except for a pedimented central window. Taylor is noted for his canted bays, of which Asgill has three, that to the front running the full height of the house. Most distinctive of all is the pyramidal roof over deep eaves, suggestive of a rare Palladian motif of a pediment within a pediment. The whole is executed in perfect ashlar, originally probably Bath stone but replaced with Doulting in the 1950s.

Taylor was always a bold planner. Internally, he used the canted front to produce two great octagonal spaces, one above the other. The ground plan consists of an octagonal hall flanked by a room to either side whilst the rear entrance leads to a tiny vestibule and oval staircase. The diminutive stair is perhaps the interior's finest moment. A

Asgill House, from the river. GLRO

serpentine doubling-back at its top leads through an arch towards an upper stair under the eaves; a second arch opposite forms a stunning cross-vista after the tightness of the main oval. A vaulted passage leads to the second octagonal room, to which a series of paintings by Casali was moved in the 19th century.

The house was extended to the rear in the 19th century. For much of the 1960s it lay derelict and prone to vandals, until in 1969–70 the Victorian wing was removed and the rest restored. The former dining room became the kitchen, and its stone fireplace, an elegant confection of classical heads within a rococo framework, was moved into the octagonal hall. Where the fireplace now is was originally a door to the garden front, with fireplaces on the flank walls to either side. But whilst the other rooms (and especially the upper octagon) are a curious mix of Taylorian and 19th-century mouldings, it is the octagonal hall that best expresses the simplicity of much of Taylor's detailing: his reliance on the spatial effects of bold planning, and his concentration of ornament on important matters such as fireplaces.

63

Syon House
Isleworth, Hounslow

1/D5   British Rail to Syon Lane or Brentford; or underground to Richmond, then bus

[A]

At first Syon appears to be just another Home Counties Elizabethan house: square, with corner turrets, refaced and given Georgian sashes. There is no clue, except for its cloistered shape, that it sits on the site of a Brigittine convent moved here in 1431. There is also no external indication that the state rooms were entirely remodelled by Robert Adam from 1761.

The Dukes of Northumberland claim descent from the Lords Percy, Earls of Northumberland, who were granted Syon by Elizabeth I. Direct succession was contorted by two heiresses. It was when the husband of the second of these was given a dukedom that Adam was commissioned to aggrandise the house. Adam planned a great rotunda to fill the central courtyard, which never

materialised. What he did produce was one of the greatest celebrations of the formal dinner in Britain: five rooms, with the dining room strategically in the middle.

Adam was encumbered by the shapes of the Tudor rooms but not, as at Osterley, by the work of any previous architect. The stone-coloured entrance hall is typically a transition between indoors and outdoors, its marbled floor mirroring the coffers of the ceiling. It is almost but not quite a cube, and Adam got over changes in level by placing steps at either end and embellishing their asymmetry with a colonnade and copies of Roman statues. The Roman theme continues through three rooms, enforcing a strongly masculine aura: they can seem overwhelming but are consummately detailed and survive perfectly, with only a little added furniture brought from the demolished Northumberland House in the Strand to clutter Adam's intentions. The ante-room, up the steps from the hall, is perhaps finest of all. Twelve columns, an uncertain number of them real verd-antique lifted from Rome, are disposed to make a square out of a slightly rectangular room. Their colour is contrasted with gilded statues placed on their tops in the manner of a triumphal arch, and by the red, blue and yellow

Syon House. The anteroom. CL

scagliola floor. The dining room, the focal point of the display, is calmer to allow digestion, with apsed ends in the manner of Kedleston or the library at Kenwood, a copy of a Roman statue in every red marbled niche.

The remaining rooms are softer in tone. First the richly coloured withdrawing room, the original carpet repeating the pattern of the ceiling set with 260 roundels by Cipriani. Finally comes the library or long gallery, which runs the width of the house and is effectively a ladies' drawing room. At 136 ft long and only 14 ft wide the Elizabethan proportions were impossible to hide; but Adam lightened them by running strong cross-lines through the lozenge-patterned ceiling and grouping his pilasters in blocks of four. Frivolous notes are the way some Percy depicted his or her ancestry from Charlemagne in portrait medallions around the walls, and two boudoirs, one round, one square, placed in the corner turrets.

For good measure the first duke also called in Capability Brown to landscape the grounds, in 1767–73. The ornamental gardens seen by the public, however, date from 1827–30, when the importation of new botanic discoveries from America was the highest fashion. The highlight is the contemporary conservatory by Charles Fowler of Covent Garden fame. Stone still has to do some structural work in the outer walls, but above soars a great glazed wrought-iron dome supported on twelve cast-iron columns. Today this great space offers tranquility for those who have run the gauntlet of gift and garden shops that now nearly envelop it.

64

Osterley Park
Isleworth, Hounslow

1/C5   Underground to Osterley

[A]   National Trust

Like Syon, Osterley is a 16th-century house transformed in the 18th century. Again, too, the chief architect of the transformation was Robert Adam, although here his work served to unite

Osterley. The portico. NT

and embellish alterations made over the previous century. As a grand sequence Osterley is less dramatic than Syon, but its smaller rooms in contrasting styles are more immediately endearing.

Whereas Syon has been the possession of an aristocratic family since the Reformation, the wealth behind Osterley came from the City. It was built on a new site shortly before 1576 by Thomas Gresham, the founder of the Royal Exchange. His house was reclad and given antiquarian turrets in the 18th century but its form dictates the present layout and low ceilings. Gresham's house was only one room deep, without corridors, though the early date of its undercroft suggests the raised courtyard was always a walled enclosure. Less altered is the stable block, its cupola and clock added in 1714.

Any owner who has commenced building work at Osterley seems never to have lived long enough to enjoy the results. Gresham died in 1579, and subsequent owners included the developer Nicholas Barbon. In 1711 it was acquired by Francis Child, the banker, but he died in 1713 without living there and it was his grandsons, Francis and Robert, who created the house we see today. A puzzle is the work

done for Francis Child (1735–63) with which William Chambers may have been associated, since fireplaces in the long gallery and elsewhere are convincingly close to drawings by him, and he seems to have also designed the Doric Temple of Pan in the grounds. Certainly the long gallery owes little to Adam's style, and its solid Palladianism would have been yet more pronounced had not the Venetian windows at each end been blocked.

It forms a grandiose interlude in the sequence of delicate rooms added by Robert Adam for Robert Child after 1763. The work continued until about 1777, and the National Trust's preferred route through the house follows Adam's chronological evolution. What hits you first is, of course, the entrance portico, the more dramatic for its incongruity against the 16th century proportions of its surroundings. Then comes the entrance hall, transitional between indoors and outdoors, with stucco decoration by Adam's favourite plasterer, Joseph Rose, grisaille paintings by Giovanni Battista Cipriani and a stone floor inlaid with slate that mirrors the pattern of the ceiling. It and the nearly adjoining Eating Room were both finished around 1766. The whole north wing is a history lesson in conservation: the delicate colours of the Eating Room, giving full expression to Adam's delicious plasterwork and furniture, are in stark contrast to the gaudy treatment Adam's library received at the hands of well-meaning restorers in the 1960s and the nasty modern copy of a Rubens ceiling painting burnt in 1949.

Infinitely more sumptuous is the south wing, and especially the antechamber to the state apartments known as the Tapestry Room. The delicate plasterwork, with inset ceiling medallions, discreetly complements a set of Gobelins tapestries dated 1775. The furniture, by John Linnell, is covered in the same tapestry, and the ceiling design is mirrored by that of the carpet. It is one of the richest and most complete of Adam's later interiors. By contrast the Etruscan dressing room is light and fun. Adam did five such Etruscan rooms, of which four were in London; this is the only complete survivor. Etruscan culture, then known mainly through its pottery, became fashionable in the late 1760s. To Adam it was a vehicle for arabesques and anthemions of exceptional purity and thinness that shows his neo-classical style at its extreme: a contrast to the relatively weighty earlier rooms.

Adam also worked in the grounds, where beyond public bounds a tiny stream is spanned by a bridge formed of huge blocks worthy of Piranesi. Its ruination amid a mass of overgrowth (rendering it invisible from but a few yards away) is at once tragic yet appropriate to its concept.

65

Kenwood
Hampstead Lane, Highgate, Camden

1/F3 Underground to Hampstead, Highgate or Archway, then bus or longish walk

[A]   English Heritage

Kenwood is the urbane northern terminus of Hampstead Heath. Best reached across the Heath, it is worth the excursion to see its cream stuccoed front

appear through the undergrowth.

Kenwood is a remodelling of an older house, probably built by William Brydges between 1694 and 1704. It was acquired in 1754 by William Murray – later created 1st Earl of Mansfield – Attorney-General, Lord Chief Justice and a Scotsman. When, ten years later, he decided to make improvements the obvious choice of architect was Robert Adam, then working at Osterley and Syon, and a fellow Scot. Kenwood was a relatively small commission, but the simplicity of the existing building and Mansfield's liberality allowed Adam unusual freedom.

Adam was restricted, however, by the shape of the earlier house. A particular feature of this was an orangery attached at right-angles, probably also for Brydges. At first Mansfield only wanted a villa for occasional entertaining and weekend use. The chief addition therefore was a big reception room to the east, mirroring the remodelled orangery on the west. Kenwood became Mansfield's permanent home only in 1780, when his tolerance towards Catholics caused his Bloomsbury house to be burnt down in the Gordon Riots.

Adam raised the house by a storey, and added a portico to the entrance facade. The garden front was remodelled with a rusticated base and an implied

Kenwood. The music room. GLRO

order of decorative pilasters in the manner later adopted at the Adelphi. Like the Adelphi, Kenwood was rendered in an experimental patent stucco, unfortunately not one of the Adam brothers' best. The garden front was refaced soon after 1793 when much of the detail was removed. The present decoration is a reconstruction in fibre-glass made from the original drawings.

The portico leads into a low hall dominated by the 'movement' of the simply decorated ceiling. To the east, the staircase hall is a smaller version of Osterley's with the same anthemion motif in the cast-iron balustrade. The fireworks are reserved for the new room on the garden front. Although called the library, books only occupy the apses, which are separated by paired columns from the central area reserved for entertaining. Most impressive is the segmental curved ceiling, an innovation of which Adam was especially boastful in his *Works in Architecture* (1773). The other rooms along the south front are those of the early 18th-century house given new fireplaces, and sometimes cornices; the present parlour comprises two rooms thrown together around 1815.

Kenwood was made into a more substantial house by Mansfield's nephew, the 2nd Earl. He lived here from 1793 until his death in 1796, long enough to add two wings to the entrance front and rebuild the service wing and stables. His architect was George Saunders. The simplicity of his work is a reaction to Adam's, making no attempt to continue Adam's mouldings. Saunders's interiors are equally stark, the dramatic highlights not the dining and music rooms that are the principal spaces but their ante-rooms: to the east the marble hall, top-lit and modelled on a vestibule by Holland at Carlton House, and to the west a surprising vista through paired columns from the orangery into the music room.

Saunders's simple rooms are the perfect foil to pictures by Rembrandt, Vermeer and Gainsborough. The collection is not that of the earls of Mansfield, sold in 1922, but of Edward Cecil Guinness, 1st Earl of Iveagh. He bought the house to prevent its

Grovelands, from the park. EH

something to Nash's training under Robert Taylor, but is most striking as a serene disposition of his favourite motifs, to be much reworked later in London. There are tripartite windows under scalloped arches, oval windows in the attics to either side, and an Ionic order stepping back and forth in pilasters and columns. Most fascinating are the materials: white stone columns and dressings juxtaposed with stucco that has never been painted but left to resemble a reddish stone. It gives the villa a crispness like the finest biscuit ceramic.

The side entrance, its vestibule sporting a dome and set with classical plaques, opens into a vast hall in which the staircase rises, splits and doubles back. The surrounding suite of drawing room, dining room and library settles back in cool submission to this great space. Only the morning room startles. Octagonal, with apses, it is a painted *trompe l'oeil*-birdcage of unknown date and set with tantalising scenes of the Campagna amid hollyhocks and mirrors: an odd contrast to the Repton park seen through the windows.

67

Red House
Red House Lane, Bexleyheath, Bexley

1/K5   British Rail to Bexleyheath

[B]   by written appointment with owners

Red House is as simple and forceful as its name. It was built in 1859–60 as a farmhouse-sized home in an orchard for the newly wed William and Jane Morris by their friend Philip Webb, having been devised on a French canal holiday taken by Morris and Webb in 1858. Today it is hard to imagine a less likely setting than Bexleyheath for the champion of the Arts and Crafts Movement (unless it is his birthplace of Walthamstow). Yet the high red garden walls still manage to keep suburbia just at bay.

William Morris had considered entering the church, but turned instead to art and articled himself briefly to the architect G E Street, for whom Webb

demolition and passed it on his death in 1927 to the London County Council, who had acquired land to the south.

The grounds are also largely by Robert Adam, who built the bath house and an eye-catching bridge at the end of the main lake that is in fact a 'sham' hiding the dam. Adam describes vistas to St Paul's and Greenwich that are now obscured by trees, securing Kenwood aloof in its own valley. Hampstead Lane originally ran closer to the house but was moved by the 2nd Earl, who corresponded with Humphry Repton. It is doubtful Repton visited Kenwood, but the serpentine paths, shrubberies and flower garden are in his style.

66

Grovelands
The Bourne, Southgate, Enfield

1/G2   Underground to Southgate

[B]

Stability was a commodity rare in John Nash's life. After early bankruptcy and a

disastrous marriage, Nash relaunched his career as much by force of personality as by architectural masterpieces. A steadying hand arrived at a crucial moment in the form of Humphry Repton, as practical a landscapist as Nash could be impractical an architect, but who shared a similar vision of the picturesque.

The partnership was brief but remarkably fruitful for both fortunes. Grovelands, built for a brandy merchant called Walker Gray, gained them particular attention by its proximity to London. The park's entrances and paths date only from 1911 when it was saved from development by the local council, but the effect of the whole remains much as Repton intended. There is a mass of trees to one side, in the valley bottom the Bourne is dammed to form a lake, while the house rising sentinel on the other is seen last of all. Repton exhibited sketches for the grounds in 1797 and Nash designed the house a year or so later. It is four-square and strong, with porticoes on three sides and a conservatory, long demolished, on the fourth. The composition owes was already working. The house Morris commissioned from his friend owes much to the ideas of Pugin and Ruskin: to Pugin's demand that there should be no decorative ornament that was not part of the construction or function of the house, and to Ruskin's hope for a quality of spiritual expressiveness through a simplified form of Gothic. These ideas had already inspired Street and his contemporary William Butterfield to produce cottages and vicarages in honest brick, with big roofs and arched windows. Webb, then only twenty-eight, developed this idiom more freely for larger houses. In so doing he helped to lay the foundations of the Arts and Crafts Movement, the Queen Anne Revival and – in the eyes of historians like Nikolaus Pevsner – even of the Modern Movement.

The feeling of the house is Gothic, as are details such as a turreted well-house and the pointed brick arches; but elements like the sash windows are classical, or rather traditionally English, in inspiration. The type and scale of each window exactly match the scale of the room behind it, just as Pugin and Ruskin would have wished. Above all Red House exudes Webb's delight in

good materials, especially brick, whether used as plain walling, as relieving arches to the windows or as crow-steps to the tall chimneys – all contrasted with old-fashioned tiled and bellcast roofs.

The house is completely asymmetrical, L-shaped around a courtyard with a well, which the monastic trait in Morris conceived as a cloister. This courtyard is the most powerful element of the design; a third side, intended as a separate wing for his artist friend Burne-Jones, was never built. The cloister idea is reflected in the plan of the corridors, which face the courtyard – hence the projecting stairwell in the angle of the two wings that is the finest space in the house. Every tread and riser of the stair is exposed and lovingly detailed. The wings are of different heights, distinguishing the relative importance of the front one; the brick-filled tympanum where they collide is a feature culled from Street. Of the principal rooms, only Morris's office has a window over the courtyard.

The main rooms are where the wings meet – in particular a first floor drawing room with a projecting bay that retains the most important piece of furniture in

the house, a huge settle brought from Morris's previous lodgings in Red Lion Square and given a gallery. Otherwise the interior has lost most of its fittings, but not the simple brick fireplaces – some arched, some with rounded mouldings, some chamfered. They are a triumph of self-conscious under-statement. Equally delightful are tiny details like the door fittings.

68

Grim's Dyke
Old Redding, Harrow Weald, Harrow

1/C2   British Rail to Hatch End, then bus

[C]

Grim's Dyke, tucked away in overgrown isolation at the back of Harrow Weald Common, is a genial specimen of the Norman Shaw country house, and the best example of the genre to be found within 20 miles of London. Its history and architecture alike make it hard to take quite seriously; about its charm there can be no doubt. Its entrance front boasts a pointed porch overhung by a large, mock half-timbered gable (the half-timbering is now painted stark black-and-white, instead of the silver-grey-and-ochre which such houses require), and a big studio wing splayed off to the left, all upon a base of pretty, pinkish-red brickwork. The side has passages of timberwork too, but the best elevation is towards the garden. Here, patterned tile-hanging bears the ornamental brunt, while the chimneybreast of the dining room inglenook, crowned with one of Shaw's delightful stacks, kinks in to give 'go' to the composition.

The house was built in 1870–2 for an orientalizing and sentimental painter of the Victorian realist school, Frederick Goodall: hence the studio, which was canted away from the main line of the building to catch the best light. The remainder of the house lies parallel to the real Grim's Dyke, a venerable earthwork which runs just north of the house and can be well seen further west along Old Redding. Mounting the

Red House, the courtyard as partially built, with well. MARTIN CHARLES

elaborate, processional oak stair and entering Goodall's studio, a lofty, waggon-ceiled hall with a little gallery at one end and a big bay at the other, one is staggered that Victorian painters could afford houses on this scale. With changing tastes, it turned out that Goodall couldn't. In 1883 he sold up to a banker who put on a billiard room with a second inglenook in a raw Gothic style (architect, Arthur Cawston) at the end of the building.

Then in 1888 a more enduring owner arrived, the tetchy comic dramatist and versifier W S Gilbert. Five years before, he had procured Ernest George and Peto to build him the richly gabled No. 39 Harrington Gardens (p. 144). In architecture as in the theatre, Gilbert knew what he wanted. At Grim's Dyke he got George and Peto to add bedrooms on top of the billiard room, which they did with a tact which pays tribute to their admiration of Shaw. He also engaged a semi-inebriate French craftsman to carve the extravagant alabaster chimneypiece in the studio, more in the Harrington Gardens manner than that of Grim's Dyke. Gilbert resided here in style, surrounded by lemurs, parrots and other pets a-plenty (Goodall in his day had kept sheep for his biblical paintings), quarrelling with neighbours and driving dangerously round the local

Grim's Dyke, the garden front. ANDRÉ GOULANCOURT

lanes, until his death in 1911. This occurred when he went to the rescue of two young ladies who had got into difficulty while bathing in the lake.

Grim's Dyke since has never been the same. After passing from one use to another, egregiously that of Gothic backdrop for horror films made by one

of the local studios, it became a country club and hotel in the 1960s. With permission, you can saunter in the pleasant grounds, dine, participate in a Gilbert-and-Sullivan singalong in the studio, or visit Goodall's former dining room, the one room still much as Shaw left it, complete with angular inglenook.

85

Parks and Gardens

The history of gardens has become, perhaps too much, a separate study from that of the buildings that created them. A garden can be any man-made landscape, from the acres of Hampton Court to the smallest former burial ground or square. Even cemeteries, being designed layouts, are gardens. The reader can appreciate the huge variety of green spaces which London has to offer, and our selection has been made only from those parks and gardens that were not developed around a house or which have long had an independent existence.

A history of English garden design could be written without venturing outside Greater London for examples. That does not mean London has the best examples of any period, with the exception of Hampton Court and Chiswick. These two serve also to explain the survival of many London gardens: Hampton Court as an example of an institutional garden that was fossilised, Chiswick as a country house garden that was saved from suburban development to become a public park.

For the small 17th-century garden embanked by terraces, Grays Inn is the most authentic example, with its two grass banks laid out to the design of Francis Bacon around 1600. The garden behind Fenton House, Hampstead, though largely a re-creation, gives a better impression of this formal, manicured style of different levels and compartments set off with low walls and box hedges. Such compartmental design lent itself to the educational beds or *pulvilli* of the Chelsea Physic Garden, established in 1673, where the garden was divided in four to represent the known continents and then subdivided into regular plots by species. Ham (pp. 72–3), another re-creation by the National Trust, shows that towards the end of the century larger gardens evolved into single compositions of hedged parterres, designed to be viewed from the *piano nobile* of the house and focusing on a single distant point.

For the formal garden at its most

extensive, Hampton Court (pp. 59–61) is without peer. The idea of opening out into the landscape is French: for kings it symbolised absolute control extending beyond the horizon to the whole nation. The *patte d'oie* of long canal flanked by radiating avenues, which Nash expunged at St James's, survives here, emanating from a semi-circular parterre now overrun with yews. The scheme was begun by Charles II, fresh from France in 1661–2, and developed by William and Mary. It extends into Bushy Park opposite, laid out with double avenues by London and Wise in 1689–99. The bold bones of the conception survive, simplified by Queen Anne and embellished with pretty formal beds when the taste for Tudor historicism took hold early in the present century. The staying power of the formal garden is displayed by Wanstead Park, Redbridge, laid out in the 1700s by George London as a huge complex of canals and geometric ponds, and scarcely softened by modifications in the 1720s. The house was demolished in 1823–4, but the water features survive amid the brambles to a remarkable degree.

The English landscape garden, as defined by Christopher Hussey to mean a collection of classical and occasionally Gothic references within a supposedly natural setting, owes its origin to the Grand Tour undertaken by so many landed young gentlemen in the early 18th century. There seem to have been two parallel developments: one centred on Yorkshire, where classical monuments are set against fortress-like bastions with views across the large-scale open landscapes, and a slightly later southern movement emanating from Burlington's circle – the writings of Alexander Pope and artistry of William Kent. Chiswick (pp. 77–8), with its formal axes and exedra broken by a serpentine lake, is a first attempt at a compromise between antique enrichment (including the spoils of Burlington's own Grand Tour) and an

Deep concentration in Kensington Gardens.
HULTON PICTURE LIBRARY

unequivocally English setting given careful facial surgery.

The balance between architectural reference and 'natural' landscape shifted decisively in favour of the latter with the emergence of the prolific Capability Brown and Humphry Repton. In London their consummate industry has been put to serve as golf courses: Brown's at Wimbledon Park, Merton, and The Park, Harrow; Repton's at Sundridge Park, Bromley. But that is to underestimate Repton's influence, egregiously on Nash's serpentine creations in St James's and Regent's Parks, but also on the development of two new institutional spaces: Kew and the Zoological Gardens (the latter now dominated by architecture in a manner not originally intended). Their embellishment coincided with the increasingly successful propagation and importation of exotic species, first from America and later from Asia, such as are found also in the arboretum at Syon (p. 81). In a competitive atmosphere of collecting and cultivating, gardens gradually reassumed formal elements to make the most of these fruits of horticultural hard labour. The contrived results are more consciously picturesque than natural, with complex walks winding through clumps of shrubs and bedding. Such walks and shrubberies half-shrouded by London planes, adopted for their resilience to the dirty atmosphere, became also the standard language of the London square. Berkeley Square claims the oldest planes, Mecklenburgh and Ladbroke Squares perhaps the most complete surviving layouts, and Bedford Square (p. 99) the best synthesis between a miniature landscape and its enveloping buildings.

Compared with the northern industrial cities, London was late in its provision of public parks. Public access to St James's and Hyde Park, though long established, was only confirmed in the early 19th century, whilst for long admittance to Kensington Gardens was restricted to the respectable and much of Regent's Park remained the privileged domain of its residents. Many squares are still private precincts today. It was left to the Commissioners of Woods and

Forests to fulfil the need for a park in the rapidly expanding East End, with the opening of Victoria Park in 1845. They followed up with Battersea and Kennington Parks in the 1850s, and provision was continued by the Metropolitan Board of Works and London County Council. Commercial development was confined to the singularly bizarre theme-park out at Crystal Palace. The Victorian public park was eclectic, labour-intensive and aggressively horticultural, a tradition that lingers in the formal bedding-out of flowering annuals. Distinctive to London are the debased cottage-garden schemes developed by J J Sexby for the LCC's parks – botanical Noah's arks of riotous colour caught somewhere between mass-bedding and the more painterly theories of Gertrude Jekyll. The best example is the walled garden of Brockwell Park, Lambeth. There is a similar indiscipline in one plantsman's garden now open to the public, at Myddelton House in Enfield, where E A Bowles established a 'lunatic asylum' for the most curious of his imported exotica.

Outside the public domain, the 1890s saw a revival of the architectural garden. The country house architecture of the Lutyens generation, who conceived house and garden as a united scheme of indoor and outdoor rooms, is largely outside the physical area of this volume. London does, however, boast one example at the most monumentally Italian extreme of the genre, The Hill, Hampstead. Its terraces and pergolas may be not so far from the Renaissance ideals of Bacon's era, given greater artistry and architectural permanence.

69

Hyde Park and Kensington Gardens
Westminster

2/B5–C5   Underground to Hyde Park Corner, Marble Arch, Queensway or South Kensington

Hyde Park originally meant the whole open space from Park Lane to Kensington, which in 1536 was

requisitioned by Henry VIII from Westminster Abbey to become a deer park. James I first admitted the public, and under Charles I and especially Charles II the eastern part developed as a fashionable parade ground for the wealthy and their horses, carriages and mistresses. Hyde Park was thus from the first a place less to see than be seen in, and this function was the chief influence on its later development. The present roads were laid out as carriage drives in about 1825 by Decimus Burton, whose Grecian lodges and screen at Hyde Park Corner are amongst the few architectural elements. In 1836 George Rennie built the Serpentine Bridge to carry the Western Carriage Drive that forms the boundary with Kensington Gardens over the Serpentine.

The sparsity of Hyde Park has its moments, but Kensington Gardens is altogether more satisfying. It owes its separate identify to having been taken back into a private royal garden in the 18th century. When in 1689 William and Mary acquired Nottingham House at the undeveloped western end of the park, they used their prerogative to enclose 26 acres as a complex series of formal parterres with box hedges. These were simplified by Queen Anne, who employed Henry Wise to enclose 100 acres as a deer paddock. In 1704 she commissioned the orangery, a greenhouse and summer supper house, designed by Hawksmoor under the auspices of Wren as Surveyor-General, with revisions by Vanbrugh. A sunken garden was also made, in a slightly different position from but presumably the inspiration for the present 1908–9 version east of the house.

From about 1727 Queen Caroline employed Wise and Charles Bridgeman to create a more naturalistic landscape. An avenue laid out by Anne was widened to form the Broad Walk, and a rectangular pond where George I had stored edible turtles became 'The Basin' or Round Pond. From this fanned a series of radiating avenues to give the gardens the cross-vistas that remain their most remarkable feature. Towards the end of the 1720s, William Kent had created an irregular-shaped lake at Chiswick; in 1730–1 Queen Caroline

Hyde Park. Water Gardens. EH

employed Charles Withers and a Mr Jepherson to produce a similar 'serpentine river'. By 1733 Kent himself was designing garden buildings, including a little temple that survives to the north of the Serpentine Gallery, formerly stables. But after Queen Caroline's death in 1737 Kensington declined as a royal residence, and William IV restored public access to the 'respectably dressed'.

An air of Victorian respectability still pervades Kensington Gardens. The *rond-points* of the 18th century avenues are now terminated by sculptures such as the Speke Monument of 1864 and G F Watts's *Physical Energy* of 1904. As telling are the glimpses of surrounding buildings, a vista down one of the avenues to Sir Gilbert Scott's Church of St Mary Abbots of 1869–72 being particularly evocative. Its tradition as a haven for nannies to bring their young middle-class charges lives on in the Peter Pan statue commissioned by J M Barrie from Sir George Frampton in 1912, and the Elfin Oak, created in 1928 by Ivor Innes. Remnants of the 1851 Great Exhibition in Hyde Park have also strayed over the border: the Coalbrookdale Gates at the entrance of the Flower Walk, and the pavilion in the Italian Gardens at the northern end of

the Long Water, created in 1861. Henry Moore's *Arch* of 1979 is a strange but not inappropriate contrast.

70
Royal Botanic Gardens
Kew, Richmond

1/D5   Underground to Kew Gardens, or British Rail to Kew Gardens, Kew Bridge or Richmond [A]

When William and Mary decided to develop Hampton Court, Richmond Palace lost its importance. But subsequent royals established smaller estates to its north, and George II and Queen Caroline laid out gardens. Their grounds form the western part of the present Kew, the boundary being Holly Walk – roughly a line drawn between the Dutch House and the Pagoda. In 1770 this landscape was remodelled by Capability Brown and his lake, river walks and rhododendron dell survive.

In 1730 Frederick, Prince of Wales, fell out with his father and acquired the adjacent estate to the east. The estates were united on the death of his widow, Princess Augusta, in 1770. In 1802 George III commissioned a fantastic

castellated palace from James Wyatt, but this was never finished and in 1828 was dynamited. That left a merchant's house at the extreme north of the site, built in 1631 by Samuel Fortrey, a merchant of Dutch parentage. It has good claim to be the first house in England built in Flemish-bond brickwork, and its curly gables are further evidence of Dutch inspiration. The epithet 'Dutch House' seems more appropriate than that of palace, though it fulfilled the latter role from 1802 to 1818.

Kew survives because of the importance of its botanical collections, originally only 10 acres, laid out for Princess Augusta by William Aiton, and developed by Sir Joseph Banks after 1772. Significant too, since some of his buildings survive, was Princess Augusta's employment of the architect William Chambers. Chambers made his name as a designer with a treatise on Chinese gardens and buildings, based on personal observation as a Canton merchant. Most famous at Kew is his pagoda of 1761–2, ten storeys and 163 ft high, and originally decorated with eighty dragons, coloured glass and gilding. But most of Chambers's buildings were classical in style, including many ephemeral wooden structures that have not lasted. Grandest is his orangery of 1761, but tucked away on the eastern boundary of the gardens are three little temples: Arethusa, Bellona and Aeolus – this last rebuilt by Decimus Burton – and a ruined arch. Four more temples and a Theatre of Augusta have gone, as has any semblance of Chambers's layout.

By 1841 the botanic collection was outgrowing its accommodation, when most of the gardens were passed to the state. Queen Victoria retained a small area including Queen Charlotte's cottage, built in 1772 and incorporated into the public gardens only in 1898. William Hooker took over as botanist, and W A Nesfield imposed the formal landscape of the main lake and its attendant ranks of massed bedding. One of the best buildings at Kew is the early 'Queen Anne' lodge designed by his son William Eden Nesfield at the eastern extremity of the gardens in 1867. It has an assured strength and simplicity in the

Kew. The Palm House interior during restoration. GLRO

pyramidal massing of its steep-pitched roof and massive dormers and chimney.

But Kew is best remembered for its greenhouses. The most resplendent, the Palm House, came first. In 1843 the Irish conservatory specialist Richard Turner produced an elaborate, probably Gothic, design with a double aisle of closely spaced columns. As consultant architect, Burton favoured something at once more functional and more like the curvaceous forms of Paxton's Great Stove at Chatsworth. His was the basis of the final design, but it was perfected when Turner devised a means of making 60 ft spans, and substituted slimmer wrought-iron 'I' beams for cast-iron. It was one of the first examples of such a system outside shipbuilding, and opened in 1848.

There was no such fusion of architectural and engineering inspiration in Burton's design for the Temperate House. This was begun in 1859 as the world's largest glasshouse, but the wings were not completed until 1898. The brief demanded the avoidance of curved sections, difficult to detail, and Hooker insisted that the roof be masked by a stone parapet. A more staid design

was inevitable. The myriad other buildings at Kew make for even more of a jumble, and many of Burton's simple brick buildings suffer from their dull materials. More recently the needs of plants have dominated over architectural aspirations, nowhere more so than at the Princess of Wales Conservatory, opened in 1987.

71

Zoological Gardens
Regent's Park, Westminster

1/F4   Underground to Camden Town or Regent's Park

[A]

The Zoo was designed as a garden ornamented by animal houses, rather as the contemporary Kew is ornamented by its greenhouses. But buildings now dominate the landscape, despite the efforts of the landscape architect Peter Shepheard. There has been a campaign to provide more natural environments for the animals, often at the expense of what Ian Nairn called 'a Noah's ark of architecture'. In the 1960s the animals

here were as famous as the Royal Family, if less noted for their fecundity. Today it is a place to observe the human species fostering its young and at play.

There are four main phases of building. The Zoological Society was founded in 1824 and soon acquired the northerly portion of Regent's Park. Decimus Burton was appointed architect to the Society and the gardens opened in April 1828. A feature of the Zoo is its division into three sections by a road and the Regent's Canal. Little survives of the original layout of serpentine paths and round beds, apart from the eastern tunnel under the road, by Burton, and his Giraffe House of 1836–7, as graceful as its occupants.

Just before the First World War the Zoo expanded its collection, and new accommodation was designed to create more natural surroundings for its display as well as increased facilities for its study, mangement and visitors. J N Mappin, partner in the West End firm of Mappin and Webb, was a leading supporter of the Zoo. The architects for his Oxford Street store were Belcher and Joass, and it was presumably through him that they became architects for the Zoo. Both Belcher and Mappin died in 1913, but Joass, amongst others, continued to design neat little red brick buildings in keeping with Burton's original Italianate conception until the late 1920s. Joass's most remarkable creation was the Mappin Terraces, built with a bequest from their eponymous benefactor. Around a tea pavilion and flamingo pool rise, successively, enclosures for deer, bears and goats, culminating in Matterhorn-like

London Zoo. Elephant and Rhino Pavilion. GLRO

pinnacles some 80 ft high. The structure is an early and unique variant of the Kahn system of reinforced concrete developed in the early 1900s to simplify the construction of car factories. The mountain goats perched on their improbable crags above the trees used to make a strange sight in Regent's Park. Underneath an early example of the red brick genre, the Parrot House of 1898, is Britain's only concrete telephone box – a prototype of 1931 that never went into production.

Recent architecture at the Zoo has made few architectural statements. But the Elephant and Rhino Pavilion of 1965 by Casson, Conder and Partners has a stark brutalism, forceful but unrefined, that suits the look of its occupants if not their lifestyle. A similar claim can be made for the elegantly simple, tensile, structure of the Snowdon aviary, designed in 1963 by Cedric Price, Frank Newby and Lord Snowdon.

This is to leave the best until last, worth the hefty entrance fee alone. In 1928 Solly Zuckerman was appointed Research Anatomist to the Society. Four years later he introduced Lubetkin and Tecton to the Zoo as architects of the Gorilla House, the first building by Britain's most advanced architectural practice of the 1930s. This was a sensitive commission because of concern about the health of the Zoo's two new gorillas. Tecton provided a drum of two parts, half sleeping area and half viewing arena from which the glazing could be slid away on warm days, with a public walkway between. It has since housed koala bears.

Tecton's greater (if physically tiny) masterpiece is the Penguin Pool of 1934. A perfect abstract composition of reinforced concrete, the pool is bisected by two interlocking ramps supported on an oval perimeter wall cut to allow the public to lean over and look in. Simple tones of white and blue add to the subtleties of light and shade. The desire of the director, Peter Chalmers-Mitchell, was for a showcase where the animals could entertain the public, a very different brief from that given architects at the Zoo in recent years. Tecton responded by creating a totally artificial environment that contrasted the

London Zoo. Penguin Pool. EH

penguins' under-water skills with their endearing clumsiness on land. The combination of delight and concern for the animals' well-being, which the Penguin Pool arouses, is representative of the mixed emotions felt by Londoners at the news early in 1991 of the Zoo's proposed closure.

72

Battersea Park
Battersea Park Rd, Wandsworth

1/F5   British Rail to Battersea Park; or underground to Sloane Square, then bus

In the first forty years of the 19th century London doubled in population, but no provision was made for more public open spaces. Local Vestries were too small and impecunious, and there was no private philanthropic initiative. A need for a new park in the East End was recognised by a Select Committee on Public Walks in 1833, but only in 1840 was the acquisition of Victoria Park authorised by the Commissioners of Woods and Forests and the Office of Works.

In 1844 Thomas Cubitt suggested that a second park be created on Battersea Fields, a bleak, marshy wasteland with an equally murky reputation, noted for its gaming and drinking dens. An Act of Parliament followed in 1846, empowering the Commissioners of Woods and Forests to form a Royal Park of over 198 acres, with housing permitted on a surrounding 120 acres. A provisional scheme was drawn up by James Pennethorne, who had laid out Victoria Park, but was not carried

out until 1855. As at Victoria Park, Battersea owed more to the imagination of the gardener, John Gibson. It was he who enlivened Pennethorne's simple rectangular shape, cut into quadrants by carriage drives, with a lake in its marshiest corner. The park opened in 1857.

Battersea is more exciting than Victoria Park. Whilst both have absolutely flat sites, Battersea was given greater interest by raising the river embankment and creating hills using earth from the excavations of the London Docks. Five miles of road were laid out, and 40,000 trees and 45,000 bushes were planted. This planting has ensured that despite splendid views across the Thames, most of the park turns its back on the river. Gibson was an early exponent of exotic foliage and carpet bedding, quintessential features of Victorian gardening that found full expression at Battersea. Most famous was Gibson's sub-tropical garden of palms, tree-ferns and bananas; this contrasted with an alpine garden around the lake, some of which survives amidst artificial rocks supplied by Mr Pulham.

In 1889 management of the park passed to the London County Council who added new lodges, gates, boating facilities and that curious London park institution, the menagerie of ageing

Battersea Park. Peace Pagoda. EH

goats and wallabies. But the 1850s landscaping of Battersea remains at variance with the looser planning and brilliant-hued bedding of later LCC parks.

Until 1950 the northern part of Battersea Park behind the river terrace consisted of open grassland and cricket pitches. Then amidst some controversy it became the pleasure gardens and funfair to the Festival of Britain. For five months in 1951 Battersea assumed the national significance that had always eluded it. The last remains of this naive fantasy, which included such delights as Rowland Emett's Far Tottering and Oyster Creek Railway, have been systematically swept away since the collapse of the Big Dipper in 1974. Little survives except the Grand Vista, a lake setting for firework displays with twisted pylons and flimsy shelters devised by John Piper. Today it leads to a football pitch. Hopefully more permanent are sculptures by the boating lake: *Three Standing Figures* by Henry Moore, and *Single Form* by Barbara Hepworth.

Meanwhile the optimism of the Festival of Britain has found expression in the more mystical form of a riverside pagoda presented in 1975 by the Buddhist order of Nipsponzam Myohogi, a confection of traditional timberwork, stone, gold and bells.

73

Crystal Palace Park
Sydenham, Bromley

1/G6   British Rail to Crystal Palace

The Crystal Palace began life as the great glass, timber and iron hall of the 1851 Great Exhibition mounted in Hyde Park to display the pre-eminence of British manufactures. Joseph Paxton dashed off the original design in nine days. The Great Exhibition lasted for seven months and attracted 6 million visitors. Paxton earned a knighthood and £5,000, but was more concerned with the fate of his building. His first aim was to keep it in Hyde Park, but in May 1852 a motion to this effect was defeated in Parliament. Anticipating this, Paxton had raised

£500,000 to move the structure to a hilltop site at Sydenham.

The original building had cost only £150,000. Paxton submitted to temptation and made the revised version even larger, with five storeys instead of three and three transepts instead of one. Whereas in Hyde Park the Crystal Palace was adapted to an existing landscape, at Sydenham it was raised supreme over two great stone terraces from which a monumental formal layout stretched downhill across the park. Paxton conceived a series of fountains 'grander than Versailles' worked by pressure from two huge water towers built by Brunel to either side of the Palace. The building itself housed Fine Art Courts, natural history collections, special exhibitions and a concert hall. The concept was to be educational as well as entertaining.

Success at first seemed assured, despite Paxton's prodigality and the high cost of upkeep. Two new railway lines brought some 2 million visitors each year. But when the north transept burnt down in 1866 it was never rebuilt, and by 1900 the building's popularity had begun to wane. In 1913 it was bought for

£230,000 and presented to the nation as an effort to save it. Restoration began in 1920, but on 30 November 1936 a fire in a lavatory spread in minutes to consume the whole building. The water towers were demolished in 1940.

The National Recreation Centre, erected in 1954–64, ironically reflects the form of the two great fountains formerly on the site. Gouging out the centre of the park, it has left it without a focus. Five feet of earth were deposited on and below the lower terrace, submerging the remaining fountains. All we have now are the terrace walls and steps, impressive in their ruinous decay, and a handful of statues. A great head of Paxton was taken from the wreckage and mounted by the sports centre to mark the line of the central vista.

Paxton's more naturalistic gardens to the north and east form the present park. The English garden, an informally planted glade, runs through the northern section, to which a maze was added in 1872. But the highlight is the south-eastern corner of the park. This was conceived as an educational display, including reconstructions of geological

Crystal Palace. Dinosaurs. GLRO

strata, of which the coal measures survive as an element in a more rugged landscape. A serpentine path leads into a narrow glade with an irregularly shaped lake where are displayed twenty-seven dinosaurs. Made of brick around an iron frame and clad in brightly painted stucco, all shapes and sizes are represented. They were built by Benjamin Waterhouse Hawkins as accurate representations of the real things, although subsequent research has revealed some errors. Largest is the iguanadon, in which twenty-one gentlemen held a celebratory banquet when it was half completed – impossible to imagine if engravings did not survive to confirm the story.

74

The Hill
North End Way, Hampstead, Camden

1/F3   Underground to Hampstead and longish walk

The Hill's charm lies in its secrecy. It is strange to find a fragment of ruinous Italy suspended above the wilderness of West Heath, at the end of civilised Hampstead. Today you have to enter from the back of the garden: this is a public park of smooth lawns on several levels, restored by the Greater London Council. Steep steps lead up to a series of raised balustraded stone terraces, carrying pergolas of Roman Doric columns slung between massive rusticated belvederes or look-out houses. The style is the Edwardian Baroque that fortified a handful of Italianate gardens in the early 1900s.

The terraces have now been reduced to romantic decay. The columns, the wooden pergolas they support, the vines, wisteria and ivy in which they are entwined, have all become one so completely that nature and architecture are no longer distinguishable. The main terraces and pergolas are roughly L-

The Hill. The end of a terrace. EH

shaped, full of little steps, *rond-points* and surprises. To the east they overlook the bedraggled lawns of the derelict house.

The house was remodelled and the garden built for the soap king W H Lever, later Lord Leverhulme, best known as the creator of Port Sunlight on Merseyside. His garden designer was Thomas Hayton Mawson, who in 1906 was given the brief of designing a garden appropriate to Lever's ambitious for the house, then being extended by E A Ould. Mawson was a major rival of Lutyens. His work was often grander and more monumental, if less fluid in composition. His robust qualities were especially suited to his native northern England, where most of his best work is. This is a rare example of a private urban scheme.

A particular need was to obscure both house and garden from the gaze of the public on the Heath. Planting would have taken too long to mature, so Mawson characteristically built a pergola; his garden for Lever at Thornton Manor, Cheshire, has one almost identical in style. An added

problem at The Hill was the slope of the site, which Mawson solved by building up the land with spoil from the construction of the underground, then being extended to Golders Green. This enabled him to hide the gardeners' sheds and propagating houses below the terrace. The part of the garden adjacent to the house remains in private hands, including the remains of the lily pond, aligned like the main terrace on the centre of the house.

The gardens were enlarged in about 1911 and again between 1917 and 1920, but Leverhulme was unable to close the lane running through the site to West Heath. So Mawson built the grandest pergola of all, sailing on a bridge high above the land and ending in a great rusticated belvedere designed to catch the best view of Harrow-on-the-Hill in the distance.

In 1928 The Hill was sold, and renamed Inverforth House after its new owner. In 1955 it was acquired by the Trades Union Congress as a hospital, from whom the London County Council acquired the public part of the gardens in 1960.

6

Squares

London's squares are a shibboleth. They are often said to represent the special strain of urban civilisation which Britain has bequeathed to the world. At the least, they seem to stand for a quality of Georgian urbanism which the Danish architect-planner Steen Eiler Rasmussen so brilliantly captured in *London, The Unique City*: the formal surrounding terraces for a certain reserve, pragmatism and propriety, the gardens in the centre for amenity and the English love of nature. Certainly they are a form of architecture and town planning if not unique to London, then never exploited to the full in other cities – though Bath, Edinburgh and Liverpool all had a good stab at it.

This image of the London square relies upon a picture of it at the high point of its development in the early 19th century. Regular terraces round the sides of a square were rare, though not unknown (see St James's Square), before the 1760s. Even after that the regularity was usually approximate, because of English architectural indiscipline; attempts to make all four sides match almost never came off, even in seemingly perfect Bedford Square. Planting in the centre of squares was non-existent till the mid-18th century, scanty and subordinate to the architecture for another fifty years after that. The dense protective thickets and towering planes which we enjoy today were products of the Reptonian garden revolution of 1800–30.

The London square is an evolving thing, and cries out to be savoured in its full historical and topographical setting. It is, for a start, mistaken to think of the square as a Georgian phenomenon. One has to accept Albert Richardson's sly formulation that 'the eighteenth century borrowed forty years from the preceding century and another forty from the nineteenth century' to make it so. Even then this leaves out Covent Garden, battered ancestor of the London square (pp. 208–9), such an exceptional creation as Milner Square of the 1840s,

and countless other examples of the 1840–80 period, dotted all over London but at their most numerous in Kensington, Paddington and Islington. You have missed an ingredient in the formula if you have not seen one of these many later chains of squares, from which we have selected the Lonsdale and Milner Square sequence in Islington. The real collapse of the square occurs in the 1880s, simultaneously with that of the great London terrace house. Attempts to recreate it after that are acts of revivalism undertaken against the grain, but none the worse for that. Courtenay Square, Kennington, of 1913, is the outstanding example. Sutton Square, of the late 1980s, is a recent attempt at the form, but on the basis of a shallower philosophy of urbanism.

The story of the London square appears different if you concentrate upon the voids rather than the solids. Open space within the city has a long, elaborate and political history. Covent Garden of the 1630s was important not just for Inigo Jones's architecture but also as an attempt, along with Moorfields and Lincoln's Inn Fields, to safeguard open space at a time of decreasing public amenity. All the early squares of London were paved and more or less open. But in an age of ineffective policing this led to encroachments, the most notorious of which was the establishment of the Covent Garden market, and a loss of value for surrounding property. So from the 18th century landlords railed off the centres of squares, at first hesitantly, in time more firmly. Over the past hundred years, public access has in places been prised back, but it remains hit and miss. Grosvenor Square, for instance, was opened up after the Second World War, and the delightful St James's Square garden is accessible; but Kensington, Bedford, Fitzroy and Belgrave Squares are all still restricted to key-holders. Much depends on the size and power of landowners. One result of the 'privatisation' of open space in London's

Covent Garden when an open square.

squares was that the city's real public spaces of assembly became profoundly un-architectural. Piccadilly Circus and Trafalgar Square are both deeply unsatisfactory places, while the unnamed intersection at Bank, 'the Hub of the Empire', has better surrounding architecture (pp. 17, 36–7, 207–8, 214–15) but no unity.

Formally, the square appears at first to define itself – four roads all round, buildings lining them and open space in the middle. Yet the variations are infinite. Many squares, especially those that were hacked out of something historically different – Charterhouse Square (p. 150) is an example – are not even rectangular; few are anything like square. There can be squares with big buildings in the middle, most commonly churches, and squares with so little between the long sides that they are really just wide streets, like the west end of Queen Anne's Gate (pp. 131–2), once 'Queen's Square'. From early on in their history they can stand alone in suburban isolation, like puzzling, charming Kensington Square, or they can be the centre of a much larger surrounding grid, like Grosvenor Square. The London square with one end open to a main road and with only two or three built-up sides, like Park Square, Regent's Park (pp. 109–12) is typical and effective. Sometimes, as at Alexander Square, Brompton, the term is arrogated to a mere terrace set back from a main road behind a garden and flanked by other buildings which project further forward. In one pretty Kensington development of the 1810s, Edwardes Square, the largest terrace turns its back upon the ample common garden, while the flanking houses are separated from it by their own conventional front gardens. From models like this stems a fine Victorian type, commonest in North Kensington, in which the visible square is suppressed altogether and its common garden snatched away and set behind or between the houses, as at Harrington and Collingham Gardens (p. 144). And at Hampstead Garden Suburb (pp. 119–20) the central square consists, strangely, of just two rival churches, an 'institute', tennis courts, trees, grass and

a single roadway. The very flexibility of the square warns us not to admire it in isolation. It is part of London's larger vocabulary of urban and estate planning, linked to the street, the mews, the crescent and the park.

Much pleasure and instruction can be had merely by examining the way in which roads come in and out of squares, and their architectural consequences. In most of the early squares (Covent Garden, St James's Square) the sides are bisected by roads, leading to shortish, staccato terraces and awkward corners. Grosvenor Square is the first to tackle this problem and set the square within a regular grid of surrounding streets; but the architectural will to achieve uniform terraces was not there and the corners remained practically and aesthetically awkward, giving a sense of the architecture leaking away. When the Grosvenor Estate faced a similar task a hundred years later in Belgrave Square of the 1820s, a fresh approach was taken by setting grand villas diagonally across the corners. Squares, too, sent out their own shock waves into the surrounding streets. By the mid-18th century, the best houses had to have their own stables immediately behind. This meant narrow mews at the back of each terrace; for economy of planning, those mews needed to be two-sided, and to serve another good street beyond, parallel with the original terrace. Rare were the landlords like the Grosvenors or the Portmans with land enough to carry through the logic of this system. The result is that most Georgian squares had better sides, fully serviced behind, and worse sides with less depth, squeezed up against a main road like the south side of St James's Square, for example. In the 19th century, as hiring horses and coaches became easier, stabling began to be reduced in scale and grouped away from houses, allowing greater freedom in layouts and, eventually, the 'North Kensington' model of common garden behind houses.

The architecture proper of the London square has seen a struggle between the forces of order and disorder, discipline and freedom, ever since Inigo Jones imposed the rigid system of the 'temple front' on the main side of Covent

Garden in the 1630s. On behalf of classical (or other – see Lonsdale Square) regularity, it is said that unified squares look smarter and that they keep up values as well as appearances. Against it, the argument is that uniformity of elevation goes against the piecemeal nature of the London development and, equally important, redevelopment process. It has been rarely achieved and, once achieved, even more rarely maintained. The grandiloquent gesture whereby old Grosvenor Square was torn down in the 1930s for the sake of a new system of uniform fronts, never achieved, now seems absurd. Besides, except in small squares with modest gardens like Courtenay Square, one cannot now 'read' all the sides of a square together. It seems right that, where possible, the different sides of a London square and, a fortiori, the competing buildings along a given side, should respect one another. But absolute uniformity has never been either practicable or desirable. Bedford Square is a golden example of what the classical ideal and an authoritarian London landlord could achieve together. But the diversity of St James's Square is equally agreeable; even so chaotic an agglomeration as the buildings surrounding Golden Square can give pleasure. In the end it is the old formula of variety within uniformity that suits the London square the best.

75

St James's Square
Westminster

2/F5   Underground to Piccadilly Circus

Among the five or six second-generation London squares built after 1660, St James's Square is pre-eminent. That is not because any of its original houses survive (the west side of Bloomsbury Square seems to be the only place where such vestiges remain), but because it kept its cachet longer than its rivals and still boasts a finer sequence of Georgian town houses than any other square in London.

The objective of the St James's

Square development, as projected by the Earl of St Albans and his trustees in the early 1660s, was explicit: the square was to be built 'for the conveniency of the Nobility and Gentry who were to attend upon his Majestie's Person, and in Parliament'. In its early days it was even called the 'Place Royale', in naked imitation of what is now the Place des Vosges in Paris. Easy words to use, perhaps. Yet despite setbacks caused by war, plague and the Great Fire of London, despite too a change of layout whereby a mere thirteen or fourteen grand 'palaces' had to be watered down to twenty-two separate plots, the three main sides of the square as built between about 1667 and 1677 were indeed in near-exclusive aristocratic, legislative or diplomatic occupation till the early 19th century. To its east was a market, envisaged as part of the original development but suppressed when Lower Regent Street was laid out in the 1810s. Northwards Wren's church of St James's, Piccadilly at the top of Duke of York Street, though not started till development was well forward, soon became integral to the square's amenities.

Most London squares until the late 18th century developed with haphazard frontages. St James's was an exception. Early views show the east, north and west sides as uniform, the houses having wooden eaves-cornices, plain brick piers and tiers of windows with plinths in between the storeys, like the later houses of Hanover Square. The Crown had some supervisory role over the development, but who designed the elevations or made the builders conform we do not know. The likeliest candidate is Hugh May, whose cousin Bàptist May, 'court pimp' (Babmaes Street perpetuates his name), was a trustee of the Earl of St Albans.

The uniformity did not last long. Since the St James's Square houses were sold freehold, there was every incentive for their rich owners to rebuild. This they did with unremitting fervour. No. 4 in the north-east corner, built in 1726–8 for the Duke of Kent with plaster window-dressings and a sumptuously plastered staircase by the robust architect, developer and (need it be added?) plasterer Edward Shepherd is the outstanding early survival. Nos 9–11, a plainer group on the north side, are of the late 1730s, by Henry Flitcroft working with Benjamin Timbrell. The

magnificently appointed Norfolk House of 1748–52 was St James's Square's most grievous loss, though its music room, decorated by Borra of Turin, was rescued in 1938 for the Victoria and Albert Museum. Continuing chronologically, one comes next to No. 15 near the top of the west side, by Athenian Stuart (1764–6) with later additions by Samuel Wyatt – important in its day for introducing the neo-classical stone front to the high-class terrace house. The idea was taken up by Robert Adam, whose No. 20 further down the same side (1771–4) is the most complete, inside and out, of his several interventions in the square. It was, however, rendered highly confusing by Messrs Mewès and Davis, architects, who in 1936 extended No. 20 four further bays southwards in the same style and stuck on extra storeys above the parapet. Adam also refronted No. 11 and rebuilt No. 33 on the east side in a quieter style. The sequence of magnificence can be followed through into the ensuing centuries with No. 12, a handsomely proportioned stuccoed house designed by an unknown hand working for Thomas Cubitt (1836); No. 18, enriched in the Genoese manner during the 1840s; and No. 7, a conscious effort in neo-Georgian self-effacement by Lutyens for the banker Gaspard Farrer (1911). Of the office blocks that began to eat up houses after 1918, the only one with much character is at No. 3, which has some jolly inter-war relief sculpture.

The centre of St James's Square began as a huge, open, paved space. As at Covent Garden, experience proved that this soon led to booths, nuisances and other encroachments. So it was 'privatised' by Act of Parliament in 1726, when a circular pond and octagonal railing were introduced. The present garden, with an enlarged circular enclosure and shrubs, is one of the lesser-known works of Nash and dates back to 1817, though the delightful trees which make sitting here such a pleasure did not arrive for some years thereafter. The statue of William III in the middle is by the two John Bacons, father and son, and was erected in 1808, having been first envisaged almost a hundred years before.

St James's Square. EH

76

Kensington Square
Kensington and Chelsea

2/A6 Underground to High Street Kensington

Squares are deemed to be an urban form of architecture, but Kensington, 4 miles west of the City, was a mere village on the turnpike road when Kensington Square was projected by Thomas Young in 1685. It had a cluster of wayside inns and a handful of prosperous residents, just beginning to live out of town after London's ordeals of plague and fire in the 1660s. What possessed Young to think he could carry off a square here? A high-class joiner who had worked at Chatsworth and other country houses, he seems to have been smitten by the speculative building bug. Evidently he saw Kensington Square as a place of suburban resort, rather like the contemporary spa at Hampstead, for to its south he laid out a 'spring garden', a bowling green, and 'an House of Entertainment (for Eating and Drinking)'. Pepys and others liked to come out to Kensington on drinking bouts, so there was some sort of excursion trade to cater for. But it was not enough.

By 1687 Young was in difficulties with his project and vanished into a debtors' prison. But an unexpected turn of events saved the square, though not its progenitor, from disaster. In 1689 the asthmatic William III decided to buy, extend and inhabit what became Kensington Palace in preference to damp and rambling Whitehall. Court officials and hangers-on needed nearby accommodation for those months of the year when the monarch was in residence. This gave a sufficient fillip for the north, east and south sides to be quickly completed and for a start to be made on the west side – not in the end finished till the 1720s. For forty or fifty years Kensington became, in Leigh Hunt's phrase, the 'old court suburb', with the square a major attraction for the transient court population. Soldiers, prelates, state pensioners and petty functionaries all lodged here.

Most of the first houses underwent reconstruction or enlargement in the Georgian period. So there are few tokens today of the square's early appearance apart from Nos 11 and 12, a pretty, mirrored pair built just off the south-east corner of the square in 1701–2. With three full storeys above ground and hipped roofs, they are higher than were most of the original houses. Do not be misled by the inscription on the shell-head over No. 11's door citing the names of the Duchess of Mazarin, Archbishop Thomas Herring and Talleyrand;

Herring had a house nearby in the 1740s, but the others were only brief visitors to the square. The grandest former house, seven windows wide with a central pediment, stood nearby on the site of the present No. 13; here William III's general, the Duke of Schomberg, lived for a time.

Kings and court deserted Kensington in the 1730s, leaving the square an amiable backwater for a hundred years. Because the freeholds were in separate ownership, changes took place haphazardly, giving each of the sides a gently variegated appearance. Front

11 and 12 Kensington Square. RCHME

gardens on the north and south sides and generous planting in the central enclosure help to maintain the suburban air. Miraculously, most of the houses are still in domestic use and many in single-family ownership – a rarity for a square as old as this one. It has helped that they are not too big. For a time the growth of Barkers department store to the north threatened to overwhelm the enclave. But commercial encroachment was stoutly and in the end successfully resisted by residents.

Houses which have more than vestiges of old work include Nos 11 and 12 (see above); No. 17 (inhabited by the composer Hubert Parry); No. 18 (the home of John Stuart Mill); No. 19; No. 29; No. 33 (lived in by the Edwardian actress Mrs Patrick Campbell); and Nos 34–37. Genteel rebuildings include No. 7 (1808–9) and Nos 41 and 42 (1804–5). Outstanding among Victorian intrusions is the Convent of the Assumption on the south side of the square, with a chunky Gothic chapel (1870–5) designed by the Catholic architect George Goldie, who lived in the square, rebuilt Nos 6 and 16 and refronted No. 5. The secluded convent garden is all the open space that now remains from poor Thomas Young's bowling green and spring garden.

77

Bedford Square
Bloomsbury, Camden

2/F3   Underground to Tottenham Court Road

Why has Bedford Square come to symbolise Georgian London at its most perfectly composed? In part this must be due to the completeness with which its houses have survived, the regularity of their composition and distinctive quirks like their door surrounds. Scholars have been drawn, too, by the survival of the records of the Bedford Estate, which still manages the square, especially as these do not entirely answer the question of who designed it. But certainly a factor, whose influence is impossible to determine, was the removal here in 1917 of the Architectural Association, to

Bedford Square. North side. EH

occupy Nos 34–36. The educational forces there in the 1920s were Robert Atkinson (who built its war memorial library) and Howard Robertson, both appreciative of Georgian proportion and brickwork. Here Steen Eiler Rasmussen lectured in 1928, and his book on the quintessentials of London architecture, *London, The Unique City*, perfectly captures the homely spirit for which London's Georgian squares and terraces have since been venerated. The AA, through its public lectures, exhibitions and bookshop, retains an influence wider than that of other schools of architecture.

Bedford Square was built between 1778 and 1783. Its first impression is of an unusual unity, its simple brown brick relieved by little save for stuccoed centrepieces with pilasters and pediments, and doorcases enlivened by boldly vermiculated Coade stone voussoirs. In the centre rise lofty planes in an intensely private circular garden complete with a rusticated summer house. Only one corner house, No. 39, was rebuilt in Victorian times.

A more studied look reveals many solecisms. Except on the south side the composition of projecting centre blocks and ends melts away into the smaller terraces of the surrounding streets. The details only serve to confuse: different size plots, different fanlights, some houses with full-length windows to the first floor, some without. There is a bewildering variety of ironwork to the first-floor balconies, most markedly at

No. 12 with its canopied verandah. The oddities are most pronounced in the central stuccoed houses: whilst No. 6 on the grand east side is of five bays, that on the opposite side has only three. Most alarming of all, the matching centrepieces on the other sides are shared by pairs of houses and so commit the mortal sin of classical architecture in having central pilasters to their pedimented compositions.

The square has been traditionally associated with Thomas Leverton, a worthy if not first-rate country house designer, who certainly built Nos 1, 6 and 10 and lived at No. 13. But it can be convincingly argued that he was only involved with these grandest houses, and that the vagaries of the square are due to the Bedford Estate surveyor, Robert Palmer, or to the builders of most of the houses, the brickmaker William Scott or the carpenter Robert Grews. No. 1 stands aside from the general layout. It is a singular composition, with a central rendered doorcase like a triumphal arch bearing arms and a curious internal plan of a hall across the whole facade with a staircase on the left side. It was built for a tobacco merchant, Lionel Lyde, and totally upstages the centrepiece of the east side, No. 6, finished by Leverton for the unknown architect John Mecluer. Many of the houses have not only delicate staircases but Adamesque ceilings to the principal drawing rooms on the first-floor front rooms, some with inset painted medallions. A good time to see them is at dusk on early winter evenings.

The views out of Bedford Square are fascinating too. It is one of the few places where you can appreciate the vast dome of Sydney Smirke's reading room for the British Library, as well as one of the many from which the view is pierced by Richard Seifert's rhythmic and underrated Centre Point of 1961–5. Most curious is the giant dust sheet construction behind No. 27 Bedford Square that covers the Imagination Gallery, conceived in 1989 by Ron Herron.

78

Fitzroy Square
Camden

2/E2   Underground to Great Portland Street or Warren Street

The name Fitzrovia began as a joke, invented in the 1940s to denote its antithesis from up-market Belgravia. It has stuck, and with it something of the Bohemian character it stood for. The Fitzroy family, earls of Southampton, began to develop their estate in about 1790, the year in which those famous speculator-architects Robert and James Adam obtained a lease to build Fitzroy Square as its centrepiece. Other features of the estate, including its chapel, were bombed in 1940, when much of the square was gutted. Yet Fitzroy Square is the best preserved of the Adams' London planning schemes: ironically so, since only two sides were begun before Robert Adam's death in 1792.

Fitzroy Square balanced monumental facades with simple interiors. This was a contrast to the Adams' earlier London developments in Portland Place and particularly at the Adelphi, the project by the Thames that nearly led to their financial ruin in 1773. There the exteriors were of unassuming proportions, with decoration confined to strips of patent cement render that gave them a delicate elegance. The Adelphi was more than half destroyed in the 1930s, while a line of much altered houses and the wide avenue give little

Fitzroy Square. The centrepiece of Adam's east side. GLRO

indication of the intended grandeur of Portland Place. But monumentality was a feature of Robert Adam's very last work, anticipating the terraces built around Regent's Park by John Nash – who also piled his effects on to his exteriors. Adam intended the square to be a centrepiece for simpler terraces along the surrounding streets, which were later added by other builders.

The east side, first let in 1792, is the most impressive. It is dominated by the giant order at its centre, and by the Diocletian windows in the end pavilions which make a Venetian formation with the surrounding fenestration. Patent

Liardet cement decoration is reserved for a garlanded frieze, whose loss in places matters little. The south side, completed in 1794, is more delicately wrought. The motifs of the centre and ends are reversed, so that the Ionic order is squashed into a tripartite window below a heavy frieze. Not only are there more friezes but also decorative roundels not found in the earlier block, giving it typical Adam movement – here at the expense of power.

The north and west sides are in keeping, unspectacular if today distinctly the more chic. The north side, now pierced by an Edwardian hospital, dates from 1827–8, whilst the west side was not completed until about 1832. Both sides show how the Adam style evolved into the flat patterning of neo-Grecian pastiche: particularly debased are the awkwardly fat columns of the giant order on the western terrace. The ensemble works, however, if largely because its disparate elements are hidden from each other by the huge plane trees in the central garden. This dates from 1815, though given its circular form only in the 1950s. The bomb site in the angle of the two Adam blocks was neatly filled in 1951–3 by Ralph Tubbs's Indian Student Hostel for the YMCA, which respects the Adams' bulk and height unslavishly. The key feature is its domed corner cupola, built as a prayer house.

The square was formerly home to many artists and writers, most notably the young Virginia Stephen and her brother before they could afford to move over to Bloomsbury. For similar reasons it was found suitable in 1913 by her sister Vanessa Bell, who with Roger Fry set up the Omega workshop there to encourage young designers imbued with the bright colours and motifs of post-impressionism.

79
Belgrave Square
Belgravia, Westminster

2/D6   Underground to Hyde Park Corner

Everything about Belgrave Square spells amplitude – its plan, its mansions, even its roadway, round which motorists like to race at rather more than 30 miles per hour after freeing themselves from the noose of Hyde Park Corner. If you enter one of its houses, you feel dwarfed by the scale of the corridors; if you peer over the railings, you fear a tumble into the depths of the basement would meet with certain death. This sense of being cowed is a by-product of upper-class urban architecture in the 1820s – not the least class-conscious of decades.

Belgrave Square gives its name to an area and is immortally associated with

Thomas Cubitt, most successful of all London builders – the man who raised to an art the mixing of speculation with rigid respectability. Yet Cubitt had more in detail to do with other portions of Belgravia and Pimlico than with the great square itself, *clou* though it was to the new suburb behind Buckingham Palace. When the Grosvenors contemplated developing their huge Pimlico landholdings, they quickly thought of a big square surrounded by lesser streets, after the model of Grosvenor Square on their earlier Mayfair estate. James Wyatt made a layout for the square, setting more or less the shape it has now, in about 1812. Little then happened for a decade, till the project of a canal up from the Thames into central Pimlico and the rebuilding of Buckingham Palace shed simultaneous lustre on development west of Hyde Park Corner. Plans for the square and surrounding streets were revised, probably by Thomas Cundy I, the Grosvenors' surveyor, and in 1824 Cubitt made an offer for three sides of the square; Seth Smith, another big builder, accepted terms for the fourth. But Cubitt and Smith, who often worked in tandem, soon laid off this part of the future Belgravia on to a City banking syndicate led by the Swiss-born brothers Haldimand. The Haldimands brought in George Basevi to design the square's

four grand ranges. These were built between about 1826 and 1837, probably by a variety of builders, though Cubitt himself put up a few of the houses. Unusually for the period, one of the buildings is signed; George Haldimand's house, No. 31, bears the inscription 'G. BASEVI, Archt. 1827'.

Basevi has the reputation of having been Sir John Soane's best or favourite pupil. The front of the Fitzwilliam Museum in Cambridge apart, why he enjoyed such fame is a puzzle. Howard Colvin dismisses his country houses as a 'dull lot'. Looking at the fronts of Belgrave Square or indeed Basevi's various later essays in unified London housing design – Alexander Square, Thurloe Square, Pelham Crescent and Egerton Crescent – it is hard to discern special talent. No doubt he was employed for his efficiency. James Elmes hit on a truth when he dismissed one of Basevi's central features in Belgrave Square as 'a poverty-stricken would-be-fine sort of effect'. Faced with the blankness of these fronts, the separate sore thumbs of their porticoes sticking out along each terrace, one remembers too Lethaby's dictum: 'a building that poses as imposing is an imposition'. Historically, Belgrave Square was prompt in taking up the planning and grouping tricks and the all-over stucco terraces that Nash had pioneered at

Belgrave Square. EH

Regent's Park. Via its example, the Nash techniques came to be applied in a second-hand way to a complete quarter of London. Basevi is the link between Nash and the acreage of debased Victorian classical housing that covers so much of South Kensington. But of Nash's manipulation of picturesque effect, Belgrave Square has not a jot.

The Haldimands never got their hands on the corner sites. Here, instead of the awkward pairs of houses built between the incoming streets of Grosvenor Square, it was decided to have grand 'villas' set at an angle. Three were built, mostly after the terraces were finished. They help to give the square some of the individuality which Basevi failed to supply. The most villa-like still is Henry Kendall's house for Thomas Read Kemp, the developer of Kemp Town, Brighton, in the south-west corner (1827–33). In the north-west and south-east angles are larger mansions for peers, designed respectively by Robert Smirke (1830–3) and Philip Hardwick (1842–5). Revised road arrangements in the north-east corner made a detached villa impracticable. Here Cubitt's office eventually put up No. 49 for Sidney Herbert, Florence Nightingale's patron, as late as 1847. Most of these grander houses, like so much of Belgrave Square, are now in diplomatic hands.

80
Tredegar Square
Mile End, Tower Hamlets

1/H4   Underground to Mile End

Before demographic changes in the mid-19th century pushed it down-market, the East End offered opportunities for building on a handsome scale, especially away from the river in Bow and Mile End. After more than a century of neglect, the more picturesque of these terraces enjoyed a resurgence in the late 1980s, owing to their proximity to the City – and none more so than the finest of all, Tredegar Square. Its special feature is its contrast of unassuming

Tredegar Square. East and south sides. EH

little houses, possessing an almost bewildering variety of builders' details, with a far more massive and composed focal point.

In 1822 Sir Charles Morgan leased all his 45 acres in Mile End to a local bricklayer, Daniel Austin. Development began on the ancient thoroughfare of Bow Road with a line of tall terraces, followed by smaller houses in the streets behind. Last of all came Tredegar Square, laid out in 1828. It is so big that it is perhaps not surprising Austin went bankrupt the next year. He sub-let each side in separate lots, though at least two and probably all four sides were acquired by a single builder, William Miller. The east, west and south sides are no grander than the streets around, copying all the latest tricks in the Georgian repertory in a simple and crude manner. All the first floor windows are set behind relieving arches, whilst the doorcases further nod at fashion with fluted Greek Doric columns embedded in the doorcases. The east and west sides were intended to mirror each other, with a weak centrepiece of incised stucco strips topped by a tiny pediment. The short south side is the boldest of the three, for elsewhere slenderer doorcases and

pretty fanlights in a plethora of arabesques creep in to disturb the supposed symmetry – especially on the east side, finished last when money was tightest.

The money clearly went on the north side, which allows no such lapses. It would be hard to credit as the work of the same builders if their authorship had not been proved. Austin, or less probably Miller, sought no less than to emulate John Nash, whose development around Regent's Park was just being completed. The terrace is arranged in three massive blocks, the centre one with projecting ends, the end ones with projecting centres, and linked by recessed two-storey pavilions – one of which has since been raised, to add to the confusion. The links are especially contorted, employing every motif of Nash's expansive York Terrace squashed together. Tripartite and round-headed windows jostle with a couple of niches to wedge themselves in and around pairs of columns set *in antis*. A Doric order is used for the porches in the links, and a giant Ionic for the main block. No amount of gentrification can soften the impact of its bulk amid the low ranges of Mile End.

81

Lonsdale and Milner Squares
Islington

1/G4　Underground or British Rail to Highbury & Islington

The development of Barnsbury, the area west of Upper Street, began in the 1820s. Its earlier squares and terraces repeat the classical forms then established for speculative building: simple rows whose classical order is expressed in columns or pilasters only at their centres or ends. Gibson Square, built by Francis Edwards in the mid-1820s, is a good example, though it indicates too how the composition could go limp if the rows were long and the architect, builder or property owner was not particular. By the late 1830s this consensus of fashion had broken down and developers were looking for alternatives. Lonsdale and Milner Squares, built to either side of Gibson Square, show how diverse was the range of possibilities.

The small estate owned by the Drapers' Company of the City hit in 1838 upon a happily picturesque option. The Elizabethan style had been much advocated, by J C Loudon amongst many, as appropriate for cottages, and examples of semi-detached villas in the style can be found in the near-contemporary De Beauvoir Square, Hackney, by Roumieu and Gough. Moreover, the Drapers' architect was R C Carpenter, soon to be in the vanguard of the Ecclesiological Revival. At Lonsdale Square, completed in 1842, he revealed his proto-Gothic hand with a square of closely packed four-storey terraced houses of grey brick, all with Elizabethan hood-moulds to the windows, steeply pointed gables set forward, and trefoils over the porches. Because there are only two entrances to the square, at each end, the effect of so close-packed a site is powerful. In some ways it is closer to contemporary workhouses than to Nash picturesque, though the manicured rose gardens in the centre tip the balance towards piquant charm.

In Islington, meanwhile, Roumieu and Gough asserted themselves in a very different manner to their work in Hackney. The Gibson estate to the east of Lonsdale Square was otherwise completed when in 1839 they began to lay out Milner Terrace, promoted to a square shortly after without an increase in proportions. Here is the antithesis of the picturesque. But this is classical gone wild – two great cliffs of stock brick facing each other across a narrow paved square that has spurned even the delicacy of grass.

The final design and actual construction of the houses date from 1842–4. Like Lonsdale Square there are only entrances at the ends, which in so narrow a square as Milner heightens the impact of a four-storey wall of some sixty stock-brick giant pilasters to either side. Proposals were briefly entertained for a church in the centre of one side, which might have eased the tension of such an unrelieved rhythm. Instead it is enforced by the recessed stucco panels between the pilasters. The attic storey, by contrast, is arcaded, an alternating rhythm of big round arches containing windows between smaller blind ones. We see too not only the demise of classical purity but of its adjutant the glazing bar, here reduced to thin horizontals as

Lonsdale Square. GLRO

Milner Square. GLRO

reductions in taxes on glass precipitated the introduction of bigger sheets of plate glass. The ensemble was fittingly described by John Summerson as 'unreal and tortured'; not even in public housing estates does so much humanity seem so close-packed. It hints at Roumieu's future as one of the most bloody-minded of Goths: his vinegar offices in Eastcheap, designed in 1868, have a mass of pointed brick gables that make them one of the most entertaining buildings in the City.

82

Courtenay Square
Kennington, Lambeth

2/H7   Underground to Kennington

Anxious to keep abreast of his subject, Stanley Adshead, professor of the young science of town planning at the Liverpool University, took himself off in 1910 with a bevy of housing reformers to visit Munich. There, he and a friend fell in with an 'unknown person who seemed to be particularly keen on architecture'. In circumstances scarcely credible even for Edwardian gentlemen, the three travelled back together, stopping off in Paris *en route*, without Adshead ever

discovering his companion's name. Back in London the mystery man reappeared, introduced himself as the Prince of Wales's secretary, Mr Walter Peacock, and invited Adshead to prepare a report on the Prince's estates at Kennington 'with a view to rebuilding'.

That was the genesis of Courtenay Square and much of the surrounding area. All budding architects and planners should have their noses rubbed in this subtlest, most contextual of English exercises in urban renewal. Yet how few know it.

The story of Adshead's appointment somewhat dramatises events. The Duchy of Cornwall had been worried for years about the structural and moral state of its Kennington estate. Developed in the mid- to late Georgian periods, its neat fronts disguised crumbling construction, multi-occupation, poverty and, worse, prostitution, especially in the two-storey streets behind Kennington Road and Kennington Lane. As and when leases expired the Duchy had already begun building small blocks of flats, easier to manage and control – for instance, in Chester Way. What may have sparked the wider initiative was the advent of a new, young and idealistic Prince of Wales and Duke of Cornwall, the future Edward VIII, in 1910.

Adshead's report is a landmark in

town planning history. At a time when the fashion was to turn as many people out of London as possible, he upheld the virtues of the modest inner suburb as a civilised place to live, so long as the right type of tenant could be found. He insisted on the value of the existing Georgian townscape and urged a restoration of the original effect, using modern materials and construction. And though Adshead proposed much rebuilding in a mixture of cottages and low-rise flats, he rejected the bulldozering, municipal approach to slum clearance, adopting instead Patrick Geddes's philosophy of cleansing individual pockets of urban decay over time while keeping the old sense of place.

All this was a little too novel for the Duchy, which felt a creditable responsibility for its poorer tenants and did not see its way to the mix of classes which Adshead hankered for. As it was, the First World War put paid to many of his suggestions. Just three outstanding, small-scale ensembles were completed. One was Denny Street and Crescent, a secluded group east of Kennington Road given to the architects J D and P Coleridge, with pert Dutch gables that Georgian-loving Adshead would never have countenanced. The second was Woodstock Court, formerly the Old Tenants' Hostel, in Newburn Street, a fetching and original quadrangle of 1914 by Adshead and his partner Stanley Ramsey. It injects new life into the almshouse tradition, with ammonite-headed capitals to the pilasters in front, a cupola over the entrance, a wooden colonnade inside and a sculpture by Henry Poole in the middle. Opposite Woodstock Court stands Newquay House of the early 1930s by Louis de Soissons, representing, despite the refinement of its brickwork, just the type of flats which Adshead refused to build.

Courtenay Square is the third little unity, the only one of three small squares proposed in 1911 that got built. Its plain, low and (be it noted) flat-roofed houses dribble out into two-storey flats along Courtenay Street and Cardigan Street northwards, and more mannered three-storey flats southwards looking towards Kennington Lane, where the porticoed former school of the Licensed Victuallers' Company (1836) proffers rhetorical contrast. Three sides of the square were started in 1912, the eastern one being added in 1919. It is a beautiful exercise in how to achieve architectural presence without height. The three-bedroom 'cottages' unaffectedly adopt the Georgian tradition, with just enough details like paired porch hoods to create charm, just enough concrete parapets, sills and ornament to give contemporary candour. The style might be dubbed 'Artisan Regency', though Adshead and Ramsey seem to have associated it with the brothers Adam. Even the plans are traditional, with the old-fashioned back extension for scullery-cum-bathroom not disdained. But the central space is open to all, something which no self-respecting Georgian developer would ever have allowed. Its simple row of limes bring verdure and shade to this most human of London squares.

Courtenay Square. EH

7

Planned Housing and Flats

A successful scheme of planned housing, we suggest, is one in which social and aesthetic aims balance and merge together. Self-consciously social intent in housing immediately conjures up an image of subsidies and building for the poor, so much so that 'social housing' has become the new euphemism for what used to be called artisan housing or the housing of the working classes. Yet all housing, working-class or otherwise, has social implications. The custom of building homes protected from market rents and forces can be traced back at least to almshouses, and even to monastic buildings beyond that. In form and intent, almshouses certainly (pp. 149–54), and perhaps too some ancient hospitals and schools, conform to our definition.

So the starting point for a history of planned housing in London is bound to be arbitrary. The creation of the first coherent suburban development at Covent Garden in the 1630s would be one possibility; the beginnings of Victorian philanthropic housing another. We have preferred to place the origins of London's modern housing traditions at the height of the picturesque movement. Our earliest example, The Paragon, is of the 1790s, so that our selection encompasses metropolitan housing endeavours of the past 200 years.

Picturesqueness in English architecture tends to be treated as a matter of mere aesthetics. But its persistence in London housing, from Regent's Park to the Alton and Span estates via Bedford Park and Hampstead Garden Suburb, suggests deeper layers of meaning. At the least, a picturesque treatment of a housing development can disguise its all-too-frequent extent and monotony. In addition, it may confer upon a displaced population some sense of tradition and roots and a health-giving chance of contact with nature.

The 'natural' motive seems to come first. The Paragon and Regent's Park are both unapologetically suburban developments. At the time they were built, other European capitals put architectural priority upon their centres, but London was uniquely large and problematic. Five miles from the City, The Paragon lay at a commuting distance which no Parisian or Viennese merchant would have accepted for such modest-sized houses. Yet Londoners were already shunning their gigantic, polluted and criminal city, for the sake of calm and health. In 1821, the very year that Regent's Park got off the mark, Cobbett made his call for 'the dispersion of the wen'. Suburbs could not restore the agricultural and village life which Cobbett thought critical to the health of the nation and the individual, but they were the next best thing. The picturesque suburb – an accommodation between urbanism and nature – was a means towards that desirable end. Suburban architecture started out at The Paragon isolated, modest in scale and stiff in conception. In the hands of Nash and Burton at Regent's Park, it grew up, escaped its urban cage and ran amok in all sorts of prophetic directions, from vast articulated terraces to the cottagey charm of the 'park villages'. The common denominator was the incursion of nature.

Trees, plants, grass and gardens mean a sacrifice of land, costly even in a suburb. So until Raymond Unwin revolutionised the science of estate layout in the Edwardian period, the benefits of nature were all but confined to the middle classes. Lord Shaftesbury and the other conscience-stricken early Victorians who started to built and run 'model dwellings' for the artisan class (never for the very poor, who could be anticipated to break up or degrade any accommodation) were obliged to build heavily constructed blocks of flats in the densest portions of London, using every available inch of ground. Parnell House, Bloomsbury, is the foremost European survivor of the type and a building of international significance. Here

Totterdown Fields, Tooting, opened by the future George V (centre) in 1903. GLRO picturesqueness plays no role; the relevant antecedents are barracks and warehouses, and the architecture matches the purpose of the block down to the last concrete lintel. Not until the London County Council's architects tackled the great Boundary Street Estate in the 1890s was there any coherent attempt to cheer up the Victorian urban working-class block of flats. This they did with a mixture of 'rationalized picturesque' architecture derived from designers like Butterfield, Webb and Lethaby, and of tree-planting and small municipal open spaces. But the cost was agonisingly high. Nor were the flats within the Boundary Street blocks conspicuously better than those of Parnell House.

Shaftesbury and other Victorian housing reformers never really believed in these barrack blocks. Like Cobbett, they wanted to see densities in London drop and working-class people live in suburbs outside. But so long as jobs were in the centre and transport was scarce and expensive, there were few alternatives to urban flats. Once suburban railways, the underground network and electric trams ramified, dispersal began in earnest. First came developments like Queen's Park, modestly pretty in its architecture but not so in layout. After 1900 a flourishing 'cottage' tradition of suburban housing established itself. Beginning with the LCC's Totterdown Fields and its three other pre-1914 cottage estates (Norbury, White Hart Lane and Old Oak), it was transformed by Parker and Unwin at Hampstead Garden Suburb; between the world wars, the strands coalesced in the myriad two-storey estates, municipal and private, of London's outer fringe. Picturesqueness reigned supreme in 'Metroland' – if less so on the council estates, where there was always less money to spend on extra 'features'. But the legacy of Hampstead Garden Suburb and the cottage tradition was more than merely sentimental. There was hard-headedness as well as sentiment and artistry in these estate layouts, with their cheap, narrow, curving roads and gaps between the houses. The long, hedged gardens were not just there for flowers but for vegetables. Gardening

The Paragon. RCHME

kept people healthy and out of the pub; it also helped national efficiency in the competitive new century. This can be hard to grasp now up in the Garden Suburb, where a Porsche may clutter the roadway in front of a cottage designed with a deserving East Ender in view.

The triumph of garden city and garden suburb ideology meant that flats were neglected too long. Ever since 1880 there has been strong demand in London for flats at all social levels; commuting cannot cater for everyone. Flats, 'luxury' and municipal alike, were much built between the wars, but they were mostly unimaginative and lumpish. Here was something which Modern Movement architects, with their zeal for minimal living, could latch on to. But the starker side of European apartment life, represented by Wells Coates' Lawn Road Flats (pp. 146–7), has never appealed. Better loved are Lubetkin and Tecton's classic Highpoint pair of blocks at Highgate, where mature

planting and (in the later block) some tongue-in-cheek frills temper the rigours of the design. What the ardent young architects of the 1930s wanted was to be building modern flats like Highpoint systematically for the working classes, as the Weimar Germans and the Viennese seemed to be doing. Lubetkin had a pre-war scheme of this kind for Finsbury which came to partial post-war fruition at Spa Green.

The context in which most post-war housing was built was that of Patrick Abercrombie's London plans of 1943–4. Abercrombie set an official policy for dispersing London's 'excess' population to government-sponsored new towns, and he fixed targets for lower densities in the centre. To fill the gaps, he preached the gospel of 'mixed development', a concept plumb in the picturesque tradition. To relieve the monotony of council estates with a single type of building, the new estates were to balance one another with a sprinkling of high flats, rather more middle-sized maisonettes and a modicum of two-storey housing, with space in between. This philosophy lies behind most LCC housing of the 1945–65 period, from rapidly built Lansbury to the overwhelming township of the Alton Estates, Roehampton. Both are avoidably shabby now. At Roehampton, the site – mature Victorian gardens at one end, rolling parkland at the other – provoked the young LCC architects to try to reconcile their native, picturesque inheritance with Corbusian technologism. If it does not quite come off, that is not just because there is too much concrete or too many tall towers, but because the picturesque ideal has declined here from an ethic into a mere aesthetic. There is little function except car parking for the acres of open space; the communion between tenant and nature is more theoretical than real. The Span Estates at Ham and Blackheath, admittedly private and much smaller, show a more refined sense of the compatibility between open spaces and modern flats.

Towers (and, let it not be forgotten, the socially even less satisfactory slabs) played their part in the mixed development idea. Early enthusiasm for them had much to do with aesthetics. The 'byelaw' street of London's poorer inner suburbs seemed intolerably dull, and a 'vista-stopper' or two might give it a fillip, it was thought; San Gimignano was much invoked. For a short period in the 1960s, tower blocks got out of control. By that time, it was the speed with which builders could put them up that was getting them built, and most architects were cured of them. One who was not was Ernö Goldfinger, whose extraordinary Trellick Tower and Balfron Tower are isolated statements of French monumentalism and concrete technique in the unexpected settings of North Kensington and Poplar. The only worthy points of comparison are the vertiginous, triangular pencils of the Barbican, an enclave which turns its back upon nature and the life of the street with equally un-English fervour. Perhaps time will make these tough developments seem to fit in better with the fertile and internationally influential tradition of planned housing in London.

83

The Paragon
Blackheath, Lewisham

1/J5   British Rail to Blackheath

Had Michael Searles built much north of the Thames, he would be one of London's best known architects. But his main activity was speculative development in underestimated South London. In truth Searles was second only to Nash in the sophisticated skill of laying out groups of Georgian houses. The Paragon is the equal of any of the Bath crescents or Regent's Park terraces, and one of Europe's most satisfactory setpieces of suburban planning.

The idea of breaking up terraces of houses into picturesque groups governed by an overall architectural arrangement started to be explored in the 1780s and 1790s. To it we owe the English concept of the semi-detached house, at first linked by porches or colonnades to the sides, later independent. It came in first not in central London but along suburban roads where ribbon development was spreading and land was less valuable. Searles's first attempts were two little speculations in Southwark, both now demolished. The second of these, also called The Paragon (1787–8), contained on a small scale the elements of the Blackheath development – groups of three-storey houses in pairs, linked by short colonnades. Searles had also designed a plainer development of grouped houses in Greenwich, of which part survives as Gloucester Circus.

The Blackheath Paragon was laid out from about 1794 on land taken by Searles from a speculating timber merchant, John Cator. The edges of Blackheath were becoming fashionable, and Searles and Cator saw their chance. Owing to a slump the project took time – till 1805 – to complete, and Searles had to relinquish his interest to Cator. There are fourteen houses altogether in seven groups of two, laid out in crescent shape. There were some separate houses to the West, of which Colonnade House along South Row is the main survivor. It

is now separated from The Paragon by a group of 1950s flats, outliers of the pioneering Span development further south around Blackheath Park (pp. 124–5).

Searles's arrangement of a crescent punctuated by colonnades is pleasurable because the curve and the breaks between the houses convey a sense of their depth and solidity, as opposed to the 'shirtfront' appearance of the normal Georgian terrace. As originally designed, the centre was supposed to have a full-height portico and pediment, but economies prevailed. The colonnades were in large part built in Coade's patent stone. The houses themselves are plain enough, but nearly all have bows at the back. Alterations over the years followed by war damage had detracted from The Paragon before the delightful, exact symmetry of Searles's design was painstakingly restored in the 1950s, when most of the houses became flats. The little lodges at the ends are of this date, not original.

84

Regent's Park
Westminster and Camden

2/D1–E2   Underground to Regent's Park, Baker Street or Camden Town

The hard-pressed tourist in search of some single piece of London both utterly English yet central to the history of western architecture can be told without hesitation, 'Go to Regent's Park'. John Nash's rich, majestic and entertaining scheme for the park's development

Regent's Park. Cumberland Terrace. RCHME

Regent's Park. Park Village West. EH

points in manifold directions. It is at once a high point in European classicism, the acme of English picturesque achievement and the original of the middle-class garden suburb. Haphazard the park certainly is, and it has taken punishment over the years. The fact remains that Nash was one of the great international masters of architectural theatre, and that his effects are still there to enjoy.

The story of Marylebone Park's transformation into Regent's Park starts with John Fordyce, the Surveyor-General of the Crown's Land Revenues. As London pressed northwards, Fordyce urged a coherent plan for developing the park, then under lease as grazing land. In 1811 John Nash and his partner James Morgan were one of two sets of official architects to present development schemes. Nash's was from the first more 'enlarged' in outlook than those of his unsuccessful rivals. It took account of the layout and the shortcomings of neighbouring developments north of the Marylebone Road; it indicated a practicable line for the future Regent Street, which Fordyce had seen was needed to make the new suburb accessible from the centre of town via the existing Portland Place; and it envisaged taking round the edge of the park the branch of the Grand Junction

Canal then being promoted to link the Midlands with the London docks.

The development plan changed much over the ten years before Regent's Park got going. Nash had first to be dissuaded by the Prime Minister, Spencer Perceval, from building largely inside the park. In his revised layout there were to be two vast circuses, one at the entrance to the park from Portland Place, the other in the centre where the Inner Circle now is. Both were realised only in vestigial form. After building had been going on for just six or so years, the Crown officials called a halt to development in 1826. So we have only a fragment of Nash's full Regent's Park conception: a stately fringe of terraces, interspersed with curiosities; a handful of altered villas in the middle of the park; a lake and some few effects of landscaping; about half the line of the canal, with one fine bridge; and the two Park Villages east of Albany Street.

A good starting point for a circumference is Hanover Gate off Park Road, half a mile north of Baker Street Station. Next to it is Frederick Gibberd's recent mosque, just the kind of anomaly that Regent's Park is so good at absorbing. Going anti-clockwise, the glorious terraces succeed one another on and round to the north-east corner of the park in a near-unbroken show of

classicism in enfilade – the breaks, recessions and stylar dress of the palace and the temple filched for the bare purposes of street-theatre and the diversion of the obliquely approaching passer-by. Today the all-over stucco of the terraces glistens in pristine cream. Formerly, the fronts may have been jointed and coloured in imitation of Bath stone, with sash bars grained to look like oak and the railings bronze-colour.

First comes Hanover Terrace – 'provocatively conventional', says Sir John Summerson. Behind it is Kent Terrace, facing Park Road. Next we encounter Sussex Place, 'more than a little wild', with a colonnade wheeling round to collide with a series of bayed towers. This alternation of the bizarre and the orthodox is typical of Nash, who like Shakespeare knew how to keep his audience's interest. Clarence Terrace is next, one of the blocks entrusted to young Decimus Burton and his father James, the speculative builder; so too was Cornwall Terrace, up against the street after Clarence Gate. Hence unfurls the long line of York Terrace, laid out by Nash after much controversy so as to create a fine axis with Hardwick's new St Marylebone Church. The back streets between this terrace and the Marylebone Road warrant exploration.

After York Terrace, Ulster Terrace takes one round into Park Square, the upshot of a change of plan in 1823. The colonnaded circus envisaged around Marylebone Road had been the one element of the scheme started in the pre-Waterloo years. But its builder, Charles Mayor, failed while building the southern half – now known as Park Crescent, and the most urban portion of Regent's Park. The Park Square houses 'continue the Ionic theme of the Park Crescent porches, though here the columns are attached to the walls' (Summerson again). Do not miss the minimalist lodges next to noisy Marylebone Road. Behind Park Square East is the carcass of the 'Diorama', an illusionist auditorium designed by Augustus Pugin senior, once an assistant of Nash's.

Now the east side commences,

muddled at first but leading to an imposing climax. It is mostly of c.1824–8, a little later than the western sector. After modest St Andrew's Terrace and Place, Denys Lasdun's Royal College of Physicians (1964) abrasively interrupts the sequence. It has qualities but it is in the wrong place, and its lack of a clear entrance is tiresome. But Regent's Park can take it. Similar objection could be taken to the intrusive, French-style Cambridge Gate, by Archer and Green (1875–6), but its Bath stone should not be censured, as that was then the colour of the ambient stucco. It replaced one of the park's original entertainment buildings, a preposterous and short-lived 'Colosseum'. After that we are back to Nash, first with quiet Cambridge Terrace, then with the two most sumptuous blocks of all. At Chester Terrace, more than 900 ft long, he improvised triumphal arches at the ends

to placate complaints about the relation between the projecting blocks and the terrace behind. Cumberland Terrace beyond, a mighty fantasy on the palace theme, divides into three grand blocks with a nakedly scenic pediment in the middle replete with statuary by Bubb. Its splendour was meant to respond axially to a tea-pavilion or *guinguette* for George IV within the park just here, but that never materialized. Then comes the last of the anomalies, St Katharine's Hospital, a Tudor-Gothic group in stone and brick, not stucco, by Ambrose Poynter (1826–8). The chapel front is of stone, while the east end facing Albany Street is in brick; had it been built a few years later, when Puginian principles ruled, it might have been the other way round. The terrace sequence ends with Gloucester Gate, on which it is alleged that the executant architect, J J Scoles, arbitrarily doubled the size of Nash's inadequate detail.

Just three villas were built and two remain round the Inner Circle, a place mostly frequented for the inter-war amenities of Queen Mary's Garden and the Open Air Theatre. Decimus Burton's The Holme is less interesting than St John's Lodge just north of Chester Road, built in 1817 to John Raffield's designs for a radical Swedenborgian, Charles Tulk, and much extended, by Sir Charles Barry in 1847 and by R W Schultz in 1891–1900 for the 3rd Marquess of Bute. Apart from Queen Mary's Garden, the lake and the remnants of the enlarged Broad Walk made by W A Nesfield and his sons in the 1860s, the park itself is rather bare. On the northern perimeter leading out to Avenue Road is one of the few remains of James Morgan's work along the Regent's Canal, the Macclesfield Bridge (1815–16), a crisp, economical structure with brick arches on fluted iron columns. The canal basin and working-class quarter built to serve Regent's Park behind Albany Street, with a market place and two squares of tiny artisan housing, have now completely vanished. Thankfully we do still have most of the two Park Villages, and they can be the visitor's last port of call after Gloucester Gate. Park Village East is a fragment now, strung along the street of that name; the rest was destroyed by the railway in the 1880s. But Park Village West, in its enticing little loop off Albany Street, is an intact miniature of its own. Here Nash the conjurer pointed forward to the world of the Victorian suburb, mixing rustic and Hellenic allusions in a display of picturesque pyrotechnics.

One lost outlier to Regent's Park sums up the spirit of the whole. That was Digamma Cottage, built on credit by the penniless Italian poet-in-exile Ugo Foscolo in the early 1820s. Its name commemorated a pamphleteering triumph by Foscolo on the subject of an archaic letter in the Greek alphabet. A stucco villa on the banks of the Regent's Canal, it stood in the vicinity of the present electricity substation in Lodge Road. Foscolo enjoyed his riparian prospect, but was pained to observe scruffy canal barges and bargees from his property rather than the ancient craft of his poetic imagination. Attended

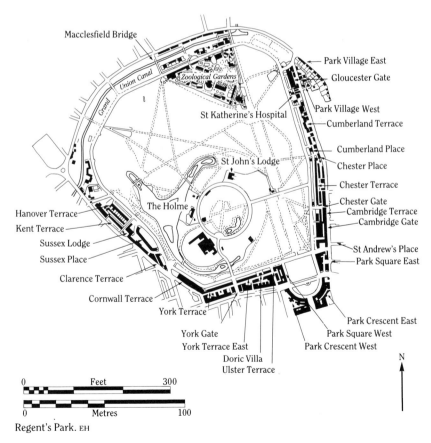

Regent's Park. EH

by two maidens in Grecian attire, the great romantic lived in Digamma Cottage all too briefly before his creditors caught up with him.

85

Parnell House
Streatham Street, Bloomsbury, Camden

2/G3   Underground to Tottenham Court Road

En route from Tottenham Court Road to the British Museum, you may remark a laconic inscription, 'Model Houses For Families', gouged out of the cement string course upon a dour, compact block of five-storey flats. This unyielding building is something more than that. Parnell House is the outstanding monument of pre-municipal efforts to reform London's housing, and may be the earliest purpose-built block of flats for the urban working class not built by a specific employer to survive anywhere.

Shocked by the facts uncovered by official commissions on the horrors of London's slums, a group of Tory evangelicals – Lord Shaftesbury is the best known of them – banded together in 1844 to form the Society for Improving the Condition of the Labouring Classes. It was the first of many such ponderously named organisations to tackle this thankless task. To begin with they knew little about their subject. The block of dwellings they first erected, at Bagnigge Wells, was savaged by the knowledgeable editor of *The Builder*, George Godwin. Nothing daunted, the society tried again. They built two more lodging houses, then the Streatham Street Dwellings in 1849–50, and then a model cottage for the Great Exhibition, paid for by Prince Albert and transferred after the exhibition to Kennington Park, where it can still be seen.

Technical and architectural knowledge for all these efforts was furnished by Henry Roberts. A Tory evangelical himself, Roberts belonged to a new brand of Victorian architectural specialists. His career started

conventionally enough with the stylish Fishmongers' Hall. But his involvement in the SICLC turned him elsewhere, and he devoted the rest of his working life to housing. Through his buildings and copious pamphleteering, Roberts set a tradition of planning and constructing artisans' flats which persisted to the end of the century and beyond. His principles were simple: the most solid kind of building and finishes affordable, in essence 'warehouse construction'; plenty of fresh air; and the maximum physical and psychological disconnection between the flats, to discourage the spread of the 'drunkenness, domestic feuds, and vice' which the SICLC feared more than disease.

The Streatham Street block, not far from the former rookeries of St Giles (the worst of all West End slums), exemplifies all this. Roberts had learnt his technics from Charles Fowler of Covent Garden Market and Robert Smirke of the British Museum, the best British architectural constructors of their day. So the building is very solid. Floors and roofs are arched between cast-iron girders, filled up with hollow bricks, covered with concrete and, in some cases, slate. The roof is flat (still a rarity in 1850), concreted and covered with asphalt. The walls are thick and faced in the hardest-wearing stocks, with heavy brick rustication marking the lower storeys where punishment is likely to be worst. The windows, conventional sashes in shape, are reduced in size because of the oppressive window tax. Timber construction is minimised, partly to avoid danger of fire, partly in case tenants choose to burn wood for their heating. In plan the building consists of open galleries for access, a single common staircase and quite generous flats – originally of two bedrooms and each with its own kitchen and WC. The basements were used for workshops, wash-houses, bath-houses and coal and potato stores, while the open internal area (now set out with flowers and fancy lamps) was a drying ground. The tenants were described as 'of the artizan and journeyman class'. Poorer people could never have paid the rent or kept to the strict rules which all

Victorian housing reformers insisted upon.

The principles of Streatham Street and the other early SICLC dwellings were to spread throughout the industrialised world. Some of them, for instance the open balcony access, have still not been utterly superseded in subsidised housing. But Henry Roberts was not to reap the credit which should have been his. This 'gentlemanly, religious, precise and quiet man,' as his one-time assistant Gilbert Scott called him, became (can it have been through his charitable concerns?) briefly involved with 'a member of the lower orders'. Chastened, he retired with his wife to Florence in 1853, and never came back.

86

Queen's Park Estate
Harrow Rd, Kilburn, Westminster

1/E4   Underground to Queen's Park

The expansive grid of streets and tiny two-storey houses which make up the Queen's Park Estate, laid out between about 1874 and 1885, represents one of the largest pre-municipal attempts to tackle Victorian London's crippling housing problems by means of suburbanisation.

The belief that working-class people could live happier, healthier lives in cheap houses of their own on the fringes of cities than in costly blocks of flats in the centre is as old as the urban housing problem itself. For Victorian housing reformers from Lord Shaftesbury onwards, the difficulty was the relation between houses, jobs and transport. Most jobs were in the centre and what suburban transport there was pitched its fares too high for the pocket of the ordinary worker. Until the issue of 'carriage versus rent' could be solved, only artisans and clerks at the upper end of the working-class bracket could afford to move out of town. It was for this section of the housing market that Queen's Park was intended.

Queen's Park Estate. Detail from Fifth Avenue. EH

and Sixth Avenues, breaks into informality at the edges, where in any case redevelopment has blurred the estate's sharp definition. But the centre is still a self-contained world of tight little cottages in two tones of brick, concrete sills and heads to the windows, bracketed Gothic hoods over the doors with the company's shield reminding tenants who owned and ruled the place, and low-pitched slate roofs broken by the insistent line of party walls. High pyramidal roofs at a few corners and a further picturesque trick or two keep monotony at bay. Recent householders have unfeelingly accelerated the process of jollification by changing windows and painting brickwork. There is some variety in the size and appearance of the earlier units before the company was reconstructed, but the later housing is fairly uniform in scale.

The architecture of the Queen's Park and Shaftesbury Park Estates is usually ascribed to a certain Robert Austin, but he seems to have been responsible only for their layout. A better claimant to the authorship of the house designs is James G W Buckle, later architect of the Theatre Royal at Stratford East. In the 1880s the better-known Rowland Plumbe was brought in to add touches of the Queen Anne style to the edges of Queen's Park. He it was who designed the clubhouse on the Harrow Road (where remnants of the estate's shopping parade can be seen) and the Methodist Church, both extant though fallen on hard times. It was Plumbe too who went on to design the Artizans' Company's Noel Park Estate, a prettier but less comprehensive venture.

87

Bedford Park
Turnham Green, Hounslow/ Hammersmith

1/E5   Underground to Turnham Green

Bedford Park, like so many Victorian suburbs, was a railway development. What is now the District Line, at first a spur of the London and South-Western

The promoters of the development were the Artizans', Labourers' and General Dwellings Company – a catch-all of a title betraying a vague breadth of aim confirmed by the company's history. It was at any rate consistent in its suburban prejudices. Before embarking on Queen's Park the company had built on the outskirts of several British towns for rent and sale. In London it had undertaken the Shaftesbury Park Estate off Latchmere Road, Battersea (1872–7). Here was established a pattern of wide roads, sanitary two-storey terrace houses, occasional architectural incident at corners, a few shops but absolutely no pubs. Queen's Park began on similar principles, but was rudely interrupted when the company's

manager, a Mr Swindlehurst, was brought to book on severe corruption charges. The board was then reconstructed on more explicitly philanthropic lines. Under this fresh management Queen's Park was finished and the last of the company's three London estates, Noel Park in Hornsey, was built.

The interest of Queen's Park is its extent. Amounting originally to nearly 2,000 houses, or twice the size of Shaftesbury Park, its density is something like twenty-five dwellings to the acre. The hard grid of streets between the Harrow Road and Kilburn Lane, psychologically stressed on the north–south axis by the un-English nomenclature of Third, Fourth, Fifth

Railway, arrived at Turnham Green in 1869. Services to London improved fast, suggesting to Hamilton Fulton (owner of Bedford House on the Green) and his effervescent young son-in-law Jonathan Carr that building on their land and adjacent property north of the station would be worthwhile. Work started in 1875 and peaked in about 1880. A crisis in Carr's affairs (p. 115) killed further development after 1883.

The character and significance of Bedford Park are hard to pin down. Though it is often called the first garden suburb, that anachronistic label is confusing and contentious. It is green enough and, unlike many Victorian developments, preserved a lot of old trees, but its layout is neither novel nor inspired. It would be better defined as the first 'community suburb' for the middle classes. Carr's priorities were to create a place where well-educated

people of moderate means could rent good-looking, up-to-date houses and associate on terms of informality. His aims, in other words, were partly social and partly architectural. Politically Carr was a Radical Liberal, temperamentally an optimist. He was inclined to cut corners and forget to pay people, which is why Bedford Park is short on consistency of detail.

Nevertheless it is engaging. Such a centre as it has is immediately north of Turnham Green Station, where Norman Shaw's St Michael's Church and his Tabard Inn and Stores face each other across Bath Road. Just to the east was the Art School, now rebuilt, while a few yards north in The Avenue is the former Bedford Park Club, where residents mingled, borrowed books and even played tennis. A regrettable loss was Jonathan Carr's own Tower House in Bedford Road just behind the club. Here

the 'promoter' continued to live in reduced circumstances after his virtual failure in the mid 1880s.

Like most of the estate's public buildings, the Tower House was designed by Norman Shaw. But that noted domestic architect had nothing to do with the inception of the suburb. Carr's first architect was E W Godwin, who merely produced a couple of house types for Carr's builders to construct. In their unamended form, these can be seen at the corners of The Avenue and Bedford Road. Following criticism, Carr got rid of Godwin and brought in Shaw. The fruits of his labours, mainly in the form of detached and semi-detached house types, can be seen in all the streets of Bedford Park, often blithely adapted in detail. No matter how mangled, they all breathe the spirit of the 'Queen Anne' aesthetic revolution which was at the heart of the estate's *Gestalt*. Red brickwork, bay windows, white trim and tile roofs are everywhere the order of the day. Occasionally roughcast appears as well, but for a more convinced use of that material one must seek out the western edge of the suburb where Voysey was later to build one of his most interesting early houses, No. 14 South Parade (1891). Carr used other architects as well, notably the firm of Coe and Robinson in The Avenue and the obscure but able W Wilson in Queen Anne's Gardens.

After about 1880 Shaw handed over the mantle of Bedford Park to his assistants E J May and Maurice B Adams. May built, among other houses, the handsome vicarage behind the church and No. 1 Priory Gardens, now the Victorian Society's headquarters. Adams lived in Bedford Park and added a chapel and hall to Shaw's church, which is worth a special look. Shaw excelled at grasping the spirit of his clients. The witty, relaxed, almost haphazard mélange of secular and religious features exactly captures Carr's intentions for the suburb. Carr had wanted to reuse the tower of a threatened Wren church at the new St Michael's, and there is no doubt that Shaw had Wren and the 17th century in mind in designing the church. It was influential too: just as Bedford Park had

Priory Gardens, Bedford Park. ANDRÉ GOULANCOURT

a broad social influence on Hampstead Garden Suburb, so the unbroken roofline of its church helped shape the roof of Lutyens's great St Jude's there. The Tabard and Stores are also a clever piece of scene-setting. There is not much original left inside them except for some passages of De Morgan tiling in the pub.

Bedford Park has come up in the world recently. Property values having risen, new white wooden fences imitating the original design fringe front gardens and Morris fabrics peep out self-consciously behind close-paned windows.

Whitehall Court and National Liberal Club (to the right) from the Thames. GLRO

88

Whitehall Court
Westminster

2/G5   Underground to Westminster

The spikes and mansards of Whitehall Court do much for the silhouette along the Thames and make a spirited complement to the outline of the Palace of Westminster. But the tangled history of these massive blocks of mansion flats is less than well known.

The making of the Victoria Embankment, outfall sewer and underground railway in the 1860s spelt the reconstruction of a swathe of Crown property in the old Whitehall Palace area, to a line set back from the Thames behind a garden. In the early 1880s the Crown's surveyor, Arthur Cates, solicited bids for the plum site facing the river. Various schemes for flats and luxury hotels were floated but collapsed. Enter in 1883 Jonathan Carr, fresh from the triumph of his aesthetic suburb at Bedford Park. Then busy promoting Kensington Court with an array of services new to Victorian houses, such as hydraulic lifts and electric lighting, Carr always had something clever up his sleeve. But he was not financially astute. Whitehall Court involved bigger liabilities than anything he had undertaken before. The fact is, he was not up to it.

All went well at first. The National Liberal Club, founded to help give

Gladstone's Liberal Party organisational backbone, took the end block next to Whitehall Place; for the rest of the site, Carr proposed 'suites of residential chambers for legislators, professional men, men about town and visitors'. As architects he chose Thomas Archer and Arthur Green, former assistants of Cates, who on the Crown's behalf imposed Portland stone elevations rather than the brick and terracotta which Carr wanted. The National Liberals opted for the better-known Alfred Waterhouse. They got on in 1885–7 with their building, a rare plunge by Waterhouse into the French Renaissance style, sporting a fine corner tourelle. Meanwhile Carr was getting into deep water with creditors. With the foundations of his flats scarcely begun, he was saved from bankruptcy by Jabez Balfour, MP for Croydon and mastermind of the Liberator Building Society. It was under subsidiaries of Balfour's that the flats were built to Archer and Green's designs in 1886–92. Carr retired to lick his wounds in Bedford Park, debt-laden for the rest of his life.

There the story might have ended. But Jabez Balfour himself foundered with huge liabilities in 1892. The Liberator's creditors were mainly small-time investors, many of whom lost life savings. A public scandal ensued: and Balfour was foolish enough to abscond from his Whitehall Court flat to Argentina, whence he was extradited for a show trial in 1895. At this, irregularities involving Whitehall Court emerged. Balfour survived a prison sentence to publish an autobiography,

courageous of its type.

Archer and Green were above-average commercial architects with experience of prestigious, French-style projects on Crown property. They had previously designed Cambridge Gate at Regent's Park (p. 109–12) and were to go on (for one of Balfour's companies) to design the Hyde Park Hotel. At Whitehall Court they rose to their riverside chance with the floridity to be expected of the 1880s. The result is not great architecture, but the heavy elevations are broken up with a firm feeling for the underlying composition. The differences between the flats and the club at the end bear witness to an uncompromising collision between competence and real ability. Whitehall Court's size marks it out as the most opulent of early blocks of mansion flats in London. Among the long list of the notable to have lived here, Bernard Shaw and his rival H G Wells are worthiest to be singled out.

89

Boundary Street Estate
Shoreditch, Tower Hamlets

2/L2   Underground to Liverpool Street or Shoreditch

Boundary Street was the forerunner of the manifold housing estates providing flats for working-class people built all over Europe and America in the first three-quarters of the 20th century. As the original of its type, it embodies a fresher feeling for urbanism than most

Chertsey Buildings, Boundary Street Estate. GLRO

first LCC housing project, but it was its largest and most important early estate. It was preceded by a few flats and cottages on either side of the Blackwall Tunnel (all demolished) and two extant blocks of flats in Shadwell (Dellow and Bewley Buildings). Architects, politicians and housing reformers all preferred cottages. But they were not realistic in inner London, owing to the cost of land, the loan conditions imposed on municipal housing by government and the need to house people near their work in the absence of affordable public transport. So the LCC took as their starting point the gloomy five-storey 'walk-up' blocks put up by private housing companies over the previous twenty years and then improved upon them with better planning, pitched roofs and vivid elevations. The earliest buildings are still stodgy; two, Henley House and Walton House, were farmed out to a private architect, Rowland Plumbe. The two-tone blocks round the central Arnold Circus, attributable to LCC assistant R Minton Taylor, adopt a stripey Queen Anne manner, but the later ones, notably Molesey, Clifton, Laleham and Hedsor Houses (1896–9) by C C Winmill, are strikingly Arts and Crafts in tone.

By the time Boundary Street was complete in 1900, twenty-three blocks had been erected and over 5,000 people housed. A laundry in Montclare Street, two schools, a sprinkling of shops along Calvert Avenue and even a series of workshops and sheds for local craftsmen and costermongers were provided. The garden and bandstand of Arnold Circus were planted on the heaped-up rubble of the notorious Old Nichol slum, which the estate had replaced. But it was all at a cost. More slum-dwellers were ejected than the number of those rehoused, and few of them could pay Boundary Street rents. They slipped away to crowd out other quarters of the East End, while Boundary Street filled up with respectable artisans, policemen and the like. The blocks were healthy, solidly constructed by the Works Department and, for those that cared about architecture, attractive. But they cost far more than anticipated and hardly dented

of its successors. But it suffered the same travails and disappointments as have beset later schemes of inner-city housing.

Housing was high on the agenda when the capital acquired its first municipal government, the London County Council, in 1889. Despite half a century of sanitary and housing reform, the health, life expectancy and living conditions of Londoners were little better. London was still getting denser and, to make matters worse, there was civil unrest in 1888–9. This gave the radicals of the new-broom county council, known as the Progressives, their cue. The second LCC Progressive administration voted in 1892 to build

municipal housing. This had only been done in a small way before, by Liverpool Glasgow and one or two other boroughs To show that it meant to keep on building till the housing problem was solved, the LCC set up its own Works Department so that it could construct to its own high standards instead of being at the mercy of private contractors, and a Housing of the Working Classes Branch within its Architect's Department. The branch attracted a series of young architects under the direction of Owen Fleming, caught up in the social and architectural 'Progressivism' that affected London in the 1890s.

Boundary Street was not quite the

the London housing problem. In 1898 the LCC switched its housing policy as far as possible to suburban cottage development, linked to subsidised transport.

Even so, Boundary Street was widely influential. It attracted visitors from all over the world. Its progeny can be found in Paris, Amsterdam, Berlin and Vienna alike. In London, where it soon proved impossible to restrict council housing to the suburbs, its ideas can be traced in the LCC's manifold later efforts, from Millbank (1898–1905) to the Alton Estates at Roehampton (1952–61), the only place where the same social ardour was recaptured (p. 123).

90

Carrington House
Brookmill Rd, Deptford, Lewisham

1/H5   British Rail to Deptford or St John's

The masterpiece of the young team of in-house architects who strove, always on tight budgets, to give Arts and Crafts qualities of honesty, originality and urban presence to the many buildings erected by the London County Council in the ardent twenty years after its creation, was arguably neither a fire station nor a housing estate, college or school, but this towering, six-storey 'single men's lodging house' in the heart of Deptford.

Accommodation for single people, drawn to the metropolis by its high wages, full employment and animation, has always been a critical aspect of London's housing problems. There was much concern about the issue in the 1890s. Following a well-publicised night spent in a Finsbury doss-house by John Benn, an activist on the LCC's Housing Committee, the Council built a first, inadequate lodging house in Parker Street, Holborn. The initiative then passed to philanthropist Lord Rowton, who as an offshoot of the housing work of the Guinness Trust built six vast 'Rowton Houses', charging 6d a night for cubicles, with cooking and cleaning

facilities and locker, smoking and reading rooms attached. The later LCC men's lodging houses, Carrington House (1902–3) and Bruce House, Covent Garden (1904–6), follow the Rowton House model quite slavishly, but with finer architecture. The LCC also contemplated lodging houses for single women, but none were ever built.

Outlying Deptford was chosen for a lodging house because of the demand for casual labour in local docks and warehouses and at a Deptford Cattle and Meat Market, centre for the growing trade in imported meat. The site had been an insanitary one and was cleared partly at the insistence of Sidney Webb, then LCC Member for Deptford. As so often, the LCC architects would have preferred cottages here but lost out to considerations of demand, economy and density. By a compromise, the modest Sylva Cottages were built on the south part of the site along the road, while the bulkier Carrington House rose closer to Deptford Broadway.

The job-architect for Carrington House seems to have been J R Stark, who may also have designed Bruce House and the crisp Webber Row

housing estate in Southwark. What Stark, then in his early thirties, and his colleagues had been looking at we do now know, but there is something at once Germanic and Glaswegian about Carrington House, with its bare-brick, deep-eaved end towers and its twin-bayed, stone frontispiece over an off-centre entrance which comes as close as anything in London to the Mackintosh style. Glasgow makes sense, since that city was among the pioneers of municipal lodging houses. Stark would have been sent there and elsewhere to find out about lodging houses; no doubt he came back from Scotland with his head full of Mackintosh. But the borrowings are beautifully integrated into the orthodoxies of LCC housing blocks, established at the Boundary Street and Millbank Estates.

Carrington House originally housed 802 lodgers and twelve porters. The upper floors were almost wholly devoted to groups of cubicles, 7 ft by 5 ft, each with a bed and blue coverlet woven with the LCC's medallion. On the ground floor the dining and other rooms were sober, tile-lined and broadly arched. Until recent years the facilities of both

Carrington House. GLRO

the Rowton Houses and the LCC lodging houses remained extraordinarily, even, shockingly, unchanged. Internal improvements have wrought necessary havoc to the original arrangements.

91

Camden Park Road and Wilderness Road
Chislehurst, Bromley

1/J6   British Rail to Chislehurst

Camden Place, Chislehurst, is one of a number of old country estates near London to have eluded total destruction by turning itself into a golf club. It was the residence of Napoleon III and his family during their glum British exile of the 1870s. A hefty granite cross on the edge of Chislehurst Common opposite Wilderness Road is the one token of the Bonapartes' time here. It commemorates their son, the Prince Imperial, killed in the Zulu War of 1879, and was put up under the direction of E R Robson of board school fame.

In 1890 the two William Willetts, father and son, bought the estate in order to develop round its edges. William Willett junior, the brains behind the firm, was the most imaginative London speculative builder of his day. He had found that the middle classes were bored with the up-and-down, terrace house; what they now wanted and could afford were solid, separate suburban dwellings with individuality. This from the 1880s he proceeded to provide, notably at Belsize Park, South Hampstead and Hove. 'Willett homes' were thoroughly furnished and equipped with services, and each was distinctive. To make them so, the Willetts employed a salaried architect – Harry Measures in the 1880s, Amos Faulkner thereafter. But they did not hesitate to go to top outside architects when the occasion was right.

Their 'Camden Park Estate' was such an occasion. The location suggested ample houses and gardens looking out over the grounds of Camden Place. The villas Faulkner at first designed proving dull, the Willetts called in Ernest

Newton, then amassing a reputation for his small country houses and suburban villas – many of them in Bromley, Bickley (where he lived) and Chislehurst. Newton was every bit as good a domestic architect as Lutyens or Voysey, but his originality was less demonstrative, more 'reasonable'. So although his houses are easier to live with, he has never enjoyed the popular or international fame of those two great Edwardian stars.

What Newton could achieve and the standard which the estate was meant to enjoy, can be seen at the top of Camden Park Road, by the drive to Camden Place. This is The Cedars of 1893, built for the younger Willett himself. The curtilage is half the pleasure of it. A dwarf wall with pretty, white-painted palings above and cedar trees behind encircles the front in an arc, broken twice by half-cartwheel gates; at the back this turns into a high garden wall, swooping coolly between piers (now

sorely dilapidated). The house is in Norman Shaw's 'Old English' or 'Sussex' country house style, brought down a social peg but sweetened for the suburbs. Its off-centre entrance, big chimney to one side, flat-topped bay and all-enveloping roof are motifs on which Newton rings the changes as he proceeds down the bumpy roadway and into the 20th century – at Derwent House, Bonchester House, Elm Bank, Fairacre and the extensions to Avonhurst. Fairacre, the furthest of the series, set far back behind fancy modern gates and a *nouveau riche* garden, is architecturally the most original house, though impaired now by open garden arches built in front.

There are just too many second-rate Edwardian and later insertions between the Newton houses for the architecture of Camden Park Road to add up to a whole. To enjoy a Newtonian ensemble, one must venture a little north-east and explore the loop of Wilderness Road, the

Cedar House, Camden Park Estate. EH

Willetts' other Camden Park development, laid out from about 1900. The houses here are smaller and on both sides of the street, the road is neatly gravelled and the hedges are more manicured. Here Amos Faulkner, having learnt his lesson from Newton, comes into his own with a series of fetching houses – Parkmore, Moorlands, The Brake and Holne Chase. They miss real conviction and originality by a hair's breadth. Frustratingly for Faulkner, that is shown up by Newton's one contribution, Copley Dene (1904), with leaded windows instead of the usual white-painted woodwork. Its demureness is broken by a projection to the side with a Shavian chimneystack bursting through the sloping roof. Is this wing a later addition?

From Chislehurst, Faulkner took the Newton style to the closer-set Willett houses of Elsworthy Road, South Hampstead – a development which had a strong and good influence on speculative architecture. Via this route Newton seems to have contributed to the evolution of the fabled 'semi-detached by the bypass'. William Willett junior too, had a wider influence upon the world. It was on strolls from The Cedars into Petts Wood nearby that he thought up the concept of 'daylight saving', first put into practice during wartime just after his death in 1915 and with us still today.

92

Hampstead Garden Suburb
Golders Green, Barnet

1/F3   Underground to Golders Green

Canon Samuel Barnett and his wife Henrietta laboured in the Whitechapel slums for thirty years. For a permanent reform of social conditions, they concluded, the only solution was a mix of classes in a healthy and attractive environment where 'the poor shall teach the rich and . . . the rich, let us hope, shall help the poor to help themselves'.

These were the ideals with which Henrietta Barnett founded Hampstead

Hill Close, Hampstead Garden Suburb. EH

Garden Suburb. Her opportunity came in 1903 when the proposed Edgware branch of the Northern Line threatened the land beyond Hampstead Heath with the monotony of speculative development. She 'got up' an influential committee which persuaded local authorities to buy 80 acres of land to be added to the Heath. Beyond and to the sides of the Heath Extension a further 243 acres, later extended northwards across Falloden Way to a total of 655 acres, were acquired by Henrietta Barnett's Hampstead Garden Suburb Trust for enlightened development on modern town planning lines. The density was to be a mere eight houses to the acre, each in its own ample, hedge-bordered garden, set unevenly along varied, tree-lined but economic roads.

These principles were those of Letchworth, the pioneer garden city just getting off the ground when the Trust was formed. So Raymond Unwin, the brains behind Letchworth's layout, was appointed architect-planner in 1905–6. Hampstead Garden Suburb, with its pleasant roads, its clever management of contour and street-crossings, its backland pathways, open spaces and belts even of woodland, is the brilliant culmination of the approach to domestic site planning initiated by Parker and Unwin at Letchworth. But it also marks Unwin's defection from the garden city ideals of Ebenezer Howard, who wanted

self-sufficient communities built well outside London, not elegant extensions to the 'great wen'. Hampstead Garden Suburb was unapologetically for commuters. It soon emerged that the Barnetts' vision of attracting temperate, vegetable-growing, working-class tenants who would travel in and out of London each day on the 'twopenny tube' could not be reconciled with the costs of the development. The garden suburb became, and has remained, a liberal middle-class ghetto. Yet the influence of its planning and architecture has been boundless. The special legislation which had to be pushed through Parliament to get Unwin's ideas about layout round local urban bylaws was echoed in national town planning acts down to 1947. A spate of pre-1914 garden suburbs, not just in Britain but all over Europe, took their cue from Hampstead, while Unwin was able to distil its lessons in the layouts recommended for council housing after 1918.

Architecturally there is plenty to examine at the garden suburb. Pride of prominence goes to the two great Lutyens churches, ranged like saving graces on opposite sides of the central square – a curious incident of environmental inanity at the heart of the suburb. Lutyens had muscled in on the garden suburb in 1907 and through influential connections procured the job of planning this central area, never

119

finished. St Jude's, named after Canon Barnett's Whitechapel church and started in 1910, boasts one of his most splendid exteriors, all enveloping roof and beautiful thin brickwork. The tower and dunce-cap steeple are North London landmarks. The interior, in a Wrennish manner, is quirkier and not flattered by its wall and ceiling paintings. The domed Free Church across the square is as well worth penetrating. On the east side of the square is the suburb's social *clou*, the Institute, mainly by Lutyens' assistant A S G Butler. The silver-grey and red-brick Wrenaissance houses lining the square's edges and the slopes of Erskine Hill and Heathgate are also from the Lutyens office. The other great episode in formality is the rugged pair of shop ranges in a Teutonic Arts and Crafts style flanking Hampstead Way at the official entrance to the suburb from Finchley Road (1909–11). Their designer was an able assistant of Parker and Unwin's, A J Penty. In a similar manner is the fine high wall which separates the suburb from the Heath Extension, apparently by another Unwin assistant, Charles Wade.

The housing of Hampstead Garden Suburb reaches so high a general level within the authorised range of material and styles that it seems invidious to single out architects and examples. Temple Fortune Lane and Hill, Willifield Way and Hampstead Way are the best streets to perambulate. A famous group is the one by Baillie Scott turning the south-east corner between Hampstead Way and Meadway. By Baillie Scott too is graceful, quadrangular Waterlow Court further south, built in 1908–9 as a cooperative development for single working women.

93

Highpoint One and Two
North Road, Highgate, Haringey

1/F3   Underground to Highgate

Highpoint One was acclaimed by no less than the maestro of modern architecture himself. In 1935 Le

Highpoint Two. Garden side. AP

Corbusier wrote 'For a long time I have dreamed of executing dwellings in such conditions for the good of humanity. The building at Highgate is an achievement of the first rank, and a milestone that will be useful to everybody.'

The developer, Zigmund Gestetner, originally commissioned Lubetkin and Tecton in 1933 to build housing for his workers in Camden Town, but failed to secure the site and instead proposed a commercial development on a hilltop in Highgate. Lubetkin envisaged an artistic community, with some low-cost housing included. The success of the development pushed the building far upmarket of these ideals.

The plan is a simple 'H' of seven stories raised on *pilotis*. Services and lifts were placed in the junctions of the arms. With the assistance of Ove Arup (who had first collaborated with Tecton on the Gorilla House in London Zoo), Tecton contrived a heavily reinforced concrete system so that the exterior walls took the structural load, and a system of sliding shuttering gave an exceptionally smooth finish. Small flats were placed in the main block and larger ones in the cross-arms. All had fittings specially devised by Tecton that were

'modern, not moderne', as annotated on a series of sketches produced for a visit by Architectural Association students. The rigid grid was then deliberately broken. Balconies to the flats were given a cyma curve, whilst on the ground floor the entrance hall billows out between the *pilotis* and a tea-room pushes out to the rear. Their kidney shapes are reflected in the concave entrance porch. The result is streamlined but strong.

So successful was Highpoint One that in 1936 the Tecton practice was commissioned to build a second block on an adjacent site, bought by Gestetner to save it from unsympathetic development. Because of the success of Highpoint One and the higher cost of the site, Highpoint Two was conceived from the first as luxury housing. Its single oblong housed four flats per floor, those in the centre with double-height living rooms. Higher quality finishes were used, and the mixture of tile, glass and render has been criticised for its lack of clarity. But the big windows and bold patterning in the central section, achieved by a more complex reinforced system, mark a clear progression from Highpoint One. It is hard to believe that only three years separate the two designs.

The original design was compromised by the need for garages, which blocked the intended ground-floor vista through glass walls to the garden. It was here that Tecton's love of breaking a grid with rhythmic convex and concave curves was intended to find its fullest expression. The entrance hall was reduced to a switchback pair of ramps and set with plants inside, and its ceiling projected outside with a giant slab: such an interplay of indoors and outdoors was a favourite modernist conceit. On one side the slab is simply stopped with a sharp aris and left disturbingly floated. On the other, conceit gives way to mischief with two caryatids. Whether these were inserted as a bit of surrealism, a dig at the conservative planning authority or as an announcement of the building's up-market pretensions is uncertain, but critics were outraged to see so important a modernist using a classical reference.

In 1938 Lubetkin added a penthouse to Highpoint Two that was his London home until 1955.

94

Spa Green Estate
Rosebery Avenue and St John St, Finsbury, Islington

2/J1   Underground to Angel

Time confirms Berthold Lubetkin as the one dynamic, form-giving British architect among the many who latched on to the Modern Movement as an answer to the troubles of the 1930s. Finsbury is fortunate in having four schemes connected with Lubetkin: the Finsbury Health Centre (p. 157), and three housing estates built after the Second World War, Spa Green, Priory Green and Bevin Court. All show a deep commitment to balancing social idealism with expressionism of form. If there is a falling-off in the later projects, that is suggestive of the post-war difficulties which induced Lubetkin to give up architecture in the 1950s.

The background to Lubetkin's Finsbury work was a relationship that grew up between the forceful architect and the little, left-wing Finsbury Borough Council in the years before the war. Finsbury was a poor borough in need above all of identity and vision. Hitherto its subsidised housing, like that of neighbouring Islington, had been entrusted to E C P Monson, a soulless producer of brick flats. Lubetkin and his ally, Alderman Riley, persuaded the council to adopt a strategy known as the Finsbury Plan, which called for new housing, nursery schools, a health centre and air-raid shelters. The housing estates of Spa Green and Priory Green (Busaco Street), though fully designed in 1938 by Lubetkin's group practice of Tecton, were postponed because of rearmament. Spa Green finally went ahead in 1946–9, to revised designs by the post-war firm of Lubetkin and Skinner.

Rigour was the keynote of the Lubetkin approach to design. That quality can be sensed straight away upon the two main slabs at Spa Green, whose potentially faceless elevations are split with crisp discipline into frame, brick infill and balcony areas. The precise pattern-making of these arrangements occupied endless office hours. But for Lubetkin rigour meant more than rectilinearity; he had learnt from his early constructivist days the power and solace of the curve. So the third, lower block, running up into the angle of Rosebery Avenue and St John Street, kinks curiously. The higher slabs too have expressionistic entrances (porch-like on the fronts, box-like and tile-clad on the backs) and a pair of curving 'aerofoil' roofs solemnly calculated to get the best profile for drying clothes. In homage to this innovation, Finsbury Council went on providing curved-roof drying areas atop many of its later flats. The results can be descried on blocks in the vicinity.

The roofs are the tip of a technical iceberg. Spa Green is replete with novelties that would have been more remarkable had the flats been built a decade before. In Bauhaus spirit, the Tecton architects had taken the working-class flat to bits for a competition of 1935. Spa Green and Priory Green followed on from that analysis. The structure, devised by Ove Arup, consisted of an interlocking concrete 'box frame' system that allowed the flats to be insulated from one another and banished load-bearing partitions within them. The kitchens received obsessive attention in the light of American efficiency studies and experimental designs made in Frankfurt in the late 1920s. Waste was destroyed by means of a trap in the bottom of the kitchen sink, thus eliminating the

Spa Green Estate. AP

dustbin – always a sordid business in working-class flats.

Spa Green is in good state today following respectful modernisation and restoration in 1980. It looks better than the larger Priory Green north of Pentonville Road, built to similar designs but reduced standards between 1949 and 1955. Students of British urban housing in the 1950s will find it fruitful to go on from Spa Green to Priory Green and hence to Bevin Court north of Percy Circus, a massive three-winged block with cruder pattern-making on the elevations but a staircase of circuitous virtuosity at its centre. The final statement in this manner is Skinner, Bailey and Lubetkin's big Cranbrook Estate between Old Ford Road and Roman Road, Bethnal Green, where the fronts become almost vulgar but the internal staircases once more leave one agape.

95

Lansbury Estate
Poplar, Tower Hamlets

1/H4   Docklands Light Railway to All Saints

Lansbury was the 'live architecture' exhibition of the 1951 Festival of Britain. Town planning was then a new science, and of special relevance to the Festival's theme of Britain's regeneration. Frederick Gibberd, involved in the construction of Harlow New Town, suggested that a bomb-damaged site could be rebuilt as the Festival's exhibition of town planning and architecture, thus making more effective use of the limited building resources available than a temporary show on the South Bank. Lansbury is important because it was completed so early, while other rebuilding schemes were still struggling for grants. It has been largely forgotten, perhaps because its manners were soon found too mild for progressive taste.

Named in memory of the Labour leader and former Mayor of Poplar, George Lansbury, the area was one of eleven 'neighbourhoods' designated for

Clock tower, Lansbury Estate. EH

comprehensive redevelopment in the County of London Plan in 1943. Only part was developed for the Festival, the area to the north being rebuilt in the later 1950s. Construction techniques were demonstrated by using different systems for the various buildings, some of which were left unfinished until the exhibition was over. A temporary display included the 'Rosie Lee' café and 'Gremlin Grange' – a lesson in poor building techniques under a stockbroker-Tudor skin.

The problem of Lansbury as a town planning scheme is that it has two centres: the market square by Chrisp Street is rivalled as a focal point by the Catholic church, massive in scale and gathering round it the best of the housing, an old-people's home and the schools. The suburban feeling is due to the small scale of the houses set back from the huge expanses of road; in contrast to other redevelopments Lansbury largely respected the original road pattern. This openness is especially disconcerting around the schools in Cordelia Street. Only in the small courtyards facing Grundy Street (by

Geoffrey Jellicoe) and especially in the pedestrianised squares around Pekin Street (by Bridgwater and Shepheard) do the houses really hang together in an interesting way. But above all Lansbury gave people real houses and gardens, what the British nuclear family seems to want most. And though it is worn, shabby and prey to the salesmen of plastic windows and stone cladding, it is a popular place to live. On a small scale it was the formula of the first New Town neighbourhoods.

The original area of shops is dwarfed by the later blocks to its south. The Borough of Poplar commissioned a clock tower and viewing platform by Frederick Gibberd, who also did the market and shops to the north. The shops seem tiny today, especially the corner 'department store', three rooms high and now mutilated. At each end of the shopping mall a pub was built, and the Festival Inn has a mirror bearing the Festival of Britain emblem. Sadly the original pub sign has gone. It depicted 'typical' Londoners dancing round a shaft of light, modelled on Powell and Moya's 'Skylon' at the main exhibition.

The area around Pekin Street and Upper North Street is dominated by its churches. The Catholic church of 1950–1 by Adrian Gilbert Scott could be a 1930s building; it has the fine brickwork and architectural massing normally associated with Adrian's

A corner of the Lansbury Estate. GLRO

brother Giles, and a greater strength and solidity than anything else in Lansbury. Inside, its elliptical arches owe much to Giles's abortive scheme for the rebulding of Coventry Cathedral. The contrast between it and the neighbouring Trinity Methodist church is educative. This, of the same date by Cecil Handisyde and D Rogers Stark, is one of the best churches of the 1950s; a small, square church with projecting cantilevered galleries, an attached meeting hall and an impressive brick tower.

96
Alton Estates
Roehampton Lane, Roehampton, Wandsworth

1/E6   British Rail to Clapham Junction, then bus

The reputation of the vast showpiece suburb built at Roehampton by the London County Council from 1952 onwards to house almost 10,000 people has risen and fallen with the esteem of public housing. What one author could in 1961 call 'probably the finest low-cost housing development in the world' had become for another commentator sixteen years later an essay in utopian *naïveté*, shot through with conceptual failures and practical shortcomings. We are now on the way to a calmer assessment of this mammoth development.

The LCC sought frantically after 1945 for adequate sites to ease London's housing crisis. Outer Wandsworth was among the few areas in the County of London with space left for building on, and several large sites were earmarked for purchase – one facing Wimbledon Parkside, the other two next to one another in Roehampton overlooking Richmond Park. Their development coincided with the reorganisation of LCC housing production and an influx of new blood into its Architect's Department. The idea was to supersede the played-out old five-storey flats in slabs still being built with a fresh and more picturesque kind of housing – 'mixed development' in the modern

Slab blocks, Alton West Estate. EH

idiom, with some blocks tall and thin, others low and long, and airy landscaping in between. Wimbledon Parkside (renamed Ackroyden) was the first site undertaken in 1950. 'Portsmouth Road' (later Alton East) followed on from 1952 and the far larger 'Roehampton Lane' site (Alton West) from 1954.

Alton East, a smallish estate whose core lies on the sloping land between Bessborough Road and the old Portsmouth Road to its south, occupies the former sites of large old Victorian villas, whose landscaping was kept and enhanced. The Alton East team of architects under Rosemary Stjernstedt were self-consciously 'social' and 'Scandinavian' in outlook. They took up the theme of pitched-roof maisonette blocks, groups of staggered terraces and occasional squarish 'point blocks', built of *in situ* concrete but clad in 'clinker-block' brickwork, first timidly tried in the flatter setting of Ackroyden. The result is humane, lively and, because of the mature planting, the reverse of bleak.

Alton West was a more formidable enterprise. In the two years that separated it from Alton East, the Corbusian ethic had gained ground in the LCC. The young architects who tackled this job under Colin Lucas wanted, in the open parkland setting facing Richmond Park, to make a grand architectural statement and to make it in concrete. Three groups of point blocks were set out, to the same plan as

those of Alton East but this time faced with concrete panels. Along and off Danebury Avenue, the estate's spine, there is a variety of incident, ranging from shops at the top off Roehampton Lane through maisonettes, primary schools and a bronze bull by Robert Clatworthy next to the bus stops, to the likeable, staggered clusters of single-storey old-people's houses – flat-roofed but with prominent chimneys to remind one that the 1950s were still the era of solid-fuel heating. The best of these groups is in Minstead Gardens.

What lifts the architectural eye and raises Alton West above the level of a Modern Movement housing ghetto is the serried rank of five slabs slamming at an angle into the hillside at the top of the estate. Here Le Corbusier's concept of the Unité d'Habitation, so beloved of architects at the time, comes in cutprice version to Roehampton. The designers wanted thicker and taller slabs, but economy and practicality ruled this out. Originally they were to face in a row along the top of the hill, with a frontal view over the royal park. It seems to have been Harold Macmillan, then Minister of Housing, who vetoed this plebeian indelicacy and so made possible the dramatic revision by which the slabs bury themselves in the slope. That this is the main virtue of their architecture is plain from estates elsewhere in London, where the LCC architects used the same type of slab on level ground to no real visual effect. What the maisonette dwellers of the Alton slabs lost through

Macmillan's edict, admirers of Modern Movement architecture gained. The view up from Downshire Field is one of the most memorable in twentieth-century architecture. But the slabs, like balcony-access slabs more than point blocks everywhere in public housing, have been socially problematic.

97

Blackheath Park
Greenwich

1/J5   British Rail to Blackheath

Blackheath Park is not, as the visitor may first conceive, the expanse of space (ideal for fairs and kite-flying) that opens out on the plateau above Greenwich Hill. It is a gated and well-treed haven south of Blackheath Village in its dell and east of the Lee Road. Here, out of

the remnants of an ancient estate, the past two centuries have carved a development that displays the elasticity of London suburban housing to perfection. Is Blackheath Park planned or unplanned? The answer is a little of both, and none the worse for either.

The layout is simple: a spine of broad, straight roads, two running east–west and three north-south, off which stem drives, lanes and alleys. Blackheath Park itself is the main axis. This is prosperous territory, you perceive, as you pass the gate; speed-bumps, Volvos, healthy pensioners on Moulton bicycles and au pairs with pushchairs abound. In fact the social composition is fairly diverse. The architectural variety is palpable right away. Short Georgian terraces, brick to begin with and then stuccoed, face two rambling houses of 1896 by Aston Webb. Further on come demure Italianate villas of about 1830, when the original development was at fullest

spate. It all hangs together. As if to prove the point, Patrick Gwynne fails to spoil things with his No. 10 of 1968, all rebarbative angles, slatey textures, tinted glass, spiral ramps and a goldfish pond in front. A few doors further on is a superior modern house: Peter Moro's modest No. 20, built by the architect for himself in 1957–8. It is of brick, with a boarded upper storey and a split-pitched roof apparent only from the side. St Michael's church opposite, of 1828–9 by George Smith in an impoverished Gothic style, suggests that early Blackheath Park put a low priority on religion. A comically ham-fisted east window under a spindly spire cheers it up a little.

Thus far the development is pretty but not exceptional. What makes it so are the pockets of 'Span' housing, tucked into villa sites in and around the estate from 1957 onwards. Span was the brainchild of two unorthodox architects, Eric Lyons and Geoffrey Townsend. Impatient with the rigidities and crudities of post-war housing, Townsend gave up architecture to become a developer, while Lyons risked his professional standing to go in with him as Span's designer. The crux of their faith was that well-designed, equipped and landscaped but unabashedly modern housing with an element of communality could sell. Nobody in the Britain of the early 1950s, least of all the building societies, believed that. As Span chose to build on 'gap sites' and Victorian gardens in London's better suburbs, it had trouble too with local authorities and amenity societies. But the struggle was worth it. First at the Parkleys estate at Ham (1954–6), then more suavely at Blackheath and in sundry other small schemes, Span broke through to make good modern domestic architecture available and popular. Nothing quite like Span has been seen since the firm collapsed in 1969.

After thirty years, the Span developments at Blackheath have reached the peak of their maturity; there can be no saner and calmer place in London for a stroll on a fine summer evening. The Hall (1957–9), south of Blackheath Park and east of Foxes Dale, is exemplary. It starts at the north end

The Hall, Blackheath Park. EH

with Hallgate, a three-storey block of flats. It is set back behind a low dwarf wall and a thicket, yet it feels open and inviting. There is a broad entrance at one end paved with York stone slabs, through which you are drawn to the region of two-storey terraces beckoning southwards behind. *En route*, you pass a strange little sculpture in the wall of a man all but crushed by upper and nether concrete lintels; the figure, *The Architect and Society* by Keith Godwin, is Eric Lyons's way of telling us that Span's achievement did not come cheap.

The houses themselves are neat, modest, white-painted boxes built in cross-wall construction, mostly window on the ground floor, jagged tile-hanging above, and split-pitched roof on top. It is less the buildings than the relation between them and their ample common surroundings – what Furneaux Jordan dubbed 'the height–space relationship' – which is striking. Even the lovely landscaping and planting, partly old but intensified by Lyons and his team, would be banal if the flats and houses were too high or too low, if there were too much or too little space between them, or if that precious space was cut up with private garden walls or left as unchecked expanse.

98

The Barbican
City of London

2/K3   Underground to Barbican, Moorgate or St Paul's

Whilst London pioneered the garden suburb, its architects have generally failed to find an equivalent solution for urban sites. Faced after the war with the redevelopment of a vast area north of St Paul's in the City itself, the first proposals were for office blocks such as formed the recently ravaged London Wall. But in 1954 the Minister of Health, Duncan Sandys, suggested the area be developed for housing and Chamberlin, Powell and Bon submitted a scheme that consciously departed from suburban picturesqueness in an attempt to create something of a city's excitement.

The Barbican. Lake from central walkway. EH

Few architects have had the opportunity to so define their own brief on so massive a scale. Chamberlin, Powell and Bon recognised that only upper- and middle-class housing would provide the required return for the area, and that special facilities were needed to attract such tenants. They identified two City schools whose existing accommodation was inadequate, and as one of these was the Guildhall School of Music and Drama they added a small arts complex that could be used by both schools and residents.

The site was flat, but riddled with deep basements and breached by the underground running east–west. Furthermore the City Corporation demanded a high-level pedestrian walkway to link with that of London Wall. The result was a multi-level development that segregates the residential areas from the visitor. The best approach is from the south, where the whole complex rises round the restored St Giles's, Cripplegate.

As formal planning the Barbican is a masterpiece. The eye is led to the spaces between the buildings, where fountains and trees are aligned in rigid ranks. The centrepiece is the long canal built over the redirected railway. Height is emphasised by three towers which, at over forty storeys, are the tallest residential blocks in Europe. Their

triangular shape together with their height made for severe engineering problems, and the pronounced corner balconies were designed to reduce wind resistance. Despite its massive scale the reinforced concrete is detailed with a preciseness and quality that could not be afforded elsewhere. By contrast, the two schools are faced in brick and the arts centre at the hub is expressed in tile and glass.

The plan built was virtually that approved in 1959, though the Corbusian-inspired elevations date from the early 1960s. Two changes were made to the original scheme. The architects wanted to incorporate, as the foyer to the School of Music, the magnificent iron rotunda of Bunning's Coal Exchange, which the City eventually simply demolished. More significantly, in 1964 the small arts centre was expanded into a complex of national importance when the London Symphony Orchestra and the Royal Shakespeare Company were identified as potential tenants. The theatre, designed in conjunction with the RSC, is the most impressive space, with four oversailing galleries giving the tight-knit feeling of a true Shakespearean theatre. Since work had already started on the rest of the site in 1963 the arts centre had to be squeezed into a tiny site originally intended only for locals. The difficult access and the complexity of the resultant plan are common criticisms made of the Barbican.

Such complaints seem trivial compared to how much was achieved. But it is a 'hard' landscape, and it is refreshing to visit the Golden Lane estate to the immediate north. This was Chamberlin, Powell and Bon's first housing scheme for the City, won in competition in 1952 and completed in 1962. It has all the ingredients of the Barbican scheme without its severity and exclusiveness: the contrast of levels, the involvement of the spaces between the blocks as part of the architectural scheme, and the incorporation of ancillary facilities, here a sports hall and community centre. The estate was then extended along the Goswell Road, where a block of shops and maisonettes anticipates the Corbusian styling of the Barbican itself.

99

Trellick Tower
Golborne Rd, Kensington and Chelsea

1/E4   Underground or British Rail to Westbourne Park

The brute force of Trellick Tower assaults you head-on from the bottom of Golborne Road. Indeed, it is one of the landmarks of West London: raw, powerful and the most sculptural of all 1960s tower blocks. It is at once beautiful and terrifying.

Ernö Goldfinger, a Hungarian expatriate who married an English girl, settled in London in 1934. But it was only after the Second World War, when he was in his mid-fifties, that he reached his architectural maturity with an office block in Albemarle Street, and he was in his sixties when he completed his three massive and controversial masterpieces: huge blocks of bush-hammered reinforced concrete composed on a taut and carefully expressed grid. The controlled and careful detailing of his material derives from Auguste Perret, under whom he had studied in Paris in the 1920s. But the monumentality of his

compositions owes more to the early post-war work of Le Corbusier, whose grid systems suggested an alternative to Perret's classical inspiration. From the roof of his office block at Elephant and Castle, Alexander Fleming House, you could see his two housing projects standing sentinel at the limits of inner London to the east and west. First, to the east, came Balfron Tower, designed in 1963 for the London Country Council. It was a prototype for Trellick at a mere twenty-seven storeys: the lift shaft was detached to reduce noise for the residents and linked by access galleries every third floor, similar in concept to the 'streets' of Le Corbusier's Unités d'Habitation. At the last minute the boiler house was enlarged and made to stick out from the top of the lift shaft like a giant boil.

In 1967 all these features were refined for Trellick. James Dunnett describes the result as 'a gain in elegance at some possible cost in power'. The lift tower was turned through ninety degrees to present the main front with a

Trellick Tower. RCHME

more slender profile, and the suspended body of the boiler house was glazed. Trellick was closer than Balfron to the ideals of the Unités d'Habitation in that it provided a fuller range of facilities: on the ground floor an old people's club and a nursery school, now a teenage centre, whilst a lower block placed at right-angles includes a shopping arcade and bank. A proposed pub instead became Goldfinger's office.

At thirty-one storeys, Trellick Tower was out of fashion before it was built, Lillington Gardens having already set a vogue for low-level high-density housing. Its exterior is as hard and crisp as ever, but the foyer has been heavily altered, a recent loss in the name of improved security being the thick, richly coloured glass set in geometric blocks which Goldfinger made a feature of his lift lobbies.

100

Walter's Way and Segal Close
Brockley, Lewisham

1/H6   British Rail to Honor Oak Park

Buildings can be special because of the way in which they either look (product) or come into being (process). For the architectural tourist, product usually wins hands down, since it can be taken in at a glance. But process is worth time and attention too, when it makes you think.

Walter Segal (1907–85) was one of the band of German architect refugees who came to London in the 1930s. He made no rapid mark, but quietly established himself as a moderate who liked to work on his own and specialised in the design and construction of humane housing. St Anne's Close off Highgate Road, Camden (1950–2) shows the quality of his early housing work. When everyone else went big and brutal in the 1960s, Segal went small, Schumacher-ite and libertarian, and started to experiment with 'self-build' methods using a simple timber structural system. Why, he reasoned, should people with little money be forced to live in either badly designed speculative housing, or oppressive public housing with a poor environment? If families could be involved in designing and building their own homes, they could create their own spaces, enjoy the satisfactions of creativity, and save money into the bargain. To make this possible, Segal's timber building system had to be flexible, economical, simple and foolproof. By the late 1970s, building little more than one house at a time, he had got there.

Had it not been for the dynamic intervention of Nicholas Taylor, author, idealist and chairman of Lewisham's Housing Committee, Segal might have gone on in the same obstinate, private way. Taylor produced for him and his fellow architect Jon Broome two small 'gap sites' in the borough, on condition that they take families from the council's housing waiting list with the courage to build for themselves. Thus did a clever idea with capabilities turn into an experience which transformed a few fortunate people's lives. The septuagenarian architect, too, had the time of his life with these schemes.

Segal Close, scene of the earlier Lewisham experiment (1977–82), is a narrow, straight little path off Brockley Park, with an unfittingly fierce notice at the end of it telling you that this is private property. There are just four houses to the right and three to the left, tucked up close together on the tiny site. They are just glorified 'prefabs', really, and none the worse for that, the better type of prefab built after the war having become much loved, as Segal well knew. But the site is on a slope, which prefabs proper could not handle. The open-void basements beneath the lower parts of the houses afford space to muck and

Segal Close. Jon Broome's house. NIGEL CORRIE

tinker about in, in the style of an American 'rumpus room'. The regular battens of the system and the flat roofs (for simple construction – flat roofs need not leak) with deep eaves (a hang-over, perhaps, from Segal's Swiss boyhood) and water tanks on top give the houses unity. But there is plenty of variety. Some people have opted for off-the-peg Georgian-style doors; one house even has a Tudor-style door, with gnomes sprinkled about the little garden to boot.

Walter's Way (the pun is good) off Honor Oak Park itself is a little larger and more self-conscious (1985–7). It was mostly supervised by Jon Broome. Here there are twelve houses set at a skilful variety of angles upon a steepish slope. Ten have a front to the private roadway, while two extra are squeezed in on a path below a tight turning triangle. Neither here nor at Segal Close is the parking fully thought out. But the

greater space is a visual advantage, allowing one to take pleasure in the variations chosen by the self-builders – different bays, colours, fences and so on. You can peep far enough inside to see that the plans vary too. The predictable (and expected) accretions are taking place: a satellite dish here, a leaded window there. Ecological zealots at No. 1 have responded by planting cabbages, beans, leeks and tomatoes, fearfully close to the petrol fumes of the main road.

It is too soon to say whether the Segal method will take on a permanently wider lease of life. Self-building cannot be the answer for everyone, but it ought to be an option for those with the time and enterprise to undertake it. The design method is there and still evolving; the political opportunity for its regular implementation is what is wanted.

8

Town and Terrace Houses

In this chapter we bring together three kinds of London houses: houses built as independent entities, but in or on the fringes of the metropolis; houses in small, self-contained groups within a wider framework; and houses of individual interest, usually for their interiors, set within the London terraced street.

What unites these different types of house is a context of constraint: in particular, the constraint of buildings next to and behind them. Spatial constraint creates urban architectural form. One has only to imagine the intensifying density of a great city like London to grasp this. In many villages of the timber-framed tradition in Northern Europe and New England, the early stage of the urbanising process can still be witnessed. As plots along the main street increase in value, houses turn their ends instead of their flanks towards it, and the spaces between them start to fill up. At first, the gable-end houses still mostly have windows and entrances on their sides. But by the time of the first detailed views of London in the 16th century, the process of infilling is complete. Gable ends jostle together, and a number of stratagems come into play to secure extra space or light: greater overall height and number of storeys, overhanging gables, tighter house plans, and a tendency to cram cottages into back courts and alleys.

Because of the Great Fire of 1666 and centuries-old pressures for redevelopment, authentic survivals from timber-framed inner London are rare now. No. 17 Fleet Street (pp. 182–3) is one of the best; for the broader picture all one can do *in situ* is to trace the archaeology of the street pattern in those few sectors of the City – like parts of Fleet Street – where plots along the frontage are still narrow and alleyways lead back to the remnants of old courts behind.

After the Fire, things change. Brick definitively replaces timber, better capitalization in the building trades means that houses begin to be built in groups or even complete rows ('terraces' from the later 18th century), while the basic format of the new houses and the relation between them are set by an evolving code of building laws – perhaps London's greatest contribution to international urbanism. One pastime for the lover of London's architecture is to savour how, over the centuries, a mysterious process of give and take between regulation and architectural fashion guides the terraced house along. First the brick-built novelties of Inigo Jones and his contemporaries, exemplified by Lindsey House, Lincoln's Inn Fields, are embodied in the post-Fire regulations. Then the rules about party walls and unprotected woodwork are slowly tightened up, so that the flush window frames and door-hoods found at the west end of Queen Anne's Gate, for instance, vanish at the other end of the street. Even in outlying developments like Kensington Square (p. 98) or Church Row, Hampstead, the builders tend to fall in with metropolitan practice.

Before the second half of the 18th century there is no authentically suburban type of smaller London house. Terraces and even squares are built in places where the constraints of urban space do not operate. This shows the conservatism of house-buyers and house-builders. But it is also a tribute to the flexibility of the brick-built London terrace house, despite the awkwardness of its different levels, restricted spaces and poor lighting. Before special building types proliferated in the 19th century, terraced houses served Londoners for offices, shops, pubs, workshops, warehouses, hotels, chambers and much else as well as for single-family residences. The silk-weavers' houses of Fournier Street, Spitalfields are the most famous example of the type's adaptability for industrial purposes. Meard Street in Soho, with its three juxtaposed grades or 'rates' of house catering for tradesmen,

Queen Anne and attendants oversee Queen Anne's Gate. EH

professionals and gentry, illustrates the same point. It also gainsays the common picture of strict social segregation in Georgian London. However much the rich and their landlords might wish to create them, exclusive ghettos were rarely a reality.

That flexibility also helps to explain why so few rich people challenged the architectural tradition of the London terrace house. Fabulous sums were spent, generation after generation, in reconstructing or redecorating the large but boxy houses of Grosvenor and St James's Square (pp. 96–7). Within that framework, architects like Kent at 44 Berkeley Square, Adam at Home House, Portman Square and, in most personal vein of all, Soane on his own behalf at Lincoln's Inn Fields contrived miracles of ingenuity in planning and delicacy in decoration. But the chances such houses offered for a coherent internal architecture and fine sequence of spaces were limited.

Why London should not have created a distinctive model for the larger town house remains a puzzle. It is not that the aristocracy would not build in London because they preferred the countryside. But the efficient housing market of Georgian and Victorian London made it easy for rich people to rent and furnish terrace houses in the latest style for short or long terms; that, coupled with the difficulty of acquiring freeholds, was a disincentive to build. Yet there *was* a tradition of the larger, more open London house, limited though it was in scope compared with the Parisian *hôtel* or Italian *palazzo*. It found early expression in the sequence of noblemen's houses along the banks of the Thames, of which Somerset House, rebuilt as offices in the 1770s (p. 37–9), is now the only token. After 1660 another sequence developed along Piccadilly, in the *hôtel* mode, with enclosed forecourts fronting the main body of each house. Here Burlington House (p. 174–5) is the pre-eminent survival. The other three outstanding West End mansions of the tradition, Devonshire House, Chesterfield House and Grosvenor House, were all casualties of inter-war redevelopment.

So the nobleman's London residence

is represented in our selection by Spencer House and Apsley House – neither villas nor yet country houses, but largeish, squarish classical mansions slotted into spacious sites close to royal parks or palaces. They do not quite add up to a genre of their own, though Apsley House belongs to a little family of post-Napoleonic, Francophile magnificence including Clarence House and Lancaster House (p. 62). This lack of a clear line of development means that when Victorian grandees build houses on the largest scale in London, one is never quite sure what to expect. Hence the strangeness of, for instance, Norman Shaw's Lowther Lodge, a building which looks as though it ought to be in the countryside and be wearing a different set of clothes, compared to the same architect's 170 Queen's Gate round the corner, where the chaste civic tradition of John Webb and Christopher Wren is reinvoked. Victorian Park Lane, before the flat-building mania of the inter-war years destroyed most of its mansions, was a cacophony of styles. Yet on the middling scale, in their Kensington, Chelsea and Hampstead houses for the professional classes, the able architects of the Victorian 'domestic revival' were confident, prolific and – almost – consistent. Generally, they were at their most inventive and original when they built for themselves (Tower House) or for brother-artists (44 Tite Street). Perhaps this was less because they had unusual licence in artists' houses than because the problems of designing a well-lit studio house in an urban context made them think harder. Again, architectural constraint seems to turn out to be an incentive.

When Linley Sambourne moved into 18 Stafford Terrace in 1874, the high-class London terrace house seemed to be going strong. A decade later even, when Ernest George and the Peto brothers embarked upon their Harrington and Collingham Gardens development, they were full of ideas for breathing new life into the genre. But in about 1890 the type suddenly collapsed. Some rich Londoners transferred into efficiently serviced mansion flats like Whitehall Court (p. 115), while others used the new suburban railway system to move

out of the centre altogether. In pockets such as Chelsea, smart middle-class town houses like the group by Voysey in Hans Road continued to be built until the First World War. But for the most part the terraced tradition lingered on in two-storeyed, artisan Victorian developments of the kind represented by Queen's Park (pp. 112–13) and in outer railway suburbs for clerks like Penge and Ilford. The terraces of the early 20th century built by housing reformers, as on the London County Council's suburban cottage estates, or at Hampstead Garden Suburb (p. 119), were usually limited in length and set back as far as possible from the street behind gardens. By then, flats were believed to be a regrettable inevitability for the city centre. When high density street terraces were revived in the 1950s, they had been all but moribund for forty years. To judge from the plethora of terrace houses built since for all classes, from the Dixons' influential group in St Mark's Road to the recent 'noddy-boxes' of Docklands, the type is alive and well in London once again.

101

57–60 Lincoln's Inn Fields
Holborn, Camden

2/G3   Underground to Holborn

'Perhaps, historically, the most important single house in London', pronounces Sir John Summerson on Lindsey House, Nos 59–60 Lincoln's Inn Fields. At first the comment may puzzle the tourist confronting this simple enough painted and pilastered facade. It becomes clearer when you know that Nos 57–58 next door, so similar-seeming, was built almost a century later, in the early 1730s as opposed to the late 1630s. It makes sense when you are told that the Lindsey House front is the only authentic survivor from the campaign by the Inigo Jones circle to reform London street architecture during the reign of Charles I.

Who designed it? On that the experts cannot agree. Its promoter was William Newton, a gentleman-speculator who in the wake of Inigo Jones's revolutionary elevations for Covent Garden piazza had procured designs in the same manner for a run of houses in Great Queen Street. In 1638–41 Newton went on to develop the fringes of Lincoln's Inn Fields, in the teeth of opposition from the lawyers of Lincoln's Inn, who had long tried to keep the area to themselves. Lindsey House was the high centrepiece (or, as it turned out, not quite the centrepiece) of the west side, known as Arch Row, and much the best house in Newton's development. Though Newton was neither the builder nor the first occupant of the house, he presumably procured the design of it. Either John Webb or Peter Mills, his agents for the Great Queen Street development, could have been the architect. Summerson prefers Nicholas Stone. What no modern scholar will countenance is that Lindsey House was designed by Inigo Jones himself, as the 18th-century Palladians universally believed.

Wrong they may have been, but their reverence for the building was such that when the site to the south came up for reconstruction in 1730, all that Henry Joynes, acting as architect for Solicitor-General Charles Talbot, could think of was to imitate it – an unusual procedure at that date. But in so doing, Joynes felt obliged to iron out what he saw as some of the older front's infelicities. By spotting small differences between the two facades, much can be learned about the chequered progress of English classical architecture.

The front of Lindsey House is stuccoed and painted, while Joynes's elevation basks in the pomp of Portland stone. Inigo Jones's followers were ashamed neither of brickwork, which was once probably exposed between the pilasters of the upper storeys, nor of stucco dressings, which convey a thicker and friendlier feeling to all the applied detailing. In the face of such robustness, Joynes's more ornamental architraves look thin and fastidious. The details of the two orders tell the same story: Stuart native vigour supplanted by Hanoverian propriety. Lindsey House's pilasters stand on pedestals, taper as they rise, and feature little swags dropping between the volutes of their tight, Ionic capitals. Another swag joins the broken halves of the pediment over the central window and allows the unknown architect to thrust in a tablet for a date or a name – a motif repeated on the window above. Such 'artisan' unorthodoxies are the reason why the hand of Inigo Jones is not suspected. By contrast Joynes has 'correct', undiminishing pilasters on low bases and an unvarying run of first-floor windows. To get better ground-floor rooms, he also raises the height of his rusticated base (certainly more effective in stone than in stucco). Besides, had Nos 57–58 not been a little higher or lower, there would have been an awkward clash of cornices and the individuality of Lindsey House would have been compromised.

One similarity the two houses have is

a curiosity. Each was divided into two when Lincoln's Inn Fields lost prestige, and each is now back in one use, as offices. The alterations at Nos 59–60 were made in 1751–2 by Isaac Ware, those at Nos 57–58 in 1795 by Sir John Soane; in both cases the buildings were gutted and replanned at the same time. Only the most thoroughgoing purist can fail to enjoy the anomaly of the double entrances at the centre of the two ground storeys. Ware made no attempt to disguise his doorcases, but Soane protected his with an elegant curving porch and iron balcony which do much to redeem the southern house from the suspicion of monotony.

102
Queen Anne's Gate
Westminster

2/F6   Underground to St James's Park

To stumble upon this most exquisite of streets between the office blocks behind Victoria Street and the royal purlieus of St James's Park is one of London's best architectural surprises. Queen Anne's Gate is the *locus classicus* for studying the subtle progress of the London terrace-house elevation between 1700 to 1840. It is also about the only place where you will see London houses of the very early 18th century in near-mint condition.

The street was formerly not one street but two – or rather a 'square' and a street. Hence the width of the western leg, and the kink in the middle of the southern side which makes Queen Anne's Gate memorable as 'streetscape'. The railing between the two portions disappeared in 1873, when the statue of Queen Anne facing westwards in front of it was squashed against the flank wall of No. 15.

Pride of place belongs to the two terraces of the former Queen Square, Nos 15–25 on the south and 26–32 on the north. Not much is known about these high-class houses ('noble hostells', one early description calls them) except their date, 1704, and the fact that they

57–58 (left) and 59–60 (right) Lincoln's Inn Fields. GLRO

131

had a chapel attached, long gone. They mark the point that fashionable West End terraced housing had got to before the stipulations of the London building acts began to bite. For their day, they are remarkably uniform. Nos 15–19 give the original scale: three storeys with an overhanging cornice of wood and pedimented windows in the attics. Elsewhere an extra storey has been added. The storeys are stressed by horizontal stone bands, and the brickwork flickers between brown stocks and red rubbers round the windows. There is more window than wall, and would have been even more if the thin end openings next to the fireplaces, blocked now, were ever fenestrated. But what most sets these houses apart from the Georgian austerity to follow is their freedom of ornamentation: the stone keystones over the main windows, quaintly ferocious, and above all the overhanging wooden hoods which, by some miracle, all but two of the houses retain. With their riot of leaf-carving, flowers, heads and acanthus and pine-cone pendants, they seem to come from the dowdier shores of late-Stuart theatre or *haute couture*. Ruskin or Morris might not have disdained their vitality.

Beyond these ranges the street sobers up. On the south one finds first Nos 5–13, a mildly old-fashioned terrace for its date (1770–1: designer probably Emanuel Crouch), flat at the back as well as the front and with neat and regular fenestration. The elevations are in grey 'Malme bricks' throughout, the red colour round the windows being a modern deception in paintwork. A string course appears above the second storey alone, for reasons of proportion, while only the pedimented doorcases with their inset Gothick fanlights project beyond the building line. Opposite, Nos 14–24 (perhaps designed by Samuel Wyatt) are a shade later, of around 1774, but grander and more up-to-date, with a relation between wall, window and storey-height set by a simple module. These houses, of varying depth, look out over the park and have bows at the back to take advantage of the prospect. Last in the series comes Nos 8–12, a suave terrace dating from 1837, just before Georgian discipline gave way to

Victorian incrustation. Here the plain yellow-brick walling outweighs the area of window opening. The woodwork of the window frames and sashbars is minimised, so as to heighten the contrast between solid and void. Cool Ionic porches and a continuous balcony sufficiently break up the flatness of elevation. Here is smart, architect-designed work. Their author was James Elmes, known also as a literary critic and editor of *Metropolitan Improvements*.

The plentiful blue plaques of Queen Anne's Gate testify to a long record of distinguished and fashionable residents. It is a relief to read in *The Survey of London* that a hundred years ago historically confused local children would sully the street's sedateness, calling upon the statue of Queen Anne 'by the name of "Bloody Queen Mary" to descend from its pedestal'. On receiving no response, they assailed it with missiles.

17 Queen Anne's Gate. EH

103

Church Row
Hampstead, Camden

1/F3　Underground to Hampstead

The terrace was the universal idiom of the London speculative builder, no matter whether his site was in central London or an open field in one of the surrounding villages. Many of London's finest urban streets are in its suburbs. One very early such survival is at Nos 52–55 Newington Green, dated 1658. Rows from the early 18th century are more common, such as Nos 39–43 Clapham Common Old Town of *c*.1705; high roofs, closely spaced windows and huge doorcases give this little group a rural air of unsophistication. How quickly the language became standardised can be seen by comparing the Old Town range with, for instance, Nos 13–21 Clapham Common Northside of 1714–20, Montpelier Row, Twickenham of *c*.1720 or Maids of Honour Row on Richmond Green of 1724. Although outside the area of their jurisdiction, all these developments responded to the prohibitions of the London Building Acts of 1707 and 1709 by eliminating wooden eaves-cornices and setting their sashes a fraction behind the brick facade. Thus did legislation generate fashion.

None of these developments is quite so completely urban in manner and scale as Church Row, Hampstead, two tall terraces that lead from busy Heath Street to the village church. Its development west of Hampstead's main street seems to have begun in about 1707, and may have been prompted by the success of the chalybeate spa nearby. Richard Hughes of Holborn was certainly buying land in 1710, and by 1713 had erected eight houses on the south side of what was then called Church Lane. By 1728 it had become Church Row and contained about ten houses on the north side and thirteen on the south.

The south side is the more uniform, a great wall of brown brick and crown glass, each house of three bays with

Church Row, looking towards Hampstead Parish Church. EH

104

2 Fournier Street
Spitalfields, Tower Hamlets

2/L3   Underground to Liverpool Street or Whitechapel

thick doors and iron railings. Within this framework subtle variations are endless: some have had their windows lengthened or 'dropped', others have lost their glazing bars and decorated doorcase brackets to later fashions; some have gained a storey or a mansard roof with dormers. No 15 is a sympathetic addition of 1924. The north side is more irregular and picturesque, characterised by the canted weatherboard front added to No. 5 in about 1800. Church Row was the scene of an early unsuccessful preservation battle in 1898 when two larger houses were demolished for Gardnor Mansions, designed by George Sherrin.

Conservationists were more successful in saving the church. The medieval church of St Mary was demolished in 1745 and a replacement, St John's, was dedicated in 1747. Its architect was John Sanderson, who designed a simple box of five bays with an altar at the east end behind the tower. Church Row gains much from this picturesque termination, set in a leafy churchyard bounded by railings and gates brought from Canons Park early in the 1750s. But by the 1870s the church

was too small and a third building seemed to be the only answer. Hampstead was home to a clutch of Victorian church architects: Sir Gilbert Scott lived on Holly Hill, whilst his son George lived at No. 26 Church Row and George Bodley, Thomas Garner and Temple Moore at Nos 24, 20 and 16 respectively. At their urging, the church was turned on its liturgical axis and extended westwards. F P Cockerell built the chancel in 1878, and T G Jackson designed new fittings. The result is a wedding-cake confection of Georgian and Victorian classicism. The Victorian work may be detected by the use of paired columns with richer capitals than Sanderson's work, whose purity is smothered by the later gilding.

By contrast to the street, the main churchyard is rural in feeling, tall trees obstructing its views over London. Occupants include John Constable and Norman Shaw, the latter's eroding tomb designed by his pupil Ernest Newton. From the churchyard you can look southward to see the back of Shaw's imposing house in Ellerdale Road nearby, built by him in 1874–6, with a later wing behind.

Spitalfields in the 1990s presents what social historian and local resident Raph Samuel has termed 'the pathos of conservation'. Demolition of the venerable houses built in its Georgian heyday as a weaving district has been stemmed but not stopped. Developers, small and gargantuan, prowl around seeking fringe sites wherewith to placate the insatiable maw of the City. Their schemes usually pay some sort of homage to history now, but their heart is not in it and it shows. Meanwhile the old shops and businesses are going or have gone. Conservationists huddle in small enclaves, proud of their over-restored houses. Only the Bengali community around Brick Lane preserves the bustling spirit and muddle of traditional Spitalfields – most resilient of London's immigrant districts.

The well-off Huguenot silk-weavers who made Spitalfields hum in the 18th century were never many in number. Most of the district was covered with the humble alleys, tenements and sheds of the poorer weavers, all long vanished. Following savage destruction in the early 1960s, there are few places now where you can see runs even of the better houses: Princelet Street, Wilkes Street and (an outlier west of Commercial Street) Elder Street. The finest parade of all is along the two sides of Fournier Street, started in 1726 north and east of Nicholas Hawksmoor's new church (pp. 14–16). The brick houses 'range uniform', with wooden doorcases, segment-headed windows and keystones, but there are endless small variations from one to the next. Several have been refronted. The most striking feature is the out-of-style run of weavers' windows along the roofs on the north side. The proprietors of Fournier Street were not ashamed to show their trade to the world.

At the end of the south side next to

2 Fournier Street, Spitalfields, from the garden. DAN CRUICKSHANK

depth within the reveals. The back is distinguished by two canted bays in fine brickwork running from top to bottom, a thing rare in London before 1750. The interior, like that of several Fournier Street houses, survives in remarkable condition, with a beautiful wooden staircase, three pretty wooden balusters to a step, taking up an extravagant proportion of the plan right inside the door. The Victorian Minton-tile floor to the hall is a reminder that the house has always been tenanted by vicars, not rich silk-weavers.

105
1–21 Meard Street
Soho, Westminster

2/F4   Underground to Tottenham Court Road or Leicester Square

Though London is often thought of as the city of the Georgian terraced house, remaining ensembles from the early Georgian period are few and far between. The value of the Meard Street development is that it preserves the gamut of house types of that time – quite grand towards Dean Street, scaling down from four storeys to three along Meard Street itself.

John Meard was a substantial carpenter-builder, wily speculative developer and Soho vestryman. He may have been involved in the latter stages of St Paul's Cathedral and certainly executed contracts under the 1711 church-building Act. Meard's Soho developments brought him into disrepute as a bad ratepayer. 'His Method' (it was alleged) 'was, to shuffle from one House to another of different Rent, so that they never knew how to charge him.' The street bearing his name was laid out not on virgin ground, but on the site of two non-communicating 17th-century courts in different freeholds, the western one reached from Wardour Street, the eastern one facing towards Dean Street. The western court became available first. Here in 1722 Meard built a pair of terraces facing one another, of which

the church is a house with a difference – No. 2, the 'Minister House'. Some think it may have been designed by Hawksmoor, who with his fellow surveyor for new churches, John James, certified payments for its construction between 1726 and 1728. More probably Hawksmoor and James cast an eye over the 'platt' and made a few suggestions. The building looks and feels like a superior and expensive (it cost almost

£1,500, a large sum) example of a London craftsman's house, dominated by the contributions of the bricklayer (Thomas Lucas), mason (Thomas Dunn) and carpenter (Samuel Worrall). The front is plain and bricky enough, but the use of stone instead of wood or plaster for the door surround and cornice is a clue to its dignity. The windows have the common rubbed-brick surrounds, but the sashes are set back to an unusual

Nos 13–21 (odd) survive on the south side. A decade later he gained possession of the eastern end, broke a street through, finished his earlier rows with Nos 9 and 11 on the south and two houses to match opposite, added the taller Nos 1–7 and four fine houses facing Dean Street, and put up tablets on the flanks of the corner houses proudly proclaiming 'Meards Street 1732'.

The northern houses have gone or been irreparably altered, but the southern ranges remain. The Meard Street houses all have two rooms to a floor and a little closet wing at the back, but the smaller western ones are built with the doors and stairs on the left, while those added in 1732 are 'handed', with the chimneybreasts backing against one another, perhaps for reasons of economy. Most of the interiors had, and some still have, good wooden staircase balustrades and fairly elaborate floor-to-ceiling panelling, as befits a carpenter's speculation. The fronts are a fascinating study in minor contrasts within the vocabulary of brown brick, red-rubbed jambs and arches and straight-headed sashes common to the development. The doorways particularly merit scrutiny. The smaller houses have or had flattish pilasters and eight-panelled doors without fanlights, but the larger ones have carved brackets, a full cornice and a fanlight to illuminate the entrance passage, all similar to the doorcases on another development by Meard at 48–58 Broadwick Street nearby. There were probably always dormers in the roof of Nos 9–21, so they had not many less rooms than Nos 1–7, though the storey

heights show a drastic difference in scale and commodity. The insertion of a modest shopfront or two, some loss of railings and the addition of a certain amount of stuccowork have not spoilt the charm of this row.

Of Meard's four showpiece houses towards Dean Street, Nos 69 and 70 have been too much altered to be of great interest but Nos 67 and 68 are among the best early Georgian houses to survive in London. They are a regular handed pair, little damaged by external alteration. A deeper basement gives slightly extra height above the Meard Street level, and requires a step or two up to the unusual stone-cased doorways. The fully panelled interiors provide an absorbing contrast in the small changes in treatment to rooms of different dignity and purpose afforded by Georgian joinery. A developer pulled out much of the panelling at No. 67 in 1988, but his misdeeds have now been set right.

Houses of the middling, Meard Street size attracted mainly what we would call 'professional' inhabitants. Music was represented here among early tenants by the presence of Burckhardt Tschudi the harpsichord-maker, Handel's amanuensis J C Schmidt, and François Philidor, the French-born chessplayer and composer. Batty Langley, the designer and pattern-book writer, and his engraver brother Thomas also lived in the street, but the tone is brought down by Elizabeth Flint, 'generally slut and drunkard; occasionally whore and thief' who had a furnished room at No. 9 in 1758.

44 Berkeley Square. Staircase. SYDNEY NEWBERY

106

44 Berkeley Square
Mayfair, Westminster

2/E4   Underground to Green Park

Berkeley Square suffered many indignities in the 1930s. Georgian houses on the east side were demolished for offices and Robert Adam's Landsdowne House was sawn in half for a road. The spoils of Adam's drawing room were shipped to Philadelphia and the square became another traffic roundabout.

The remaining line of Georgian houses on the west side, developed after 1737, are easily overlooked, disparate in size and variable in degree of alteration. No. 44 is amongst the lowest and narrowest. Its strength is its simplicity. Just three bays wide and three storeys high, with a central door crushed under heavy voussoirs by a wide sill band, it is dominated by three pedimented first-floor windows. A dormer pokes forward from the pyramidal roof. Stand back in Berkeley Square amidst the plane trees – planted *c*.1780 and thought to be the oldest in London – and a glazed dome can just be seen on the right. It gives only a little clue to what lies within.

Palladianism is somehow perceived as a masculine architecture, for heavy dining rooms, not boudoirs. Yet the client here was Lady Isabella Finch, known as Lady Bel, who needed a house for entertaining as part of her social position as a member of George II's court. Her house was built in 1742–7, though she moved in in 1744. Because

1–21 Meard Street, Soho. From *The Survey of London*

Lady Bel had no family, most of the space could be given over to reception areas, though, with only one small and two large rooms on each of the two principal floors, that was not much. Her architect was William Kent, the least muscular and most animated of all Burlington's progeny. The progress of Kent's career can be charted through his work in London: from his uneven early murals at Kensington Palace via his gardening at Chiswick to his late flowering in the 1740s as an architect of both spatial imagination and decorative delicacy. Kent the pretty, playing with cupolas and little projecting wings in search of the quintessentially English public building, can be seen at the Horse Guards in Whitehall. For Kent making profit from his sojourn in baroque Rome, thirty years previously, come here.

The entrance hall, together with the little study to one side and the dining room across the back of the house, is assertive and bold, with big cornices and bigger overmantel mirrors culminating in swan-necked pediments. Anyone well-enough versed in the Inigo Jones tradition might have had a go at them. But, in between, the staircase that breaks across the full width of the house is one of London's finest surprises. The entrance hall opens into a narrow vestibule. To one side is a concave screen, cut by open niches supporting statues of Roman emperors and now masking a bar. On the other a stair leads up, breaks, and winds back on either side, its entwined wrought-iron balustrade twisting itself proudly round the tight oval space. But the shock is reserved for the turn on the half-landing, when you look back to see that the screen has continued up a storey also and – in reaction to the space – has thrust forward a convex bulge. Behind it writhes a little attic stair, precipitously cantilevered from an upper landing.

Lady Bel's apartments, the redecoration of which in the later 18th century is attributed to Henry Holland, are disappointing in their neo-classical platitudes. The saloon across the front of the house is not. It is for this room that the windows of the *piano nobile* seen from the street are so large, and those

above them are blind: for inside there soars a gigantic coved and coffered ceiling, set with a swarm of roundels depicting classical figures painted in grisaille. After so much staircase, originally painted in a warm stone or ochre colour and now cream and gilded, the drama of the saloon is heightened by the use of colour: green, blue and especially (and originally even more so) crimson. It is a miniature of the cube rooms Kent was designing at the same time at Holkham and at No. 22 Arlington Street. One wonders what Lady Bel would have made of the high-tech gaming tables now set around her saloon, and whether they are really so inappropriate.

107

Spencer House
St James's Place, Westminster

2/E5   Underground to Green Park

[B]   Sundays

On New Year's Day 1755, Henry Bromley, Lord Montfort, made his will

and shot himself. Amongst his creditors thus inconvenienced was the architect John Vardy, from whom he had commissioned a mansion close by Green Park. So Vardy took the lease himself, and the next year passed it on to a new client, John, later Viscount, Spencer.

Young, newly wed and flashy in his tastes, Spencer seems to have had an enthusiasm for the antique that approached Lord Burlington's in its fervour for exactitude. Vardy, a pupil of William Kent's, was a capable Palladian; but Spencer also brought in Colonel George Gray, an authority on Roman antiquity, to check Vardy's revised scheme for impurities. As Spencer acquired more land overlooking Green Park, so in 1756 Vardy's original plan was turned into a parade of grand rooms along a show front, leaving the entrance front on St James's Place to be extended with ancillary rooms later. It never was, and only a single pilaster on its eastern flank indicates the intended symmetry. The facade to Green Park is raised above a terrace built over a yard. Curious, too, is the way a bow window peeps out to the south. As it is, the five-bay pediment is stretched rather wide for its height. But with its attic window set with palm

Spencer House. The painted room. GLRO

Plate 1 *All Saints', Margaret Street, looking towards the chancel (entry no. 17).* GLRO

Plate 2 *St Cuthbert's, Philbeach Gardens (entry no. 23).* EH

Plate 3 *The Hall, Natural History Museum (entry no. 35).* MARTIN CHARLES

Plate 4 *Horniman Museum (entry no. 38).* EH

Plate 5 *Parnell House, Streatham Street (entry no. 85).*
PEABODY TRUST

Plate 6 *St Mark's Road (entry no. 118).* JEREMY DIXON

Plate 7 *Stonebridge Primary School, Stonebridge Park (entry no. 132).* EH

Plate 8 *Oakland Infant School, Barnet (entry no. 135).* MARTIN CHARLES

Plate 9 *Hackney Empire (entry no. 159).* EH

Plate 10 *Royal Festival Hall, river front before alteration (entry no. 164).* AA

Plate 11 *Smithfield Market (entry no. 168).* RCHME

Plate 12 *Hoover Factory, executive entrance (entry no. 186).* GLRO

Plate 13 *Paddington Station (entry no. 190).* MARTIN CHARLES

Plate 14 *Albert Memorial (entry no. 204).* EH

leaves and dramatic roof-top statuary, it is nevertheless the most imposing facade of any private town house to survive in London.

Sequences of ante-room, great room and closet were heading out of fashion by the 1750s, but the term is appropriate for the arrangement arrived at through Spencer's extra purchases. On both floors the closet rooms are the most breath-taking. That by Vardy on the ground floor, known as Lord Spencer's Room and recently restored, is broken into two halves by a colonnade lusciously enveloped with palm fronds. The near-oval space beyond is divided into apses, with in the centre a dome set with quadrangular coffers diminishing in size to give perspective. Crisp and newly regilded, the room shows how Palladianism could be bold, spatially innovative and breathe movement into the most antiquarian conceits.

Lord Spencer rewarded Vardy's inventiveness by in 1758 dismissing him in favour of James ('Athenian') Stuart. Though lazy and alcoholic, Stuart had spent the years 1751–5 in Greece and no other architect was such an authority on the pure neo-Grecian ornament then coming into fashion. He then took eight years over the decoration of the upper floor and the barrel-vaulted stairwell, pushed between the solemn entrance hall and main front. Stuart not only introduced greater delicacy, with his garlands and anthemions, he also brought colour to the house. Stuart's finest room is the closet over Vardy's, also comprising square and oval spaces divided by a colonnade. But where Vardy went for dramatic relief, Stuart chose paint. Walls and ceilings are alike adorned with scenes of love and drinking set amongst urns and flowers.

Spencer House has since been altered several times. Henry Holland in 1785 and 1791 remodelled Vardy's ante-room and dining room, and in the 1850s Philip Hardwick hung flock wallpaper and put in plate-glass sashes. In 1927 the house was leased as offices and all removable fittings were carted off to the Spencers' country seat at Althorp, Northamptonshire. From shabby neglect, in the late 1980s it was lavishly restored and filled with paintings and furniture. This new museum to 18th-century taste seems brash, however, compared with the clean-cut lines of its neighbour, No. 26 St James's Place of 1959–60. This is the most satisfying of Denys Lasdun's London flats, cunningly proportioned and expensively finished.

108

Home House
20 Portman Square, Westminster

2/D3   Underground to Marble Arch
[B]

Neighbours and local traders dubbed the Countess of Home 'the Queen of Hell'. What possessed this imperious widow, noted for her foul language, to expend her Jamaican fortune on a house when she was in her seventies is not clear. Her niece by marriage had recently made a match with George III's second son, the Duke of Cumberland, and perhaps this connection prompted her to become a society hostess. Certainly the main drawing room was designed around portraits of the royal couple. The Countess chose Robert Adam as her architect and interior designer. Building proceded slowly from 1772. The Countess moved in in June 1776 and the house was completed in 1777.

As at 44 Berkeley Square there was no need for family rooms, so the two main floors could be given entirely to display. Moreover, a client with little taste of her own left Adam free to explore his own fantasies. The 1770s were the high point of his London career, and of his conception of interiors as an interplay of pretty neo-classical themes set within apses and semi-circles: the delicacy of the library at Syon unconstrained by straight lines. The contorted planning produced an array of odd cupboards and false doors but cannot fail to excite.

Adam was aided by the large site: five bays instead of the three usual in London building. The only clue the exterior offers to the internal disposition is the offsetting of the door to right of centre, giving Adam three bays for the principal front rooms. Otherwise the facade, altered by the raising of a storey and the addition of a balcony and French windows in the early 19th century, is identifiably Adamesque only by the line of stucco plaques and banding over the first floor. The games played inside announce themselves on entering the hall, with its fireplace set in an apse and sweep of elegant doors – only one of which leads anywhere. The walls are painted to imitate Sienna marble, of almost Kentian grandeur but uncertain date. This continues into the staircase hall, as at Berkeley Square the centrepiece of the house. It is top-lit, a necessity consummately exploited by being made round. The upper reaches of the drum, broken by a single viewing point on the second floor, are a birdcage of arabesques, the iron scrollwork of the lantern repeated in stucco below. Sterner, antiquarian motifs take over lower down, with grisaille painting and Ionic columns. But the greatest conceit is the staircase itself, rising up one flight then curving back in two. The balustrade, decorated with brass and lead on an iron frame, is Adam at his most sensual, disarming criticisms of frail prettiness.

On the ground floor Adam behaves himself. More apses, those in the rear parlour incorporating semi-circular doors, echo the staircase form, except in the front parlour where only scagliola columns relieve the rectangularity. The fireworks are in the ceilings, awash not just with arabesques but with rows of medallions by Anthony Zucchi that reach prolific numbers in the library or 'asylum'. Was their programme of Virgilian themes the Countess's idea, or Adam's? Both main floors have a large and a small room to the front and a long and a short room to the rear. On the upper floor Adam begins enjoying himself, exuberantly so in the music room to the front. Each window is set in an apse, and mirrors heighten the contortion of space. The long room to the rear, intended for the portraits, slackens off after the apsed entrance and its columns may be later. Beyond lie the remains of an Etruscan room, heavier than Osterley's, alternatively intended as a third drawing room or the Countess's

137

bedroom. A sinuously winding stair climbs to the second floor, vamped up in the 1920s by Philip Tilden who added silver ceilings and a monumental marble bathroom.

109

Sir John Soane's Museum
Lincoln's Inn Fields, Holborn, Camden

2/G3   Underground to Holborn

[A]

Emerson saw in Sir John Soane's Museum a microcosm of England, or rather in England a kind of macrocosmic Soane Museum – 'well packed and well saved . . . stuffed full, in all corners and crevices, with towns, towers, churches, villas, palaces, hospitals and charity-houses'. Certainly there is something in this most freakish of London's architectural delights that epitomises the national culture. The Englishman's quirks and crotchets, his obsession with detail, fantasy and privacy at the expense of rational organisation, his pride in possessions, his sentimentality, his humour and his melancholy are all legible in the strange residence of Sir John Soane.

A private Act of Parliament promoted by Soane himself during his lifetime (1833) established that his house and collections should be shown to posterity in unaltered state. The great architect printed notes of his own for visitors, which happily have been embodied ever since within successive editions of the guidebook. Architects are not always the best interpreters of their works, so Soane's remarks are valuable chiefly for the information he gives as to the provenance of his collections, and for his pragmatic attitude towards the jumble of objects crammed into his treasure-house, as 'studies for my own mind' which he hopes may be of future benefit too for the furtherance of art and architecture. For an explanation of the

Home House, Portman Square. Dome over staircase. A F KERSTING

Sir John Soane's Museum. The breakfast room. RCHME

house's atmosphere, he offers only a vague clue – his desire to demonstrate 'the union and close connection between Painting, Sculpture, and Architecture, – Music and Poetry'. The added words are the interesting ones. Soane wants his house to strike the visitor's soul with as vivid an emotion as a Beethoven quartet or a Heine lyric. In this romantic purpose it can hardly fail.

Romance and architectural drama are possible without confusion. The muddle of the Soane Museum arises because its creator was not a very rich man, and had to build it up by degrees and in a small space over forty-five years. The story begins in 1792, when he built No. 12 to the left of the present entrance to the museum, using the back premises as his office. In due course he extended behind No. 13, and in 1812 he swapped houses with his neighbours, so that he had No. 13 and the backs of both houses. But the development of his home into a fully fledged museum-cum-shrine occurred only after the death of Soane's much-loved wife in 1815. As work went on, it became a kind of private therapy-through-mourning for the lonely and ageing architect. That is why the place is so imbued with a sense of mortality – a staircase in the shape of a coffin, for instance, and a mock-medieval tomb for Mrs Soane's dog. The present T-shaped

extent of the complex was attained in 1824, when Soane acquired No. 14, rebuilt it, let the front to tenants and added the Hogarth Room behind. In that year he acquired his greatest treasure, the sarcophagus of Seti I of Egypt. Its installation in the 'sepulchral chamber' at the back was celebrated with a three-day reception.

The boxy projection of the street front, with its nervy incised detail, its corbels filched from old Westminster Hall and its Coade stone caryatids, is a sufficiently eccentric prelude to the museum. As built in 1813–14 it was open on all floors, and intended as the left-hand wing of a composition stretching eastwards to cover Nos 13–15; Soane filled in the openings in 1824. After this, the ground-floor dining room and library seem sane and calm. They convey to perfection the sombre tones, furnishings and linearity of advanced Regency taste. Behind the stair is the little breakfast room, Soane's miniature masterpiece in lighting effects. The architect had spent years of his career recasting narrow, ill-lit London town houses, so the room represents the culmination of a lifetime's experience. Its devices include hidden top-lighting at the sides, hidden side-lighting at the top and a scatter of strategically placed mirrors. Were these supposed to help

Soane see his opponent's cards?

Dining room, library and breakfast room, if well stocked with curios, retain some semblance of domesticity. The drawing rooms above are polished and orderly enough too. But once behind all this, Soane lets violent rip with the aesthetic of the emotions. The visitor squeezes between jam-packed pictures, trinkets, urns, busts and fragmentary friezes, negotiates niches, cells and monk's parlours, and switches from Classic to Gothic to Egyptian and back again. At last one escapes into the calm and simple-seeming Hogarth Room, to enjoy the originals of those satirical masterpieces, The Rake's Progress and The Election. Then at a word the attendant steps forward, unlatches two screens, and a further spatial dimension to Soane's contorted genius is revealed.

110

Apsley House
Hyde Park Corner, Westminster

2/D5   Underground to Hyde Park Corner

[A]

Apsley House is the one place where you can still grasp how the English aristocracy laid out, lived in and embellished their grand London houses – and that in their palmiest period, after the defeat of Napoleon. The fact that its occupant was the Duke of Wellington, Napoleon's vanquisher, gives more spice to its contents than individuality to its style.

Isolated, formal and cased in dressed stone today, the mansion looked different when Wellington took it on from his brother in 1817. It was a five-bay, square brick house, built in the 1770s by Robert Adam for the Earl of Bathurst and strung on to the line of houses at the extremity of Piccadilly. Wellington at first had a few changes made by Benjamin Dean Wyatt, a specialist in the highest class of London house. He it was who did much to popularize brownish Bath stone (brought up the Thames via the new

Apsley House. Waterloo Gallery. V&A

Kennet and Avon Canal) for fronting London buildings, and to make French froth all but *de rigueur* for aristocratic London drawing rooms – a fashion to obtain until the First World War. Lancaster House, Londonderry House (these two Wyatt's), Grosvenor House, Clarence House and Buckingham Palace were all built or rebuilt in this manner during the 1820s. Not to be outdone, the victor of Waterloo decided to upgrade Apsley House to the same scale of lapidary grandeur. Besides, Decimus Burton had just constructed an opulent columnar screen as an entrance to Hyde Park right next to his house. So Wyatt was called back in 1828–9. He obliged by

adding an extra wing on the west, putting on a Corinthian portico in the austerest modern French taste, and cladding the front and new wing in the mandatory Bath stone. The high iron railings are the most vigorous feature of the front, and the only one upon which the contemporary Greco-mania explicitly intrudes. The east side, still up against other buildings, was left untouched. Not until 1962 was the house unhappily cut off from everything around it by the broad roadway made to let Park Lane debouch directly into Hyde Park Corner, and its east front cased in matching stone.

The ground-floor rooms are quiet.

One ascends Wyatt's U-shaped steep staircase with its railings of proto-Victorian floridity, past Canova's 11ft statue of the naked, mop-haired Napoleon at its base. The Emperor had never liked it. The Prince Regent handed it over as a spoil of war to Wellington, who probably did not want it and so had it put in the only place where he did not have to see it for too long at any one time; heroic nudity can be trying. Plushness and sparkle indeed, rather than military heroism, are the keynotes of the Apsley House reception rooms. The smaller ones retain a few of Robert Adam's doors, fireplaces and ceilings, but Wyatt subdued his predecessor's colour effects in favour of French white-and-gold. The grandest room is the Waterloo Gallery, running along the west front, top-lit and ornamented in a mixture of plasterwork and papier mâché. Its Louis XIV-style windows can be transformed into mirrors at the push of a panel. The walls, once a festive yellow, are now a cautious red. At the other end, the gloomy dining room of 1819 seems truer to the Iron Duke's lonely later life. It has curved corners, scagliola columns and, on a 26 ft-long table, a portentous display of silver given him by a grateful Portuguese nation.

111

Linley Sambourne House
18 Stafford Terrace, Kensington and Chelsea

1/E5   Underground to High Street Kensington

[B]   **Wednesday and Sunday afternoons**

Although the home of an artist, the *Punch* cartoonist and book illustrator Edward Linley Sambourne, 18 Stafford Terrace typifies the upper-middle-class suburban terrace house of the 1870s and 1880s. In this its survival is unique.

Stafford Terrace was developed in 1868–74 by the builder Joseph Gordon Davis, whose Italianate track-record in Pimlico manifests itself in the design. It looks like half a hundred streets, until you spy the glazed window box or

Wardian case projecting from No. 18. A sign on the brass letterbox indicates that Mr Sambourne is 'not at home'. To step inside is to enter a hushed and darkened atmosphere that has barely changed for a hundred years.

Almost claustrophobic is the clutter of furniture, paintings and prints, and the ferocious means taken to exclude every chink of sunlight from the south-facing rear rooms with stained glass, heavy curtains, and an aquarium on the landing. The ground-floor morning room, behind the dining room, is characteristic. Much of the furniture is imitation Sheraton, popular with all but

the most advanced taste of the time, added to which are bookcases, a Moorish table to give a touch of the exotic, and a morass of objects to confuse the eye. The Morris wallpaper is original, as in most of the rest of the house, but densely overlaid with paintings by friends such as Luke Fildes, minor old masters and family photos. The drawing room occupying the whole of the first floor is still more eclectic. To grasp how respectable mid-Victorians decorated their homes, look no further than these dull gold dadoes and red embossed papers. But again the wall surfaces are all but concealed by the work of

18 Stafford Terrace, interior. GLRO

Sambourne's more successful friends, most of them also Kensington residents. Otherwise the taste is chiefly for reproduction Regency and Louis XVI furniture, brimming with curios and mementos. The only 'aesthetic' touch are the blue and white 'pots', which had become an accepted fashion by the 1870s.

A photograph of Linley Sambourne at work hangs by his desk at the rear of the drawing room. But his personality is revealed most clearly on the stairs and landing, hung with his sketches, and in the bathroom, where in the 1950s some of his photographs were displayed over the marble, coffin-like bath where he did his developing. The mild titillation of some of his studio studies adds a bizarre note to so much Victorian sensibility.

Linley Sambourne moved into Stafford Terrace on his marriage to Mary Anne Herapath, just as his career was commencing. His father-in-law donated funds to buy the house. Sambourne's imaginative talent seems always to have been constrained by the format and deadlines imposed on a cartoonist, and perhaps only his book illustration hints at his potential. The survival of the house is due to his bachelor son Roy, who lived in Stafford Terrace until 1946 without making any changes to the decoration apart from adding photos of actresses to the walls of his own room. Afterwards the house passed to his niece, the Countess of Rosse, a founder member of the Victorian Society in 1958. It is therefore appropriate that the house should now be managed by that sterling body.

112

Tower House
29 Melbury Rd, Kensington and Chelsea

1/E5   Underground to High Street Kensington

Holland House, badly bombed in the Second World War, was formerly the centre of a great Kensington estate, the vestiges of which survive as Holland Park today. But despite such valuable

Tower House, Melbury Road. GLRO

land assets the family was short of cash for much of the 19th century, and was forced piecemeal to develop their estate. In 1874 it passed to the Earl of Ilchester, who managed to preserve the house and its immediate grounds from development while promoting expensive, architect-designed houses on the open land to the south.

The Melbury Road area had already become a fashionable haven for successful academic artists, of whom G F Watts was the first. But the tone of the neighbourhood was set by the arrival in 1864 of Frederic (later Lord) Leighton, who built himself a house and studio in Holland Park Road with the assistance of George Aitchison. The future President of the Royal Academy exerted his influences most markedly on the interior, particularly in the Arab Hall added to display his collection of eastern tiles – complete with fountain and a frieze by Walter Crane. Next door Philip Webb designed a studio house for Val Prinsep. Other artists gravitated to the area in the 1870s. On opposite sides of Melbury Road Norman Shaw designed two studio houses in 1875, No. 8 for Marcus Stone and No. 31 for Luke Fildes.

Very different is Luke Fildes's neighbour, No. 29. As the house of an architect, it required no large-windowed studio. What is more, that architect was William Burges, one of the few who in the 1870s remained wholly true to his medieval principles. Begun in 1875, it was his last major attempt to recreate a

13th-century fantasy world. It was occupied in 1878 but its decoration was still incomplete when Burges died in 1881. The exterior has none of the prettifying effects of Shaw's urbane Queen Anne style with its elegant sashes and tall stacks. Burges's rich red brick is severe, his massing powerful: a single great gable faces the street bang against a staircase tower perfectly positioned on the bend in Melbury Road. Taming his tendency to go over the top, Burges proved here that he could produce a simple and unwhimsical design that perfectly fitted its site.

Whimsical is too slight a word for the interior. It is a precious miniature of Burges's work for the third Lord Bute at Cardiff Castle and Castle Coch. Baronial Gothic of gargantuan strength is a backdrop for ebullient fireplaces set with figures sculpted by Thomas Nicholls and realistic painted friezes. Each room has its own iconography: literary themes pervade the library, fame and fairytales adorn the dining room, while Burges's bedroom boasts a giant seascape. There were even nurseries, though Burges was childless; this element seems in odd contrast to the bachelordom of the rest. As always in Burges's secular schemes it is the detail that captivates, in stained glass, tile, paint and furniture. An army of decorators and carpenters was employed, and some 400 drawings survive for the interior alone.

113

44 Tite Street
Chelsea, Kensington and Chelsea

2/D8   Underground to Sloane Square, or bus down King's Road

The serene presence of the Chelsea Hospital offers the perfect starting point for a stroll westwards among the 'Queen Anne' houses of the late Victorian era along Tite Street, Chelsea Embankment and Cheyne Walk.

Tite Street must be the first stop. Though ravaged by demolitions and banal enough now, in No. 44 it still boasts the most bohemian of London's

Victorian artists' houses, recently restored to something like its original appearance. Tite Street's southern leg was developed when the Metropolitan Board of Works laid out the Chelsea Embankment in the 1870s. In a moment of prosperity, James Whistler built a house for himself here in 1877–8. Bent on flouting convention, he procured from his friend Edward Godwin a design all but bereft of historical trappings – a Japanese-influenced 'arrangement of line, form and colour', like one of his nocturnes. But the Board of Works, as freeholder, found the house 'ugly and unsightly', and to architect's and artist's mutual dismay made them add ornament. Not all of this had been carried out when Whistler sued Ruskin in 1878, went bankrupt and had prematurely to give up his new house. Alas, it has been demolished.

Yet Whistler was the kind of artist to attract a 'set', and in his wake a succession of painters built or took studios in the street, moving around with confusing rapidity. One of these was Frank Miles, a young society painter who introduced various species of Japanese flower to England and another exotic original, Oscar Wilde, to London society. Wilde and Miles lived together between 1877 and 1881 and it was probably for Wilde's taste though with Miles's money that Godwin designed the surviving No. 44, built in 1878–9. *Pour épater les bourgeois*, Godwin tried on the Board of Works a yet more dramatic elevation than Whistler's, in a kind of Greco-Japanese style, all asymmetry and blocky balconies destined to have Miles's oriental plants trailing over the edges. 'Why, this is worse than Whistler's,' cried the Board's architect on seeing the design. It was turned down in committee only by the chairman's casting vote. So Godwin had to amend this second design, grumbling against 'retired farmers and cheesemongers' daring to 'sit in judgement on my work'.

As it stands today, the elevation of No. 44 is a good deal different from the elevation Godwin submitted to the Board. The tall gable covering the studio, the three-sided bay with its wooden balcony, the fiddly ornament over the entrance and the mouldings of

the deep parapet all show Godwin caving in to conventional 'Queen Anne' taste of the 1870s. Nevertheless the self-conscious relation between bare wall and window and the spareness, one might say crudity, of the detail, make the Frank Miles house even in its amended version the most authentically Japanese house of the Queen Anne revival. Inside, a stick-like staircase and an inglenook with built-in settles are just about all that is left, but convey the same feeling.

Godwin designed other houses for

Tite Street, some never built, others haplessly demolished. He was, however, not only an unlucky architect but an uneven one. It comes as a surprise to discover that the strange, coarse tower of studio-flats next to No. 44 is also his. Built in 1885, the year before his death, it seems to lack concentration. Not much more convincing are his Nos 4–6 Chelsea Embankment of 1880, round the corner. For better houses, excepting just No. 31 by R W Edis, one must get beyond Tite Street. Down at the corner, the handsome River House is one of

44 Tite Street. EH

Bodley and Garner's few secular jobs (1879–80). Along Chelsea Embankment, two good groups of Norman Shaw houses are separated by the Chelsea Physick Garden: first Nos 8 (Clock House), 9–11 and then Nos 15, 17 (the famous Swan House, now gutted) and 18 (Cheyne House) on the corner of Royal Hospital Road. Here the Georgian houses of Cheyne Walk begin, including those of George Eliot and of Rossetti, who started the whole Japanese craze and has a memorial in the gardens directly in front. West of Oakley Street, Nos 38–39 Cheyne Walk (1898–9) are the only surviving houses in the locality by another Chelsea architectural innovator, C R Ashbee. Hence you can turn up Cheyne Row past the house of Carlyle, the intellectual guru of Victorian Chelsea, to ponder at the next corner the enigmatic reserve of No. 35 Glebe Place, the best-preserved Philip Webb house in inner London, built for the water-colourist G P Boyce in two phases, 1868–9 and 1876. Its quiet originality is equally distinct from Godwin's striving for effect, Shaw's slickness and Ashbee's historical self-consciousness.

114

Harrington and Collingham Gardens
Kensington and Chelsea

2/A7   Underground to Gloucester Road or Earl's Court

The exuberant 'Dutch' houses of Harrington and Collingham Gardens look as rampantly individualistic as anything produced by the Queen Anne movement in architecture. Yet they are also an attempt to rethink the high-class London house by a master of Victorian domestic architecture, Ernest George. Had terraces and squares not given way to mansion flats and suburban villas after 1890, the deep originality of these houses would be clearer.

Protagonists in the saga of Harrington and Collingham Gardens were the five well-connected Peto brothers, sons of the Victorian railway

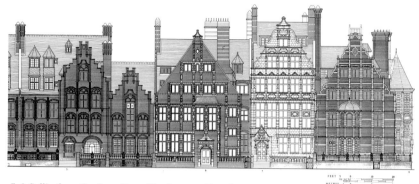

5–9 Collingham Gardens. From *The Survey of London*

contractor Sir Morton Peto. Between 1872 and 1891 their firm, Peto Brothers, was one of London's most enterprising building concerns. But one brother, Harold Peto, went into architecture and teamed up with a rising star, the deft but reticent Ernest George. In 1880 Peto Brothers secured smallish 'takes' of land on either side of Harrington Gardens, hitherto a preserve of huge, porticoed houses in the fag-end of the Kensington Italianate tradition, and called in brother Harold and his partner to see if they could do better. They could.

The scheme started quietly, with the two pairs of houses Nos 20–22 and 24–26 on the north side of the road and a common garden between them. There is little flamboyance here, though the houses are skilfully planned. In 1881 work began opposite on Nos 35–45 Harrington Gardens. As these plots were shallow and backed on to another communal garden behind, they were given uncommonly broad frontages of some 60 ft each and the backs were made as good as the fronts, without the rear extensions that made the average London terrace so shabby. This reduced the number of houses to six very costly ones, four of them arranged in pairs. It also gave Ernest George the chance to get out his travel sketchbooks, bulging with details of old Dutch, Belgian, German – and English – house-fronts.

The agility with which these florid motifs of the Northern Renaissance – stepped and straight gables, chimneys, balustrades, mullions, leadwork and ironwork – are strung together hides the discipline involved in George's design.

That is easier to grasp in Collingham Gardens, where Peto Brothers next, in 1883, obtained a simple rectangle to build nineteen houses on, split in the orthodox Kensington way into two terraces with a garden between. Here individualism is once more the keynote, with fronts of varying width, grouping and height and a range of styles and materials (terracotta included). Again the backs are as pleasing as the fronts. A look at the plans shows George taking pains to give fresh charm to the terraced house arrangement by breaking the levels and giving the better rooms good light, deep bays and attractive corners. No two houses are remotely the same, but all are planned to a set of consistent formulae.

If one of these houses is to be singled out, it must be No. 39 Harrington Gardens, built for the playwright and balladeer W S Gilbert in 1882–3 out of his profits from *Patience*. Behind its nineteen-stage gable topped by a galleon (a reference to Gilbert's alleged ancestor Sir Humphrey Gilbert, *not* to *HMS Pinafore*) is an interior which still has its chief features: a panelled hall with a blue-tiled inglenook and painted glass, a coarsely Gothic dining room, and a drawing room all the way along the back with an ornamental chimneypiece in alabaster at one end.

Harrington Gardens was a big success, Collingham Gardens less so. After the bottom dropped out of the market for large London houses in the late 1880s, such very expensive ones proved hard to let. Terraces so grand and so ornamental were never again built in

London. The Petos' great experiment proved a glorious dead-end, and they gave up building in 1891. Harold Peto left Ernest George soon afterwards, to make his eventual mark as a landscape designer.

115
170 Queen's Gate
Westminster

2/B6   Underground to South Kensington

Once there were four Norman Shaw houses in Queen's Gate, all remarkable, all red-brick, all a reproach to the stuccoed uniformity around them – and all different. No. 196 near the top was the first (1874–5), an ornate, Flemish-looking front squashed between orthodox terraces. This survives, but the door has been moved and the low-ceilinged interiors have disappeared. The others were all on corners. No. 180 (1883–4), with its Morris interiors, has been destroyed, as has No. 185 (1890–1), which had a powerful plan. In the interim Shaw built No. 170 (1888–90), a house at once original and unoriginal. Its story began with Fred White, scion of a prosperous cement manufacturing firm. Like others of Shaw's Queen's Gate customers, White was a collector and connoisseur. He knew what kind of home he wanted – a respectable-looking brick house of late 17th-century type; and he went so far as to make some elevational sketches and to take them to Philip Webb. Webb gently told White that he could not work that way, which is how White beat a path to the door of Norman Shaw. Here he found a warmer welcome, partly because Shaw was less fastidious than Webb as to style, partly because he was bored with the high jinks of his youth and hankered after a more august architecture.

The sketches which White took to Shaw were translated with surprising faithfulness into the front of the symmetrical, hipped-roof No. 170 which we have today, down to the single-storey billiard room at the side. In this way the client influenced his architect to produce a house which was to prove seminal to English neo-Georgianism. Yet Shaw was no cipher. By this stage of his career, planning was the part of domestic architecture he most relished. The layout of the house was all his, and in its day as revolutionary as the facades. The reception rooms were all kept down to ground-floor level, and finished and furnished in a deliberately cool taste – the taste of Inigo Jones, as was then supposed – at odds with the forced and quirky classicism of the earlier Queen Anne revival. But Shaw's ingenious individualism could never quite be suppressed. It manifests itself here chiefly in the way in which he wraps the staircase round the back of the elegantly top-lit hall. The staircases of all four of his Queen's Gate houses were *tours de force* of planning. It is sad that only No. 170's remains to bear witness to their inventiveness.

Outside, Shaw seems to have left a lot of the detailing to his trusted chief assistant W R Lethaby, to whose hand we certainly owe the lovely leadwork and probably also the cornice details (carried out in the White firm's Portland cement) and the elongated proportions of the entrance door and windows. The shutters may have been Fred White's idea. Was it also his suggestion to use

170 Queen's Gate. Front door. RCHME

cement too instead of stone for the quoins at the corners? Shockingly they are a mere skin, having no depth and being backed by brickwork. Shaw was capable of such tricks, but the moral Lethaby cannot have approved.

116
12–16 Hans Road
Brompton, Kensington and Chelsea

2/C6   Underground to Knightsbridge

In the twenty years before the First World War C F A Voysey built a series of small English country and suburban houses admired the world over: clean, low, simple in outline, white-walled, mullion-windowed, and devoid of stylistic excess. The edges of London have a few of them: one in South Parade, Bedford Park, another in St Dunstan's Road, West Kensington, a third (built for Voysey's father) in Kidderpore Avenue, Hampstead, and a fourth on North Drive facing Tooting Bec Common. Their invariable style suited the suburban context, but it would not do for central London. To see what Voysey could do in the city, Hans Road – a narrow, unpromising street that suffers from the proximity of Harrods – is the only place to go.

Voysey had as yet built little when he came to grips with Hans Road, and the history of the commission betrays a certain inexperience on his part. The site of the three houses, Nos 12–16 (even), was part of a strip taken for development in 1891 by Archibald Grove, a Radical Liberal MP, magazine editor and property speculator. Grove wanted a house for himself at No. 12 and two slightly smaller houses for letting next door at Nos 14 and 16. Voysey went away and produced a design of epoch-making elegance and simplicity for the group of three, based on Norman Shaw's group at 9–11 Chelsea Embankment but with all the elements purified and translated into the stripped Tudor idiom which he had already made his own. At first he wanted his usual roughcast elevations. On revision he either changed or was

145

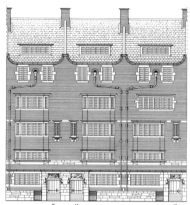

12–16 Hans Road. Voysey's original design. From *The Survey of London*

persuaded to change his mind, and accepted red brick with a base, bands and dressings of Ketton stone. Duly, Nos 14 and 16 were built in 1892–3. But when the time came to proceed with No. 12, Grove and Voysey had fallen out – certainly over money, but perhaps over other things as well. Voysey indulged in a rather piffling law suit for costs against his client, who meanwhile had turned to another architect, A H Mackmurdo, to design and build No. 12. Mackmurdo, founder of the Century Guild, was as fascinating a figure and as important in the English Arts and Crafts Movement as Voysey, but not, it must be frankly said, as good an architect. His No. 12, built in 1893–4, toys with some of Voysey's motifs and genuflects subtly to the Queen Anne architecture of nearby Chelsea, then much admired. But it fails to complete the group in the coherent way which Voysey had intended.

The fronts of Nos 14 and 16 survive quite well, though the bay window on No. 14 has been lowered and an extra mezzanine window added. Do not miss the animal reliefs (by Conrad Dressler) within the porches. The plain brick backs of the houses, rarely seen, are interesting too, with the same curving parapets as on the front; the first-floor drawing room windows project just a touch, to make modest oriels. Inside, not much more than the tapering-balustered stairs survive from what was once a characteristically cute and economical job of house planning on Voysey's part.

117

Sun House
Frognal Way, Hampstead, Camden

1/F3   Underground to Hampstead

The early Modern Movement in Europe meant more than a vogue for reinforced concrete and flat roofed 'white boxes'. Its houses expressed a healthier outdoor life, with a sun terrace if not an open sleeping porch. Inside it implied big windows and a sculptural interplay of connecting spaces, often enhanced by fitted furniture, in which there was place for only the choicest possessions. The movement hardly reached England before 1930. The few architects turned on by the English translation of Le Corbusier's *Towards a New Architecture* in 1928 were young and lacked friendly patrons. A boost was the arrival in 1933–4 of three of its greatest exponents from Nazi Germany: Marcel Breuer, Erich Mendelsohn and Walter Gropius. To work in Britain the immigrants had to go into partnership with Englishmen: Breuer with F R S Yorke, Mendelsohn with Serge Chermayeff and Gropius with Maxwell Fry. For these young architects this tutelage was an inspiration.

One place to see the results is in a pair of houses in Old Church Street, Chelsea. No. 66, with a curved balcony, is by Gropius and Fry, whilst its longer, squarer neighbour, No. 64, is by Mendelsohn and Chermayeff. They date from 1936. But both hide their main fronts from the street, and the Gropius house has been badly reclad.

What Fry could do on his own by

Sun House, Frognal Way. AP

then can be glimpsed through the trees of Frognal Way: the evocatively named Sun House of 1935–6. The treatment of the house is the consequence of its south-facing aspect having also the best views. Its composition transposes the curves of the Old Church Street house on to a single facade, behind which are placed all the principal rooms. The proportions of the horizontal bands of glazing were much admired by Pevsner. But the strongest image is the steep curve of the driveway and garden wall swinging up to the garage, over which sails a terrace roof supported on slender steel posts. It appears a more vertical composition now that the bulk of the house is obscured by trees. The main roof sports another terrace, with screens to give shelter whilst allowing views through pierced openings. Inside, Fry designed most of the furniture, much of it fitted, and there were murals and sculpture.

Frognal Way is a wide gravel roadway lined with a mismatch of architect-designed houses, a few in the comic hacienda style. The other Modern Movement house is at the corner with Frognal, on which it is numbered. No. 66 was designed in 1937 by Connell, Ward and Lucas, whose High and Over in Buckinghamshire initiated the genre here in 1929. It uses the same ingredients of semi-basement garage, balconies and roof terrace in a far more brittle manner: more striking but less fluid, as tended to happen as the 1930s progressed.

The ideals of modern living lent themselves even more to blocks of flats, where to the precepts of simplicity could be added the other great chestnut of communal eating and recreation spaces. Few were prepared to finance such projects, but one of the best examples hides just down the hill from Hampstead, in Lawn Road. It was the idea of Jack and Molly Pritchard, who in 1932 formed the Isokon company to promote the minimum flat: a studio with a specially designed sofa-bed and fitted furniture, its own bathroom, dressing room and balcony, intended as a better alternative to lodgings. After a model 'minimum flat' had appeared in exhibitions, the Lawn Road flats were finally built in 1933–4, with Wells Coates as architect. Inhabitants included Gropius and Breuer, and later Agatha Christie.

118

105–23 St Mark's Road and Cowper Terrace, St Quintin Avenue
Kensington and Chelsea

1/E4   Underground to Ladbroke Grove

The 1970s produced much that was good in public housing. The ideal shifted from Lillington Gardens-style courtyards to tastefully unassuming terraces, many for housing associations, small in scale and dictated by inflation. Jeremy and Fenella Dixon were amongst the first to give the formula a style and identity by judicious borrowings from traditional London building.

Their two lines of gables at 105–23 St Mark's Road and Cowper Terrace derive from the humblest early 19th-century terrace, the touches of coloured glass from Soane through to the Edwardian town house. It is too easy to label the terraces, completed in 1979–80, post-modern classicism. They work because there is no purposeless pastiche: Victorian references there may be in the concrete gable copings and massive geometric gatepiers, but there are no gratuitous sashes or panelled doors. Instead the coloured panes march in Mondrian-like grids across the projecting porches. Boldest of all is the use of vivid colour, heralding another 1980s idiom, here a sequence of yellow, turquoise, blue and green.

Low-cost housing was the brief, for the Kensington Housing Trust. The cost factor may explain why some of the painted surfaces have decayed so rapidly. Ground-floor flats face the street, with above each a real house that pushes out to the back at an angle and thereby grabs the garden. There are thus four units per gable. Sandwiched into the corner between the two terraces, No. 105 St Mark's Road is a block of old-people's flats.

44 Britton Street. Corner view. AP

119

44 Britton Street
Finsbury, Islington

2/J3   Underground or British Rail to Farringdon

Janet Street-Porter was one of the most ebullient figures of the 1980s, proving that style bought with money could still be style if carried off with prominent front teeth and a strident accent. Of all TV personalities it seems most appropriate that she should have expressed herself by building a new house close to the City, especially since she had herself studied at the Architectural Association with Piers Gough.

The partnership of Campbell, Zogolovitch, Wilkinson and Gough personifies 1980s attitudes. Two are developers, only two are design architects. They aim to shock, yet build in brick and post-modern classicism is the source of all the jokes. Finished in 1989, Janet's house spices up the surrounding area of run-down offices and warehousing with tact as well as verve. Here we have four shades of brown brick, suggesting either the evolution of the house over decades or a loosely implied order, whilst the concrete log lintels pay tribute to the Abbé Laugier's theories on the origin of Doric. Seeing it nestling under its saddleback roof of blue pantiles one might agree with the *Architects' Journal*'s surmise that the joke must have failed since it got planning permission.

A set of prominent steel lattice grilles form the grid of the building, shaped to the front like one of the client's or architect's more outrageous pairs of spectacles. The bridge-piece is a projecting, fan-like balcony. The plot, and the ancient lights of an adjacent property that was then promptly demolished, suggested the plan. The sawn-off street corner and curved rear wall create a series of odd-shaped rooms rising from octagonal ground-floor billiard room to roof-top office, their tricksy furniture played off against bare concrete finishes. Most satisfying is the short side elevation, for its simplicity: just a round stairwell lit by glazed bricks.

9

Health and Welfare

Before the Reformation, charities concerned with health and welfare were managed under religious aegis; since 1948 their role has been taken by the State. In the intervening 400 years the sick and elderly survived as best they could, on a mixture of bequests, on subscription hospitals supported by community fund-raising and, *in extremis*, on the parish.

Into the vacuum left by monastic orders there stepped self-made merchants out to acquit their souls, livery companies, national institutions and prelates – of all of which London had an exceptional supply. Thomas Sutton's adaptation of real monastic buildings, such as the Charterhouse, was a particularly logical solution. Only in the 18th century, as advances in medicine made treatment a realistic concept, did the term 'hospital' arrive at its present and more limited curative meaning. Before then, almshouses for the elderly might just as easily be called hospitals or, equally confusingly, colleges. Not all such foundations were for the most destitute of the parish and our examples suggest a preference for the widows of the respectable.

With many professions thus rewarded for virtuous endeavour, there arose in the reign of Charles II the question of what to do as Britain's first professional servicemen reached their dotage. Thus to London's impressive collection of almshouses were added the two military hospitals at Chelsea and Greenwich, funded by the State, of unique size and architectural distinction but in concept no different from contemporaries like little Trinity Hospital in Mile End. At Chelsea Hospital communal living survives not just in the dining hall and chapel, but extends to uniforms and dormitories as well. Ex-sailors seem to have preferred a pension and their independence, for in 1869 Greenwich Hospital closed to become a training school instead.

Three hospitals in the modern sense survived the Reformation with the support of the City of London. Only one, St Bartholomew (p. 3), is in its original location, rebuilt to a design by James Gibbs between 1730 and 1759 that is an appropriately humble version of Palladianism. Bethlem Hospital went to Surrey in 1929, whilst St Thomas's moved upstream from London Bridge to Lambeth in the 1860s. The most fascinating survival of these institutions is not a true hospital building but an imaginative rooftop addition: the operating theatre of old St Thomas's Hospital, fitted into the attic of a church in 1821. All these were, or became, teaching hospitals, supported by fees and voluntary donations.

Because they were better funded and dealt with a narrower range of ages and ailments, military hospitals were often at the forefront of medical and architectural innovations. The pavilion plan hospital, with long narrow wards linked by a corridor, though based on an earlier French concept, was launched upon every parish thanks to its promotion by Florence Nightingale coinciding with increased public provision for the sick poor. Alongside Nightingale's involvement at the prestigious Herbert and St Thomas's Hospitals can be counted scores of new infirmaries, fever and smallpox hospitals built by parish unions and the Metropolitan Asylums Board under an 1867 Act that attempted belatedly to deal with the new scourges of London: cholera and typhoid. Until 1867 parish relief for the sick and elderly was confused with a minimum provision for all those incapable of supporting themselves, with the emphasis placed on deterring the indolent by making aid conditional on work. The system was originated in 1601, and though the workhouse only became universal in 1834, London boasted many earlier examples, of which a survivor is that in Manette Street, Westminster, built in 1770–1. The 1867 Act recognised that most claimants were genuinely in need of health and welfare, and thus were

Pensioners' Dormitory at the Royal Hospital, Chelsea, 1922. RCHME

149

built the hospitals that form the basis of London's provision today. St Charles's Hospital in North Kensington, built in 1881 to the design of the prolific hospital architect Saxon Snell, is perhaps the most alluring. Near the centre of London there grew also an assortment of specialist and teaching hospitals, many of them rebuilt around 1900. Architecturally, the most impressive is University College Hospital, where a small, square site suggested that the pavilions be arranged in a cruciform plan.

Always separate, in terms of both finance and planning tradition, was the treatment of the mentally ill. The term 'lunatic asylum' was banished from official usage only by Act of Parliament in 1930. Over the previous century, the justices of Middlesex and Surrey followed by the London County Council had ringed London with mammoth institutions holding up to 3,000 souls declared too 'melancholic' or 'manic' to cope with the pressures of urban life. For the incurably handicapped the Metropolitan Asylums Board erected even larger encampments still further out, and an old-people's hostel in Tooting Bec.

To the almshouse and hospital may be added, from the late 18th century, the charitable dispensary for the relief of those at home. The clinic followed from around 1900. The existence of so many separately underfunded institutions is difficult to contemplate now that they have been crudely amalgamated under the National Health Service. What to do with small dispersed units, a particularly acute problem in the poorer central areas, was briefly in the 1930s a local authority concern. Only Bermondsey and Finsbury tackled health care with any commitment. We include the Finsbury Health Centre as an example of a pre-war clinic that anticipated the era of the NHS in both its medical and architectural solutions. Medical knowledge and our expectations of health care have advanced far ahead of the disparate and makeshift building stock inherited in 1948, whose maintenance seems to come last in any budget. Are our expectations at fault, or is there some more fundamental question of policy?

120

The Charterhouse
Charterhouse Square, Finsbury, Islington

2/J2   Underground to Barbican

[B]   Summer Wednesdays and Sunday services

Charterhouse Square is a British muddle of buildings fringing an irregular green sward. Set back from its north side, a squat tower with a wooden cupola and an angled Tudor range betray the secret of one of London's most venerable architectural ensembles – Sutton's Hospital in Charterhouse.

The London Charterhouse has changed its spots almost as often as the Vicar of Bray. The Carthusians founded their extra-mural priory here in 1371, only to have it part torn down, part taken over and part rebuilt for his own house at the Reformation by Sir Edward North. The 4th Duke of Norfolk elaborated the new mansion just before he was beheaded in 1572. In the early 17th century Thomas Sutton converted the buildings into an almshouse, a

Sutton's Hospital in Charterhouse. The chapel tower from Charterhouse Square. THE MASTER OF SUTTON'S HOSPITAL

school and a joint chapel. Charterhouse School migrated to Surrey and was replaced by Merchant Taylors' School in mid-Victorian times. When the Merchant Taylors moved away in their turn between the world wars, St Bartholomew's Hospital took the eastern portion for its medical school, leaving the older buildings for charitable use. Then bombing gutted the complex. A sensitive reconstruction of the 1950s at the hands of architects Seely and Paget restored something of its ancient quaintness. Little of what is seen behind the fronts today is wholly authentic. The older portion now houses a mixture of pensioners' residences and discreet offices.

The entrance, through a gateway next to No. 17 in the square, is a picturesque jumble of late-medieval flint, ragstone, brick and timber with brick upper storeys of 1716 on top. Hence you either veer right towards the main group of ancient buildings, or pursue an unpromising-looking lane northwards, which opens out to reveal Preacher's and Pensioners' Courts. These, built in 1826–9 to the designs of Edward Blore and R W Pilkington, are London's prettiest instance of late Georgian institutional Tudor-Gothic, in a comfortable brown brick with drip moulds over the windows. Pensioners' Court is a closed quadrangle with a garden behind, Preacher's Court an open, irregular space formerly joined to the main ensemble; both are nicely planted out.

Back to the earlier ensemble of Master's Court, Wash House Court and Chapel. They are built in the Oxbridge collegiate mode, mainly out of ragstone. The date 1611 over the entrance to Master's Court refers just to the foundation of Sutton's school and 'hospital'. The oldest element and completest surviving portion of the monastery buildings is the sweet Wash House Court, formerly the lay brothers' quarters, all brick and chimneybreasts at one end, random stonework at the other. It was finished just before the monastery was dissolved. The larger Master's Court is early Elizabethan, started by Sir Edward North and continued by the Duke of Norfolk, who

fitted out the Great Hall. The hall screen and roof are more or less authentic, while the adjacent staircase represents Seely and Paget's best efforts to recreate the spirit of what was a magnificent Elizabethan interior before bombs gutted Master's Court. Behind it a closed-in arcade mixed up with remnants lead to the Chapel, which escaped the worst wartime devastation. Though its core is medieval, it belongs essentially to 1613–14, just after Sutton's death; Francis Carter, an officer in the royal works, was the 'Surveyor or Contriver' of the job, with Edmund Kinsman the mason under him. It consists of a flat-ceiled nave and north aisle separated by a handsome round-arched arcade, with extra seating in west galleries and in an early-Victorian transept to the north. The whole is white-painted and dark-panelled in austere Protestant taste. In a corner is a fine monument to Thomas Sutton by Nicholas Stone and Edmund Kinsman. Sunday Service at 9.45 am, one of the few times the public can see the Charterhouse, reveals a Trollopean scene, with a dozen or so old men – the pensioners – sitting remote from one another and the organ droning lugubriously from the loft.

121
Bromley College
London Rd, Bromley

1/J7 British Rail to Bromley North or South

[B] by appointment with the chaplain

Bromley, a paradigm now of the suburban town engulfed by London, was once the amenable seat of the Bishops of Rochester. From here John ('Willie') Warner, defiant Laudian and royalist, exercised his uncompromising episcopate between 1637 and 1666. Despite a reputation for parsimony, Warner was a wealthy prelate. Amongst his many charities, picturesque Bromley College, founded by the terms of his will in order to house 'twenty poore widdowes being the relicts of Orthodox and loyall Clergie-men', is the

Bromley College. Main entrance. GLRO

conspicuous memorial.

Quadrangular almshouses were nothing new in the late 17th century. What distinguishes Bromley College and its South London companion-piece, Morden College at Blackheath (established for 'decayed Turkey merchants' by Bromley's treasurer), is the scale of the foundations and their aspiration to the status of 'college'. Clergy widows and Turkey merchants were not the deserving poor. They were respectable middle-class folk who expected a certain level of accommodation and service in return for living in community. The former style of life at Bromley and Morden would have been much like the Oxbridge pattern, habits of study apart. A servant and a spinster daughter for each widow were the rule rather than the exception.

Architecturally, the original quadrangle of Bromley College is a trifle old-fashioned for its date of 1670–2. The front is set back from the noisy London Road behind a high wall, Georgian wrought-iron gate, stone piers with mitres on top instead of the usual pineapples, and a screen of trees. It has a deep, overhanging roof with heavy chimneys, old-style casement windows and projecting houses at the ends so that the chaplain and treasurer may supervise comings and goings. The buttresses and dormer windows are later additions to what must have been a plain enough frontispiece – excepting one fine

151

feature, the pedimented entrance to the quadrangle, enough to betray that Bromley College was not due to some unlettered provincial builder. Its 'Surveigher' (and therefore presumed designer), a certain Captain Richard Rider, was one of many shadowy figures in the world of mid-17th-century London building. But the mason Joshua Marshall, and the joiner, William Cleere, are better-known names; they were both much involved in rebuilding City churches, Marshall at St Paul's, the Monument and Temple Bar too. The entrance and the disciplined stone colonnade round the quadrangle surely reflect Marshall's taste and knowledge as much as Rider's. Yet the lean-to roof on top of his columns and the little windows behind give the quadrangle a rustic feeling.

Behind the quadrangle is the chapel – not the 1670s one, but an enlarged Victorian Gothic apsidal affair with encaustic tiling and crisp stained glass, supplied by Messrs Waring and Blake, architects, in 1862–4 to cope with the college's increased numbers. A second court had been added by Thomas Hardwick between 1792 and 1805, to designs unusually faithful to the spirit of the original for their date. Also in the college's grounds is the former Sheppard's College, a T-shaped Tudor-ish block built in the 1840s to house homeless clergy daughters. Retired parsons and their wives as well as their widows now profit from Bishop Warner's forethought, in greater comfort than of yore after a radical modernisation of the college in the 1970s.

122

Chelsea Royal Hospital
*Royal Hospital Rd,
Kensington and Chelsea*

2/D8   Underground to Sloane Square

[A]

Chelsea Hospital has none of the fireworks of its naval counterpart at Greenwich, but greater charm. It is still used for its original purpose as an almshouse for retired soldiers and has

Chelsea Royal Hospital. North and east sides of the courtyard. A F KERSTING

an air of monasticism tinged with the fraternity and tradition of a barracks. This is the home of the distinctive red-coated Chelsea Pensioners. Until the Commonwealth, England had no standing army and only under Charles II did the responsibility of providing for aged servicemen become a concern. The building of the Hôtel Royal des Invalides in Paris, 1670–6, prompted the English Crown to follow suit, first at Kilmainham in Dublin, begun in 1680, and a year later in London. The latter's promoter was Sir Stephen Fox, who had made a fortune as Paymaster-General of the army and who, in addition to personal donations, formed a fund for the building out of deductions from army pay. Christopher Wren suggested the Chelsea site, an unwanted gift to the Royal Society of which he was then President. Wren also supplied designs for the buildings, completed in phases between 1689 and 1691.

The hospital has been maligned as a simple and occasionally clumsy work, for at the age of 50 Wren was still maturing as an architect. Yet it is the severity and height of its facades that are most telling, to which the arcade across the centre block of the main three-sided courtyard – facing the river – contrasts a massive gentleness reminiscent of a cloister. The materials too, brown brick with red brick dressings apart from the Portland stone porticoes and arcade, are those of humble domestic architecture as well as Wren's City churches. The centre block contains the dining hall and chapel, linked by an octagonal vestibule the full height of the building

that is distinguished by a giant portico to back and front and a central lantern. The south-facing portico with free-standing Doric columns particularly impresses for its huge, assertive scale. A more awkward but picturesque contrast is the lantern, set with columns at the angles and a neo-baroque foretaste of Wren's later church towers. Last to be finished were the lower side courts that set off the main block so well.

The chapel is City church architecture writ dramatically large and light, the closest comparison being the free-standing St James's, Piccadilly. The benches are now set sideways in collegiate fashion, with choirstalls authentically by Grinling Gibbons. Their intricacy, however, is overshadowed by the huge barrel vault and a Resurrection, added by Sebastiano Ricci for Queen Anne. The dining room has a spartan nature, afforded no relief by a pedantic allegory to Charles II by Verrio. The atmosphere of a barracks is strengthened by the list of battles on the wall panelling – with half a wall still empty in the distressing anticipation of future conflicts. The wings each contain three floors of wards, every pensioner given, then as now, a tiny oak-walled cubicle, with more wards in the dormered attic storeys. The end pavilions contain residences for officials, the governor getting the most lavish woodcarving.

In 1783 Wren's casement windows were resashed under the stewardship of Robert Adam, and John Soane, a later Clerk of Works to the Hospital, also made alterations. In 1810 Soane was asked to make additions. His infirmary was bombed in 1941, but his stables and official residence of 1814 survive. They show an austere grace which Wren at his simplest could not match for refinement.

123
Royal Naval College (formerly Hospital)
King William's Walk, Greenwich

1/H5   British Rail to Greenwich or Maze Hill

[A]

The rise and fall of English baroque architecture may be charted in this one building. For the rise, it is best to view the work from the riverside walk or Island Gardens on the opposite bank. Charles II began rebuilding Greenwich Palace, formerly on this site, in 1664 with John Webb, the pupil and nephew of Inigo Jones, as his architect. Webb completed only one wing, which can be identified because it has the only pediments that were ever sculpted, topped with crowns on flat brackets. This block, called the King Charles Block and one of Webb's few surviving works, has a massiveness in its full-height rustication and giant columns totally alien to Jones.

As William and Mary preferred the healthier air of Hampton Court, Wren was called in to provide a naval hospital that was to be a grander version of Chelsea. In 1699 Wren revised his design to produce essentially the present plan: the Queen's House was no longer to be blocked by a big new centrepiece but was itself to be the tiny centre – framed by two pairs of blocks, the rear pair stepped forward, given domes and linked by colonnades. The colonnades and domed towers have the paired columns and measured spatial rhythm of St Paul's Cathedral. The controversial part is that which confronts you when you enter the complex. The King William Block, hidden behind King Charles's from the river, seems to be by another hand: instead of Wren's even pairings,

aedicules and voussoirs crash together and, especially on the east front behind the colonnade, columns and pilasters writhe for space where they need not even be. Since the block was erected in 1701–2, before Vanbrugh became involved, the designer was probably Wren's assistant, Nicholas Hawksmoor. This is as baroque as English architecture got. In 1718 Wren was deposed as Surveyor-General and the Queen Mary Block was completed by Thomas Ripley in a dull Palladian manner and, a service court by Hawksmoor apart, the rest merely copies Webb.

There are two major interiors: one baroque, one classical. The painted hall is a magnificent sequence of three unfolding spaces, soon deemed too good for the sailors who were banished to a sub-basement below. The wall and ceiling paintings, done in two phases, in 1708–12 and 1718–28 by James Thornhill, evolve naturally through the sequence, commencing with lists of benefactors in the vestibule, through William and Mary enshrined on the main ceiling – with William's foot firmly planted on the back of a miserably

jaundiced Louis XIV – to an undistinguished George I at the top of the upper hall, upstaged by Thornhill's self-portrait in the foreground. The main hall is remarkable for its *trompe l'oeil* fluted columns and sheer bravado of space but in the darker upper hall you can get right up to the paint and feel enveloped by it. Thornhill blocked all the windows on the north side of the hall with more paintings: these were removed in 1824, and now only one on the south side of the upper hall hints at their effect.

The chapel lacks the scale of the painted hall; it is shorter and has an enclosed dome. The original scheme by Ripley, completed in 1752, was destroyed by fire in 1779. The renewed interior by James Stuart or his clerk of works William Newton, completed in 1789, is lavishly neo-Grecian, frosty in feeling despite its rich patterning, gilding and the surviving Corinthian columns from Ripley's scheme.

The hospital closed in 1869, so there are no Greenwich pensioners to add life to the architecture as at Chelsea. Instead, in 1873, it became a military training college.

Greenwich Royal Naval College. River front. J ALLAN CASH LTD

153

124

Trinity Hospital
Mile End Rd, Tower Hamlets

1/H4   Underground to Whitechapel

Tucked safely away behind a wall in a raw sector of the East End, Trinity Hospital has the distinction of a special niche in conservation history to vie with its intrinsic prettiness and placidity. It was built in 1694–7 with money provided by Captains Richard Maples and Henry Mudd for aged sea-captains, river pilots and their widows. The powerful Trinity House, which controlled navigation around the shores of Britain, already had almshouses at Deptford. Mudd, the prime mover, must have felt that seafaring families north of the river deserved their own refuge. Hence the simple group at Mile End, originally twenty-eight little dwellings in two rows facing one another at a slight angle, each with a basement kitchen and a living room above. At the back is a tiny cupolaed chapel, broader than long at first. William Ogbourne, a master carpenter, built and probably also designed the group. Samuel Wyatt added an extra court at the back, destroyed by enemy action in the Second World War.

The almshouses enjoyed an uneventful history, despite the encroachment of working-class housing all around, until 1895, when the Trinity House Corporation proposed demolishing the place. Its timing was bad. There had been growing sentiment among the young social reformers of Toynbee Hall in Whitechapel over the East End's loss of cultural amenity and identity. C R Ashbee, who was running his high-minded Guild of Handicraft from a house near Trinity Hospital, was the leader of this movement. He had just set up a 'Watch Committee' of vigilantes to look out for buildings in danger and hoped to publish a register of everything in London of historic and architectural interest. Here was a godsend for his cause. Ashbee got up an influential protest and forced the Trinity Corporation to back down. He then published *The Trinity Hospital in Mile End: An Object Lesson in National History* (1896). This was the forerunner of the series eventually to become *The Survey of London*, which continues to this day. So not only was the Trinity Hospital saga an early conservation victory; it also marked a start to the systematic documentation of London's buildings.

Ashbee himself was hardly interested in the precise architectural history of the almshouses (on no better basis than personal hunch he misattributes their design to the joint hand of John Evelyn and Christopher Wren). What concerned him more was their contribution to the social fabric of the East End. He saw in them a survival of medieval physical arrangements and patterns of community, not just providers of bed, bread and dole. So his monograph includes sketches of top-hatted pensioners playing chess and draughts as a reminder of the spirit of charity, the loss of which Ashbee regretted in his own day. Most graphic of his illustrations is a plate showing 'Trinity Ground' hemmed in on all sides by the smoky, artisan housing of the *laissez-faire* culture he so despised. That housing has gone now, and the general disappearance of its scale and type from the East End is in its turn regretted. Trinity Hospital, heavily restored after bomb damage, is surrounded instead by post-war council housing, including a slab block very palpable behind the chapel. Have we made any progress?

125

The Old Operating Theatre
St Thomas's St, Southwark

2/K5   Underground or British Rail to London Bridge

[A]

Straight off a noisy Southwark pavement, you step into a church porch and embark upon a tight, winding staircase which ought just to lead to a belfry. Parting with a pound in a boxy ante-chamber, you climb a little further. Suddenly you stumble into a roof landscape, the apparatus of which is not ecclesiastical at all but bizarrely medical. Amidst the purlins and principals of the church roof, a cosy attic museum explains the early history of Guy's and St Thomas's Hospitals. But behind the tower lurks something altogether stranger, like a film set: a complete, top-lit operating theatre of 1821, equipped with railed tiers for student onlookers, a stark slab for the victim in the middle, and a Latin tag, 'Miseratione non Mercede' ('for pity not profit'), on the back wall.

Trinity Hospital in 1895. From C R Ashbee's monograph of 1897. GLRO

The Old Operating Theatre, St Thomas's Street. GUY'S HOSPITAL

What is it doing in this limbo? The answer lies in the tangled history of St Thomas's Hospital. An ancient monastic foundation to the east of Borough High Street, it was reconstructed in a neat series of courts over a twenty-year period from the 1680s. One of these abutted south upon St Thomas's Church, which did double service as parish church and hospital chapel. St Thomas's was rebuilt in plain brick style in 1702–3. The best part of it is the north elevation, visible from a yard behind London Bridge Street and the only surviving fragment of the hospital quadrangles. The court nearest the High Street disappeared in the 1830s because of the widening of the approaches to London Bridge, when modern wards in Portland stone replaced it. Then in 1862 the whole hospital was displaced to Lambeth by the slamming-through of the railway line from Waterloo to London Bridge. Most of the older buildings were demolished, but the more southerly new ward block (of 1842–4) survived, along with the church in St Thomas's Street and the women's operating theatre, tucked in behind the church tower at the level of the former Dorcas Ward in the second court behind, from which it was reached. When the quadrangle disappeared, that access was just bricked up. The room remained unused for almost exactly a century, until it was rediscovered in 1957.

It would be pleasant to pretend that the theatre remained equipped and in aspic during those hundred years. In truth, the place had been stripped so bare that most of what one sees apart from the walls, the giddy circumference of raised 'standings' included, is a

scholarly recreation of the 1960s based upon archaeological clues and a full inventory. So the sensation of a film set, of an outlier from Madame Tussaud's or the London Dungeon, is not accidental, nor lessened by the chilling talk given by guides from the operating table. Yet to know that in this raw space the surgeon's knife was wielded upon the poor (and only the poor – the rich had operations at home) keeps one's sense of make-believe at bay. The English hospital before Lister and Nightingale was more than a quaint and charitable institution; it was a place, as the poet Henley puts it, 'of wrath and tears', as terrible in its particular way as any prison or workhouse.

126

Friern Barnet Hospital
Friern Barnet Rd, Barnet

1/F2   Underground to Arnos Grove, or British Rail to New Southgate

The Second Middlesex County Pauper Lunatic Asylum, better known as the Colney Hatch Asylum, is not a building for the faint-hearted. The menacing grandeur of its massive Italianate facade

with its water towers and central dome reflects the minutely ordered institution it contained. The extensive grounds with their mature trees provide a *cordon sanitaire* that locks Colney Hatch into its own world. London is ringed by a score of such institutions built by the Middlesex, Surrey and London County Councils for those who through poverty and illness could not survive the pressures of urban life.

Lunatic hospitals, later called asylums, originated in London with that of the order of St Mary of Bethlehem founded in the 14th century – Bethlem or Bedlam, the second rebuilding of which, dating from 1815, survives in part as the Imperial War Museum. But there was no public provision for the insane in London until an Act of 1828 compelled Middlesex to build an asylum, erected at Hanwell in 1828–9. Its architect, William Alderson, died an inmate there in 1835.

Hanwell, now St Bernard's Hospital, rapidly became overcrowded, its 2,000 inmates a remarkable concentration of people at a time when only the armed forces had experience of organising such numbers. Most asylums still controlled unruly patients with chains, armlocks and patent mechanical devices such as rotating swings, although these had all been abolished at Lincoln Asylum in

Friern Barnet Hospital. The entrance front. EH

1838. In 1839 Hanwell acquired a pioneering new superintendent, John Conolly, who immediately abolished all forms of mechanical restraint there. In its place, he imposed a rigid system of classification by complaint, with a curative regime based on good food, healthy exercise and hard manual work; padded cells were provided for those having fits. His *Construction and Government of Lunatic Asylums*, published in 1847, established Conolly as the world authority on asylum planning. His ideas were expounded further in the Second Middlesex asylum.

Colney Hatch was built with extraordinary lavishness by Samuel Daukes in 1848–51. Men and women were separated in two wings divided by a central block containing offices, a ground- and first-floor chapel (mostly gone), a huge exercise hall, kitchens and laundry. Internally the most impressive features are two long corridors along the front of the building, lined with fire resistant tiles and together a third of a mile long. Off it, on two or three floors, were wards for different categories of patients: acute (curable), incurable or violent, each with their own recreation yard.

Within five years this model asylum was declared structurally unsound and its design out of date. Yet in 1857–9 it was nearly doubled in size by Lewis Cubitt, who added a second line of wards to the rear, and it was extended again in 1896 and 1908–13. As a community it was almost self-sufficient, with its own laundry, bakehouse and workshops where the patients worked, and its own recreation hall with stage facilities. Water was supplied from an underground reservoir, marked by a tower in the form of a garden shelter.

Since 1930 there have been successive attempts to deinstit-utionalise Britain's Victorian asylums by changing all their names, demolishing enclosing walls, and abandoning the idea of hard work as a cure. The grandeur and grimness of hospitals such as Friern Barnet cause concern, but recent experience in putting the severely ill back into the 'community' suggests there is still a place for the 'asylum' in its strictest sense, as a refuge.

University College Hospital from Gower Street. GLRO

127

University College Hospital
Gower Street, Camden

2/F2   Underground to Euston or Euston Square, also British Rail

When University College was founded in 1826 as a non-denominational alternative to Oxford and Cambridge, the provision of medical training was an important aim. Two years later a small dispensary was founded in Gower Street. This rapidly proving inadequate, a public subscription was raised to build a hospital, begun in 1833 to the design of Alfred Ainger. First known as the North London Hospital, in 1837 it was renamed University College Hospital following the reconstitution of the college the previous year. Extensions were added piecemeal, but by 1895 it was realised that a new and far larger hospital was required. The governors chose Alfred Waterhouse as their architect.

Since the building of the Herbert Hospital on Shooter's Hill, Woolwich, in 1861–5 with the determined backing of Florence Nightingale, hospitals erected on new sites had almost universally adopted the pavilion plan. The pavilion hospital had an English precedent, the

naval hospital built at Stonehouse, Plymouth, in 1762, but its evolution was essentially French, via Bordeaux (1821–9), Beaujon (1837–44) and the Lariboisière in Paris (1846–54). Old St Thomas's, demolished in 1862 when the railway was extended to Charing Cross, had had pavilion wards added to it in 1842–4. Long, narrow and linked together only by a corridor or open arcade, they were considered the last word in segregation and cross-ventilation, crucial at a time when 'miasma' or foul air was thought to be the cause of most disease. Nurses like Nightingale admired them too because they were easy to supervise, each being the clearly defined domain of a sister. The plan's status was confirmed with its adoption for the rebuilding of St Thomas's on a prominent South Bank site in 1868–71. It offered a timely model for the London Poor Law authorities who had been authorised to build hospitals in 1867. Hospitals such as the Brook, built by the Metropolitan Asylums Board next door to the Herbert Hospital in 1895, show how little the formula was changed in thirty years.

But at University College Hospital, Waterhouse was faced with a tight, square site. The hospital Secretary, Newton H Dixon, and a staff physician, Dr G V Poore, suggested that pavilions be adapted as four radial wings reached via spurs from a central circulation core. Their initiative is a measure of the profession's preference for the pavilion plan even after the discovery of bacterial infection in 1867 had dismissed many theories of miasma.

Nevertheless, University College Hospital, built from 1897 to 1905, is unmistakably a work by Waterhouse. The hard, red Lancashire bricks and terracotta dressings are wholly characteristic, as are the tourelles topping the end of each wing. When it was officially opened in 1906, it was criticised for being so out of keeping with its classical surroundings – the very quality that gives the building so much character today – though the planning and airiness of the wards were much admired. Perhaps the Waterhouse idiom was realised to be out-of-date stylistically even as the building was completed. Waterhouse himself died in 1905 and the adjacent and more classically compromised Medical School built that year was wholly the work of his son, Paul.

128

Finsbury Health Centre
Pine St, Finsbury, Islington

2/H2   Underground to Angel or Farringdon; or British Rail to Farringdon

Whilst for parts of London the 1920s and 1930s were a boom period of growth and consumption, in many inner boroughs conditions were no better than in Victorian times and in dockland areas often worse. In 1934 it was shown that about one in eight of London's working class was still living below the level of poverty defined by Charles Booth in the 1880s.

Poverty meant not only poor housing, but bad nutrition and poor health. In the 1930s progress was made into the causes and prevention of disease, into radium, insulin and cures for tuberculosis. But until the formation of the National Health Service in 1948 the only public clinics were provided by a few philanthropists, and socialist boroughs which defied the national government's commitment to economic stringencies. The relics of this municipal interest in health are a clutch of swimming pools and open air lidos, and a few health centres. In Peckham a subscription clinic for better working-class families led to the building of the Pioneer Health Centre by Owen Williams in 1935, and the Borough of Bermondsey opened a solarium for the treatment of ricketts and TB, followed by a health centre in 1936. But the finest monument to nascent clinical provision in Britain is the Finsbury Health Centre, built by Lubetkin and Tecton, conceived in 1935–6 and opened in 1938.

Finsbury was one of the most overcrowded boroughs in London. It is hard today to imagine the health centre in its original setting of tiny terraced streets, since all have been replaced by new blocks and a public park. It was intended as the centrepiece of the 'Finsbury Plan' proposed for the borough's redevelopment by Alderman Harold Riley. When in 1932 Berthold Lubetkin had formed his Tecton group of young Architectural Association graduates, he had tested their skills in rational planning with a project for a TB clinic. Dr Katial, Chairman of the Finsbury Public Health Committee, saw this scheme as a basis for the new health centre which was to centralise and improve facilities that had evolved piecemeal in the borough. Provision had to be made for doctors' and dentists' surgeries; maternity, chiropodist's, X-ray and TB clinics; a solarium, disinfection rooms and a mortuary.

These facilities were planned around the communal spaces placed at its centre, such as the reception and waiting area, staircases and a first-floor lecture hall. The principal space is the waiting area, stretching the width of the convex front and given a subtle diffused light by a wall of glazed bricks. It is controlled by the reception desk right opposite the door and backed by a concave screen originally decorated with a map depicting Finsbury as the heart of London. Alongside, Gordon Cullen designed another mural, that impelled everyone to 'live out of doors as much as you can.' This ideal is born out by the roof terrace above, behind which floats the domed roof of the lecture hall. The noisome facilities for delousing were placed in the basement, with a separate rear access. This central block, with its *pilotis* and expressed roof anticipates the form of the Royal Festival Hall a decade later.

The clinics and offices were placed in wings, angled to admit the maximum amount of daylight, with corridors tapered on the assumption that there would be less traffic towards their ends. The offices and clinics were given movable partition walls and ducting was placed behind panels on the exterior to maximise flexibility. Because of the dirty atmosphere the supporting concrete end walls were tiled, and the sides were clad with tiles and thermolux panels. By contrast to the boldly articulated centrepiece the wings are flat planes.

The success of the health centre has been its flexibility, for it is still heavily used. It has survived, too, without proper maintenance: tiles have fallen, windows and timberwork rotted and steel reinforcements have been exposed. It has also been swamped by the trees planted round it. Yet the bold front, described as a 'megaphone for health', still expresses the visionary commitment with which it was founded.

Finsbury Health Centre when new. AP

10

Schools and Colleges

Perhaps no English buildings have gone through such frequent shifts in form as those devoted to education. That is because people can never agree what teaching and learning are about. London plays a special role in that pattern of diversity. The wealth of the capital, its size, its concentration and its symbolism have made it central to most trends in national education, especially vocational and technical training. On the other hand its great university arrived late and has grown in a piecemeal, disconnected way, frustrating from the physical and institutional standpoints alike. Shortage of space, too – space increasingly valued for health, recreation and the broader development of the individual as well as for mere expansion of facilities – has cramped the planning of London's schools and colleges. Most of the schools we describe are to be found on more or less suburban sites, where ampler space allows freer rein to modern ideas about education.

When we think of early English education we think first of Gothic courts or quadrangles, in other words of the Oxbridge ideal, much revived in the 19th century. Those courts and quads reflect old patterns not so much of education as of communal living. They are better preserved in the capital's palaces (pp. 53–69) and almshouses (pp. 149– 54) than in its schools and colleges. Yet the image does stand for one enduring strand in educational thought: that teaching, learning and living should be indissoluble. In ancient form, that ideal lives on in the still-functioning Inns of Court, the Inner and Middle Temples (p. 170), Lincoln's Inn and Gray's Inn, where barristers learn their trade, dine and work together in conditions that go back to the medieval need to teach literacy to lawyers.

'Public schools' like Westminster and Harrow have come over the centuries to embody another version of the teaching-and-living philosophy, by plucking children from their homes and housing them in or near the place where they are taught. Westminster School, created out of the spiritual and physical wreck of the Abbey's monastic buildings, is a graphic example both of continuity and of what architects call 'loose fit' – in other words, education's ability to make use of any old premises added to in any old way. Ashburnham House is just a fine old building comfortably adapted for school use; Lord Burlington's dormitory may be magnificent, but it was never convenient. By contrast at Harrow, where the school's thrust to social status came in the 19th century, living is represented by C F Hayward's big, purpose-built houses respectfully ranged around a grander core of teaching and institutional buildings (a chapel, library, speech hall, etc.).

Another way of solving the teaching-and-living riddle is represented by Crosby Hall. Citizens cannot often live where they work or learn. Universities and colleges, coping with people halfway to maturity, must always find some of them places to live. 'Halls of residence' are too often isolated, sterile dormitory blocks. Patrick Geddes's response was to rescue a great medieval hall to put next to his bedsitters, in the hope of stimulating some sense of community. Our final example of the theme is little-known Whitelands College. Here the combination of a teacher-training college with a lively communal life, a forthright principal, urban pressures and the need to protect and nurture young women, led in the 1920s to a single massive building which was a landmark in the development of women's educational architecture.

There is another side to the coin. Learning requires discipline and concentration, as pre-Victorian pedagogues were not afraid to stress. The harsh atmosphere of Harrow's Jacobean schoolroom conveys an educational reality impervious to any amount of styling. At mid-Victorian Dulwich, Harrow and in most church-supported schools of the era, this naked reality is given a becoming Gothic dress.

Coming out of assembly, Westminster School. CL

159

Then after 1870 came the slow dawning of educational liberalism and with it the Queen Anne style – a symbol in schools of freedom from church control. The Butler Museum and Music School at Harrow show it at its lavish best. But its testing ground was the elementary school of the London School Board, national flagship of the grand movement for universal, secular education. In early board schools, by no means free from Gothic influence, the lively elevations hide fairly primitive arrangements for teaching. As time goes on the fronts become more assertive, while the schools get extra facilities and more elaborate plans. Early or late, formidable or charming, their striking image and high-walled playgrounds were meant to cut them off from their environs and make them seem secular churches, oases of civilisation within the urban desert. Teachers could be trusted to impart the right values, whereas working-class parents could not. So teaching and living were kept apart.

Not until after the Second World War is any trust generated between state schools and the community. There follows a loosening-up of school planning and architecture in London. The 1945–65 period is the true moment of 'sweetness and light' in English school architecture, though due to restrictions on cost, the light is often more apparent than the sweetness. Much educational and architectural ferment takes place at this time. Schools open out into their grounds and the walls around them come down. Some are gather up into a few great blocks, others dissolve into inchoate units. In primary schools, classrooms fuse with corridors; in secondary ones, social and technical facilities are added. To illustrate this, we choose two schools at opposite ends of the scale: one a primary school in a corner of Greater London that formerly belonged to Hertfordshire, and therefore fell within the famous Hertfordshire school-building programme; the other, one of the London County Council's vast comprehensive schools of the 1950s. Little Oakland shows that experiment in the architecture of education does not always go hand in hand with imposing

elevations. The shocking slab of Tulse Hill is a reminder that fine external architecture and right educational arrangement are not the same thing.

We could have called this section 'Academic'. That would have suggested a selection of university buildings; but most of the University of London – University College, King's College and the academic buildings of Bloomsbury and South Kensington – are an architectural disappointment. The best of the Bloomsbury buildings are Holden's over-bearing Senate House and the School of Hygiene and Tropical Medicine nearby, by Percy Morley Horder and Verner O Rees (1926–8). The University of London has failed to create a coherent architectural tradition; nor have its successors within the London region done better. For good buildings devoted to higher education, one must seek out piecemeal the modest technical institutes, polytechnics and 'monotechnics' founded to promote and improve training for Londoners. Mountford's Northampton Institute in St John's Street, Clerkenwell (1896), now the headquarters of the City University, is one; the LCC's joint building for the Central School of Arts and Crafts and the London Day Training College in Southampton Row, Holborn

(1907), another; Goodhart-Rendel's additions for a cookery school to Westminster College, Vincent Square (1952–3) a third. The LCC's Edwardian architects in particular created a range of fine monotechnics to service the once-flourishing industries of London, from the Bolt Court School of Photo-Engraving and Lithography just off Fleet Street, to the Poplar School of Navigation, still existing but bereft of its original function in deepest Docklands.

129

Harrow School
High St, Harrow on the Hill

1/D3   Underground to Harrow on the Hill

[B]   Wednesday afternoons and school holidays

Ten miles north-west of Charing Cross, Harrow Church's spire protrudes from the trees atop Harrow Hill, a far-descried haven amid suburban infinity. A select haven, too; for the hilltop is host to Harrow School, the most varied and attractive of British 'public schools'.

Harrow's buildings are not drably collegiate or quadrangular. Instead, they are dotted about the hillside and on

Harrow School. Old Speech Room. RCHME

either side of the busy road that threads through it. Five cluster together to form the school's distinctive centre; Speech Room, Memorial Hall, the chapel and library, all by the roadside, and, a level above them, the Old Schools, angled insouciantly away from the library but joined to the group by an elaboration of steps and balustrades.

The Old Schools have a commanding pair of crow-stepped gables, a three-part Gothick porch and a cupola on top. The building looks like an early Jacobean revival job, and most of it is, of 1820 by C R Cockerell. But the left-hand wing is genuine Jacobean work of 1615 (as the brickwork on its flank reveals) and a token of the days when Harrow was a proper local grammar school. It houses the Old Schoolroom, unaltered since the mid-19th century and surely the most extraordinary relic of British educational history. At the end there is the master's throne, before which hard rows of forms run lengthwise. The atmosphere is bare, merciless yet deeply affecting; in those days education was not meant to be 'child-centred'. The famous and obscure who have carved (or caused to be carved) their names on the panelling in the schoolroom are legion; every inch is covered. In the answering wing is a little museum-cum-gallery.

Below, the chapel and the Vaughan Library sit in un-Harrovian formality on the flat and at right-angles to one another. They are by Sir Gilbert Scott in his prickly mode, and make a study in levels of Victorian-Gothic decorum. The library (1861–3) is in red brick, with diapering on the walls and roof. The earlier chapel (1855–6), end-on to the road and apsidal, achieves the added dignity of flint walling, richer stone dressings, an unusually ornamental *flèche* and an alternation of plain and scalloped tiles on the roof.

Opposite and a little to the north lies the Speech Room, for which the school deserted Scott and applied to the bouncier William Burges. The bludgeoning Gothic front is unexceptional, in part because of its long building-history (main facade 1874–7, towers added in 1919 and 1925). Inside, Burges comes into his eclectic own with a Greek hemi-cycle plan

Harrow School. General view, left to right: Old Schools, Memorial Hall, Speech Room and Chapel. EH

tucked tightly into the slope. There is a wonderful wooden roof, flat-ceiled in the centre, vaulted round the edges behind a ring of cast-iron columns. The decoration is mostly post-Burgesian. Between the 'Speecher' and the Old Schools is Herbert Baker's Memorial Hall (1926), the architectural *clou* of the group. Its conservative mixture of Tudor-style brick, flint and stonework, pull the four other arbitrary buildings together perfectly. Here, Baker's self-conscious contextualism is vindicated. A short war memorial cloister is hollowed out of the south end and linked to the steps above.

Away from here, the school buildings dissolve into individual statements, blending southwards into the old Harrow village. The one series that stands out is the set of fierce brick Gothic boarding houses of the 1860s and 1870s designed in a Scott-ish style by C F Hayward. The best lie along Peterborough Road and Grove Hill, north of the central cluster. But for Harrow's finest architecture you must go downhill just beyond the Speech Room, into Football Lane. Here the Biology Schools occupy the former Butler Museum, a kind of enriched and refined London board school designed by Basil Champneys, always an elegant architect, in 1886. The towering, hillside

front with its two high-placed oriels is specially dramatic. Below this, half-hidden by hedges, is Edward Prior's equally noble Music School of 1891. Its refined treatment of red brick and white sash windows foreshadows the best Edwardian architecture. The strongest elevation, a great three-sided apse, again faces down the hill.

130

Westminster School
Little Dean's Yard, Westminster

2/G6   Underground to Westminster or St James's Park

[B]   College Garden open Thursdays, seasonal hours

Go through the arch beneath Broad Sanctuary, Sir Gilbert Scott's Victorian-Gothic range next to the west end of the Abbey, and you come into Dean's Yard, a quiet square with a pleasant assortment of churchy buildings around it. Most arresting of these is Church House at the back, Sir Herbert Baker's headquarters for the inter-war Church of England (1936–40). It is a highly self-conscious piece of contextual architecture, mixing flint, brick and the odd symbolic fragment of ancient stonework. Over the arch in the corner leading out to Great College Street is the chapel.

Turn left by way of a little opening in the east range of Dean's Yard, through a short but ancient rib-vaulted passage, and you come into a smaller Chinese box, Little Dean's Yard, quaint and irregular, with a magnificent plane tree in one corner and the Victoria Tower of the Palace of Westminster beckoning powerfully behind. This is the core of Westminster School, one of London's semi-secret delights.

On the right are various school houses, Georgian-looking but with a complex building-history. The farther fronts are of 1789–90, by R W F Brettingham; the nearer one of 1897 we owe to T G Jackson in neo-Georgian mood. The back of the yard is a curious muddle. Just off-centre is a free-standing Palladian gateway of 1734, leading up to the school hall and hacked about in vandalistic public-school manner with inscriptions cut by 'Old Westminsters'. To its right, unimpressive from this side, is the

bricky, much-restored end of the former Dormitory of the Queen's Scholars. To grasp its size and quality you must choose a Thursday, penetrate the murkier passages behind the Westminster Abbey cloisters and emerge into the College Garden. The dormitory was first planned in Wren's office, but eventually built in 1722–30 to Lord Burlington's designs. A fine, plain, fifteen-bay stone statement of early Palladian principle, it would make more architectural sense if the ground floor were still the open arcade it was until 1846. Amazingly, there was above the arcade originally just one lofty and chilly storey for the scholars to sleep in, lit by the small upper windows; the first-floor openings were blank niches, fenestrated in 1895. There is nothing now worth seeing inside, the dormitory like the rest of the school having been sorely bombed in 1941.

One fine interior is, however, worth making the effort to see. That belongs to Ashburnham House, the unpromising U-shaped house on the Abbey side of Little Dean's Yard. Like other buildings round the yard it incorporates medieval foundations and fragments, here of the former prior's house. But the core of the present buildings belongs to about 1662–5, when the King's Cofferer, William Ashburnham, took a lease and carved out for himself a north-facing entrance, spectacular stair and series of first-floor rooms. For some years in the 18th century it sheltered the King's Library, and the school acquired it only in 1882–3.

Ashburnham's architect is traditionally said to have been Inigo Jones's former assistant John Webb, though John Harris has lately proposed that the building is nearer to the style of William Samwell. Pedants may continue to enjoy arguing about this while the visitor enjoys the architecture – a magnificent, virtually unaltered staircase leading to a series of more ambiguous first-floor apartments. The style, ponderous but succulent, is midway between that of Jones and that of Wren. The staircase begins outside the main compartment, then turns elaborately by means of broad steps and a bulbous, wide-spaced balustrade into a

Westminster School. Dome over staircase, Ashburnham House. RCHME

panelled rectangle lined with an Ionic order and crowned by an open, oval drum whose balustrade carries thin triplets of columns supporting a little lantern. The detail has that earnestness of intent and vigour of execution that English 17th century classicism still possesses, 18th century classicism usually lacks. Of the first-floor rooms the largest is the south-facing drawing room, once crowned by another dome before an extra storey was added above. The fireplaces here and elsewhere are not original.

131

Dulwich College
Dulwich Common, Southwark

1/G6   British Rail to West Dulwich

Dulwich College. Central block. GLRO

Dulwich is an estate village, an oasis of greensward and rigid conservation policy in suburban South London. The estate was purchased in 1605 by Edward Alleyn, actor, impressario and brothel-keeper, to endow Alleyn's College of God's Gift – a school and almshouses for the poor of Bankside. His original foundation is the little three-sided block next to the Picture Gallery, mauled by successive restorers, with almshouses and chapel in one half and boarding house and schoolroom in the other. Opposite Sir Charles Barry added a grammar school in 1841, equally tiny.

Suddenly, in the mid-19th century, the charity found itself immensely wealthy as London expanded in its direction. Renowned as a 'hot bed of speculation', it received a windfall of £100,000 in compensation for three railway lines cut through the estate. This prompted an investigation by the Charity Commissioners, and in 1857 the foundation was reconstituted. In 1866–70 a new day school was built for middle-class gentlesons, a school of unusual size.

The architect was Charles Barry junior, who succeeded his father as estate surveyor. His experience with Sir Charles at the Palace of Westminster and the fruits of extensive travels in

northern Italy show throughout the building, if imperfectly assimilated. The exterior comprises three blocks that would be symmetrical if one wing did not have a campanile and the other a squat Italianate tower. The north and south wings housed the lower and upper schools respectively. The pleasure and exuberance of the building lie in its materials, red brick contrasted with buff and pale blue terracotta supplied by Blashfields, with whom Barry had worked in Kensington Palace Gardens. So extensive a use of terracotta, still a costly and experimental material, was rare in the 1860s. Barry seems to have got the idea from the Charterhouse at Pavia. Stripy chimneystacks and iron crestings were removed in the 1960s, and the connecting cloisters have been glazed; but there remains a superabundance of decoration, much criticised by purists at the time. Best of all are a line of rather jaunty terracotta heads, at odds with the Venetian fenestration above and below, ranging from Aristotle and Plato (both twice) through Shakespeare to the Muses.

The principal rooms are on the front floor of the main block. The centrepiece

is the Great Hall, modelled on the double hammerbeam roof of Westminster Hall, with a waggon roof copied from San Fermo Maggiore in Verona placed on top for good measure. A central lantern owes something to Barry senior's Birmingham Grammar School as well as to his Palace of Westminster. Otherwise the interior lacks the frivolity of the exterior and is in need of restoration: the arabesque decoration on the ceilings has gone and the honours boards on the walls have been papered over. Better preserved is the Masters' Library, which retains its bookcases and a fireplace formed from panels of *Piety* and *Liberality* supposedly acquired by Alleyn from Elizabeth I's state barge. The composition is balanced by the board room on the other side of the Great Hall. The ground floor contains memorials to two old boys: the new P G Wodehouse Library and, in a cloister, Ernest Shackleton's whaler the *James Caird*, unbelievably small to have survived Cape Horn and the Antarctic. Today the original building is occupied only by the older boys; most teaching takes place in the 1960s blocks half hidden behind it.

163

132
Board Schools

Some buildings mean most if you can look at a number of them. London's board schools are like that, so we break from our usual format and suggest a range of them to visit.

The urban school board system held sway between the years 1870 and 1904. The revolutionary Forster Act of 1870 laid the foundations for universal elementary education in England. Local, directly elected, secular boards ran the schools in cities. Much the grandest was the School Board for London, the capital's first democratic institution. In the teeth of awesome problems, the Board set out on a crash programme of school-building, which had reached 469 schools and was still not exhausted when the Board handed over to the London County Council in 1904. Most of this took place in the poorer districts of London.

For reasons of space and of image the Board decided to build high – three stacked storeys usually, towering over the houses around them and girdled by tall walls. The schools were thought of as colonies of health and enlightenment. 'Each school stands up from its playground like a church in God's acre ringing its bell,' said Charles Booth. But symbols of religion had to be avoided. Gothic was soon discarded as too 'churchy', and in came the secular red brick and big white windows of the 'Queen Anne style', which school-building helped to define. There are three main phases of London board school architecture. For the first few years a variety of architects contributed individual designs. Then E R Robson took over, producing with a staff of assistants some superb and many mechanical schools. From 1884, T J Bailey presided over the most ebullient phase of the programme. Gradually the schools got bigger and more specialised. Their architecture became more symmetrical but also started to deviate from standard 'Queen Anne' vocabulary, rising often to a flurry of wildly detailed turrets above the roofline.

Joseph Lancaster School, Southwark. EH

Southwark is the best borough in which to track down survivors of the early phases of board school-building. **Joseph Lancaster School** (2/K6) in Harper Road off the New Kent Road, by R W Edis (1872–3), is the finest of the schools built by private architects. Austere and economical, it is on the cusp between the Gothic and Queen Anne styles. It was well added to by Bailey at the back, to enlarge its facilities. Behind it, to point a modern comparison, is Chamberlin, Powell and Bon's striking Geoffrey Chaucer School (1958–60), with a hyperbolic paraboloid roof. More amiably Gothic is **Riverside School** (1/G5) of 1873–4, visible from Bevington and Janeway Streets north of Jamaica Road. It is by M P Manning, a minor architect always worth a second glance. Again there has been a careful early addition at the back. After these schools, the shock of the advent of 'Queen Anne' is well conveyed by Robson's **Southwark Park School** (1/G5) Southwark Park Road (1874–5), a fetching, gabled front with paired windows and pretty plaques showing idealised little boys and girls willingly learning.

Clerkenwell has two examples of schools built by Robson in his prime. The earlier one, now the College for Distributive Trades in narrow **Eagle Court** (2/J3) off St John's Lane, long, low, hemmed in and plain, was selected in Robson's 1874 book on school architecture to show the difficulties of site and social condition that the London School Board faced. More graceful and conspicuous but not so

different in plan or height is the former **Bowling Green Lane School** (2/H2) 1874–5, now studios occupied by the likes of Zaha Hadid. The brickwork is pinker, there is a relaxed ratio of wall to window, and the gables are delicate and distinctive. Here one may surmise the influence and maybe even the hand of Robson's friend J J Stevenson, briefly linked with him in the design of these schools. A stone's throw to the east, but an architectural and educational world away is the mightly Clerkenwell Centre of Kingsway–Princeton College, formerly T J Bailey's **Hugh Myddleton School** (2/H2) of 1892: three big blocks deep, with extra facilities fringing the playground entered from clearly marked gates. Terracotta-clad towers with hipped roofs thrust up with bald confidence at the ends of the front. The school occupies the site of the former Clerkenwell House of Detention, remnants of which may be found by torchlight in the basement.

So much pleasure and incident do London's board schools afford their districts that a list of them could be extended on and on. We end with four schools that have qualities not touched on above. **Beckford School** (1/E3) in Broomsleigh and Dornfell Streets, West Hampstead (1886 and 1891), is typical of the board school around which, by virtue of its siting and its authority, the life of a neighbourhood seems to revolve. **New End School** (1/F3), close to Heath Street, Hampstead, is a meaty late-Bailey design (1905–6) which takes on the drama of a high-rise slab by virtue of its enclosure and the way the land falls away in front of it. Outlying districts too formed school boards as they became urbanised, and some of them built with style, relying on the London model. The Willesden School Board, one of the best, dotted what is now Brent with a splendid series of schools designed by G E S Laurence, of which the one in **Wesley Road** (1/E4), off Hillside, Stonebridge Park (1898) is perhaps the best. Lastly, there is the one-time Drew Road School (1/J4), put up in Silvertown by the West Ham School Board in 1895. Through chance survival in the wilderness next to the entrance of the London City Airport, it has become the first or last architectural impression of England some visitors will receive. The indestructibility of London's board schools is not the least impressive thing about them.

133
Crosby Hall
Cheyne Walk, Kensington and Chelsea

1/F5   Underground to South Kensington, then bus

Americans move their buildings around like nobody's business. The English do not do it so much, but an egregious exception is the 15th-century grandee Sir John Crosby's imposing hall, spirited away from the City of London and re-erected on the Thames embankment next to Battersea Bridge as the centre of a Chelsea college hostel in 1909–10.

Crosby, a wool merchant and envoy in the reign of Edward IV, built his stone hall with a matching great chamber at right-angles to it in about 1466–70, at the back of a timber court of buildings on the east side of Bishopsgate. It seems to have been meant for entertaining fellow traders and foreign dignitaries. Sir Thomas More was briefly the tenant of Crosby Place in 1523–4, and it was to be because of this tenuous association that the hall ended up in Chelsea, More's suburban home. After a fire in 1672 the great City mansion fell on hard times. Its hall became successively a conventicle, a warehouse (with an inserted floor) and, after restoration, a pioneering Victorian restaurant for City businessmen, where banquets could be held in an authentic setting. As such it might have remained to this day but for the value of City land and the tardiness of preservation laws. When a bank bought the site for rebuilding in 1907, there was nothing for it but to record the remnants of Crosby Place and rescue the hall if possible.

The story of its coming to Chelsea is curious. There were three competitors. Gordon Selfridge seriously proposed putting Crosby Hall on the roof of his Oxford Street department store. Lord Leighton's daughter wanted it as an art school in the back garden of her father's Kensington House. And Professor Patrick Geddes, the polymathic Scots scientist, sociologist, planner and educationalist, wanted it to boost More Hall, a communal university hostel he had started a few years earlier with extravagant ambitions on Cheyne Walk. Thus far he had managed only to have a decent block of student flats, More's Garden, built at the corner with Beaufort Street (architects, Dunn and Watson of Edinburgh, 1903–4). But Geddes, a great enthuser and persuader, invoked the spirit of Sir Thomas More and won the battle for Crosby Hall. With the technical help of a young antiquarian architect, Walter Godfrey, it was re-erected on the eastern part of the More Hall site facing Danvers Street. It was supposed to be integrated into a complete quadrangle, but this never quite came off. Geddes used the hall for his famous Civics Exhibition of 1911, but it was not until 1925–6, when the British Federation of University Women took the place over the built the northern range of Godfrey's design, that it had any physical connection with the rest of the hostel. The style of the boxy residence up against the hall's south end and of the wing along the embankment,

both of the 1950s by the successor firm of Carden, Godfrey and Macfadyen, is unfortunate.

Crosby Hall changed a good deal in its translation to Chelsea. The rubble core of the walls was supplanted by a neat brick modern one, while the Reigate stone ashlarwork, already much patched with Bath stone, largely gave way to the smooth Portland facing which gives the building so cool a look. The north end and south end, the lantern, the screen and the invisible structure of the roof are all Godfrey's. But the visible timberwork of the roof is old, as are the fenestration of the superb west-facing oriel lighting the dais, the oriel's little bossed vault, and most of the other windows. The oak roof – really a false ceiling – is the chief magnificence, with a forest of little arches in either direction dropping into pendants. The hall of Eltham Palace, built a decade later than Crosby Hall, is the closest equivalent. The roof can be hard to make out in the gloom, but some colouring tastefully added by Walter Godfrey's son in 1966 has cheered things up.

134
Whitelands College
Sutherland Grove, Wandsworth

1/E6   Underground to Southfields

The spectacular feature of Whitelands College is its southern front, a *tour de force* of English neo-Georgian architecture. Its broad extent is cut back into a deep series of tiers and pavilions, falling, flat-roofed terraces and overlapping planes, all expressed in a vocabulary of purplish-red handmade brickwork, pantiles and wooden sash windows on top of reinforced concrete construction. It is a superb blend of scholarly traditionalism and modernity, of a kind which architectural critics used to worry about but which we ought to find it easier to accept today.

The architect of Whitelands, built in 1928–30, was that modern traditionalist Sir Giles Gilbert Scott. His design

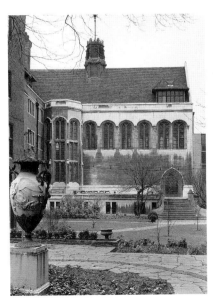

Crosby Hall. EH

165

responded to the college's proud sense of identity. A Church of England teacher-training college for women, Whitelands had functioned from a house in King's Road, Chelsea since its foundation in 1842. In the 1880s Ruskin became interested in the place. He gave books, engravings and watercolours, secured Morris and Burne-Jones to make glass for the college chapel, and instituted the May Queen festival (still kept up at the college) which climaxed in a precious piece of Arts and Crafts jewellery being conferred upon the most virtuous student – virtue being construed in an all-round sort of a way.

Winifred Mercier, one of Britain's most remarkable educationalists, became Principal of Whitelands in 1918 and soon saw that the expanding college would have to move. She secured the 12-acre site off West Hill, Wandsworth in 1924, and Sir Giles Scott as architect in 1926. Scott was brilliantly briefed by the meticulous Mercier, who wanted teaching and living integrated in one great building rather than a series of dormitories strung around a lifeless teaching and administration block. Hence the original plan: a broad spine from the entrance to the middle of the south front, with dining hall and assembly hall on either side; a cross-corridor behind that front giving access

to the main teaching spaces; and a series of internal perimeter corridors above giving access to student and staff bedrooms, many of which retain the wholesome wooden furniture specified by Scott. As many as possible of these bedrooms communicate with the south-facing roof terraces, which were conceived as an integral part of the college's space, to be used for teaching, social life, outdoor sleeping and soaking up the fresh air and sun so much stressed in inter-war educational thought. Winifred Mercier was no puritan, and a summertime visit to Whitelands confirms how enduringly successful the terraces remain.

Attached to the main block on the north by an arch between the two entrances is the chapel, an afterthought paid for by private subscription. It is in Scott's handsome brick Byzantinising manner and just predates his similar chapel at Lady Margaret Hall, Oxford. Old fittings from Chelsea were incorporated, and the size of window openings was set by the fine Morris and Company glass of 1885–93 (mainly designed by Burne-Jones) translated from the chapel there. Shamefully, most of Scott's stalls were ejected a few years ago. Despite, indeed to some extent because of, the chapel, whose relation to the main block leaves something to be

desired, the Whitelands entrance front lacks the distinction of the other end, nor are the sides of greater interest. Hostels of the kind Miss Mercier loathed now fill up much of the space between the main buildings and West Hill, where Scott provided a fine double lodge over an arch which led into the former college driveway. One of the two leaves of the wrought-iron gates within this arch is 18th-century and comes from Chelsea; the other is a copy.

135

Oakland Infants School
Daneland, East Barnet, Barnet

1/F1   Underground to Cockfosters, or British Rail to Oakleigh Park

The pilgrimage to suburban East Barnet must not be made by anyone in search of architectural dramatics. Oakland Infants is an austere, rather rambling, single-storey school clad in concrete panels that look flat enough on a grey day. Its interests lies not in what it looks like but in what it feels like – inside especially, on a working school day – and in what it stands for.

Because parts of the London Borough of Barnet used to be in Hertfordshire, a handful of its schools, Oakland Infants among them, were built as part of Hertfordshire County Council's post-war primary-school building programme. Children came first in this famous campaign, mounted against a background of labour and materials shortages, urgent demands and calls for economy. Out went rigid, pre-war classroom layouts; in came flexible, well-lit 'teaching spaces', child-sized furniture, and small things to encourage the growing child to learn from experience and activity – tiny gardens, areas for messy wet work, and accessible works of art. The schools were all built on a simple, evolving, prefabricated system of steel uprights and girders clad with concrete panels. No two schools were the same, but the same building elements, fittings and furniture were employed throughout the

Whitelands College. South front and terraces. EH

programme. To understand Oakland, it is worth visiting other Barnet schools built on Hertfordshire's '8 ft 3 in system' as well: the excellent Livingstone School in Baring Road, East Barnet, for instance, designed by James Cubitt and Partners; or the less successful Whitings Hill, in Whitings Road, Arkley. The London County Council also built primary schools using their own version of the same system, but the results were never so crisp. As with any language of building, you could design well or badly in it.

Most of the Hertfordshire schools were designed in-house by the county architects. But Oakland, built in 1950–1, was one of a number farmed out to private architects to see what they could make of the system. It went to the Architects Co-Operative Partnership (ACP), a socially conscious group practice. Leo de Syllas, the partner in charge, put much effort into making the system more 'architectural' than usual. The entrance approach, with the blank end of the hall to the left and a tipped little canopy over the door, has excellent presence. Inside, one moves through a sequence of fresh, colourful, ample and airy spaces, taken for granted in primary schools now but breathtakingly new at the time. Four of the low-height classrooms cant away in a staggered line to the east – a clever fusion of semi-open space borrowed from the corridor and semi-closed space for intimate teaching. Light enters each of them from contiguous sides for easier, more flexible working, while the toylike wooden furniture and lockers give each enclosure a Froebelian feeling still palpable after forty years of hard wear and changing teaching methods.

In the centre, the columns and miniscule lattice girders of the steel frame dominate the dining hall, separate from the square assembly hall next to it. Upon its end wall is the most striking of the many works of art commissioned by Hertfordshire for its post-war schools: a part-ghostly, part-exotic mural in greens, purples and browns by Fred Millett, depicting children wandering in a secret garden. It blends the style of the Festival of Britain with the spirit of Maurice Sendak.

136

Tulse Hill School
Upper Tulse Hill, Lambeth

1/G5   British Rail to Tulse Hill

The secondary schools built in the wake of the Butler 1944 Education Act are a muddled but stimulating bunch. Should people build comprehensives, technical schools or secondary moderns? Ought a school to be very big, so that all subjects could be taught, or small enough for pupils to have some sense of identity? All this was left for local education authorities to decide. Even the London County Council, usually sure that it knew best, was confused. The LCC opted for comprehensive education, but could not decide about size and arrangement. In the end the Conservative government of the early 1950s helped out by ruling that urban comprehensives should be as large as possible, over 2,000 each, so that they could be divided into separate grammar and secondary modern schools if policy changed!

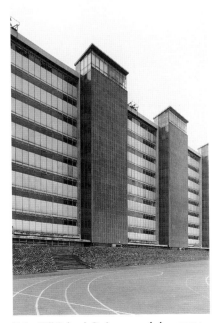

Tulse Hill School. Staircases and classrooms.
EH

The upshot within the old County of London was a phase of little-known architectural experiment. The best of these schools are in South London. Kidbrooke, in Corelli Road, Greenwich, by private architects Slater, Uren and Pike, with a Festival of Britain feeling of delicate, naive adventurousness about it, was the first LCC comprehensive to open (1954). Hard on its heels came Malory School in Launcelot Road on the Downham Estate, Lewisham, by Bridgewater and Shepheard. Then the LCC Architect's Department took over most of the work, papering over differences of educational approach with a common system of curtain walling. Big and angular Eltham Green, again in Greenwich and opened in 1956, paid candid homage to 'Soviet realist' planning models. Best of all (and exceptionally an omission from the near-flawless *London 2* volume of the *Buildings of England*) is Elliott School (1955–6), built within a dip in Pullman Gardens on the Ashburton Estate in Putney – a fine, clear, cruciform statement with a swept-roof assembly hall in front.

Tulse Hill (originally Strand Comprehensive), also opened in 1956, makes all these schools look timid by virtue of a monstrous piece of effrontery – that of stacking all the teaching rooms into a nine-storey slab serviced by lifts up the back. It was a more than questionable experiment, and the Ministry of Education's experts were appalled. Yet the slab is of high architectural quality, with the *pilotis* clear at the base and the box of the concrete frame above crisply enclosing the flat surface of the patent glazing, which is set in chequerboard colours. The whole thing makes many so-called brutalist housing slabs of the time look weak and fussy. The approach means that most views of the block are end-on, but it is worth getting further away for a fuller look, especially at the back, where the lift towers supply vertical vigour.

Tulse Hill started with a role of more than 2,200, mercifully much reduced over the years. J M Kidall was the LCC's job-architect. A more familiar name connected with the school is that of Ken Livingstone, an early alumnus.

11

Professional and Corporate

If the assemblage of buildings included in this section has a cohesive theme then it is one of educative fellowship, as work-related leisure, in which the palliatives of food and drink are rarely far away. Within that brief the buildings here run the gamut from privileged social club, through home, workplace and public exhibition space to charitable foundation. Some combine several of these elements.

Being Astronomer Royal must have been a lonely business, especially before more assistants were recruited at the Greenwich Observatory late in the 19th century. His is the unique establishment in this section, combining home and place of work but with no place dedicated to fellowship with colleagues. The difference is due, of course, to the paucity of professional astronomers by comparison with lawyers, goldsmiths, architects and gardeners. The institutionalisation of the City's traders and craftsmen began early: goldsmiths were among many groups fined around 1180 for forming illicit associations. Undeterred, the livery companies set up codes of practice and training, and secured monopolies of City trade; in the 14th century most celebrated their success by building halls, from which date that of the Merchant Taylors survives in part. Their robes of office and association, or liveries, bear strong resemblance to university gowns.

Far greater in terms of lasting power and architectural impact was the establishment of the Inns of Court, in place a century earlier. For the similarity of their arrangements of rooms, in quadrangles around a central core of hall, chapel and library, to those of the colleges established at Oxford and Cambridge in the same period, our examples could have been fitted into the section on education (pp. 159–67). The Temple is included here instead as a paramount example of the benefits of professional and sociable association. Though lawyers' chambers are primarily places of work rather than academic

learning, they were traditionally residences also and members may still lunch in fellowship together, perpetuating the tradition of collegiate-based universities as well as the 'working lunch'.

Learned associations for the study of history and the sciences were set up in the later 17th century. A good many gravitated to Burlington House where Banks and Barry provided a phalanx of libraries and lecture halls either side of the new headquarters of the Royal Academy of Arts, founded in 1768 as a school and exhibition space for painters, sculptors and architects. Although the conversion of an older building, the Royal Academy's premises fulfil the same requirements of fellowship, though the need for lecturing and exhibition spaces and increasing public access has pushed the 'feeding' and social intercourse to the sides. Much the same is true of the buildings of the Royal Horticultural Society and Royal Institute of British Architects, where library and meeting facilities take precedence over hospitality. But where the public are rarely admitted, as at the Law Society, and in the livery halls in their more charitable 20th-century guise, the true spirit of the professional club as social centre and dining hall survives uncompromised.

For professionals working alone or in only small groups, a national institute remains an important source of knowledge, status and networking. And the natural location for these headquarters remains London, giving the capital an incomparable range of little-known formal spaces, from 14th century Middle Temple Hall via Apothecaries' Hall, built in 1688, through a galaxy of 19th-century classical spaces, from which we have chosen Goldsmiths' Hall and the headquarters of the Law Society, to the more flexible spaces erected for the Royal Horticultural Society and the RIBA in the 1920s and 1930s. The post-war rebuilding of many livery company

Taking commons in Middle Temple Hall.
GLRO

169

halls reveals a continuing need for such association, just as the increasing number of learned and campaigning societies continues to require appropriate homes.

How then does little Mary Ward House fit into this selection? The settlement was a late-Victorian attempt to bring the benefits of education, improving entertainment and association with the 'better' classes to the poor of London's working-class 'ghettos'. This meant a corporate lifestyle of bedsitting rooms and communal dining and recreational facilities for the worthy young graduates who chose to exorcise their social conscience by living in poor neighbourhoods such as St Pancras, with a library and meeting hall shared with the locals. Here was education through fellowship in an especially pure form.

137

The Temple
Middle Temple Lane, City of London

2/H4   Underground to Temple or underground/British Rail to Blackfriars

The Inns of Court make up for London's lack of a medieval university. Their enclave between Westminster and the City has a collegiate feeling never developed in Bloomsbury. Most gracious, perhaps, is Lincoln's Inn, dominated by the picturesque composition of Philip Hardwick's New Hall of 1843 against the greensward of 17th-century New Court. But an older and more complex development is the Temple.

Magna Carta fixed the Court of Common Pleas in London. Schools of Law had been established in association with City churches, the students living in hostels and taking their main meals together. But from 1207 the clergy were forbidden to practice in the secular courts and in 1254 were prohibited from teaching the Common Law. Meanwhile

the Order of the Knights Templar had settled near the Thames in about 1160. After their suppression in 1308 their possessions passed to the order of St John which, however, had already set down roots in Clerkenwell. The area had been leased to the legal profession by 1400. Communal dining continued, with the lawyers grouped in surrounding chambers. The tradition of the Inns of Court owes much to Oxbridge, but with vestiges in their ritual of the Templars and City livery companies.

The Temple has suffered from the sometimes unadventurous architectural choices of its Benchers in the 19th century, and most particularly from a bombing raid on 10 May 1941. But careful post-war restoration and recreation has re-established its character of little courtyards, and important medieval and 17th-century buildings survive. There is no distinct division between Inner and Middle Temple. A rule of thumb is that Middle Temple lies generally west and Inner Temple east of Middle Temple Lane, although part of Pump Court (north side *c.*1686, south side 1951–3 by Sir Edward Maufe) and the Cloisters (1949–50) are Middle Temple outposts on the wrong side of the track. Inner Temple comprises two large quadrangles, Inner Temple Gardens and King's Bench Walk, and two smaller ones hard by its central hall. Middle Temple is a more complex sequence of little courts stepping down to the river.

The earliest building is Temple Church, shared by the two Inns. Its nave is constituted by the Round Church, one of four surviving churches in Britain modelled on the Templars' Church of the Holy Sepulchre in Rome, and consecrated in 1185. It has Romanesque round-headed windows beneath a Gothic pointed vault. The west doorway is a riot of Romanesque carving, whilst the use of Purbeck marble columns was the first in London. The chancel, a rebuilding of *c.*1220–40, is similar in style to the retrochoirs of Winchester and Salisbury Cathedrals but is a 'hall church' with aisles the same height as the body of the building. In 1841–2 Sydney Smirke threw out the box pews and Wren

reredos. The church was entirely gutted in 1941, and the meticulous restoration by Walter Godfrey included the replacement of all the Purbeck shafts and the relining of the chancel walls. The reredos was recovered from the Bowes Museum and reinstated.

Apart from the shared church, the two Inns are entirely separate, each centred on its great hall. Inner Temple's was rebuilt by Sydney Smirke in 1866–70 and by Sir Hubert Worthington in 1955, following bombing. But both Smirke and Hitler spared a tiny 14th-century range called the Buttery, whose irregular ragstone adds incident to Maufe and Worthington's worthy but unimaginative quadrangles. Middle Temple Hall has survived, with much restoration, from the 1560s. It is a quirky and instructive blend of the medieval great hall meeting the Renaissance. The layout of the hall separated by a screen from the entrance cross-passage and service butteries is medieval, as is the form of the double hammerbeam roof, though not its Serlian finials. The great oak screen is classical, with strapwork and caryatids. The doors are later, while the wooden louvre was added as late as 1732 and rebuilt after the Second World War.

The Temple escaped the Great Fire of 1666, but suffered conflagrations a decade later: hence its tradition of fine late 17th-century chambers. Grandest are Nos 2–7 King's Bench Walk, built by Christopher Wren in 1677–8. Middle Temple employed Dr Nicholas Barbon, whose simpler New Court dates from 1676. In 1684 Roger North, an amateur who is otherwise remembered for his writings on architecture, produced a striking gateway with four bold Ionic pilasters at the entrance to Middle Temple Lane from the Strand. Adjacent is an odd contrast in style though not in date: No. 1 Hare Court is a timber-framed building with two jetties dating from 1693.

J P St Aubyn and the Smirke brothers were the most favoured 19th-century architects. Sydney pops up in an

Middle Temple Lane. Archway through Temple Gardens. GLRO

unlikely guise, adding frilly Elizabethan to Robert's severe Paper Buildings of 1838. Even more outlandish is Edward Barry's contribution, the only chambers divided between the two Inns: his Temple Gardens Building of 1878 closes the vista down Middle Temple Lane with full-blown Renaissance vigour. Barry's panache is in contrast to the rest of the lane, where even T G Jackson was relatively self-effacing; his extension to Hare Court is the only Queen Anne contribution to the complex, and typical of the way the Temple's character owes far more to its tight-packed jumble of buildings and spaces than to any one masterpiece.

138

Old Royal Observatory
Blackheath Avenue, Greenwich Park, Greenwich

1/H5   British Rail to Greenwich or Maze Hill

[A]

Off-centre to the august line-up of the Queen's House and the Royal Naval Hospital down by the river below, nothing could be a less plausible definition for the axis of the world than the Royal Observatory. The turrets that peep cheekily over the brow of Greenwich Hill seem to signal some romantic fortlet rather than a powerhouse of astronomical endeavour. The romanticism is not quite arbitrary. There *was* a little castle here, an offshoot of Greenwich Palace, and its foundations serve the observatory. Also, before this purpose-built home was created for the first Astronomer Royal in 1675–6, John Flamsteed had used one of the turrets of the White Tower at the Tower of London for his observations, and materials from an old gatehouse there were incorporated in the new Greenwich building. Is it too fanciful to see in the 'pompe' which Wren admitted injecting into the design a miniature version of the Tower?

Closer to, the fetching silhouette gives way to the set of separate, modest buildings which make up the former Royal Observatory. It is a group of

exceptional significance for British history. Before Charles II, badgered by the Surveyor-General of the Ordnance, Sir Jonas Moore, set Flamsteed up in this watch-tower (as the Latin inscription on the side of his house calls it), no navigator could be sure of his bearings at sea – an uncertainty which had profound effects upon trade, war and colonial policy. Such was the precision of Flamsteed and his eminent successors in 'rectifying the motions of the heavens, and the places of the fixed stars' that British sailors after 1725 steered with navigational data in a class of their own. The accolade of 1884, when the Greenwich meridian was selected to serve the world from a medley of national alternatives, testifies to the primacy of Greenwich's astronomical repute.

How Wren and his collaborator Hooke, scientists both every bit as much as they were architects, must have relished designing Flamsteed's house! The front to the hill is largely an 'eye-catcher', with two sham windows flanking the long one in the centre from which Flamsteed made northward observations. The basic shape of the building, as the back reveals, is an octagon, with long mullioned windows (in wood disguised as stone) turned towards the main and subsidiary points of the compass. There is something of Wren's Sheldonian Theatre in it, translated into homely tones of brickwork. The turrets come in handy, one of them equipped with a big mast

Flamsteed House, Old Royal Observatory. EH

and ball dropped at one o'clock to help ships in the river with their time-keeping. Inside, everything is subordinate to Flamsteed's octagon, a stately, tall room of palpably Dutch feeling, with telescopes mounted by the windows and holes cut away in the panelling for timepieces by Tompion. Poor Mrs Flamsteed and family had to suffer the poky basement apartments underneath. They were refurbished in about 1790 and then extended southwards for the fifth Astronomer Royal, Nevile Maskelyne. The additions now contain the observatory's most technical displays, where earnest fathers may be overheard discoursing to their fidgety offspring on matters chronometrical.

Flamsteed's major observations were carried on not from the house but from a pair of sheds in the garden behind, known as the Quadrant House and the Sextant House. Though totally rebuilt, they form the basis of the present Meridian Building, extended eastwards from 1720 onwards as successive Astronomers Royal added new equipment. Thus the Greenwich Meridian, first fixed by Flamsteed's Mural Arc on the wall of the Quadrant House in the 1680s, gradually crept east, till it came to rest on the line of Airy's Transit Circle, completed in 1851. The front and the roof of the building open out here to allow the great telescope free range, slicing through a classical facade on the line of the meridian so as to give dramatic meaning to the concept of the broken pediment. The tower at the end through which visitors enter the complex dates from 1857. Its dome, one of three on the observatory's lesser buildings, houses a large refracting telescope and dates in its present form only from 1973.

Further south, a lumpy, cruciform but far from charmless building in brick and terracotta, built in 1894–5, is now used as a planetarium ('Please, no under-sixes,' says the notice on the gate, 'they get scared or chatty'). By a practice once common in the architecture of science, the names and dates of eminent astronomers bedeck the cornice. Tucked into the bowl of the hill between here and Flamsteed's house is a delightful garden, entered from a path to the west. Less easy to miss is the fine prospect from the hill, with London off to the left. For once, the view is enhanced rather than spoilt by the looming tower of Canary Wharf behind.

139
Goldsmiths' Hall
Foster Lane, City of London

2/J3   Underground to St Paul's

The City livery companies have had profound impact on the appearance of London. They developed huge estates, built or ran a plethora of almshouses and endowed more than thirty schools. Yet in their original powerbase of the City, they have long underplayed their physical presence.

There are ninety-four livery companies, representing traditional trades and crafts, and, since 1930, new professions also. Their medieval purpose was to institute apprenticeships and quality control through holding monopolies. From the senior liverymen are elected the Lord Mayors of London; otherwise, the companies lost power as trade controls eased during the 18th century. But enough shrewd investments were made and bequests received, mainly in the 16th and 17th centuries, to ensure the continuity of the major companies as ceremonial and charitable clubs, centred on their livery halls.

The Fire of 1666 destroyed most of the medieval halls, and there followed a rebuilding similar to that of the City's churches. Their annihilation in the Second World War was even more thorough. But the livery halls adopted no new form in the 17th century, remaining inverted from the street in medieval style. It was only those rebuilt in the early 19th century that evolved a language of display, along with a coherent plan. The Fishmongers, displaced by John Rennie's new London Bridge, got a prominent new site on its northern flank and a sober new hall by Henry Roberts, which opened in 1834. Its Grecian restraint is remarkable

Goldsmiths' Hall. Staircase. A F KERSTING

enough for Roberts, still more so for his assistant, Gilbert Scott, and a reminder of how flexible young architects in the 1830s had to be.

Goldsmiths' Hall is the more impressive because it lacks any such purity of style. Designed by Philip Hardwick in 1829 and built in 1830–5, it replaced a 17th-century structure so overburdened by additions that it was declared unsafe. Hardwick's plan resembles that of Fishmongers' Hall but focuses attention more emphatically on the principal rooms: a central staircase under a dome, the great banqueting hall, and the Court Room where the

Prime Warden and liverymen have their meetings. But Hardwick's fruitier classicism is apparent even on the outside, in the armorial devices festooned beneath the mighty hexastyle portico tucked up narrow Foster Lane. The rear, in Gutter Lane, admits the further solecism of round-arched windows with, tucked in front, the assay office from whose work the term 'hallmarking' derives.

Luckily it was the front block of Goldsmiths' Hall that received the inevitable bomb. The rooms recreated by Fernand Billerey and C H James have a coolness at odds with Hardwick's work behind. But even those interiors palpably Hardwick's are not unaltered, for later redecoration has tipped his Empire style towards full-blown Victorian eclecticism. The staircase hall, a galleried two-storeyed courtyard similar to those of Barry's clubs – here pierced with a double-flight stair – was once decorated with green scagliola, swags and swirling iron balustrades. The marble inserted in the 1870s gives a greater haughtiness. The main hall, by contrast, was enlivened by its redecoration in 1892 by George Aitchison, whose rich colours are least altered in the trabeated ceiling. The room glows with gold leaf and heraldic glass, the latter set into the round-arched windows facing Gutter Lane. But the brightest notes are its chandeliers, repeated to infinity in huge mirrors. In a building devoted to the crafts of metalworking, and with its own magnificent collection of silver gilt, it is ironic that the glassware glitters brightest of all.

140

Burlington House
Piccadilly, Westminster

2/E4   Underground to Piccadilly
[A]

Burlington House started badly. It was begun in 1665 by Sir John Denham, the poet whom Dr Johnson thought wrote the most beautiful quatrain in the English language. Before it could be completed, Denham fell out with his wife, went mad and they both died (Lady Denham believed she had been poisoned 'in a cup of chocolate'). The house was bought and finished by the first Earl of Burlington using Hugh May, perhaps also Denham's architect. A good deal of that carcass survives, but nothing can be seen of it. For from about 1716 the third Earl of Burlington, young, rich and influential, opted to turn his house into the first London showcase of revived Palladian architectural principle. What chiefly remains from Burlington's reconstruction is the casing in stone of the lower two storeys of the south front facing on to the court by the pushy Scots

Burlington House. Entrance from Piccadilly. EH

architect Colen Campbell, and elements of the first-floor rooms behind – notably the fine saloon, with a ceiling painting by William Kent. Campbell, taken up early by Burlington but dropped in the 1720s, provided a frontispiece more in the style of Inigo Jones than of Palladio, whom he understood imperfectly. Yet he set the tone for everything that followed. Such was Burlington's mystique that architects repressed their individuality in the face of the mighty Palladian

patron. So Burlington House became a repository of respectful but lifeless neo-Burlingtonian architecture.

Samuel Ware, not a well-known architect, inaugurated this tradition of homage. He it was who in 1815–19 built the much-loved Burlington Arcade to the west so as to make enough rents to save the house from demolition. Ware also rearranged the interior for Lord George Cavendish in tactful taste. His one big gesture was the staircase up from the entrance, with its florid, Regency cast-ironwork; less easy to guess as his are the long Reynolds Room and the Assembly Room, both on the first floor.

In 1854 the government bought Burlington House, thinking to install the learned societies. Owing to what Gladstone called 'vacillation, uncertainty, costliness, extravagance, meanness and all the conflicting vices that could be enumerated', it took twelve years to decide what to do with the place. Under the final carve-up the University of London got the back, now Burlington Gardens, to build offices upon (Sir James Pennethorne, architect, 1866–9), the Royal Academy took Burlington House proper (top storey, portico and galleries by Sydney Smirke, architect, 1867–9), while the societies were given the forecourt; here they built three-storey ranges replete with grave libraries and conference rooms (Banks and Barry, architects, 1868–73). Pennethorne's block, now housing the Museum of Mankind, is a lively enough job looking down Burlington Street, but his colleagues were too frightened of Burlington. So the courtyard and Piccadilly front are rather lugubrious Victorian affairs. It is a relief to focus on Alfred Drury's sprightly bronze of Reynolds in the middle of the court (1931) after the weight of academic statuary on Smirke's second-floor front behind.

Inside Burlington House, every academician-architect given half a chance has had a go at rearranging things. The entrance hall, inset with paintings by Angelica Kauffmann and Benjamin West brought from Somerset House, has most to do with T G Jackson (1899–1900) but was de-Victorianised by Raymond Erith (1962); the Friends' Room to the right, once the library, is chiefly by W Curtis Green (1927); the restaurant and adjacent stair are by Norman Shaw (1883–5). Most recently (1990–1), Norman Foster has threaded a lift and a stair in the well between the old house and the Smirke galleries behind, rebuilt three exhibition rooms on top, and reset the Royal Academy's prized possession – the Michelangelo tondo.

141

Mary Ward House
Tavistock Place, Bloomsbury, Camden

2/G2   Underground to Russell Square

Mary Ward House is the masterpiece of two young architects, aged only 29 and 24 – Dunbar Smith and Cecil Brewer. Opened in 1898, its bold use of simple, cheap details defies stylistic description, though it owes much to the ideals of Philip Webb and especially W R Lethaby, who designed a fireplace, as did C F A Voysey, Ernest Newton and Guy Dawber.

In the 1880s the poverty and seeming depravity of parts of inner London were in part put down to a lack of middle-class guidance. So high-minded young professionals came to live in 'settlements' in a few districts which had lost their social mix. The settlement theory was that these enthusiasts would pursue their careers by day but devote their spare time to running an educational and social centre for local inhabitants and live alongside it. Best known and most successful of such projects was Toynbee Hall in the East End, which flourishes still.

The 'Passmore Edwards Settlement' in Bloomsbury was another such, situated in a working-class area conveniently close to University College. It was the progeny of Mary (Mrs Humphry) Ward, a best-selling novelist widow of an Oxford don and intellectual, who had been deeply influenced by the charitable philosophies of T H Green. Financial backing was provided by Passmore Edwards, a newspaper proprietor who gave his name to dozens of public libraries he founded in London and his native Cornwall. It is their initials which adorn the doorplates and fireplaces in the building, though since 1920 the building has been named after Mary Ward herself. Since 1961 it has been the headquarters of the National Institute for Social Work.

In 1895 Mary Ward acquired a site in Tavistock Place, and A H Mackmurdo produced a design. This proved too expensive and instead a competition was held, which was won by Smith and Brewer who had already been involved with the Marchmont Street centre. On to a small site, altered from that of the original competition, they packed a hall, library, meeting rooms underneath and a block of bedsitting rooms to the rear. The hall's blind side walls and end staircases dictated the composition of the front. The living quarters have their

Mary Ward House. Detail of front. MARTIN CHARLES

own entrance at the side and share central dining and common rooms. Between the two halves is a lightwell, under which was once a basement gymnasium.

Mary Ward said she wanted a 'House Beautiful' as an inspiration to all who used it. Despite the conversion of the bedsits to offices, the building retains a homely atmosphere. The key features are a modest scale and careful detailing. To the careful brickwork and traditional sashes championed by Philip Webb are added a few classical elements such as the Venetian window in the first-floor entrance hall, complete with squat columns and flattened capitals, and – most powerfully – symbolic touches inspired by Lethaby's *Architecture, Mysticism and Myth*, published in 1892. Lethaby sought to give a philosophical or spiritual base to the belief in craftsmanship. This is seen most obviously in the main entrance, aggrandised not by an order but by two eggs representing creation. The Lethabite spirit suffuses the whole building: it is present in the segmental doorheads with dying hood-moulds, in the expression of the steel roof joists in the deep overhanging eaves, in every exaggerated hopper head, every picture rail and in the simple, architect-designed tables and fitted cupboards (these survive especially well in the dining room, now a coffee shop). Most beautiful are the green-tiled fireplaces, a reminder of the contrast between soft greens and whites once found throughout the public spaces.

142

The Law Society
113 Chancery Lane, Westminster and City of London

2/H4   Underground to Chancery Lane

Whilst the four great Inns of Court remain the spiritual and physical bastions of the British Bar, London's solicitors are a largely rootless bunch. The lesser Inns of Chancery from which

The Law Society, from the north. GLRO

their profession evolved, such as Furnival's, Serjeants' and Staple Inns, were already in decline when the Law Institution, later renamed the Law Society, was founded in 1825.

The core of the Society's premises, opened in 1831, is neo-Grecian at its coldest and most attenuated: a young Lewis Vulliamy outstripping his master Robert Smirke in severity. The giant Ionic columns of the portico are carried through to the hall-cum-reading room behind to be repeated massively in cast-iron, wrapped in red scagliola. They support the library above, extended to either side in 1849 and 1857 in furtherance of Vulliamy's original conception. A comfortable club house the result is not, despite the imposition of coloured glass and mementoes from the demolished Inns of Chancery.

In 1902 the architect H Percy Adams was commissioned to build an extension. For Adams, however, read his inspired young assistant, Charles Holden, for whom 1903 was an *annus*

mirabilis. John Summerson has defined a small group of British architects playing with blocky massing and squared-off surface patterning much like Frank Lloyd Wright at a similar date. Chief of the group were Mackintosh and Holden. Mackintosh's Glasgow School of Art, begun first, was completed after Holden's Bristol Central Library, and the famous west elevation to the School of Art owes something to Holden's similar treatment at Bristol. The Law Society extension, completed in 1904, has a stone staircase ascended under a low arch, with an identical enveloping quality as at Bristol. But in the exterior Holden forsakes the free-Tudor square rhythms of his contemporary work for classical mannerism. Summerson considered it 'based on Michelangelo, seen perhaps through the eyes of Alfred Stevens'. His angled mouldings and dripping keystones anticipate those of John Joass, whose work with John Belcher is a distinctive feature of the Edwardian West End. Holden foreshadows Joass too in the use of sculpture set under thin canopies: at the Law Society Truth, Justice, Liberty and Mercy, all by Charles Pibworth, squat under arches that disrupt the rusticated base. Better known because more controversial were the suitably anatomical figures supplied by Jacob Epstein for Holden's British Medical Association, now Zimbabwe House, on the Strand, completed in 1908.

The Law Society also has a surprising skyline – smooth faces of Portland stone with set-back corners that we with hindsight can liken to Holden's Flanders war memorials and to No. 55 Broadway. The interior, staircase emphatically excepted, is unsatisfying. The ground floor has been mutilated, whilst the first-floor common room is dominated by square columns of Cipollino marble in violent peppermint stripes that overwhelm the quality of the fireplaces and other fittings. It seems that the even more discordant feature, a Della Robbia frieze by Conrad Dressler, was insisted upon by the Society.

A third breed of classicism, this time Palladianism given an Egyptian batter, can be found to the other side of Vulliamy's block. This is the former Law Fire Insurance Office, built in 1859 by Thomas Bellamy, an attractive building to both front and back.

143

Royal Horticultural Hall
Greycoat St, Westminster

2/F6   Underground to Pimlico, St James's Park or Victoria

[C]

The first-time visitor to a flower show or other event at John Murray Easton and Howard Robertson's Horticultural Hall (1926–8) encounters no dramatics on arrival. The building has a neat, neo-Georgian front, its symmetry a trifle awkward in view of the corner site. There is a high stone plinth, delicately bowed outwards to enlarge the entrances to the foyer, then four storeys of purplish brick above. The craftsmanship is refined, and in the

pretty gilt flowers on the entrance canopies you can recognize the hand of someone who has made the pilgrimage to Stockholm to see what Ostberg, Tengbom and Asplund were up to. Then you pass through to the hall itself, and the mood is transformed. Virile, flat-faced elliptical arches in concrete bound from one side of the hall to the other, bearing with them no less than four stepped tiers of windows on longitudinal girders. There are domed openings up in the high apex of the roof, and further

ones in the low aisles behind the arches. Gantry-like lights of functionalist aspiration hang down on thin wires to illuminate the exhibits. It is like the contrast between St Pancras Station and the hotel in front – a paean to modern methods of construction obscured behind an essay in urbane historicism. Only here the architects of front and back are one and the same.

In reality the pedigree of the hall is as complex and scholarly as that of the front, and Sweden again comes into the

Royal Horticultural Society Hall. GLRO

picture. Big halls with stepped tiers of windows, to obviate the deadening effect and 'greenhouse'-type heat of crude top-lighting, go back to the Crystal Palace. They seem first to have been combined with elliptical, reinforced-concrete arches in the Wroclaw (Breslau) Market Hall of 1906–8, which Easton and Robertson may not have known. What they did know was the temporary Congress Hall erected for the Gothenburg Exhibition of 1923, where a church-like effect similar to that of the Horticultural Hall was achieved with laminated timber arches, not concrete. The flat haunches of the Gothenburg arches excited the English architects, who resolved to emulate the effect in London and in concrete. But since there were aisles to their building, they could not afford to waste valuable ground-floor space with wide-spreading bases to the arches. So the great arches were made to descend on to thin and all but vertical columns, their thrust being laterally absorbed by the flat roof-slabs of the aisles. This was the contrivance of Oscar Faber, the engineer for the project.

The impact of the Horticultural Hall's stepped section and elliptical arches earned it rapid progeny in the form of municipal baths, of which many were built in London during the 1930s. Some architects followed Easton and Robertson's lead and fitted their baths within a historicist frame; such was Kenneth Cross's elegant St Marylebone Baths, Seymour Place (1936–7). Others, like the municipal architects of Poplar and Willesden (Poplar Baths, East India Dock Road, 1932–4; Granville Road Baths, Kilburn, 1935–6), took the line that functional-looking halls should be preceded by functional-looking offices. None, however, had the space or scale to let the hall obtrude upon the elevation. To follow the working-out of the concrete-arched hall as a building type, one must look to a succession of inter-war European market and exhibition halls, for instance at Frankfurt, Rheims and Brno – buildings of greater span and structural significance than the Horticultural Hall. But none has the intensity induced by the high lifting of the arch at Greycoat Street and the swimming pools that followed it.

144
Royal Institute of British Architects
66 Portland Place, Westminster

2/E3   Underground to Regent's Park, Portland Place or Oxford Circus

[C]

In the midst of the recession of 1931, the announcement of an open competition for the headquarters of the British architectural profession aroused immense activity: 284 architects submitted entries. If there were few wholly modern designs, there were surprisingly few wholly traditional ones. Those commended generally opted for something in between, most choosing a stripped, precisely ordered style in the fashionable Swedish idiom inspired by Gunnar Asplund's Stockholm City Library and Ragnar Ostberg's Stockholm Town Hall. Nobody followed the style more closely than the winner, Grey Wornum, who had led an Architectural Association excursion to Stockholm in 1930, when he had met Ostberg.

Wornum won less for his elevations

Royal Institute of British Architects. The Staircase. RIBA

than because his plan successfully fulfilled the brief for a lecture hall and exhibition gallery that could both be reached without lifts. His then revolutionary elimination of corridors created a tight, economical plan and a wonderfully exciting central space. The original building was only five storeys, two more being added in 1957 when the adjacent property was finally also redeveloped. Wornum's revised scheme was approved in April 1933 and the building opened in 1934, the Institute's centenary.

Today the RIBA adds a note of refinement to the remains of the Adam brothers' Portland Place, its severe white stone profile broken only by a great Asplund-inspired window cutting through two floors and by two detached pylon figures. However, the success of the building remains its interior spaces. The most dramatic is the staircase, its

massive marble columns towering through two floors and giving an impression of darkness and solemnity from which the eye is drawn into the light Henry Florence Exhibition Hall beyond a glazed wall. The other major spaces are the lecture hall below and the double-height library above.

Not only did the RIBA headquarters take its design and finishings from Sweden, but its use of symbolic decoration closely followed Ostberg. Wornum and his wife, Miriam, installed a group of young sculptors, glass engravers and craftsmen in lodgings next door, just as Ostberg and his wife had gathered a team of disciples in Stockholm. The chief sculptor was Bainbridge Copnall, who produced the relief of 'Architectural Aspiration' over the central window; his work is best seen in the Henry Florence Hall, where his depiction of 'Man and his Buildings

throughout the Ages' tellingly includes reliefs of Stockholm Town Hall and Scott's and Lutyens's Liverpool Cathedrals, as well as vignettes of the craftsmen employed on the site. The other principal decorators were James Woodford, who carved the pylons and designed the images of London buildings for the bronze entrance doors, and Jan Juta, whose etched glass is a major feature of the building. Miriam Wornum decorated the library. Best of all, though little seen, are a pair of etched and opaque glass doors on the fourth floor, designed by Raymond McGrath to depict the six great periods of architecture.

So much decoration combined with so many marbled and walnut-veneered finishes make the RIBA a complex and atmospheric whole, a worthy compromise between classical and modern that succeeds on its own terms.

12

Eating, Drinking and Sleeping

Time was when the main roads of London and the outlying villages that lay along them were packed with hostelries for eating, drinking and sleeping. Supplying the wants of the body is the prime service industry in any community; and when work, travel and the basic conditions of life were more physically arduous than they are today, there was need for frequent and accessible places of refreshment and rest. We should not be tempted to romanticise them. Most were small, some no better than tiny, noxious hovels. The respectable medieval traveller, if he were lucky or wise, would prefer the protection and hospitality of a friend, a monastery, a guild or a great man's hall and table. The respectable medieval (and much later) workman would either sup at home, or have food and drink brought in to him from one of these small establishments and eat at his bench. The urban take-away service is older than the restaurant.

There were also, of course, numerous decent hostelries, some with a meeting or dining room upstairs. Prince Henry's Room in Fleet Street of 1610–11 is the outstanding survival. Lloyd's coffee house, original rendezvous of the great broking business (pp. 217–18), was a development of this kind of building in the securer City of the period after the Great Fire with private rooms or booths to do business in. And a few suburbs boasted large inns. Southwark is specially associated with them, because of Chaucer. Being suburban, it had space enough for stabling, and it lay on a key main road. Pilgrimage to Canterbury was just one of London's many travel-related businesses; Bishopsgate, Aldgate, Holborn and, later, Islington and Knightsbridge, attracted inns too. But it is in Southwark that London's one example of the old inn-type survives, in the courtyard of the George, Borough High Street (c.1680). The George is described below as a 'coaching motel': that is to say, it dates from the days of the 'stage'

and the 'post', when four-wheeled vehicles were introduced for long-distance travel, allowing greater comfort and regular schedules. The proportions of the George's yard and of its accommodation reflect this. Yet its timber construction and galleried arrangement remain Tudor or earlier in origin, of a type found all over northern Europe.

London pubs or inns underwent no great changes in the Georgian period, as the prints of Hogarth mordantly confirm. But at the upper end of the market, these were the years when the smart coffee house or gaming house transformed itself into the club. The type rapidly concentrated in St James's (though there were City examples too). The St James's clubs divided themselves into two clear phases. The early ones in St James's Street itself (chief survivors Boodle's, by Crunden, 1775–6; Brooks's, by Holland, 1776–8) masquerade as more or less private houses, in which political discussion is a by-product of eating, drinking and gambling. Post-Napoleonic clubs, led by Robert Smirke's short-lived United Services Club, assumed civic airs of increasing pomposity, reaching a climax in the sequence of Athenaeum, Travellers' and Reform Club along Pall Mall. It was Charles Barry's genius to discern that the Italian Renaissance *palazzo* suited this mood perfectly. From the moment that public self-consciousness triumphed over private pleasures, standards of club architecture tended to go up, those of club cuisine to go down.

Clubs, it is sometimes forgotten, are private hotels as well, and their architectural idiosyncrasy presages a new look to the hotel too. It is hopeless to distinguish accurately between early hotels, clubs, inns and lodgings. The term 'hotel' is first applied in London to sets of West End private houses, each of which could be hired with complete staff, for a minimum of several weeks. Claridge's started out in this way (as Mivart's), and there were others in the

Enjoying a drink at the Prince Alfred, Formosa Street. EH

181

Bond Street area. They were not distinctive, since discretion and privacy were their hallmark. Brown's Hotel perpetuates the tradition. In due course the chic French name is transferred to the inn-type. The Golden Cross, a major coaching inn rebuilt by Sir William Tite in 1832 as part of the Trafalgar Square improvements, stands at the point of transition. It is superseded by the railway terminus hotel, which first appears in the 1850s and in two decades changes the plan, scale and style of urban hotels.

Because the railway hotel is usually built by a railway company, it tends to be all but on top of the station, with all the dirt and inconvenience that this brings. Open to all respectable comers, its reception rooms are designed to impress, allowing the traveller to dream that he dwells in marble halls (though its bedroom floors are generally anonymous). It is in the 'coffee rooms' of the railway hotels that women, hitherto barred from respectable places of public refreshment, begin first to make inroads, and the modern restaurant starts to evolve. As to style, the name 'hotel' suggested France, and food snobbery pointed the same way. Few entrepreneurs and architects could resist a mansard roof – useful in any case for stuffing in extra bedrooms. Surviving examples of the style include the Great Western (Paddington), the Grosvenor (Victoria) and the Charing Cross; there were once several more. The Great Northern (King's Cross), a feebler performance, is more than overweighed by its outrageous neighbour, Sir Gilbert Scott's Midland Grand in front of St Pancras (pp. 238–9) – queen of railway hotels and climax of the secular Gothic Revival. There is one afterthought: Edis's sumptuous Great Central Hotel in front of Marylebone Station (1898–9), now reopened to the public after decades of office use. May the same fate soon overtake the Midland Grand, far too long left to decay!

It took until the 1880s for grand hotels to catch on in London elsewhere than at railway stations. When they did, they soon surpassed their models in smartness. But if Claridge's, the Connaught, the Savoy, the Dorchester

and their lesser rivals are mostly grave and atmospheric places, none amounts to first-rate architecture. The nearest a London hotel comes to that quality is the Ritz, a wholly derivative Edwardian building which has some claims to originality of structure but none of style or decoration. London's clutch of high hotels built in the late 1960s is, regrettably, of low quality, and nothing since augurs better. It is a type to which the British have yet to contribute much that is distinctive.

With the pub, we are on firmer ground, for here is something native to London. But beware endeavouring to date an old London pub. From the Prospect of Whitby by the river to Jack Straw's Castle up on Hampstead Heath, it is fiendishly hard to distinguish the original from the sham. Old-looking panelling or cut glass are rarely good guides to a pub's authenticity; sawdust on the floor guarantees a fake. There are many London pubs with 17th-century bits and pieces, but few make any show of it because the remnants tend to be structural. Where drinking takes place, nothing ornamental lasts very long. It is better to choose your pub for its character and beer than on grounds of architectural purity. Nevertheless there are still plenty with a genuine Victorian feeling, even if the little spaces into which almost all were once divided have been opened up now into 'saloon' and 'bar'. We counsel a crawl in the Maida Vale area; but anyone with initiative and a good eye can construct his or her own itinerary. Many of the most egregious and enjoyable pubs, outside and in, were products of a pub-building boom of 1896–9, the vigour of which beggars belief. It was the brewers' architectural revenge for the gradual closing-down of one little hostelry after another by Victorian reformers and health fanatics.

For politer, 'family' pub architecture one must go to the suburbs – starting, perhaps at Norman Shaw's Tabard Inn, Bedford Park (p. 115). The Arts and Crafts Movement, however, had little beneficial effect on the London pub, the outlandish Black Friar apart. Perhaps this was because it was too closely linked to teetotalism. At Streatham, in front of the old silk mill (pp. 223–4), you can see

the strange juxtaposition of a pub and a reformed coffee tavern, The Beehive. This was designed by one of the best late Victorian domestic architects, Ernest George, for a teetotal manufacturer who wanted to discourage his workers from going to the pub. It is the coffee house, naturally, that has closed.

145
Prince Henry's Room
17 Fleet Street, City of London

2/H4   Underground to Temple
[A]

Ancient timber buildings in central London have a habit of turning out to be half-bogus. Staple Inn in High Holborn, the biggest, most picturesque example, has been shifted bodily once and reconstructed twice behind the front. The gateway to St Bartholomew the Great formerly displayed a cladding of sash windows and mathematical tiles. The overhanging front of 17 Fleet Street, too, is more scholarly Edwardian recreation than true Jacobean timberwork. But here a venerable and mildly mysterious upper-floor room which can be seen free any weekday

17 Fleet Street before the restoration of 1905.
GLRO

afternoon more than makes up for any external inauthenticity.

Just as Roger North's suave and scholarly Middle Temple Gateway of 1683–4 fronts the entrance to Middle Temple Lane a few yards further west, so 17 Fleet Street strides over the entrance to Inner Temple Lane. The contrast is instructive. Whereas the pink brickwork and pilastered classicism of North's gateway were commissioned by the Benchers themselves, 17 Fleet Street belongs to an earlier world, that of private-enterprise timber-building along the narrow, commercial street fronts of Jacobean London.

There were two houses here in the 16th century, one at least latterly a tavern, like so many buildings along Fleet Street. They were rebuilt as one in about 1610–11, either by John Bennett, a sergeant at arms, or by William Blake, a vintner. The premises were then called The Prince's Arms, so it is likely that they went on being used at least in part as a tavern – as was certainly the case in the 1660s. The Prince in question was Henry, James I's eldest son, Prince of Wales from 1603 until his death in 1612; that is confirmed by his initials and Prince of Wales' feathers in the centrepiece of the ornate plaster ceiling on the first floor, and by further feathers upon the front. There is, however, a puzzle. Seventeenth-century pubs were generally crude places; the elaborate kind of timberwork and plasterwork we see at No. 17 was usually reserved for persons of status or ambition. The answer may lie with the Duchy of Cornwall, Henry's personal fiefdom. In the 1620s the Duchy's Council was meeting somewhere in Fleet Street. What seems likely is that the Duchy fitted up the first floor of the rebuilt No. 17 as its Council Chamber, perhaps meeting here regularly till the time of the Civil War. But it cannot be proved.

The 19th century, with its customary confidence, had no doubts about the building's history. 'Formerly the Palace of Henry VIII and Cardinal Wolsey' announced a huge placard hiding the whole top storey. Having briefly been used for a waxwork museum, by the 1870s No. 17 had become a fancy Fleet Street barber's where you could have

17 Fleet Street today. GLRO

your hair brushed by steam power. Its front had been completely transmogrified with sash windows and pilasters, queerly incorporating some of the old wooden panels from beneath the windows.

In 1905 the need to widen Fleet Street threatened the building. In one of its first practical historic buildings operations, the London County Council came to the rescue and bought the property. The LCC's architects proceeded to set the ground floor back by 5 ft, including the gateway to Inner Temple Lane (do not miss the wonderfully solid doors – seemingly of 1748). They then added an unobtrusive new block along the lane behind, and restored the front on the basis of remaining timberwork and old engravings. They made a convincing fist of it, even if some details of the hanging oriel windows may be questionable. Within, 'Prince Henry's Room' itself was restored with the help of South Kensington Museum experts. Armorial glass by Burlison and Grylls was inserted in the new windows, notably a stained-glass version of the first LCC seal (a Walter Crane design). The walls are lined with a mixture of Jacobean and Georgian panelling, and there is a good Georgian fireplace, but the low plaster ceiling is what holds the attention. Today this old-world room is set out with a display of objects belonging to the

Pepys Club, which also supplies the courteous custodians. There seems to be good reason to believe that Samuel Pepys drank here in his time. What London hostelry did the diarist not patronise?

146

George Inn
Borough High St, Southwark

2/K5   Underground or British Rail to London Bridge

[C]   National Trust

The George today is Shakespearean and Dickensian Southwark personified. Spurious as these associations may be, they account for the George's lone survival as an example of a galleried inn in London.

The first reference to the George appears on a map of about 1542, where seventeen inns are shown around the Borough Market. The inn was rebuilt in about 1620, only to be totally destroyed by fire in 1676. The ungalleried brick frontage is that immediately rebuilt by Mark Weyland. The galleried section followed soon after, and was continued round the courtyard. Early illustrations of the borough give no clue to when the George assumed its courtyard and galleried form and, despite historians' proclivity for drinking, the evolution of the English inn remains obscure. The earliest surviving examples rarely have galleries, though they are common in examples of the 16th and 17th centuries – in Europe as well as England. Both courtyards and galleries, the latter providing access to lodgings, are a feature of coaching inns, and the George flourished as such a motel throughout the 18th century.

The opening of London Bridge Station in 1844 put paid to the coaches. The George struggled on, serving the hop dealers who established themselves in the area. The courtyard and surrounding buildings became themselves warehouses and in 1874 the whole site was acquired by the Great Northern Railway Company. In 1889 the galleried ranges to the north and east of

183

The George Inn. GLRO

the courtyard were demolished for a new depot. Chaucer's Tabard had been demolished in 1878 and the rest of the George seemed equally doomed.

It was then that the Dickens legend came to the rescue. Despite a mere one-line reference in *Little Dorrit*, the manageress, Amelia Murray, was convinced that the George had been a haunt of Charles Dickens and she and her daughter Agnes traded on its nostalgia. The Shakespeare Society, Dickensian Fellowship and Tabard Players gathered here and the courtyard lent itself to Shakespearian re-enactments. In 1934 the George passed to Harold and Leslie Staples, nicknamed the Cheeryble Brothers from *Nicholas Nickleby*. They attempted to restore the inn but found its structural condition beyond their means and in 1937 the railway company offered it to the National Trust. The present arrangement of ground-floor bars and first-floor function rooms owes little to historic arrangements but everything to venerable panelling and smoke-enriched atmosphere.

147
Athenaeum, Reform and Travellers' Clubs and Institute of Directors
Pall Mall, Westminster

2/F5   Underground to Piccadilly Circus or underground/British Rail to Charing Cross

The ponderous clubs along Pall Mall proclaim the growing self-awareness of the post-Napoleonic ruling classes. Here, in four clubs in a line (there would be a fifth, had the Carlton Club not been bombed), you can trace the rapid institutionalisation of spirit and architecture that divides the world of George IV from that of his niece Victoria.

The sequence starts in 1826–30 with the stuccoed smartness of the United Service Club (now the Institute of Directors) and the Athenaeum, flanking the corners of Waterloo Place. The United Service people came first by a hair's breadth. The core of their

membership was the upper-officer class, demobilised after Waterloo and with time on its hands. Their competitor, the Athenaeum, was a club of newer creation and of scientific and literary bent. The prime sites the clubs acquired at the bottom of Waterloo Place derived from George IV's decision to destroy Carlton House, the original termination of Regent Street, when he commissioned Nash to rebuild Buckingham Palace. In its stead Nash, with his instinct for improvising urban scenery, planned the two Carlton House Terraces. In front of this were to be grand new building sites along Pall Mall with backs as well as fronts ranged in line, and an ample garden in between. To simplify things, the United Service Club chose Nash as its architect; the Athenaeum opted for his erstwhile protégé, Decimus Burton.

At first sight the clubs look much the same, and their lavishly proportioned fronts bulk together handsomely. They were supposed indeed to correspond exactly, insisted Nash at the outset. He then failed to keep his side of the bargain and ended up saying he had wanted differences all along. So the United Service Club had a double-height portico, pedimented windows and an extra portico at the back. Their rivals took vengeance by adding enrichment in the form of the Parthenon's Panathenaic frieze, on the grounds that the United Service's portico might 'throw an air of inferiority over the Athenaeum'. This, with E H Baily's gilded statue of Athena over the porch, gives a plausible Hellenism to what in truth is a still very Italian pair of buildings. The Athenaeum's frieze was carried out in Bath stone (not plaster, as might be supposed) by the Henning family. Years later, Burton scored again. Called in by the United Service Club to alter Nash's building, he added a fancy frieze there too.

West of the Athenaeum are the Travellers' and Reform Clubs. Their creation by Charles Barry in the 1830s began the transformation of Pall Mall into a street of oligarchical *palazzi* – Victorian England's answer to Genoa's Via Nova. The Travellers' is the smallest, prettiest and cleverest of the four buildings. Barry's first great public success, it ushered in the scholarly 'Italianate' architecture that was to supersede the impure Greco-Italian idiom of Nash and Burton. Recollections of Florence, Rome and Venice come sweetly together in a design calculated to impress on the club's well-travelled members the diligence and depth of Barry's own grand tour. The back, with its arched windows and its excrescence in the roof for smoking, is livelier than the front. Beyond the Travellers', the Reform Club (1838–41) completes the series. Its larger scale, portentous stone front and political purpose seem light years away from its neighbour. Here we stumble into the self-conscious world of Victorian public architecture.

Inside, all four of the clubs have big, tripartite rooms at the back for lounging, gossiping, dining or reading, decorated according to their function and date. But there are differences too. Nash sacrifices almost everything to an enormous central stair, probably because at one stage the United Service Club anticipated rescuing the grand staircase from Carlton House. The Athenaeum has a simply planned interior in Burton's best Greek manner, gingered up by a committee of Royal Academicians in the 1890s. The Travellers' again wins hands down for originality. Here Barry brings in the atrium plan, in a form not unlike its use in office buildings of the 1970s. The stair sneaks round the back of a square lightwell, and rooms are reached from its edges. But the atrium at the Travellers' has been eaten into, so one must go next door to savour the full effect on a *palazzo* scale. The Reform interior has grandeur and is of great interest for its structure and servicing, but it is a little wearying. Luckily the club employed Alexis Soyer as its first chef, in specially arranged kitchens, to save members from the puddingy effect of its architecture.

148
Prince Alfred
Formosa St, Maida Vale, Westminster

2/A2   Underground to Warwick Avenue

[C]

The architectural pub-crawler is profitably directed to Maida Vale. First call is in Formosa Street, where the Victorians showed two ways to end a terrace: on one side the blind side wall is relieved with giant pilasters and a great scrolled console over a blind arch; on the other is a pub. The building dates from about 1860, its interior from c.1890.

The Prince Alfred has been elevated from the ordinary to the sublime because it is a lone survivor of the typical late Victorian pub interior. It has all the once-common characteristics: a horseshoe-shaped bar with a central free-standing high counter holding the optics, from which radiate a series of little snugs, a public bar and a larger saloon bar leading to the billiard saloon. Each bar has its own street entrance and is internally connected only by waist-high doors cut into the panelling under the glass screens. Privacy in the snugs was further ensured by the glass 'snob' screens at eye level, with just enough space below for the drinks to pass through, and these survive along one side. The result is a medley of brown staining – from the lincrusta ceiling to the oak-grained panelling – and glass, acid-etched or embossed with opaque decoration. Gilding is reserved for the capitals of the slender iron columns that support the structure above. The architectural forms are simple and coarse: great broken pediments with urn finials and strapwork that might just owe something to Serlio.

Victorian reformers particularly objected to the snug or private bar for the opportunities it presented for salacious or illegal antics. They could do little to quell the drinking habits of the proletariat, but the magistrates could and did encourage the rebuilding of a single massive edifice in an area at the

Clubs in Pall Mall. Right to left: the Reform Club, the Travellers' Club and the Athenaeum. Beyond Waterloo Place: the Institute of Directors. EH

The Prince Alfred, Formosa Street. The public bar. EH

expense of two or three lesser locals. This policy suited the large Burton-on-Trent breweries, then beginning to make inroads into the London market; as the London breweries stretched themselves to beat the new competition, so pub architecture reached new heights of glitz and bravura. Thousands of pubs were rebuilt for fabulous sums between 1896 and 1899, when the inevitable financial crash came. Examples can be found all over London, recognisable for their imposing facades and huge saloons. They marked the arrival to dominance of the saloon bar. A good one within calling distance of Formosa Street is the Warrington Hotel in

Warrington Crescent, refitted in about 1899. Its tiled central entrance porch is impressive and its saloon more so, with a great coved frieze over the bar, frescoed with Rackhamesque lovelies in 1965, an Ionic arcade and much lincrusta and coloured glass. The decoration extends upstairs to the dining room, with its heavy plaster frieze of paired cherubs.

Still more elaborate is the Crown, across Maida Vale in Aberdeen Place, now called Crockers after its first landlord, the ambitious Frank Crocker. In 1898 he commissioned Charles H Worley, a more serious architect than most publicans resorted to, to produce a

lavish confection of baronial Queen Anne. Its interior has lost much of its atmosphere to thick carpets and upholstered sofas and its billiard room was dismantled in 1974, but its saloon retains handsome marble-lined walls and fireplaces as well as embossed glass in its entrance, here curved. As the *Licensed Victuallers' Gazette* remarked in 1899, 'one would fancy that it was the hall of some magnificent modern mansion rather than the saloon of a tavern'.

149

The Ritz
Arlington Street and Piccadilly, Westminster

2/E5   Underground to Green Park [C]

The Ritz, standing dramatic and sentinel where Piccadilly meets Green Park, is not so large as its imposing facades suggest. The massiveness of its construction, however, cannot be denied, for there lurks behind it a steel frame of unusual sophistication for its date in London.

César Ritz, a Swiss waiter, got on in hotel management by recognising a need for American standards of luxury and respectability in the hotels of the most expensive French and Swiss resorts. He and his winning formula, along with his chef, were brought to London by Richard D'Oyly Carte, who opened the Savoy Hotel in 1889. Claridge's and the Carlton Hotels followed, and under Ritz's management established themselves as smart social centres for the rich and titled and the West End as their national location. In 1898 Ritz realised the ambition of his own hotel, in Paris, but in 1902 he had a nervous breakdown and had no personal involvement with the London hotel that also bears his name, planned the same year. It repeated his formula, however, in respect of both its creature comforts and its architecture.

The architect for the Paris Ritz was Charles Mewès, whose practice was as international as his banker and playboy clientele. In 1900 he took the Beaux-Arts trained Arthur Davis as his London partner. Together they added a palm court to the Carlton and were the obvious choice for the London Ritz. Their planning is best appreciated entered from Arlington Street, from which unfolds a sequence of formal spaces breaking from the across a spinal corridor. This axis, clinging to yet shielded from Piccadilly, cannot hide the narrowness of the site, but the interplay of shapes and levels is an imaginative Beaux-Arts performance. French also in inspiration is the decoration supplied by Waring and Gillow, most exotic in a writhing fountain called *La Source* set back from the deep coves of the central Palm Court in its own gilded niche, and in the dining room at the culmination of the sequence, overlooking Green Park. Here the oval coffering of the ceiling, inset with painted clouds, seems to swell the room and mask its rectilinearity. Best of all perhaps is the domed entrance hall, cut into by a high drum giving glimpses of the upper floors, and which leads to one of the sinuous stairs

Mewès and Davis excelled at. To gain space and prominence in the street, the Ritz throws its upper floors over the pavement in an arcade resembling a length of the Rue de Rivoli.

That Mewès and Davis had so much freedom in the size and disposition of their rooms was due to the system of construction adopted. This was not French but American, organised by the Waring White Building Company – a consortium that had been set up by Samuel Waring and an American engineer, James Gilbert White, to build Waring and Gillow's store in Oxford Street (now Mothercare). For the Ritz they imported a Swedish engineer, Sven Bylander, who had built steel frames in America and Germany. The Ritz was not Britain's first steel-frame building, but it was London's earliest prominent example of the species, erected in the teeth of anomalous restrictions: to comply with the letter of the London Building Act, the Norwegian granite and Portland stone of the fronts had, absurdly, to be of load-bearing

thickness. The foundations, too, were wholly new for London. Instead of the concrete raft, long commonplace, Bylander used piles together with the 'Columbian system' of reinforcement for the floors, to allow maximum flexibility in loading. The timing of the contract and the technical detail of the structure, carefully pre-planned by an engineer rather than an architect, warranted a series of special progress reports in the technical press throughout 1905. Bylander was to use a similar system for Selfridge's department store, begun the year the Ritz opened, 1906. As a result of these pioneering efforts, the London Building Acts were at last amended to permit easier and more logical use of steel frames.

150

The Black Friar
Queen Victoria St and Little Water Lane, City of London

2/J4   Underground to Blackfriars
[C]

Seven to seven-thirty on a weekday evening, when the clientele is changing, is a ripe moment to drop in to the Black Friar. Young City pups and their girls tend to be finishing a drink just then and debating whether to go on to food and fun in the West End or to slope back to their suburbs, leaving the field to hardened topers. Some romance or other will usually be pursuing its course in the Grotto, the protagonists oblivious to the ambiguous mottoes ('A Good Thing is Soon Snatched Up'; 'Industry is All'), comic scenes and marble extravagance enveloping them. Oblivion to its unique and puzzling décor seems a mark of most Black Friar patrons. For the place is a genuine working City pub still, not an aesthetic tourist trap.

The puzzle is how this banal, squashed-up and externally quite ugly pub marooned on its cleft of land north of Blackfriars station, should have become a show-case for Arts and Crafts pub decoration. Arts and Crafts *aficionados* did not on the whole like drink, and when they did have to do with pubs they tried to reform them by

The Ritz. Palm Court. THE RITZ HOTEL, LONDON

bringing in the family, seating people on high wooden settles, getting cocoa sold and other earnest stratagems. The strident vulgarity of the London pub boom of the 1890s, much relished today, was anathema to the decade's artistic ideologues. Yet the Arts and Crafts Movement was always a broad church. Among its latitudinarians must be counted H Fuller Clark, the obscure architect brought in by Alfred Pettitt in 1904–6 to cheer up his new-bought pub, put up in 1875 on a fag-end site left over when Queen Victoria Street was laid out, and trickily sandwiched between road and railway. Pettitt and Clark decided to turn to dramatic account the name of the little hostelry, taken from the big Dominican priory once to be found northwards of the pub. The 'Merrie England' theme, with its mixture of nostalgia and innocent satire, is strong in minor Edwardian literature and art. But nowhere is it celebrated with such rollicking, high-polished bravado, in variegated marble, brass, mosaic, wood and copper relief, as on the Byzantinising walls of the Black Friar.

The copper panels of friars getting up to every imaginable antic are what most strike the eye. Soberer observers may

note a measure of restraint in the mixture of materials and the poking of fun at friars in the main bar (originally divided into sections) as compared with the inner sanctum of the Grotto. This is because the Grotto was an afterthought. Warming to their task, Pettitt and Clark decided in 1913 to add extra space behind, excavated from a railway vault and therefore windowless. It was not carried out until 1917–21 – very late for this kind of thing. The Grotto is superior to the main bar area, not just because it has been less altered but also because the panels are the work of a better sculptor, Henry Poole, RA, in place of Frederick Callcott. Here 'the drinker is bombarded with visual wit and entertainment', comments pub historian Robert Thorne. Poole's friars do sillier things than Callcott's, the moral impact of the beautifully lettered inscriptions is bewildering, while the enclosed, vaulted, marble-lined space hints at a chapel. The side-chapels of Westminster Cathedral, just being embellished at the time, may just have had some bearing upon the Grotto of the Black Friar. It has an aura of harmless but concentrated profanity, not to say secular-religious schizophrenia.

The Black Friar. Main bar. EH

151
F Cooke's Eel, Pie and Mash Shop
41 Kingsland High St, Dalston, Hackney

1/G4 British Rail to Dalston Kingsland
[C]

Eels are a peculiarly metropolitan delicacy. Perhaps it was because little else could readily be found in the muddy Thames estuary, especially once it became polluted. Certainly there were travelling eel-sellers by the 17th century. But, unlike the equally traditional shell-fish which may still be found on stalls in markets and outside public houses, sometime in the late 19th century the eel-sellers moved indoors.

The pie and mash shop as a cheap source of nutrition is unique to London and its seaside off-shoots like Southend. It seems to have owed its genesis to a handful of families, such as the Cookes, Manzes and the Burroughs, now all intermarried. Like other popular traditions their highpoint was the 1930s, but shops have held fast to their support in East and South London despite a strictly limited menu. Minced beef pies, mash, and live eels – stunned, decapitated and gutted in a single motion – is the choice, all served dripping with lasciviously green parsley sauce. The cowardly may opt for rhubarb and custard.

Robert Cooke opened a shop in Brick Lane in 1862. In 1910 his son Frederick took a second premises in Kingsland High Street, in a building erected in 1902–3 by the local architect James Hood. It is the culinary equivalent of the music hall: big mirrors, easily cleaned walls tiled in blue green and white, and marble-topped tables. The tiles include Delft-like scenes of wherries and ketches harvesting the catch. A coffered dining room was added to the rear in 1936, perhaps the date of the art deco counter. More recently the mirrors have been secured with clips in the form of intertwined eels. The atmosphere is neither friendly nor inviting, but as a

F Cooke's Eel, Pie and Mash Shop. EH

piece of social history, the pie and mash shop is one of the experiences of London.

152

Jack Straw's Castle
North End Way, Hampstead, Camden

1/F3   Underground to Hampstead
[C]

Jack Straw or Rackstraw, a comrade of Wat Tyler in the 1381 Peasant's Revolt sparked by the imposition of a poll tax, set up an encampment on Hampstead Heath. By the 18th century Jack had been commemorated by an inn at its highest point. The present building has all the trimmings of antiquity, a weatherboarded timber frame, sash windows – some with Gothic tracery – and two castellated turrets. Enter the yard, through an arch resonant of the pub's former coaching days, and there is a gallery to the upper floors, with, in a corner, an alcove complete with a Tudor arch and Gothick finials. Yet the whole confection dates only from 1962–4. It is entirely the creation of Raymond Erith, best known for neat and historicist Georgian houses.

It replaced a largely 19th-century building that had been badly bombed. The brewers, Charringtons, wanted to

restore its one-time prestige as a restaurant and sought something worthy of the location. Erith was happy to oblige, and had long been interested in traditional timber construction. But in the puritan 1960s it caused a row. Jack Straw's Castle is exactly contemporary with Centre Point, yet it is hard to imagine a greater contrast between two buildings of the same date. Hampstead Borough Council called Erith's scheme 'ostentatious and ridiculous'. The modernists of the London County Council, surprisingly, gave it their blessing without demur. In retrospect, Erith liked to say that he

achieved this by conning the LCC into the belief that he was promoting a 'new' and exceptionally versatile prefabricated system.

But by no means everyone was against Erith's traditionalism, as he sometimes liked to believe. The best assessment was made by Ian Nairn in the *Daily Telegraph*: 'It is just what a genuine Georgian designer would have done in the same circumstances – something that feels quite different from the pallid Georgian copies which are still going up in nearby streets of Hampstead Garden Suburb.' The exterior is convincing because its palimpsest of styles is held together by the simplicity of its profile and the basic elements of weatherboarding and longitudinal windows, and because it takes no obvious detail from any one period. Only the Gothick alcove in the courtyard is a simple pastiche, the frivolousness of which highlights the strength of the main composition.

The ground-floor retains some historically minded curiosities such as a pair of dated firebacks, but lost much of its character when the saloon and public bars were thrown into a single space in 1971. The restaurant and tower bar on the top floor survive better, though their fittings seem oddly conventional until you remember their date.

Jack Straw's Castle. AP

Entertainment

This section deals with auditoria. There are few sights in architecture more profoundly moving than a vast empty hall rippling with curved seat backs, waiting to serve up a few hours of mass escapism or culture; and little so optimistic as the prospect of filling them all. For in Britain entertainment buildings have been almost consistently financed by knife-edge speculation.

Purpose-built theatres grew out of the inadequacy of other halls to provide scenic effects. Indeed, for some historians of the theatre, the auditorium is secondary to the stage and the machinery required to mount the action upon it. From the Middle Ages dramatists have demanded floor traps, some kind of 'heaven', balcony or fly tower, and from the Renaissance, a way of creating perspective. The form of the Rose Theatre, built in 1587 and excavated in 1989, was not so very different from that of the later theatres selected here. It was polygonal, of timber on the shallowest masonry foundations, with narrow galleries round a solid-floor, raked stalls area or pit. The narrow stage thrust forward and had a 'tiring room' over, used not only for changing but for suspending scenic effects and 'flying' actors. Much of this knowledge comes from contemporary descriptions or prints, as does our information on 18th-century staging. Even Victorian stage machinery survives rarely and fragmentarily, with one exception. That is the theatre at Normansfield Hospital, the only surviving working example of a 'groove' scene-changing system in Britain and equipped with a unique collection of painted scenery.

The nature of theatres from even so recent a period as the 1860s and 1870s is now difficult to determine. The near-round drums of the Royal Opera House, Covent Garden and (though a concert hall) the Albert Hall, offer rare clues on a magnified scale to the awkwardness of theatre construction before balconies could be cantilevered. A history of

London theatre architecture must necessarily dwell on the two playhouses built under royal patents granted in 1663, Covent Garden and the Theatre Royal, Drury Lane, whose series of rebuildings chart the development of the British art of theatre construction. Their monopoly of serious drama did not mean that other theatres were not built before these patents were revoked in 1843: buildings such as the Haymarket Opera House of 1704–5 by Vanbrugh, and Sadler's Wells, originating in 1683, got round the restrictions through music licences. Yet the theatre 'took off' as popular entertainment only in the 1860s, and reached its height only a little ahead of cinema, between 1890 and 1914.

That so little survives from before 1890 owes much also to fire, and its resultant legislation. In 1898 Edwin Sachs, an architect as obsessed with fireproof construction as with the theatre, reckoned that there had been thirty-five serious fires in London theatres in the previous hundred years – in other words, that a theatre was destroyed every three years. Moreover, a huge percentage of these fires occurred in the twenty years from 1870. Other European cities suffered similar theatre fires, but none quite so many. What distinguishes London's subsequent theatres from those of the continent is the enthusiasm with which steel cantilevers were adopted, to pack more people in more rational fashion closer to the stage. Plans in Sachs's *Modern Opera Houses and Theatres* show what tiny sites London theatres occupied compared with those of the smallest European city, while even Her Majesty's Theatre, Haymarket, could fit on the stage of the Paris Opera House. The London County Council, for whom theatre design was an early preoccupation, insisted that half a theatre's external walls be open to the street, as a fire precaution: Sachs considered this too little. Only the Palace Theatre on Cambridge Circus

Matinée at the Avenue, Northfields, 1973.
GLRO

191

paid for a wholly island site – indicative of its intended status as an English Opera House. To cope with the complex regulations and demands of developers for quickly built, cheap buildings, there sprang up a small band of theatre specialists. Though little rated by more academic practitioners of the art of architecture, designers like C J Phipps, Frank Matcham, W G R Sprague and Bertie Crewe delivered the goods with vivacious panache.

Theatres purpose-built for high-brow entertainment really belong to the euphoric era of post-war public subsidies. Hence our selection pays tribute to more popular forms of entertainment such as the music hall, of which only the Hoxton Hall and Wilton's survive as more than fragments, and the variety hall that superseded it. Of the many Empires, Empresses and Alhambras that once adorned the inner-London suburbs, we have chosen the Hackney Empire as the one closest in feel to the mixture of vaudeville and concert entertainment these provided until the onslaught of first cinema and then television. Meanwhile concert halls relied on subscriptions, as at the Albert Hall, or interested sponsors, such as the piano-makers Bechstein at the Wigmore Hall.

Allied to the arrival of public subsidies was the idea of opening up the theatre 'out of hours': of providing eating, drinking and exhibition facilities not only for the greater comfort of those attending shows but to attract more transitory punters also. The classic example is the Royal Festival Hall, funded by the London County Council as the centrepiece of the Festival of Britain and the only building there intended to be permanent, with its hall enveloped in a great shell of subsidiary space. The unjustly maligned National Theatre by Denys Lasdun that followed, also with municipal sponsorship, is more difficult to penetrate but worth doing for the contrasting muscularity of its central foyer.

This century, popular culture has passed to other art forms. The first cinema exhibition in London was at the Regent Street Polytechnic in 1896. Because of the inflammability of nitrate

Theatre Royal, Drury Lane. Upper foyer. RCHME

film, cinemas were even greater fire hazards than theatres, though legislation controlling their building was passed only in 1909. A spate of cinemas followed, from whose fragmentary remains the Electric, Portobello Road, stands out. London is richer in examples from the second wave of cinema-building, which followed the arrival of 'talkies' in 1928. These cinemas replaced the hierarchical tiers of galleries found in theatres with a single huge circle, often slung over a grand foyer, tea room and/or ballroom. Here the losses have been still more severe, and it is those large auditoria that have passed out of cinema use that best survive: as legitimate theatres, such as the New Victoria, Wilton Road; as

dance halls, like the former Avenue, Northfields and the Forum, Kentish Town (now the Town and Country Club); and as bingo clubs, like the Granada, Tooting. Whilst theatres are slowly being returned to their original use, the alteration and destruction of cinemas continues.

Equally, popular opinion has yet to accept sports stadia as worthy of serious architectural attention. Again, sport as popular public entertainment dates only from late last century, and its structures mostly from the earlier part of this. Unfortunately, their building has tended to be piecemeal and cheapskate. Only cricket has ever had the cash, or cachet, to employ architects of repute at its national showcase. Lords has gained much from the employment of Frank Verity, Herbert Baker and, most recently, Michael Hopkins. Football has been particularly prey to commercial considerations, with only Arsenal and Chelsea building with any style for the millions who have supported them. At Wembley Owen Williams's stadium stands shabby if nostalgic, and his swimming pool languishes as the worst of all concert venues.

153

Theatre Royal, Drury Lane,
Westminster

2/G4   Underground to Covent Garden
[C]

The Theatre Royal enjoys an elevated status amongst London theatres. Its right to stage plays derives from letters patent granted by Charles II and there has been a theatre on the site since 1663. Just as it charts the development of English dramatic art, so the theatre encompasses the history of theatre design as developed by major architects.

The theatre has been completely rebuilt four times, and the auditorium remodelled on many more occasions. The first building only occupied the centre of the present island site. Such a site proved far too small, and in 1791 the Duke of Bedford agreed to buy up the surrounding freeholds and lease them to the theatre. Only after the fourth theatre was built in 1812 was all the land secured, so that the theatre turns its back on the street whose name it bears. The design of the first theatre, erected in 1662–3, has been attributed to Christopher Wren, but he is now thought only to have been involved with its rebuilding after a fire, in 1674. His design was subsequently much remodelled, most especially by Robert Adam in 1775. In March 1794 a new and vastly enlarged building by Henry Holland opened. It boasted a horseshoe-shaped auditorium, with an extra tier and far more boxes, and a huge stage supplied with elaborate machinery. Particularly handsome was the front of house, a series of saloons that included

an 'Egyptian Hall' behind the pit. Elaborate fire precautions included four water tanks, iron fire plates to protect the timber-framed shell, and an iron safety curtain. Yet in 1809 the theatre was almost completely destroyed by fire.

Benjamin Dean Wyatt built the replacement, which opened in 1812. The plan, again with three tiers of boxes and an upper gallery ringing the auditorium, was more semi-circular than Holland's, and introduced the idea of an elaborate proscenium arch as a frame to the spectacle on the stage. This concept was subsequently adopted elsewhere. More important, since it survives, is Wyatt's front of house. The boxes and grander seats were reached via two great cantilevered double-flight staircases arched round a domed and columned rotunda. One staircase was dubbed the 'King's' and one the 'Prince's', since George III and the Prince Regent were provided with separate boxes facing one another – a tradition that lives on today. They form a worthy processional sequence and perhaps the grandest art gallery in London, for the Theatre Royal has an impressive collection of theatrical paintings and sculpture.

Two distinctive features of the facade are later additions: the Doric portico attributed to both James Spiller and John Soane, put on in 1820, and the long Ionic colonnade facing Russell Street that was added by Samuel Beazley in 1831. The auditorium is later still, although its plan and the smallness of its top gallery were dictated by Wyatt's walls: it was rebuilt in 1921–2 by J Emblin Walker, F Edward Jones and Robert Cromie. Wyatt's auditorium had been much altered, but one can mourn the loss of his curtained boxes supported on slender cast-iron columns. They were replaced by three cantilevered tiers. The fronts of the lower boxes are in a Wedgwood-style classicism found in cinemas of that date, but above it burst forth bigger-boned and more lush mouldings, supposedly inspired by the Empire lines of Wyatt's work but in places neo-Egyptian. The decoration has a stilted grandeur of imitation lapis lazuli and bronze gilding, especially in the massive light fittings, unlike any surviving theatre or cinema, yet closest

to a Hollywood epic in feeling. What does survive from an earlier period are the complex system of wooden traps and other 'machinery' under the stage, and a rare scene painting shop to the rear where the backcloths are raised and lowered on vertical frames over 40 ft wide.

154

Royal Opera House
*Bow St, Covent Garden,
Westminster*

2/G4   Underground to Covent Garden
[C]

Three venerable theatres have stood on this site. Of these the present Royal Opera House is not – in auditorial terms – the biggest. The palm belongs to Robert Smirke's Covent Garden Theatre, a lavish Greek Revival project built in 1808–9 and burnt to the ground in 1856. That in turn replaced the much smaller Theatre Royal, Covent Garden, dating back to 1732 and renowned as a venue for early pantomime and for Handel operas and oratorios. Smirke's theatre carried on this high reputation with a mixture of Shakespearean tragedy and romantic opera, but proved hard to make pay and was often hired out. When therefore Frederick Gye, lessee of the building and manager of the Royal Italian Opera Company, set about rebuilding after the conflagration of 1856, he did so with an eye to economy. That is why Britain's premier opera house has stucco fronts and stingy public spaces. By contrast it has an auditorium which in acoustical and aesthetic terms is second to none.

Chronically short of money, Gye brought to the rebuilding the idea (more familiar now than then) of using part of the site for commercial purposes wherewith to subsidise his theatre. This was the origin of the iron-and-glass Floral Hall, immediately south of the Opera House. By renting it out to Covent Garden Market traders and others, Gye hoped to recoup his building costs on the theatre. But the plan turned out badly. The Floral Hall failed, proved a white elephant, then was half-lost in a fire and is now a shadow of its former self, though its partial restoration is now in prospect. Its main practical effect was to constrict the theatre.

There is a structural relation between the buildings too. Gye was in a hurry to reopen and needed a 'fast-track' rebuilding; this prompted as much iron construction and off-site work as possible. So he hired not just an architect but a complete building team, all of whose members had worked on the Houses of Parliament. Charles and Thomas Lucas, experts in railway construction, were the contractors for the two buildings; Henry Grissell supplied and designed the ironwork; and as architect Gye chose E M Barry, Sir Charles's twenty-six-year-old son. The theatre which this team built at top speed in 1857–8 is in part a concealed iron building. Huge iron girders span the building from side wall to side wall. The elegant saucer dome and arches of the auditorium ceiling, far from being structural, are hung from these girders above by means of a wooden framework prefabricated at the Lucases' works in Lowestoft. The auditorium itself is a largely independent internal structure of iron, its galleries being canted out with a system of columns and girders.

How much independence young Barry, an able and underrated architect, had is hard to say. He certainly designed the elevations including the main portico (which Gye wanted to leave off as an unnecessary expense), as well as the modest foyer, staircase and first-floor crush room. Of these only the staircase survives in unaltered form. The deft lines of the auditorium, based in part on an internal reconstruction of Smirke's theatre undertaken only ten years before, must be Barry's too, as is the proscenium arch. But Barry had to contend with Raffaelle Monti, an Italian sculptor brought in by Gye as decorative consultant for the auditorium. By Monti are the swelling lines of the box fronts, the nymphs that adorn them and the 'Portland Vase'-style relief over the proscenium. Despite various changes to the auditorium, the general appearance and plush colour scheme, including the 'cerulean' blue of the ceiling, reflect the original choices.

One thing that has utterly changed is the stage, originally designed with a slope, traps and other mid-Victorian devices. The advent of Wagnerian opera made a more flexible stage and high fly-tower imperative. These were furnished in 1900–1 by Edwin Sachs, a clever Anglo-German architect with a passion for theatrical technicalities. Having been struggling along with modifications of the Sachs stage ever since, the Royal Opera House is at the time of writing in the throes of a drawn-out reconstruction which will, among much else, see everything behind the proscenium arch disappear in favour of an ampler stage. The big block of rehearsal and dressing rooms behind the theatre, designed by the GMW Partnership in 1979–82, is the completed preliminary to Jeremy Dixon's development plans which aim to bring the whole swathe of property southwards down to Russell Street and west to the Covent Garden Piazza within the opera house's ambit. The quality of Dixon's architecture promises to be high, but the scheme has hurdles still to jump.

155
Hoxton Hall
Hoxton St, Hoxton, Hackney

2/L1   Underground or British Rail to Old Street or Liverpool Street [C]

The Hoxton Hall opened on 7 November 1863, erected by a Mr James Mortimer with the objective of 'affording to the humbler classes an entertainment that shall combine instruction with amusement'. *The Era* recorded the hall as providing 'a good drop of beer' in 'an elegantly fitted and brilliantly lighted hall', and music worthy of a 'second-class concert room'. Its singing and magic shows were intended to be vaguely improving. Clearly this did not work, as it became instead a dance school.

In 1868 the music hall was reopened by James McDonald, former manager of Collins's hall on Islington Green. With a repertory of comics and singers the Hall was successful until 1872. Why it then lost its licence is uncertain, but the sheer number of rival halls may have been a determining factor. Unlike most halls, Hoxton was never attached to a pub, so there was no steady source of income.

Royal Opera House, Covent Garden. GLRO

Hoxton Hall. GLRO

The Hoxton Hall changed dramatically in appearance in its short life as a music hall. Under Mortimer it was a low hall with Corinthian pilasters and a small gallery raised on wooden columns at its western end. Entrance was from the side, and the hall was reached from stairs at the stage end. Under McDonald the hall was heightened and two galleries raised round the room on cast-iron columns. For some reason the cast-iron fronts are of different designs. The hall is still tiny, and uniquely vertiginous. The original stage has been replaced but it remains otherwise much as McDonald left it, effectively a tavern song room without a tavern. Comparison with the only other surviving music hall, Wilton's, off Wellclose Square in Tower Hamlets and essentially of 1859, suggests the Hoxton Hall was old-fashioned when built; nevertheless both look spartan when contrasted with the lavish variety theatres that superseded them.

Like Wilton's, the Hoxton Hall has survived because it passed quickly into a completely contrasting use. It was acquired in 1879 by the Blue Ribbon Army, a Christian temperance movement sponsored by the biscuit manufacturer, W I Palmer of Reading. It became a mission hall for meetings and services, and a community centre for organisations such as the Girl's Guild of Good Life. It was presumably the Blue Ribbon Army who ripped out the ledge for drinks fitted behind the railing of the first floor gallery, of which only the brackets survive. The Army died with Palmer, who in 1893 bequeathed the hall to the Bedford Institute, a Quaker

movement engaged in similar community work. So the Hoxton Hall maintained its social function, and in 1910 was enlarged by Lovegrove and Papworth. A passageway was made from Hoxton Street, and stairs at the rear of the hall inserted; the present entrance through a former shop dates only from 1981.

Community work remains the principal function of the hall, particularly for young people and pensioners. Since the 1960s it has also become a centre for dramatic societies and workshops, with special music hall evenings. It is still run by the Bedford Institute, who restored it in 1977.

156
Royal Albert Hall
Kensington Gore, Westminster

2/B6   Underground to South Kensington

[C]

The 1851 Great Exhibition held in Hyde Park made £186,000. Just as he had initiated the Exhibition, Prince Albert determined what happened to the profit. The aims of the Exhibition were to be perpetuated by a permanent centre co-

locating technical training schools with museums of art and science, concert halls and facilities for learned societies. Land was purchased in South Kensington, but none of the major established institutions could be persuaded to move out there.

The one success was to attract the Government School of Design, founded in 1837 on principles close to the Prince's own and run by many of those involved in the Great Exhibition. Henry Cole, its Secretary, even shared Albert's mistrust of established artists and architects. When the School moved in 1855–7, military engineers were employed, chief of them Captain Francis Fowke, who produced a series of brick buildings intended to be richly decorated as funds permitted. With a vast body of assistants and draftsmen it is almost impossible to determine who did what at South Kensington. But the result was a distinctive style of simple red brick forms relieved by fine decorative terracotta, seen most clearly in the central courtyard and Henry Cole Wing of the Victoria & Albert Museum facing Exhibition Road – and on the Royal Albert Hall.

The genesis of the Albert Hall was the death of the Prince from typhoid fever in December 1861. Cole considered a concert hall more appropriate to Albert's ideals than a monument, and though

Royal Albert Hall from the Memorial. GLRO

the public subscription raised was eventually entirely devoted to Sir Gilbert Scott's memorial (p. 253), he did not give up. His first idea was for a small multi-functional hall with shops, flats and galleries to provide revenue. But a grander concept of a great amphitheatre won out early in 1865. The scheme was to be financed instead by selling boxes and seats.

Fowke designed a cigar-shaped hall dominated by apsidal ends; but in December 1865 himself died. The form of the interior, a flat floor with banking on either side rising to three storeys of boxes around the wall, seems nevertheless to have been largely his. The exterior and the final elliptical shape were most likely the work of Lieutenant-Colonel Henry Scott, though, as elsewhere in South Kensington, a confusing array of assistants was employed. Most impressive structurally was the iron and glass roof engineered by J W Grover and R M Ordish, the latter fresh from working at St Pancras Station.

The interior is stunning for its size and simplicity, best seen from the top walkway, intended originally as an exhibition gallery. There are only the simplest mouldings to the cast-iron stanchions and no decorative elaboration. The grandest feature is the organ, installed by Henry Willis and then the world's largest. The surrounding corridors and even the bar have the starkness of a cheap railway hotel. Decoration was reserved for the exterior, whose most lavish feature is a terracotta frieze running round the building under the main cornice. It was made in 800 slabs by Minton, Hollins and Company, assisted by the ladies of the South Kensington Museum's mosaic class. Above it runs a huge inscription describing the laying of the foundation stone by Queen Victoria in May 1867 and her opening of the building in March 1871.

On its completion the Albert Hall was left without endowment, and with the burden of hundreds of seats already sold in perpetuity. It has chiefly been used for music, but its finances are still bolstered by an extraordinary range of uses that include sport, balls and conferences.

157

Normansfield Hospital Theatre
Kingston Rd, Teddington, Richmond

1/D6   British Rail to Hampton Wick

Although the study and certification of mental illness was well established by the 1860s, there was little provision for the incurably handicapped, then termed 'idiots'. An early pioneer was John Haydon Langdon-Down, for ten years the medical superintendent at Britain's first large institution for the handicapped, the Royal Earlswood Asylum in Surrey. In 1866 he produced his paper on 'Mongolism', the condition today known as Down's Syndrome. This established his reputation, and in 1868 Langdon-Down opened a private asylum for the handicapped offspring of the upper and middle classes in a new villa in Teddington.

By 1877 the asylum had been expanded to house 115 patients. Large asylums usually had both a chapel and a recreation hall, the latter usually with a stage but otherwise very plain. At little

Normansfield Hospital Theatre. GLRO

Normansfield the two functions were incorporated into one building, so greater elaboration was perhaps to be expected. But, additionally, the Langdon-Down family had a passion for the theatre that included the founding of a local amateur dramatic society as well as the production of entertainment by and for their patients. Mrs Langdon-Down was 'acting manager' for the residents' performances, which were open to the public, and their son and successor, Dr Reginald, encouraged acting as therapy. The architect was Rowland Plumbe, who seems to have secured the commission through his mother, an early supporter of Earlswood.

The 'entertainment hall' at Normansfield is the most lavish in any British hospital. The high, richly decorated proscenium and a gas 'sunburner' in the middle of the hall breathe the atmosphere of a real theatre in this unlikely spot. Otherwise the architectural treatment of the hall would be equally appropriate to a chapel: the heavy hammerbeam roof, the cast-iron gallery to the rear, and the painted figures set under Gothic canopies to either side of the stage. But the hall's special significance lies in the survival of its Victorian working stage, with its groove system of wings intact, gas-lit footlights and over a hundred pieces of 'stock' scene paintings – the largest collection in Britain.

Normansfield was run by the Langdon-Down family until 1951, when it was sold to the National Health Service. As the hospital is now threatened with closure, the future of the theatre is uncertain.

158
Palace Theatre
Cambridge Circus, Westminster

2/F4   Underground to Leicester Square or Tottenham Court Road
[C]

The interior of the Palace Theatre today leaves two striking impressions. One is how strong was class distinction in the

Palace Theatre, newly restored. EH

Victorian theatre. There is a world of difference between the cheery stalls bars, now a brasserie, and the bare formica counter serving the vertiginous gallery or 'Gods' hundreds of winding steps above. As you climb from one to the other so the decoration and scale of provision, seating, sightlines, waiting areas and bars are carefully graduated. The other impression is that this is glorified pub architecture: lincrusta ceilings, encrusted plasterwork, all now in the murkiest of browns. Only when your eyes have adjusted to the gloom can you appreciate just how lavish the auditorium is (though from the Gods, with its plain brown tiles, much is out of sight), and count all the cherubs on the curving balcony fronts. It was not always so murky, and the recently restored facade shows just how sumptuous the interior will be when similarly treated.

The cutting of Shaftesbury Avenue through the slums of Soho coincided with a boom in building bigger, better equipped and safer theatres. Its north side is lined with theatres that exploited new developments in steel construction so that balconies could be cantilevered rather than supported on columns. This meant that balconies could be much bigger, and that all patrons were assured of an unimpeded view of the stage. The

Palace Theatre, built between 1888 and 1891 by G H Holloway, with T E Collcutt brought in to provide the decorations and imposing terracotta facade, was the first London playhouse to employ cantilevers confidently. There were three great circular cantilevered balconies, the uppermost replaced in 1908 by one with a serpentine front. The planning, on an awkwardly shaped site, is particularly neat. Offices and dressing rooms shielded the tapering auditorium from the noise of Shaftesbury Avenue, and the tier of foyers and bars provided similar protection from Cambridge Circus.

The scale and innovation of the theatre reflect the ideas of its builder. It was the great commercial failure of Richard D'Oyly Carte who, having achieved lasting fame as the progenitor of Gilbert and Sullivan's light operas, tried to go up-market. The Palace was erected as the Royal English Opera House, an opportunity for Sullivan, too, to fulfil a cherished ambition of writing 'serious' opera without the distraction of Gilbert's comic lyrics. His *Ivanhoe* opened the theatre in January 1891 and flourished briefly, but there was no English opera with which to follow it. By the autumn D'Oyly Carte had to fall back on French operetta, and in 1892 to mount a season with Sarah Bernhardt to inject much-needed cash. In December 1892 he sold out to Augustus Harris, who reopened this monument to a higher art-form as the Palace Theatre of Varieties – little more than a music hall.

159

Hackney Empire
Mare St, Hackney

1/G4   British Rail to Hackney Central or Hackney Downs; or underground to Highbury & Islington or Bethnal Green, then bus

[C]

The Hackney Empire was built in 1900–1 as part of Britain's unprecedented theatre boom. A few entrepreneurs recognised a demand for an alternative to music hall, bringing a more consistent standard of programme and more lavish surroundings to the local high street as well as the West End. Variety theatres were large, safe and comfortable – working-class and low-brow, but aiming above the alcoholic

Hackney Empire. Euterpe returned to the rooftop. EH

rowdiness and vulgarity of the music hall. A few artistes like Marie Lloyd, who lived nearby, objected to the monopolies of the new theatre companies, but most accepted the more secure touring contracts they offered.

One of the foremost entrepreneurs of the variety theatre was Oswald Stoll, whose mother inherited a music hall in Liverpool when he was fourteen. He later formed a circuit of variety theatres with two former rivals, Edward Moss and Richard Thornton. In 1900 this became a public company, Moss Empires Ltd. Their regular architect was Frank Matcham, Britain's most prolific theatre designer, who fulfilled their demands for quickly built and eyecatching theatres superbly. In a career of just under forty years, Matcham built some eighty new theatres, and remodelled another thirty. The Hackney Empire is one of his few surviving variety theatres and stands comparison with his grander London commissions, the Coliseum (1902–4) and Richmond Theatre (1901). The statistics of Matcham's career and the fact that the Hackney Empire was completed within a year testify to the cut-throat competition of Edwardian theatre. In his day Matcham's over-the-top confections were condemned by critics as popularist and un-archi-tectural: today they are revered for these very qualities.

The Hackney Empire was built for 2,500 people, yet there is always a feeling of intimacy with the performance. This must be due not only to Matcham's expert planning but also to the decorative treatment, which reaches to every part in an Alhambran encrustation of motifs and gold paint. There are three tiers, all richly fronted, with boxes to the side and behind the grand circle. Matcham's panache reaches its height where these meet the proscenium: on each side robust cherubs support the board giving the numbers of the variety acts, with a pair of Indian domes tucked above them for good measure. The original painting scheme was destroyed in 1979; murals, oddly sub-Gainsborough in style, remain over the proscenium arch and in the front vestibule, where Haydn, Handel and Mozart are depicted. This entrance

was for patrons of the stalls and grand circle only; lesser mortals had to enter round the back.

The facade was denuded of its rampant terracotta domes in 1979, but these and a statue of Euterpe were replaced in 1988 after a successful prosecution led by theatre historian Robert Thorne on behalf of the Greater London Council. The return of these features restored the facade's vitality and excitement. Best of all, the Hackney Empire has been returned to its original function as a variety theatre, interspersed with concerts and a Christmas pantomime. Much work still needs to be done to the auditorium but it is already the best live venue in London, a tribute to the perseverance and imagination of the preservationists and performers who have brought new life to it.

160

Wigmore Hall
Wigmore St, Westminster

2/E3   Underground to Bond Street or Oxford Circus

[C]

Wigmore Street was a fashionable shopping street that got upstaged by tawdry Oxford Street. That has been its salvation, and perhaps also that of the Wigmore Hall built between 1899 and 1901 at its centre. It lurks opposite Debenham and Freebody's first store, hidden behind a spirited group of terracotta-clad buildings and distinguished only by a projecting glazed canopy. A narrow marble passageway leads to a ticket window, a little foyer dominated by an alabaster staircase bigger than the balcony it serves, and a simple auditorium.

The Wigmore Hall is ideally suited to the string quartet and recital. Mahogany, marble pilasters, a barrel-vaulted roof with a skylight; you can still imagine how they looked by gaslight, for which a few fittings survive. The platform is raised in an apse at the far end, with golden wallpaper and more mahogany doors. But look up and the

Wigmore Hall. Mural in proscenium arch. RCHME

sense of homeliness is dispelled. The dome of the apse is engulfed with gold leaf and metallic paint, as impassioned a piece of symbolism as a Wagner opera. An androgynous Soul of Music bursts from the sun-like rays of the Genius of Harmony, flanked by a composer and musician assisted from a tangle of thorns by encouraging angels. The contrast between hall and mural symbolises the late Victorian era of fraught gentility, every frustation of a Henry James or Edith Wharton novel, better than anywhere else in London.

A Wagnerian, or at least a Germanic, reference is not inappropriate. The Wigmore Hall was originally known as the Bechstein Hall. In the late 19th century Germany and the United States became the centres of the first large-scale factory production of pianos. In 1853 Bechsteins opened a showroom in Berlin, followed by one in London in 1879. In the 1890s they followed the pattern set by, amongst others, Steinway in New York, by building their own concert hall for recitals in Berlin. In 1899 the London showrooms followed suit, building a hall behind the adjacent property at a cost of £100,000. The architect was T E Collcutt and the muralist was Gerald Moira; they had previously worked together at the P&O Pavilion at the 1900 Paris Exhibition. In 1904 Bechsteins acquired the premises in front of the hall, which they rebuilt to the designs of Walter Cave.

On the outbreak of the First World War Bechsteins put their property in the hands of a receiver and manager; nevertheless in 1916 the hall, showrooms and 137 pianos were sold by order of the Board of Trade for only £56,000, to Debenhams. In 1917 the concert hall reopened as the Wigmore Hall, and apart from some new light fittings little has changed since. It is still valued today for the quality of its acoustics.

161

Electric Cinema
Portobello Rd, Kensington and Chelsea

1/E4   Underground to Notting Hill Gate or Ladbroke Grove
[C]

When it opened in February 1911 the Electric Cinema Theatre in Portobello Road was just one of many thousands of little cinemas being built to a fairly standard design. All were simple rectangular halls, though the more grand among them had balconies. Typical is a barrel-vaulted roof decorated with bands of fruity plasterwork that continue down the sidewalls, which were given the effect of panelling, but in plaster. Because there was no sound amplification the screen could be placed

directly on the end wall – indeed it often was the end wall painted white. An attempt at grandeur was usually made by building a proscenium arch with a little segmental pediment or central cartouche, a couple of columns and a few swags. Similar eye-catching ornamentation was given to the entrance front, usually rather crudely, and there was often a dome or tower, and sometimes two.

The architect of the Electric, Portobello Road, was Gerald Seymour Valentin. He followed this formula almost to the letter, though the auditorium's rich panelling is much more elaborate than most. The hall is tiny, almost square. The proscenium at the Electric is like a picture frame, the moulding running along the bottom as well as the top and sides of the screen. One or two theatres also went in for this unusual device, but there are few survivors.

Since legislation was only introduced to regulate the showing of films in 1909, following a series of fatal fires caused by the explosive nitrate film, it is impossible to determine where London's first cinema was. The Electric's feat is to have kept its form and fittings intact, gas-lights and all. Most early cinemas smartened themselves up in the 1930s to compete with the super cinemas and built wider prosceniums when sound

The Electric, Portobello Road. GLRO

and bigger picture sizes arrived, but here there was never the money. The cinema gained popularity in the late 1960s as an 'arts' cinema, showing films never usually screened in a mainstream cinema, and has struggled on since then, with this formula.

162

Wembley Stadium and Arena
Olympic Way, Wembley, Brent

1/D3   Underground to Wembley Park, or British Rail to Wembley Stadium

[C]

On both occasions, Britain has advertised its ability to survive a World War by staging an exhibition. More than this, in 1919 it was decided to demonstrate her continued dominance over an empire, with the British Empire Exhibition held in 1924. More survives of the 1924 buildings at Wembley than of the 1951 Festival of Britain on the South Bank. The Wembley site is also a much-mauled testament to Britain's greatest modern exports: football and rock music, neither of them accepted symbols of national pride. The pervading squalor is not for the high-minded.

For the Empire Exhibition each colony was given a building of a size proportionate to its perceived importance. These were eclipsed in scale by two massive British palaces dedicated to industry and engineering, placed fairly symmetrically to either side of a central double avenue leading to the only structure intended to be permanent: the stadium. For all these buildings concrete was chosen as cheap, quick and appropriately modern. The commission was shared between the architect Maxwell Ayrton and the engineer Owen Williams, the latter's first prominent work. Williams's structure was subservient to Ayrton's architectural pretensions, the *in situ* concrete cast with masonry lines with Williams's expressive imagination allowed vent only in the interior stanchions. Concrete was presumed to be a suitably temporary medium. But

Wembley Stadium. The twin towers. MARTIN CHARLES

when the exhibition closed in October 1925 and the site was sold off piecemeal the economic climate was so far deflated that many buildings drifted into industrial uses. The Palace of Industry survives as one of Britain's more monstrous warehouses. It has a brutishness worthy of Mussolini topped with the lions of Empire in concrete.

Wembley Stadium is used for many sporting and music functions, but is most famous as football's national shrine. Outside, the twin towers are resonant of late-empire baroque at its most debased, whilst inside is a cavernous oval of terracing, the pitch distantly perceived beyond a running track and the greyhound course that brings Wembley much of its regular

revenue. The ends of the terracing were covered over to complete the oval roof only in 1963. Grubby and out-dated it may be, but to the football romantic none the worse for that.

Sadder is the state of the British Empire Pool, now the Wembley Arena, constructed by Owen Williams for the 1934 Empire Games. It makes a pointed contrast between what Williams the engineer could do when masked by the architectural embellishment of others, and the more inspiring forms he could achieve when allowed to bare his engineering forthrightly. The brief was for a huge pool that could be floored in as an arena, with a clear span – in the event of 236 ft 6 in. The solution was a toast-rack of cantilevered concrete frames, supporting both the pitched roof and upper terracing, that are expressed externally as a line of projecting, counterbalancing fins. At each corner tiny towers perch like bird-watchers' huts. The shame is that Williams's stepped and ribbed glazed ends have been so assaulted with tatty posters and temporary huts.

163

Granada Cinema, Tooting
Mitcham Rd, Tooting,
Wandsworth

1/F6   Underground to Tooting Broadway

[C]

'The picture theatre supplies folk with the flavour of romance for which they crave . . . While there they can with reason consider themselves as good as anyone, and are able to enjoy their cigarettes or their little love affairs in comfortable seats and amidst attractive and appealing surrounds.' So wrote a Russian aristocrat, trained architect and successful stage designer called Theodore Komisarjevsky, in 1930. He sums up what the cinema in the 1920s and 1930s was all about.

In England 'talkies' and the depression arrived at about the same time, and there was little incentive to create the vast fantasy palaces or 'super cinemas' such as were built in the United States. Perhaps the one English entrepreneur with a truly American sense of the grandiose was Sidney Bernstein. Beginning in 1930 he created a small chain of cinemas named after his holiday location of that year, Granada. Most were in the London suburbs. Bernstein used a series of architects, but all the cinemas bar one were built to roughly the same plan, all displayed his strong belief in rich fittings and a sense of tradition, and all had interiors by Theodore Komisarjevsky.

Komisarjevsky's first cinemas were in a Moorish style appropriate to their name, and that at Walthamstow survives. He has also been associated with a mock-hacienda style cinema built by Cecil Masey in Northfields Avenue (p. 190) and dubbed 'Spanish City'. Then, in one of London's least-inspiring suburbs, Komisarjevsky produced a Gothic masterpiece. Surviving drawings suggest Komisarjevsky worked more closely with Masey than with other cinema architects, but at Tooting the facade gives no clue to what lies within. To enter through the double doors is to be transported to a Doge's Palace: a

double-height entrance hall bristling with rich plasterwork and sparkling chandeliers makes ludicrous comparison with outside reality. Swish up one of the elegant flights of the double stair into a hall of mirrors, ascend a little stair or vomitory, and you enter a Gothic cathedral opened to the skies.

The transformation works despite the bizarre touch brought by bingo: bright lights, brighter bar signs and the clatter of money being poured down slot machines. The mighty Wurlitzer organ is buried beneath the bingo caller's rostrum. This is no longer Hollywood, but Las Vegas SW17. For a sense of what the effect of so much plasterwork and gold paint must have been like in near-darkness try Komisarjevsky's surviving cinemas in Harrow and Walthamstow, both now part of the Cannon circuit.

164

Royal Festival Hall
Belvedere Rd, Lambeth

2/H5   Underground or British Rail to Waterloo

[C]

Space, that elusive architectural goal of the Modern Movement, is the great thing about the Festival Hall. The building has elegances a-plenty, outside and in. But in the context of the bad British tradition of parsimonious public space, its supreme achievement is the multi-level foyer beneath the sloping floor of the auditorium. Here you can circulate, drink, eat or merely gaze about – in a setting undreamt of in British architecture before 1951. The word for its atmosphere is 'civilised', a quality which the merchandising of the foyer space in recent years has detracted from but signally failed to destroy.

The Royal Festival Hall was conceived and built in a hurry, as the London County Council's contribution to the Festival of Britain and the one permanent South Bank feature of that unique post-war jamboree. Plans for a cultural centre in the area go back to the 1930s, when the LCC bought land in connection with the rebuilding of

The Granada, Tooting. GLRO

Waterloo Bridge and, it was then hoped, Hungerford Railway Bridge as well. Such a centre was sketched out in Abercrombie's 1943 County of London Plan, when the National Theatre was expected to be its first element. After the war Charles Holden made a layout for the whole complex and fixed the precise site for the concert hall, but no quick action was anticipated. Then suddenly the Festival of Britain materialised. The LCC and the music world, bereft of a first-rate concert hall since the bombing of the Queen's Hall, saw their chance. But who could design and build a premier international concert hall in less than three years?

Robert Matthew, the strong-minded LCC Architect, was determined to keep the project in-house and to have nothing stale and old. The time-factor played in his favour and he had his way. Leslie Martin, a modernist with a reputation as an intellectual, was appointed to lead the LCC Festival Hall team. Martin in his turn called in Peter Moro, a fastidious designer who had worked with Lubetkin; and Moro brought in to assist him a bevy of young architects whom he had been teaching at the Regent Street Polytechnic.

The site set by Holden was painfully small. Hence the brilliance of Martin's concept, 'the egg in the box'. Uniquely, the auditorium would be raised *on top of* the public spaces, which would wrap round and under it; in this way too it could be protected from the noise of the trains passing so close by. It was germane to the concept that the 'egg' should be articulated within the 'box'. That is why the curve of the auditorium roof rises clear within the frame, while the skin of its walls is enclosed by a cladding of Derbyshire fossil marble, polished within, unpolished on the outside. The box itself was faced with a mixture of Portland stone, ample fenestration for views in as well as out and – originally – tiling. It was left to Moro and his team to work all this out in time for 1951. The result is a masterpiece of humane modernism, showing something of the influence of Le Corbusier in its separation of supports from walling but far more of Lubetkin and Aalto. The details of the foyer, above all the staircases and the famous green 'Net and Ball' carpet, always running in the same direction, are particularly Scandinavian.

The auditorium was an unnerving technical test. Its unprecedented size (nearly 3,000 seats) provoked the first scientific acoustical enquiry preceding the building of any major international concert hall. The great fear was too much resonance, like the Albert Hall; in the event the fault lay somewhat in the other direction. But the hall is generally judged an acoustical success. Peter Moro's interior has been little changed since the 1950s and proffers a mixture of clean, restful lines and the slight fiddliness typical of the Festival of Britain spirit. Incident is provided by the queer, cantilevered boxes with their fine scarlet hangings behind, the Aalto-like acoustical reflector in elm and Leslie Martin's rather discordant organ front with its pipework – most of which, curiously, is false.

Unlike the egg, the box has changed dramatically since 1951. The plan, overtaken by the rush to completion, was to build a second small hall with rehearsal rooms under and behind the main auditorium. This was never done. Instead, the desperate need for extra service space was satisfied in 1963–5 by the LCC architects adding on a whole new front and back to the building and correcting what were felt to be *naïvetés* in the original elevations. The result is a blander, more Corbusian and more homogeneous Festival Hall, easier to use but lacking the colourful brio of the original.

165
Mound Stand, Lord's Cricket Ground
St John's Wood Rd, Westminster

2/B2   Underground to St John's Wood

[C]

If Thomas Lord did not begin cricket's obsession with its own history, he at least did much to foster it. On being kicked out of his original ground in St Marylebone by the developers of Dorset Square, he took the turf with him. When moved on again in 1812 by the builders of the Regent's Canal, he transported it to St John's Wood. His hallowed ground has since been built up piecemeal with benches and boxes as needs and money allowed, its pavilion and grandstand bigger but no more adventurous than the better county grounds over which it claims precedence. Meanwhile it has been outgrown by its own traditions, as

Royal Festival Hall. River front after alteration. GLRO

furthered by *Wisden* and embellished by the old hands on Radio Three.

The buildings of Lord's reflect the eras of great English batsmen in which they were erected: the Pavilion is all W G Grace bluster, of 1889–90 by Thomas and Frank Verity; the Grandstand and Grace gates as stolid and self-confident as Jack Hobbs and built in 1924–6 by Sir Herbert Baker, who added the weathervane of Old Father Time as a personal whim. Corporate sponsorship crashed into this sedate world along with the one-day game sometime in the 1960s. On county grounds it meant the arrival of the hospitality tent. At Lord's that ethos has been pushed into the sky and made permanent, suspended over Frank Verity's 1899 Mound Stand. It is pleasing that some semblance of the ground's late-Victorian encompassment has been permitted to survive, with Verity's arcaded retaining wall cleaned up and continued along St John's Wood Road in 1985. Michael Hopkins and Partners then hung their independent structure on top during the winter of 1986, on a mere six thin tubular steel columns, with a girder slung between them at mezzanine level. In a supremely hierarchical structure, it is the hidden mezzanine at the back containing the watertanks and washrooms that does the work. It carries the upper debenture seats, and from it are hung the best boxes below. On top are perched the dining and drinking facilities, an ocean

Mound Stand, Lords. MARTIN CHARLES

of hospitality floating under plastic-coated canvas. The average fan, clutching six-pack and transistor, hunches between the columns on the old Mound Stand below.

Like a tent, the structure protects you from the extremities of sun, wind and rain, but not from a sense of being outdoors. And like a tent also, it is a structure elegantly created of tension and occasional compression, anchored at the back by steel ties and at the sides by cross bracing. The columns rise as masts and push out spars in alternating

patterns which, with galvanised steel cables, hold all that canvas disquietingly taut. In the current architectural climate of stretcher-bond vernacular and classical cladding, it is exciting that a high-tech solution has been so successful in this bastion of tradition and chauvinism. Hopkins's practice has made a feature of tented structures, following on from its Schlumberger building outside Cambridge, but here it is beautifully appropriate for all that is most quintessential – privileges and all – about the game of cricket.

14

Exchange

Of the western world's major capitals, London is the one whose past is most bound up with exchange. Before it was the seat of government or the centre of English civilisation, the city was 'a meeting place of traders who come to it by land and sea' (the Venerable Bede's words). That was why the Romans founded London where they did. It soon justified the logic of their choice by outpacing rivals – and not just in Britain. Londinium was a more important and cosmopolitan Roman city than its position on the fringes of empire suggests. Every new excavation testifies to the exceptional nature of the place. Its great strategic value as an entrepôt was maintained and enhanced in the medieval period. In unified countries, medieval kings were usually strong enough to subjugate their capitals to the royal will and the royal image. Such were the power and prestige of London's traders, however, that the relation between Crown and City soon became warily symbiotic, with consequences that have haunted Britain since.

Exchange connects in one direction with manufacturing (pp. 221–31), in the other with transport (pp. 233–45), both critical functions of the London economy. What distinguishes it from these activities is the need for independent parties to meet on a footing of clarity, mutual respect and – if necessary – equality. That is why not only ancient markets but also ancient banking and trading transactions were carried on in the street, even in so inclement a climate as London's. Outside or inside, the principle of the meeting place or emporium was not diluted before the growth of office-building in the 19th century. Since then, armies of specialist staff have had to be housed; the telegraph, the telephone and sundry other incremental aids to communication down to the fax machine have invaded the craft of negotiation; and the concept of commercial secrecy has run riot. Even so, the urge to meet remains irresistible.

It is visible in the brief for so obsessively technological a building as Lloyd's, and in the successful resistance of the City of London to the centrifugal forces of rational location and land-use recently flung against it.

Shopping has shown an almost equal resistance to relinquishing the street. There are still plenty of street-markets in London, if not with the scale or verve found in the cities of more demonstrative cultures. Few of them have architectural apparatus. Where London scored was in the rehousing of its enormous, unruly wholesale markets. In the 19th century they were brought in from the streets under cover, usually of iron and glass, only to spill out again when their new premises proved insufficient. Covent Garden Market, reconstituted in the famous piazza in 1828–31 but soon overflowing into annexes, is the exemplar. Billingsgate, bizarre Borough, Leadenhall, Smithfield and Spitalfields follow. All are architecturally enjoyable, though none of them reached the standard of Paris's lamented Les Halles or, for that matter, the finest covered markets in northern English towns. Smithfield must be counted the best of them because of its size and unimpeded site. Today, Billingsgate, Covent Garden and Spitalfields have been abandoned by their traders, while the rest are shadows of their authentic selves.

Retailing is an elastic phenomenon, carried on in settings of widely differing size and type. Historically, it cleaves to two distinctive species of London building, the party-walled house and the warehouse. Houses, infinitely adaptable, need little alteration to fit them up for exchange; the front parlour on the ground floor simply becomes the shop. If you want to expand, you knock through to the back and make the shop deeper, or take in the house next door and demolish the party wall. If you want to display your wares, as begins to be the fashion after about 1700, you hack away the ground-floor front wall and put in an

The Great Room, Lloyds. MARTIN CHARLES

arresting shop window. So light are the walls of a London house that a few stout posts and bressummers will serve most purposes. The spectacle of upper walls seeming to stand directly upon glass always troubles architects, who juggle with the formula to make it look less peculiar. But it never seems to concern traders and shoppers, who worry only if piers or arches diminish their precious display space. Such premises were enough for even the largest London shopkeepers down to about 1875. Purpose-built rows of small shops like Thomas Cubitt's pretty terrace in Woburn Walk south of St Pancras Church, the ranges of Mount Street, Mayfair, or even the florid Edwardianism of Sicilian Avenue in Holborn are still conceived as houses or chambers with retailing annexed.

Harrods, Selfridges, Liberty's and the other mammoth shops of the golden age of the urban department store differ from this model less than one might think. The London department store amalgamates two traditions: the covered bazaar or emporium, which those consumption-loving nations, the French and the Americans, were the first to make really large, lavish and open, and the London warehouse. The size, enrichment, display and technology of the great stores originate in Paris, New York and Chicago – in Selfridge's case, the founder does so too. On the other hand, their relative internal enclosure is native to London. That is because the London fire brigade long insisted that buildings of the 'warehouse class', to which stores generically belong, should have frequent party walls as fire breaks. Harrods even had flats on the upper floors when first rebuilt, so strongly was domesticity linked to shopping, and so unforeseen the consumer explosion to come. Only in the chain stores of the 1930s onwards, after building legislation changed, does unrestricted openness invade the architecture of London shopping. With the proliferation of suburban, single-storey Sainsburys (pp. 223–4), Asdas and Tescos it has reached a new phase – rarely of architectural merit.

If shops and markets stand for the public face of exchange, London banks

Bank of England. A F KERSTING

and offices struggle with the enigma of trying to reconcile dignity, privacy and safety with the maximising of business opportunity. So their architecture is a little self-contradictory. It starts with Sir Thomas Gresham's long-vanished Royal Exchange of the 1560s, half open arcade and half little rooms off, and a building which did much to boost London's international expertise in finance. A century later came the beginnings of modern banking, insurance and stock-broking, in which coffee houses played an important role as meeting places. Still, most merchants found their homes adequate for trading from. The first

people to break out were the Georgian businessmen who ran the Bank of England. The Bank's original Palladian front (1734) was as domestic as the Lord Mayor's Mansion House opposite (pp. 36–7). Security and separation of functions were the key to its architectural novelties, furnished first by the underrated Sir Robert Taylor, then by the genius of Soane. Memory of the Bank's grand screen did much for the elevational architecture of banking, to be felt still in the ardent classicism of even so late a building as Lutyens's Midland Bank of the 1920s, close by. Yet the Bank of England also encapsulates another strand of commercial thinking, a Dombey-esque discretion which the merchant banks such as Barings or Rothschilds were specially keen to uphold. To the present day, the older City merchant banks have gone on pretending that they operate in a 'house'.

Early Victorian insurance companies were the first to diffuse an opulent commercial architecture in London, projecting (in a memorable phrase of Sir John Summerson's) 'the image of upright, prudent men banded together to arrest the cruel hand of fate'. Their ornate mini-*palazzi*, like the Law Fire Insurance Office in Chancery Lane (p. 177), soon escape the City itself and are imitated by others. But by 1870 the most interesting kind of office has become the speculative or semi-speculative block, of which the owner occupies part at most while letting off the rest. C F A Voysey's grandfather is said to have designed London's first such building, long gone, in 1823. Its development was less dramatic and ruthless than in Chicago or other cities with a milder record of restraint in building codes, but just as fascinating. Ingenuity in stowing accommodation into the modest cubic capacity and height allowable, and in securing the best possible light, direct or 'borrowed', was the hallmark of such famous buildings as Norman Shaw's New Zealand Chambers.

In due course, considering the value of London land, something had to give. So 20th-century office buildings get first broader, then taller. Height, conspicuous from afar, is what usually evinces comment, but it is as easy to shatter the feeling of a London street with breadth. Even such proud buildings as the inter-war Daily Telegraph and Daily Express in Fleet Street (pp. 228–9) damage their context. Charles Holden's 55 Broadway, making intricate use of a corner site, does better (p. 242). Taken as a whole, London's best modern offices are not those that tackle the tall building in itself well or badly, or try to mimic the stripped classical or modern idioms of Chicago or New York – usually on meaner budgets. They are those that address the issue of context in some new

way, reactive or otherwise. To represent this eternal problem of London architecture we have chosen Raymond Hood's Palladium House, with its fresh, smart and American approach to image as well as to context; the Economist Building, which manages to create an environment of its own without destroying everything around it, as so many ham-fisted City offices do; and Richard Rogers's Lloyd's, whose rebarbative outline is like the naughtiness of some clever, spoilt child. Canary Wharf, the latest addition to this commercial clan, has the advantage of not having a context worth respecting. Instead, it beckons half of London's attention to itself from afar by means of an egregious, enormous tower.

166

The Bank of England
Threadneedle St, City of London

2/K4   Underground to Bank

[A]   museum only

Consider poor Sir Herbert Baker's dilemma. You are asked by Montagu Norman, Governor of the Bank of England, to enlarge and update the premises of one of Britain's most vital institutions, upon whose efficient functioning the nation's economic fortunes depend. You are confronted with a fortress, bounded on all sides by roads. Security must be maintained at all costs. To expand on to neighbouring sites is inadmissible. You cannot dig downwards, because the basements are replete with gold-filled vaults. All you can do is build up, behind the line of the perimeter walls. But this means covering over a set of single-storey halls, the acknowledged masterpiece of Sir John Soane. They can hardly be preserved because they are domed and top-lit, as well as being unadaptable. They are also in an eccentric style of classicism unsuitable for multi-storey building, so they give an uncertain lead for the new work.

All this should be remembered when one is tempted to fall into the cliché of cursing Sir Herbert for what he did to

the Bank between 1925 and 1939. Never did architect inherit a trickier brief. Where Baker scored was in transforming Soane's unyielding screen into the outer ring of a great *rocca* in the manner of Sanmicheli or Vauban, while domesticating the style for the inner, fenestrated 'ward' of the fortress. His one error here was to assume that such a non-urban *parti* could be easily read, given the restricted street-level views. Where Baker, a self-conscious personality, failed was in having too much residual respect for Soane. Having destroyed most of the great halls, he would have done better to strike out on his own. It was his shilly-shallying with the Soane style inside the Bank that provoked Pevsner to fury and talk of 'egregious diddling'. But that goes unseen by the visitor.

The Bank of England is one of those urban predators that start small and gradually eat up everything around it. It had arrived in Threadneedle Street in 1734, forty years after its foundation. Its original Palladian front was stretched to the corners of Princes Street and Bartholomew Lane by that fine mid-Georgian architect Sir Robert Taylor (whose youthful efforts at sculpture may still be seen in the pediment of the Mansion House opposite). It was Taylor who started the tradition of top-lit offices for the Bank with his Reduced Annuities Office. His Court Room, recreated at a new level by Baker, survives. In 1788 Soane succeeded him, and over the thirty-five years from 1792 made additions piecemeal as required. Their complexity was hidden by the great perimeter wall, whose completion in 1828 marked the Bank's acquisition of the whole quadrilateral up to Lothbury. This screen shows a side to Soane's personality different from the sombre gloom of the interiors or the nervous, flickering, linear quality of his smaller buildings. Here Soane is the unblushing public architect, pulling out the classical stops with the assurance of a Schinkel but at some cost of individuality. The 'Tivoli Corner', where Lothbury meets Princes Street, is the strongest point. Baker's little dome behind, surmounted by Charles Wheeler's gilt statue of Ariel, does no harm.

Daylighting, security and fireproofing are the keys to comprehending the lost sequence of Soane halls at the Bank of England. In these days of uniform electric lighting, it is hard to grasp Soane's obsession with getting a special quality of daylight within a tight urban space, in order both to ease the bank-clerks' work and to create a strong architectural mood within a small compass. His successive bank offices are perhaps better read as experiments in lighting effect than as essays in stylistic development. Recently the Bank has opened up sufficiently to create an estimable museum on the Bartholomew Lane side of the building. Here you will find the place's functions, history and architecture explained in exemplary detail. Photographs and drawings a-plenty of Soane's extraordinary interiors and Baker's 'diddling' pastiches may be examined; and, sandwiched between two of Baker's domed halls, Soane's Bank Stock Office has been recreated in full-scale replica. But artificial lighting makes the interior misleading.

167

Covent Garden Market
Westminster

2/G4   Underground to Covent Garden

Covent Garden Piazza is now just an obstinate construct in the historical mind. Of the epoch-making buildings raised round its edges by the Earl of Bedford in 1631–9 to Inigo Jones's design, the one element with a claim to authenticity is the deep-eaved portico of St Paul's Church on the west side. The arcaded Victorian blocks of Bedford Chambers on the north, and the answering group to be set round the north-east corner by Jeremy Dixon as part of the Royal Opera House extensions, are both reasoned responses – of their own period – to Jones's original inspiration.

For conservatives and classicists, what matters about Covent Garden is the royal architect's bid to impose order

Covent Garden. The old market from the air. A F KERSTING

and degree upon London's development – an initiative that came to maturity in the London square. For the activists who campaigned to save the area from crass redevelopment in the 1970s, another view of its history finds favour. They argue that the piazza responded to fast-growing Stuart London's need for public space, a guarantee given at Moorfields by royal fiat in 1607 and later extended to Leicester Fields, Lincoln's Inn Fields and Covent Garden. From that standpoint, the market buildings in the piazza's centre and their populist, consumerist use today are the special and enduring aspect of the place.

A market first encroached upon the open space of the piazza during the ill-regulated period of the Civil War. Traders sheltered under the Earl of Bedford's garden wall on the south side, then slipped past the flimsy wooden rails protecting the central space and set up a few apologetic shacks within them. The Bedfords managed to get things under their control in 1670 by procuring a royal charter for a market selling 'fruit, flowers, roots and herbs', as market historian Robert Thorne pithily puts it. From then on, as the West End grew and found the market excellently situated for

its fruit and vegetable supplies, there was no holding the marketmen. By the 1820s retrenchment and containment were inevitable. The Bedfords were concerned to protect their lucrative market rents but unwilling to lay out capital. A lump sum they received for giving up land for widening the Strand made the difference, and Charles Fowler, author of the nearby Hungerford Market, was called in.

Fowler's market, built between 1828 and 1831, is the basis of what one sees today. Its three parallel ranges, constructed out of hard-wearing granite and York stone in a workmanlike, colonnaded Greek Revival style, took a mixed approach to market accommodation. Shops in the ranges were let to established retailers and wholesalers, while in between lay open space where the casual traders could pitch their stands. The square lodges in the corners, meant for refreshment, seem quickly to have been taken over as shops. The open colonnade along the east end carried a terrace with conservatories for garden plants on top. Under the whole ran ramifying cellars.

These buildings soon proved inadequate. Airy iron roofs were put up to cover the unsheltered spaces between Fowler's ranges by William Cubitt and Company, in 1874–5 and 1889. Yet still the market grew, spawning iron-and-glass offshoots. The first of these, E M Barry's Floral Hall of 1859, was a money-making venture connected with the Royal Opera House and never went right. Only fragments remain of its architectural splendour, though its ornate Bow Street front is to be recreated as part of the Dixon scheme for the Opera House. The Flower Market of the 1870s and 1880s (now the London Transport Museum) and the Jubilee Market Hall on the south side are of lesser interest.

By the post-war period, the central siting of Covent Garden Market had become a picturesque but ludicrous anomaly. In 1974 its traders retreated with mixed sighs of relief and regret to Nine Elms. Intense argument over the buildings ensued. Finally the Greater London Council, once in favour of razing the whole quarter, committed itself to a faithful restoration of the central market and its return to small-scale retailing. Scrupulously undertaken by the GLC's Historic Building Division, this mammoth task was completed in 1980. One large change was sanctioned – the gouging out of basement space

Covent Garden, as restored. GLRO

beneath the iron roofs to make more selling space. The staggering commercial success of the result is now part of the history of modern international urban tourism.

168

Smithfield Market
Smithfield, City of London

2/J3   Underground to Farringdon or Barbican

Smithfield just misses being a masterpiece among market buildings. If it lacks the rigour of the late-lamented Les Halles, the grandeur of the Milan Galleria or the charm of the covered markets in a few English towns, it retains its scale, its completeness and (more vital) in great part its original use. Here alone in London you can still savour the echoing rawness of wholesale market life in a setting of metropolitan dignity.

As a site of markets, fairs and executions, extra-mural Smithfield goes back at least to Norman times. In 1638 the City Corporation, then as now the authority for most London markets, formalised provisions for a cattle market in the great square south of the present buildings. In due course shops and shambles spread all around, chaotic and unhealthy. So in 1855 live sales and slaughtering removed to a new Metropolitan Cattle Market west of Caledonian Road, Islington, where only the central tower and corner pavilions of City architect J B Bunning's spacious layout remain. Bunning expected to build the new Smithfield too. But the project was delayed by wider replanning schemes, including the formation of Farringdon Road, the making of new streets to its east, and the creation of the Metropolitan Railway (opened 1863–4), which was intended to serve the market. Sidings for the trade were indeed constructed under the meat market.

The Metropolitan Meat and Poultry Market, as the long building which holds the eye at the centre of the complex was named, fell in the end to Bunning's

successor Horace Jones, architect also of later City markets at Billingsgate and Leadenhall. It was built in 1866–8. Jones inherited a clean, unencumbered rectangle, 625 by 240 ft, which he enclosed with a humdrum series of brick and stone Italianate bays, redeemed by thin copper-domed cupolas at the four corners. In these turrets were bars in which porters could slake their thirst and traders could bargain, as well as hydraulic accumulators to work the hoists from the basement sidings.

A broad, north–south thoroughfare breaks the building into two. Its entrance arches are crowned by allegorical figures of London and Edinburgh on one side, Dublin and Liverpool on the other, while venomous post-war griffins – emblems of the City but looking well able to pollute the meat – writhe in the spandrels. The noble feature of the building is the intersection of this roadway with the narrower Central Avenue, which presents a diminishing vista behind robust cast-iron gates. But what at first blush appears to be an iron market interior turns out on closer inspection to be a complex compromise between ironwork (mostly blue-painted) and woodwork (mostly buff-painted). Over the roadway, the roof goes in for some strange hammerbeaming. The Central Avenue has two storeys of ironwork surmounted by a trussed timber roof. Because of changes in the brief during construction, the two-storey shops and offices are set behind in an unintegrated way, like separate structures within the building. Changes currently planned will not, one hopes, neuter the palpable presence of meathooks, sawdust and carcasses.

Smithfield Market is more than just the Horace Jones building. Its Victorian extensions facing Farringdon Street and Road, Charterhouse Street and Snow Hill have mostly been much altered. More impressive is the Poultry Market just west of the Meat Market. Built to designs by T P Bennett and Sons in 1961–3, it has a wide shell-concrete, saucer-domed roof without intermediate supports. Among commercial premises nearby note the Central Cold Storage Building at 53 Charterhouse Street, a beefy (it is the only word) Edwardian business in white brick and Portland stone set off by a terracotta cartouche in the centre. C Stanley Peach was its architect.

169

National Westminster Hall
15 Bishopsgate, City of London

2/L3   underground to Bank or underground/British Rail to Liverpool Street

In 1864–5, when the National Provincial Bank of England built its Bishopsgate headquarters, to erect a single-storey building on a prominent City site was to say something about money: that you had plenty of it, but were prepared to forgo pecuniary advantage for the sake of prestige. Values have changed since. Right behind this proud piece of street architecture rears the 600 ft National Westminster Tower, raised in the 1970s as if to make up for lost profit.

The National Provincial consisted from its foundation in 1833 of a network of provincial banks with note-issuing rights. There was no London branch at first. But from early days central administration was carried on from a fine Georgian mansion, Sir Robert Taylor's former Salvador House, Bishopsgate. On this site, enlarged to the north, the bank determined to build a new headquarters that would stake the National Provincial's claim to status. The result is the Victorian City of London as one feels it ought to be – opulent, portly and conservative.

John Gibson, the building's designer, was the National Provincial's regular architect and one of mid-Victorian England's ablest classicists. Cheap or costly, all his banks are pleasurably dignified. For Bishopsgate he was asked to pull out the stops. Gibson's starting point was the Bank of England, the *ne plus ultra* of single-storey, top-lit office space behind a grand stone wall (pp. 207–8). The years since the completion of Soane's masterpiece had

seen an increase in the taste for mercantile display, which Gibson enjoyed indulging. Hence the enrichment of the street facade – a screen of engaged, 30 ft columns marching along Bishopsgate, an entrance on the curve where Threadneedle Street commences, reliefs over the windows, a deep entablature reserved for the bank's name in big bronze letters, and larger-than-life statuary along the parapet. From south to north, Manchester, England, Wales, Birmingham, Newcastle-under-Lyme, Dover and London are the arbitrary choices for personification, while the panels show the arts, commerce, science, manufacturing, navigation, shipbuilding and mining. The north-ernmost two bays are additions of 1878.

Gibson had an awkward site from which to carve out his banking hall. Neither the end nor the side walls are parallel, nor is the hall aligned with the front. These irregularities are disguised with a gorgeous, Italianate display of columns, screening arches at the ends and a high, gilded coving. The roof, framed in iron, supports three dishlid domes of glass shielded above by an

invisible skylight. Originally each dome swooped down in the centre into an elaborate gas 'sun-burner'. The polished columns against the walls are of Devonshire marble. Deep plaster panels depicting cherubs run all the way round between them. Some illustrate 'the growing riches of the land and sea', while on the end wall the putti play at banking, smelting gold and other pursuits which children would be wise to come to later in life.

Up to 1980 any National Westminster Bank customer could do business in Gibson's marble hall. In the wake of the building of Richard Seifert and Partners' tower behind, the bank elected to close the hall, refurbish it and turn it into a private function room. Commendable though the restoration may have been, it has deprived the hall of much of its meaning. Open space, chairs and a tawdry carpet are no substitutes for banking counters, clutter and chatter. One must now seek one's cash from a sordid little banking foyer just north of Gibson's great building. Opulence, it seems, is not to be shared with the customer any more but reserved for the banker.

National Westminster Hall. GLRO

170

Thomas Goode and Company
17–22 South Audley St, Mayfair, Westminster

2/D5   Underground to Green Park, Bond Street or Marble Arch

[C]

Goode's is the archetype of the unchanging Mayfair shop so often exposed in American travel magazines. But South Audley Street is off the beaten consumerist track, so the place retains some shreds of old-world discretion, as well as one of the earliest and best Queen Anne Revival fronts in London.

Thomas Goode the china merchant came to South Audley Street in 1844. After his death in 1870 his son, William James Goode, started to expand and give the business its aesthetic orientation. Shops tend to develop by degrees, and Goode's was no exception. The middle of the block between Chapel Place and South Street was rebuilt in 1875–6, followed smartly by the South Street corner. Then in 1889–90 Goode added the range at the north end running round into Chapel Place, 'in order to exhibit goods immediately after the French Exhibition'.

The architects for all this were Ernest George and Peto, a firm celebrated for their clever way with the Queen Anne style. In fact the centre of Goode's was the first design Ernest George ever made in what we today call 'Queen Anne'. It was the ground landlord, the Duke of Westminster, who prodded Goode and George to build in gabled red brick. The style suited the tradesman's desire for aesthetic display very well. The earlier portion is fresher and more inventive. Over a granite ground storey comes restless, cranky brick walling, its redness set off by spidery green ironwork and niches bearing large blue pots. Two tight, shaped gables drop to a lower level at the South Street corner, where cut-brick reliefs by Harry Hems adorn the return wall; above them sails an ardent chimney, caparisoned with the aesthetes' symbol of the sunflower. The northern end is drier, confirming that in a mere fifteen years the fertility of the

Thomas Goode's. GLRO

Queen Anne style had largely evaporated. What distracts most visitors, however, is not the architecture but the huge china elephants in the windows and (for those of a mechanical turn of mind) the automatic entrance door, a contraption almost as old as the front.

The showrooms within have seen much change since the 1890s but still keep a Victorian feeling, with skylights that shed a serviceable sheen upon the china. Several piers display Minton Hollins tiles, while in one corner is a mysterious aesthetic sanctum with leather paper on the walls, a painted frieze incorporating birds, and some first-rate secular stained glass of which one would like to know more. Martin Harrison, the stained-glass expert, believes it may be a rare design by the Scottish artist Daniel Cottier.

171

Sicilian Avenue
Southampton Row, Holborn, Camden

2/G3   Underground to Holborn

[C]

The cutting of Kingsway through a slum area by the London County Council in 1900–5 caused the Holborn area to be regenerated with offices. The Duke of Bedford's estate recognised the opportunity for shopping and in 1906 began to clear the valuable corner site between Southampton Row and Vernon Place.

The replacement blocks of shops and offices designed by Robert J Worley caused problems for the LCC Architect's

Sicilian Avenue. EH

bows and bays of the office windows, turning into brick tourelles at either end. Two towers studded with pinnacles guarded the Vernon Place entrance until their removal in the late 1950s. They are the principal loss. Otherwise, the shopfronts, lattice glazing and encrustation of detail survives intact.

But the chief delight of Sicilian Avenue is in its materials: strong red brick in the upper storeys contrasted with Doulton's Carrara terracotta lavishly displayed in every element of the ground floor and every moulding above. The arcade was originally paved with marble, first intended to be black and red but revised to black and white in 1908. It has been suggested that the marble, perhaps actually from Sicily, was the cause of the change of name in 1909 from Vernon Arcade to Sicilian Avenue. Whatever, the moniker encapsulates the romantic conceit of the street as assuredly as 'Carrara' does Doulton and Co.'s cream-glazed ceramic. Indeed Sicilian Avenue, finally opened in 1910, perfectly captures the bounce and *joie de vivre* of its age.

172

Selfridges
Oxford Street, Westminster

2/D4   Underground to Marble Arch or Bond Street
[C]

Precious little can be said in architectural favour of Europe's longest shopping street. The old Waring and Gillows, John Lewis and D H Evans are no more than respectable buildings, while over the whole south of Oxford Street a veil is best drawn until one comes at its western extremity to Hereford House (the former Gamages), saved from banality by the consulting hand of Sir Edwin Lutyens in 1928–30. Westminster City Council's pavements, street furniture and ever-changing clutter are, if possible, worse; they are just the kind of thing Britain does shamefully.

All the more needful then are the orderly bulk and colonnaded magnificence of Selfridges, wrapping

Department, who had to administer the 1894 London Building Acts. Although covered shopping arcades had become popular following Samuel Ware's successful Burlington Arcade, built in 1815–19, the idea of a pedestrian street with shops and offices that was open to the skies was new. Thankfully the LCC waived its dictum that buildings could not be higher than the street was wide and allowed the projecting bays and tourelles that are a striking feature of the upper levels.

The beauty of Sicilian Avenue is the completeness of its conception. The sense of envelopment gains much from the Ionic screens at each end, which denoted that the Bedford estate retained possession of the right-of-way. Even the flower beds are part of Worley's initial conception, which also included a central fountain. The more serious nature of the larger shops facing Southampton Row is reflected in their conventional shopfronts; those in the arcade have jolly bows that project between giant Corinthian columns. Oversailing these are the three-storey itself round the long block from Orchard Street to Duke Street. Selfridges matters not only as a fine building and a reproach to its context, but as the harbinger to profound American involvement in British urban design and influence on London's streetscape.

Harry Gordon Selfridge from Wisconsin started with Marshall Field's fast-expanding Chicago department store in 1879, worked his way up the ladder, then retired from the partnership, rich but not yet fifty, in 1904. In these years he saw H H Richardson's Marshall Field Wholesale Store rise and a start made on rebuilding the Retail Store to D H Burnham and Company's designs. Before making his spectacular leap across the Atlantic to London, he had briefly bought and sold Louis Sullivan's new Schlesinger and Mayer store. So he had intimate experience of the best and most up-to-date department-store architecture in the world. Selfridge needed all the experience he had, for his decision of 1906 to locate in London was a colossal risk. Department stores usually grow from small beginnings; it was unheard of to start on a grand scale from scratch. At the time, too, proud Harrods and other London stores were also expanding and rebuilding. In its early years Selfridges did indeed nearly fail, but somehow the founder's enthusiasm, publicity stunts and grandiose vision saw his project through to virtual completion.

Who designed Selfridges? The story is complex, and not quite clear. Francis Swales, a young American Beaux-Arts architect knocking about Europe at the time, took the tycoon a sketch for the giant Ionic order which strides so superbly along the street, punctuated by bronze and glass interstices. Albert D Millar was then sent over from the Burnham office in Chicago to plan the building and hang Swales's front on a steel frame, but he had to be helped over manifold problems with the strict London building regulations by a local, Frank Atkinson. This team built the south-east corner of the store, nine bays towards Oxford Street and seven to Duke Street, in 1907–9. The rest of the front followed on in phases between 1920 and

1928, under the direction of Sir John Burnet and Partners – in other words 'Tommy' Tait, whose firm Scottish hand can be discerned in the detailing of the entrance. Most of its bronze sculpture is by Sir William Reid Dick, but the ultra-sentimental clock in the form of the Queen of Time on the prow of a ship, bearing a globe with yet another ship (that of commerce) on top was added by Gilbert Bayes in 1931. Sundry plans by Selfridge to build a central tower or dome behind the entrance proved so many castles in the air, as did his ambition to take the store right up to Wigmore Street. But his rooftop garden and restaurant, a borrowing from New York department stores, did come off. Though it has long gone, it had many descendants, including the remarkable Derry and Toms roof garden of 1936–8 in Kensington High Street – still there although the store which created it has disappeared.

The interior of Selfridges was supposed to be in the Chicago tradition, open and unimpeded with distant counters visible between a forest of columns. Tough London fire regulations put paid to that, with the result that the interior was always split into smallish divisions. Though the main entrance area still has some spaciousness and

style, it has lost something since the removal of its gilt bronze lifts panelled with Art Deco signs of the zodiac. One of these has found its way to the Museum of London.

Selfridges showed commercial London architects how to build big and strong, after years of fiddly fronts. The impact of its giant order on other shops was immediate – upon Walter Cave's clever Burberrys in the Haymarket, or Whiteleys in Queensway, for instance. Almost every building along inter-war Regent Street betrays its influence while, in a final accolade, the Selfridges articulation was sheepishly adopted for the back of Harrods in 1929–30.

173

Liberty's
Great Marlborough St and Regent St, Westminster

2/E4   Underground to Oxford Circus

[C]

Liberty's stands apart from other department stores. When Arthur Liberty opened his first little shop on Regent Street in 1875 it was to sell the Japanese silks made fashionable by the Aesthetic Movement. Pots, furnishings and other oriental imports quickly followed, supplying the commercial end of the developing art goods market and the craze for all things Japanese that had begun in the 1860s. From this bonanza Liberty and Company evolved their own range of more robust fabrics with distinctive bright patterns, which for many years were produced at mills in Merton. Something of the excitement of entering a bazaar lingers in the merchandise today – until you look at the price tags.

Liberty's ideals were at odds with their two premises on Regent Street, the swathe of high-class shopping emporia cut by Nash from 1811 to link Regent's Park with his developments along The Mall. By the late 19th century not only were the shops thought poky, but Nash's architecture was especially singled out for revulsion by Ruskin and his

Selfridges. EH

followers. They particularly objected to his 'dishonest' use of stucco and his unscholarly detail. Already parts of the street had been demolished and much more mutilated to make bigger shopfronts when in 1905 Norman Shaw was appointed to rebuild the southern block known as the Quadrant. His monumental baroque design set a trend more or less followed in the total reconstruction of the street which took place after the First World War, approved by the Crown Estate and the freeholders all along Regent Street, but the resulting heavy-handedness suited the Liberty image even less than had Nash. However, the firm had acquired

the block between Great and Little Marlborough Streets and Kingly Street, as well as a fresh Regent Street frontage. Here, with their side if not their back to Regent Street, they could do what they wanted. This they proceeded to do in 1922–4 by erecting a strange new building to the designs of Edwin T and E Stanley Hall.

Somewhere the oriental and exotic image had got caught up with nostalgia for traditional English craftsmanship. The Rows of Chester were said to be a model. Most imposing is the facade to Great Marlborough Street, symmetrical in the centre with flanks of Portland stone around the main doors before

diving off into a row of half-timbered gables that nod most convincingly on the corner-turn into Kingly Street. It is a common fallacy that traditional English timber-framed construction reused ships' timbers. Here, however, is the exception. The exterior teak and interior oak came in large part from two men-of-war, *HMS Impregnable* and *HMS Hindustan*, properly morticed and tenoned on the outside although supported by a brick backing. Inside are three central galleried halls – the idiom of the George Inn writ extra large and solid and a contrast to the flimsiness of many of the goods.

E Stanley Hall completed the new Regent Street block, schizophrenically different in idiom, in 1926. Its curved colonnaded front and high frieze of Britannia receiving the goods of all nations shields not only floors of offices but emphasises the more ponderous nature of the men's departments contained within. The two halves are linked by bridges, which contort the internal arrangement but cleverly mask Kingly Street. As elsewhere on the building, the workmanship of the Portland stone is especially pleasing in its slightly rough texture. Here it is set off with another piece of 1920s medievalism, half hidden: a clock designed by E P Roberts of Liberty's cabinet department, complete with a George and Dragon that do battle on the hour.

174

Midland Bank, Poultry
City of London

2/K4   Underground to Bank
[C]

You have to stand well back to appreciate the best bits of Lutyens's Midland Bank exterior. These are the attic storeys, with great end windows – like those of the Mansion House nearby – set in an otherwise smooth acreage of white Portland stone. In the centre the attic is unexpectedly topped with one of his shallow domes simplified from the

Liberty's. A contrast in styles. RCHME

New Delhi prototype. Lutyens's top-knot works best as a surprise, seen from Walbrook, next to the Mansion House, and from Moorgate.

The elevations, banking hall and the suites of directors' offices and conference rooms on the upper floors are by Lutyens, but the intervening floors and overall supervision were carried out by Gotch and Saunders of Kettering, the Midland Bank's usual architects. There are two heavily rusticated elevations, to Poultry and Princes Street, built piecemeal from 1928 and completed only in 1939. At either side of the Poultry front, completed years after the central bays, William Reid Dick sculptured a boy strangling a hapless goose, supposedly a reflection on the street's name.

The two fronts between them squeeze Edwin Cooper's National Westminster Bank into a tight corner. The banking hall is a basilica of white marble walls and green African verdite columns richly finished with Corinthian capitals. They punctuate counters made of African walnut that envelop their bases, and which are founded on marble footings – so solid that they seem to have grown out of the floor. But because of Cooper's building, Lutyens was forced to make a sharp turn through 45 degrees – a difficult thing to do with pairs of arcades. The beauty is that Lutyens simply did not care. On one side the hall is symmetrical, with a round arch leading to a marble stairway; opposite he just piled in more columns at the turn with a couple more arches for good measure and little purpose. Given the reflective properties of well-polished marble, not to mention a few big mirrors, the ensemble dissolves into a green-trunked forest from which it is difficult to unscramble the underlying logic.

It is well worth descending the marble stair to the safe deposit: the door of the vault alone weighs 35 tons. The stair is perhaps Lutyens's best moment, with a heavy marble balustrade offset with travertine walls and, at its foot, a little colonnade. Behind the stair a shallow niche contains a bronze version of Reid Dick's boy and goose sculpture, in which the goose at last attempts to

Midland Bank. Poultry front. GLRO

fight back. The marble work, the panelling and the columns are all featured again on the fourth floor and, especially, the fifth, where the huge window on the Poultry front lights the colonnaded entrance to the Board Room.

Lutyens was involved in four projects for the Midland Bank, three of them in London. The commissions grew out of his association with Reginald McKenna, chairman of the Bank from 1919 to 1943 and the husband of Gertrude Jekyll's niece. Whilst the other City branch, in Lombard Street, is all gusto in Portland stone, the earliest commission is a quaint brick box in a Wrennaissance style designed to harmonise with Sir Christopher Wren's St James's Piccadilly, next door.

175

Palladium House
Great Marlborough St and Argyll St, Westminster

2/E4   Underground to Oxford Circus

External colour is rarely an architect's strong point. All the more helpful then are the few attempts to think through a philosophy of architectural colour suitable to London's skies. In this respect Palladium House, though damaged by extension and alteration, still offers food for thought.

This is the one European building of Raymond Hood, wittiest and most thoughtful of the inter-war New York skyscraper architects. Hood's time in the sun was brief. Between winning the Chicago Tribune competition in 1922 and his death in 1934 he designed five great tall buildings and a medley of smaller, odder things. Palladium (formerly Ideal) House is the best of these lesser commissions. Built in 1928–9, it was a spin-off from Hood's second skyscraper, the American Radiator Building facing Bryant Park in Manhattan. There, partly as an experiment in urban colour, partly to advertise the fact that his clients were in the heating business, Hood had clothed his building in black, with gold trimmings to symbolise coal and flames.

The London building, designed as a simple showroom for the American Radiator Company's British subsidiary with offices to let above, combines Hood's interest in colour with two other preoccupations of his: how to handle urban corner sites without losing rental space, and how to finish off the tops of buildings well. As first built, it had its present width of frontage towards Great Marlborough Street but was only four windows deep along Argyll Street. That gave a compact block, which Hood coolly crowned with a recessed storey in orientalising taste. This deft effect was destroyed in 1935 when Gordon Jeeves, the English architect who had been employed to supervise the original building, added seven further bays

northwards along Argyll Street – a gross blunder. Later the trimmings of the Argyll Street doorway disappeared, to find their way to the Victoria & Albert Museum.

Despite these barbarities, Palladium House still holds its own as a shocking but far from brash approach to the problems of London street architecture. Local conditions seem to have suggested to the intuitive Hood that the black and gold American Radiator livery was worth trying again. The London climate of the 1920s was very smoky. Working for a company claiming to produce clear heat, Hood applied lateral thinking. If buildings quickly get grimy, why not make them black but shiny and cleanable, and extend the polished granite cladding of the American Radiator base all over the surface? That surely would give a smarter and longer-lasting look than smudgy Portland stone. Hood reacted, too, against the London architecture of the 1920s. With ponderous Dickins and Jones and sentimental Liberty's rising nearby, he determined to teach Londoners a lesson in what New York interpreted as modern architecture, before the Modern Movement became a moral cause. Hence the stripped, Loosian lines of the building – a reference far from accidental. One of Hood's closest cronies, the designer Josef Urban, was a Loos pupil from Vienna, and the ridicule Hood felt for the shops and offices of

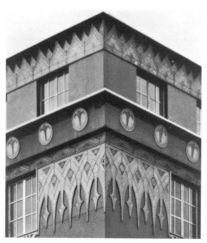

Palladium House. The cornices. AA

rebuilt Regent Street echoes Loos's distaste for Austro-Hungarian architectural pomposity. Yet Hood was no puritan. His enjoyment of ornament is proclaimed by the exotic gold and green art deco detailing of the top storeys, mercifully immune still from mauling.

'The Moor of Argyll Street', as Trystan Edwards dubbed the building, had an immediate impact. In Oxford Street alone, the Pantheon Marks and Spencer and the remnants of wicked Gordon Jeeves's Drages Store, near Tottenham Court Road, attest its influence. In Leicester Square there is the 'black Odeon', while some sixteen black Montague Burtons have been spotted. Thereafter, Hood's commercial modernism was felt to be frivolous, so London's best art deco building has never enjoyed the respect it deserved.

176

Economist Building
St James's St, Westminster

2/E5   Underground to Green Park

Alison and Peter Smithson have written much but built little. Their ideas on the form and layout of social architecture dubbed them the 'New Brutalists' in the 1950s, but their Economist Building is in many ways an unassuming piece of conservation architecture.

The centrepiece of the disparate east side of St James's Street is Boodle's Club, designed in 1775 by John Crunden with a distinctive stucco fan surround to the upper Venetian window. Opposite, a simpler pastiche had already been built 'in keeping', in 1933 by William Walcot, best known as a perspectivist. In 1960 the Smithsons won a competition for the site next door to the club. Their brief was for a commercial development, to include offices for *The Economist* magazine, that would be in keeping with the tone of the street. The brief also included flats for Boodle's, since the London County Council demanded some residential use. Additionally, the Smithsons also enlarged a dining room in the club, with a bay window that breaks forward of the blank side wall constraining the site. The other elements were each placed in a separate block at the corners of the site, each a different height. The development epitomises the late 1950s ideal of building tall to free the ground for public use, and the architectural press at the time made much of the little piazza thus created.

To St James's Street is a bank over two shops, set behind which rise fifteen storeys of offices for *The Economist* itself, whilst hidden at the rear is the eight-storey residential block. The blocks are treated in identical manner. Square, with canted corners, each has a simple rhythm of banded glazing between mullions that run the height of the building, and their proportions, though different, harmonise together. Most striking is the contrast between the tall *piano nobile* of the banking hall facing St James's Street and the lower floor levels in the Economist office block behind. The aluminium window frames continue round the soffits to give a very flat treatment to the mullions. Hard though it is to envisage these as engaged columns, there is a classical tautness to the composition. The reinforced concrete frame is, apart from the bottom foot, clad with Portland Roach, the large fossil formations of which were previously thought to make it unsuitable for grimy London. The effect is as stately as so smart yet so conservative a magazine as *The Economist* could have wished for in such a setting. Internally, the flats and offices were similarly arranged around a central service core, the offices given flexible partitioning to enable the staff to work in small teams.

The areas between the blocks were opened up into a raised courtyard, running through to Bury Street behind, paved in more Portland Roach. Note the ramps for disabled access, commonplace now but novel at the time; the then editor of *The Economist* used a wheelchair. The Smithsons considered the courtyard route as important a part of the scheme as the buildings themselves, all supposedly inspired by the approach to the Parthenon. Hopes were raised in the 1960s that it would

Economist Building, from St James's St. RIBA

evolve into a real piazza with seats, plants and sculpture, but it has never stood a chance in select St James's.

177
Lloyd's
Leadenhall St and Lime St, City of London

2/L4   Underground to Bank or Tower Hill, or British Rail to Fenchurch Street

Remember the 'Big Bang' intended to make London the epicentre of the world's financial markets? Its outfall can hardly be avoided. The City is fringed with giant cranes, shoehorning new offices around the old. The variety of cladding cannot mask their monotony, for these are buildings as speculative as the markets they serve. For all it is a monument to the 1980s, and the ultimate charismatic building as marketing image, Lloyd's is different. Not just because of the choice of an architect of international class, Richard Rogers, but also because it was built for a specific and idiosyncratic user. Speculation rarely produces great architecture. That is the problem with modern London, and why there are not

more buildings like Lloyd's.

Yet tradition plays a large part in the design. From the late 17th century, Edward Lloyd's coffee house proved congenial for business between merchants and underwriters because it functioned as a gathering-place for information, particularly shipping news. In 1769 the underwriters moved to a separate house and their work has since expanded to encompass most forms of insurance. In 1928 they installed themselves in a new building on the present site designed by Edwin Cooper, and in 1958 moved to a larger building by Terence Heysham next door. Both were dominated by a Great Room, in which each syndicate conducted its business from booths not unlike those of a coffee house, and between which the insurers' agents scrambled for the best deal. But in 1977 the Great Room in the Heysham building was in turn declared too small. The brief demanded a space capable of expansion for 50 years. It also sought to include a Robert Adam interior bought in the 1950s from Bowood, Wiltshire, for the members' committee chamber in the Heysham building.

In 1978 Richard Rogers and Partners were the surprise winners of a limited competition. Building began in 1981. Outwardly the solution was a development of the Beaubourg in Paris, its facades delineated by exposed service ducting, stairs and glazed lifts. Even the lavatories and meeting rooms are 'pods' thrust on to the ends. Some argue that such systems, serviced by cranes and gantries on the roof, are less efficient than if they had been put within the building. That is to assume that 'high-tech' architecture should work as a machine first and as architecture second. Such criteria may suit Norman Foster's work, with whose contemporary Hongkong and Shanghai Bank Lloyd's has often been compared, but they certainly do not work for Rogers.

But Lloyd's is a building conceived from the inside out, around the dominating Room. It is an atrium, glazed at one end above the sixth floor, and ringed elsewhere with galleries. By the time the building opened in 1986 four of the twelve main floors had become the 'Room', connected by pairs of criss-crossing escalators with exposed yellow mechanisms looking like Meccano. They add immeasurably to the theatre of the great space. With up to 5,000 people using the Room at any one time the difficulty of running between all the booths and other teething troubles prompted a deluge of criticism. Yet only by building upwards could the brief for expandable space be filled. At present the next two floors are occupied by the society's offices, floors 7–10 by tenants in related businesses and the top two floors house executive suites, decorated in unnervingly traditional fashion by Jacques Grange and centred on the Bowood Room. A further symbol

of tradition is the Lutine Bell, in the base of the well, which is rung when a ship is lost.

Behind the stainless steel, by 1990 looking a bit grimy, lurks a reinforced concrete frame engineered by Ove Arup and Partners. A steel frame was rejected by the Greater London Council's fire officers. The structure, a series of upturned U-frames mounted on only eight internal columns, is stunning for the precision of its casting and smooth-as-stone finishes. Much use is made of opaque glass, which adds to the building's glow at night. For it is then, bathed in lilac light, that its jagged profile and serried ranks of new-age curves are most truly thrilling.

178

Canary Wharf
Isle of Dogs, Tower Hamlets

1/H4   Docklands Light Railway to Canary Wharf or Heron Quays

Few Londoners have reason to go near Canary Wharf. But millions are beginning to get acquainted with its central tower, at 800 ft the tallest in Britain. Its shining, pyramidal top leers up at you in the most unexpected places, especially across South London.

The imposition of three overweening towers upon Canary Wharf, in the neck of land between the old West India Import and Export Docks, caused an outcry when announced in 1985. It could not have happened had not the creation four years before of the London Dockland Development Corporation contemptuously reduced planning controls in the Isle of Dogs and surrounding riverside areas. But as the improbable became reality, so Londoners have been assuaged by the grotesquely fascinating spectacle of the first and much the largest tower going up in 1989–91. The cheek and success of 'DS7' (its only name at the time of writing) lie in its breadth, which confuses one's sense of scale at a distance. Even close to there are few human points of reference, few 'natives to give scale', in the surreal landscape of this Fortress Finance. The tower's sheer and simple bulk, sheathed in stainless steel, mocks the contorted post-modern detail and stone cladding of the surrounding ten- and twelve-storey blocks.

Much has been made of Canary Wharf's North American progeniture. The developers, Olympia and York, are Canadian, whilst the overall design is by that colossus of American architectural practice, Skidmore, Owings and Merrill (SOM), working with Hanna-Olin. Cesar Pelli of New Haven has furnished the design for DS7. The planning is formal, piercing the long peninsula with a long axis centred on the Pelli tower and reached from a circular plaza off West India Dock Road at its western end. The

Lloyd's. MARTIN CHARLES

Docklands Light Railway, cutting through immediately west of the tower, provides a cross axis. Though raised on stilts, it emerges between Kohn Pederson Fox's two blocks as if through a great chasm. The tininess of its trains and the delays in the proposed underground connections to Canary Wharf cast a shadow over its commercial future. Moreover, once you finally get there, would you want to work in such an *ersatz* environment?

The artificiality of Canary Wharf is pointed up by London's second new commercial centre, which has evolved around Heathrow over the last thirty years piecemeal, almost by stealth. Its viability depends upon the car and the aeroplane rather than London's enfeebled modern public transport, and it opts not for showy height but for low-lying buildings set in parkland. So its buildings are as invisible to the passer-by as they are pleasing to the green-belt planner. An early and noble example is Heinz's UK headquarters of 1962–5 (in Hayes Park, off Hayes End Road), the only British building designed by Gordon Bunshaft of the selfsame SOM's New York office, in the days when their architecture was dynamic as well as successful. In similar vein but different style, IBM in 1979 acquired London headquarters from Norman Foster at Greenford Green. There are now many other specimens of this mode of corporate architecture tucked away in green pockets of outer West London.

The richest and most recent collection is at Stockley Park close to Heathrow, just a few hundred yards north of Junction 4 on the M4 motorway. Stockley Park was started (on the site of a rubbish tip) only in 1984, yet its cool, lush landscape, curling roads, lake and golf-course already

Canary Wharf. As envisaged in 1991, from the west. SKIDMORE, OWINGS AND MERRILL

soothe the computer-based industrialist's soul. Its scatter of discrete buildings is a showcase for smart British architects who have kept faith with the modernist creed, notably Arup Associates (who planned the place) and Foster Associates. Verdure notwithstanding, all the buildings sit on, not in, their landscapes, and their reliance on the car (the architectural problem of car-parking seems as far as ever here for happy solution) has caused the *Architects' Journal* to liken Stockley Park to a freeway strip. Yet their success has been proven; Canary Wharf's has not.

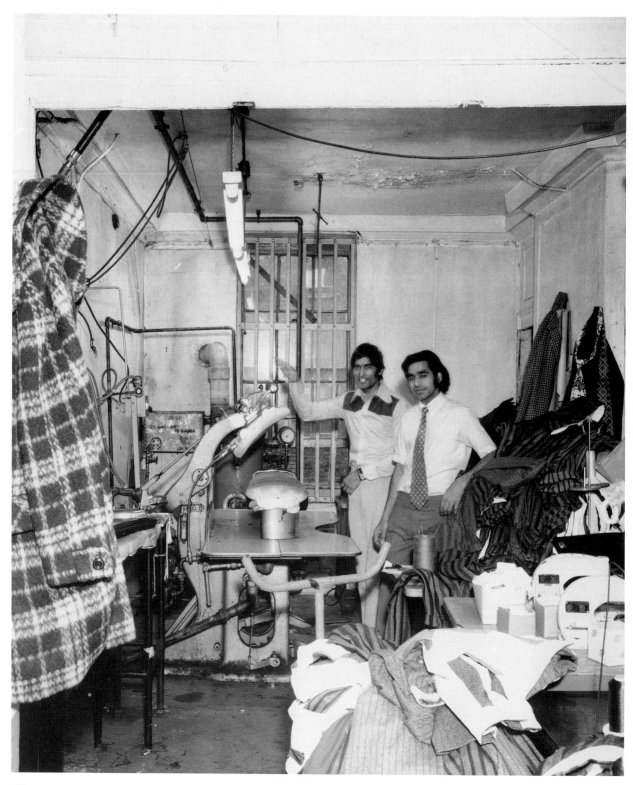

15

Industry and Warehousing

Urban industry is unsentimental about its architecture; it has to be to survive. When it is small, it makes do with whatever ramshackle premises it can find, wherever it can conveniently find them. As it grows bigger, it shows no compunction about devouring or polluting its neighbours. Eventually it shifts (or is turfed out) to a 'green-field site' or 'industrial estate', better for production, better for the city, better (perhaps) for the workforce. But the technological wheel races round ever faster. Soon enough the purpose-built premises are razed, converted or abandoned to suburban dereliction – a phenomenon every bit as wasteful and lamentable as inner-city blight.

That is the lesson of London's industrial architecture. A factory not obsolete after fifty years is rare. Plants built for the 'utilities' – gas, water, electricity and sewage disposal – have the best chance of survival. The exotic pumping stations at Abbey Mills and Crossness, the only buildings in our selection still in original use, are not just a testimony to the foresight of those who redesigned London's main drainage in the 1860s, they are a reminder of the intractability of sewage; you cannot simply hook up a few pipes and wires and begin again. The King's Cross gasholders, built in the 1880s, served London for nearly a century, Greenwich Generating Station (pp. 241–2), of 1902–6, for eighty years; Battersea Power Station, begun in 1929, for some 60 years; and Bankside, last, grandest and largest of the London power stations, for a mere forty. Such is the increasing speed of obsolescence. In the productive sector of industry, conditions are even harsher. Modern Art Glass, our latest building (1972–3), has already changed hands; it is an attribute of the design that its architect, Norman Foster, expected its life to be short. It is reassuring to turn from this smart but ephemeral shed to the noble endurance of the Harmondsworth Tithe Barn, where wisps of straw can be found among the timbers after centuries. But then Harmondsworth is hardly a London building at all.

None of this means that London has few industrial buildings, or that those that survive are of poor quality. On the contrary, it cannot be often enough stressed that London owes its greatness as much to crafts and manufactures as to commerce, and that for most of the 18th and 19th centuries the city was the world's largest manufacturing centre. Many architectural reminders of that old supremacy remain. But the visitor must not expect to find in them any more than a noble shell, structure or front. Behind that front, as often as not, now scurry the minions of today's computer-based commercial and industrial activities, destined doubtless to be as short-lived as their predecessors.

The history of London's industrial architecture has never been written, but would be worth the attempt. Even a date at which it becomes distinctive is difficult to hazard. Scale is the critical factor. The many craft industries of medieval, Stuart and early Georgian London, working in small units, needed no special premises or source of power. The one prerequisite for the more delicate processes such as watchmaking, weaving and print-setting was good daylight. For this reason skilled workers tended to float up to the tops of houses, unskilled ones to gravitate to the bottom, where storage and heavier processes took place. The most graphic evidence of the quest for light is the pragmatic run of wide attic windows along the Georgian weavers' house-tops in Spitalfields (pp. 133–4). With an eye for rooflines you can spot later examples all over inner London, notably in the former printing district of Fleet Street.

The solid, severe form of brick construction for mills, warehouses, workhouses, barracks and prisons – building types all linked with one another – had established itself nationally by 1800. It was not a development specific to London, where

Industry taking over a Georgian house in Fournier St. GLRO

employers tended to be many and small-scale rather than few and highly capitalised, like the pioneering Midlands cotton-mill builders. Flour-milling and brewing were the first London industries on a large enough scale to take it up, with early results that can still be seen in the charming Three Mills complex at Bromley-by-Bow, tucked away near the mouth of the River Lea, and in the original core of Whitbread's Brewery in Chiswell Street, Barbican. But the great London instance of 'mill construction' were the 'stacks' of bonded warehouses built by limited companies to line the new, enclosed docks along the Thames after 1795. So profligate have the capital's decision-makers been with them that we now have only George Gwilt's stacks at West India Dock across from Canary Wharf, a fragment of the London Dock, and the mauled St Katharine's Dock to convey the stark sublimity of these exceptional buildings.

One reason we know so little of London's industrial architecture is the scant pride scholars and others have taken in it. But another is the secrecy with which old-style manufacturers have invested themselves. Government is among the worst offenders, using the pretext of defence long after it is indefensible. The Royal Small Arms Manufactory at Enfield, first built during the Napoleonic wars and reconstructed on a vast scale in the 1850s due to the poor performance of British arms in the Crimea, is only just becoming known, while the even more remarkable Woolwich Arsenal, in terms of industrial archaeology one of the most important sites in the kingdom, is still all but a 'no-go' area at the time of writing. For practical reasons, these places are not included in our selection. One that is is the intriguing former silk mill of the 1820s in Streatham, buried in the midst of an accretive rubber factory and utterly forgotten until the early 1980s, when it was saved in the nick of time and annexed to a supermarket. Can there be other such discoveries to make?

By late Victorian times expanding factories in Central, South and East London had succumbed to steam (and hydraulic) power, adding their tithe of smoke from tall chimneys and noise

from enlarged engines to the metropolitan dirt and din. Most of these factories were on unplanned sites, and so despoiled their environs as they grew. In a few cases, there was some unofficial 'zoning'. Some of the Metropolitan Board of Works' new streets, notably Southwark Street, were lined with fine new warehouses and industrial premises, while south of Fleet Street the City Corporation laid out a grid of roads in the 1880s which helped to contain the burgeoning printing and newspaper industry for some years. Again, there are remnants, but increasingly only remnants, of all this to be seen.

By the turn of the century industrial dispersal had begun, on grounds of welfare and efficiency alike. Electricity made it possible – electric power for the clean, new factory, and electric transport which allowed workers to travel further to and from work, and saved them from living in a perpetual close embrace with their source of livelihood. The fresh, suburban start for industries which this opportunity brought suggested also a fresh image – one of openness, light and air in reaction to the sooty brick enclosure of the inner-city site. Hence the lovably flashy and naive facades of the celebrated inter-war factories along the Great West Road, Western Avenue, Eastern Avenue, the North Circular and other new arterial roads: this group includes Beecham, Glaxo, Firestone and, above all, Hoover, many of them designed by the ebullient Wallis, Gilbert and Partners. They were signs of London's prosperity in the 1930s, while the rest of the country languished in the slump. America supplied these buildings with the imagery of advertising, efficiency and cleanliness, and perhaps too the concept of a 'show' facade, very few feet behind which the reality of production began. The advantage of this nakedly meretricious approach to architecture is that when the use changes, the front can stay.

Very different was the earnest post-war approach to industrial architecture. In the early days of the welfare state, architects were much concerned with social equality in the workplace and with introducing techniques of prefabrication

to factory building – twin preoccupations to be found in an excellent but little-known run of buildings built by Edward Mills for the drug manufacturers May and Baker at Dagenham from 1942 onwards. Later on, attention shifted to creating simple, quickly built single-storey industrial buildings which could serve their purpose for a few years and then be thrown away. Some saw in that the negation of architecture altogether; others, like Norman Foster at Modern Art Glass, regarded it as a sufficient challenge. Even on grander projects like Nicholas Grimshaw's Financial Times printing works in Docklands, there is the same implicit acceptance of obsolescence. Architects of standing, indeed, are more involved in London's industrial buildings today than they ever have been in the past. But that, given history's ruthlessness with the factory, will hardly guarantee their survival.

179

Harmondsworth Tithe Barn
High St, Harmondsworth, Hillingdon

1/A5   British Rail to West Drayton, then bus

Almost all the agricultural lands of Middlesex disappeared under tarmac early this century. The position of Harmondsworth at the west end of the Heathrow runways makes its fen-like rurality the more remarkable. There is a good church that is a stylistic clutter of all periods from Norman to Perpendicular, and next door is the tithe barn, haunched like a great whale.

In 1391 the manor of Harmondsworth was given by Richard II to William of Wykeham, who made it part of the endowment of Winchester College. College records show that a new barn was under construction at Harmondsworth by 1424, and studies of the structure as well as dendrochronology tend to support such a date.

London has little natural building material, and timber was the usual means of construction until brick began to take its place from the late 15th other incised markings, most particularly a paired W that may refer to Wykeham.

The barn at Harmondsworth is remarkable not only for its great length, at 192 ft the second-longest remaining in England, but for the survival of almost all its original timber, including much of the weatherboarding. Despite a long-standing eastward list, its condition is very good. Feel along the sill plate and you can yet find old wheat grains. Today it is still used occasionally for storage; ironically, the oldest building in this section is the one whose function has changed least.

180

Sainsbury's (Streatham Silk Mill)
496 Streatham High Rd, Streatham, Lambeth

1/G6   British Rail to Streatham or Streatham Common

[C]

Until the mid 1980s, few people had visited the factory site occupied by Cow Industrial Polymers behind the west side of Streatham Common. More familiar was the contrasting pair of buildings fronting the High Road: the stuccoed Pied Bull pub, and the Beehive coffee tavern, slapped down next to its neighbour in 1878 with all the moral effrontery of the Victorian temperance movement by the factory owner, Peter Brusey Cow, to keep his workmen out of the pub. The Beehive had long been defunct and its pretty front, by Ernest George and Peto, had suffered mutilation, while the Pied Bull had recently been voted Evening Standard Pub of the Year. Behind the factory gates were the remnants of a little housing development, and a disused Victorian school designed, as it turned out, by Sir Gilbert Scott. The core of the factory lay further back, hidden from the road.

The Cows left their Streatham site and the buildings were scheduled for clearance and replacement by a Sainsbury's store. What should emerge from the muddle of additions but an

Harmondsworth Tithe Barn. GLRO

century. The lack of decent stone in the area can be seen by the use in the plinth here of 'fericrete', congealed gravel resembling concrete dug in huge lumps. It appears in a few buildings in the area, such as Bedfont church; Harmondsworth is one of the last examples. By contrast, the base of each pier is an ashlar block, variously said to be of clunch or Greensand.

The timber-frame construction is intermediary between the crown-post universal around London in the 14th century and the development of side purlins with decorative windbracing to the principal rafters. There is no collar purlin and the crown-post is reduced to a strut. The church-like feeling is heightened by the arch braces to the aisles. Odder still is the form of assembly. There is no one principal threshing floor reached on both sides, but three openings on one side. With an even number of bays, these are necessarily asymmetrically spaced, but whereas most timber frames turn a fair face towards the central threshing floor, here the massive timbers are tenoned into the centre of the tie beams every time. The huge number of carpenters' marks show that the building was erected south to north. There are many

J Sainsbury's, Streatham. EH

entire three-storey mill building dating from about the year 1820, of a type familiar in the industrial Midlands yet utterly unheard of in London? This factory, research revealed, had been erected by a rather sinister industrialist, the silk-weaver Stephen Wilson, seemingly in an attempt to break the monopoly and high wage-rates of the Spitalfields handloom weavers. Wilson wanted to introduce the factory system into London silk-weaving, by keeping his weavers under his personal control in a remote, suburban location and by using the Jacquard loom, the secrets of which after some elaborate industrial espionage he contrived to steal from France. In all this he failed. Changes in fashion, tariff regulations and competition from other British silk-weaving towns caused the rapid decline not only of Spitalfields but also, it seems, of Wilson's Streatham enterprise in the 1820s. The factory passed a decade later into the hands of a rubber goods manufacturer and hence descended to

Cows. At the end of its life it had been reduced to making hot-water bottle stoppers.

After a fiercely fought public enquiry in 1986, Sainsbury's agreed to amend their plans so as to keep the 1820s core of the factory. In this lonely looking buffer between car park and store, Streatham shoppers can now sip coffee after making their weekly purchases and admire drawings and old photographs of the mill so nearly lost to posterity. David Gibson's restoration has the virtue of showing where new brickwork has been necessary because of the removal of adjacent buildings. The ends are mostly new, and so is a great deal of the lower portion of the south side, where a boiler house and handsome factory chimney (by Ernest George and Peto) once stood. But the character of the rugged building has not been betrayed. It is a narrow affair, divided into a centre block and slightly lower and wider wings. Upon the roof sits the traditional type of wooden factory cupola for a bell or clock. The

internal construction between the walls is of timber and not exceptional. It is likely that the tall looms – Jacquards and others – nestled up against the windows on either side of a central passageway. There are more than a hundred windows to the building; if each was occupied by a loom, that would imply an ambitious level of production.

In compensation for the loss of their chimney, Ernest George and Peto's Beehive has now been restored to something like its original state, with a cheerful wooden-bowed front window. Behind its front is a temperance meeting hall, still looking for an up-to-date use. Scott's school and the remnants of Factory Square, alas, are no more now than so many patches of tarmac. A conservation victory was only half won here.

181

Gwilt Stacks
West India Docks

1/H4   Docklands Light Railway to West India Quay

Tobacco Dock

1/G4   Underground or Docklands Light Railway to Shadwell

St Katharine's Dock

1/G4   Underground or Docklands Light Railway to Tower Hill/Gateway

London had the largest system of docks in Britain until 1968–70, when most closed suddenly and dramatically. The survivors went in 1980–1. Their redevelopment can at best be comprehended as the latest phase in the history of an area that has changed more frequently in the past 200 years than perhaps any other in London. Created in the early 1800s, subject to great changes in use and in demography from the 1860s, then heavily bombed, the area is a shrine to 1980s enterprise. Conservation continues to lose out to a commercial culture that still wants history to be either sanitised or obliterated.

By the late 18th century the Thames was overcrowded with shipping. The only official berths were in the Pool of London, with high tariffs and without storage facilities. The idea of enlarging the Thames's capacity by building large-scale docks dates from 1793, and enabling legislation was passed in 1799. The area from the Tower to Blackwall and Rotherhithe was thus transformed to create docks and bonded warehouses, where goods could be stored without paying duty. For security all the docks had impenetrably high walls, whose loss alone has completely transformed the area. Only in Rotherhithe does a sense of the area's evolution survive.

The West India Docks, begun in 1800, were not only the first but architecturally probably the finest. The engineer was Ralph Walker, with John Rennie as consultant. Two great rectangles were created, the Import and Export docks, to which further docks were added in 1868. The main range of warehouses lay along the north side of the Import dock, and were designed by George Gwilt, father and son, in 1802–3. Two survived bombing in 1940 together with the dock office. Like most early warehouses, they were of timber within a brick skin, such as survives in the interior of the Dickens Inn at St Katharine's Dock, a warehouse of about 1800 to which the 1970s exterior bears no relation. Cast-iron stanchions were inserted into West India Dock No. 2 Warehouse in 1814, because the timber columns were overloaded with the weight of sugar stored there. Sugar and grain warehouses are recognisable for their low ceiling heights, so No. 2

Warehouse contains six floors while No. 1 has only five, within the same total height.

To the west, London Docks have fared even less well and have largely been filled in. The architect was Daniel Asher Alexander, who put his admiration for Piranesi and experience of building Dartmoor gaol to great effect. The warehouses closed in 1969, were promptly vandalised, and have been demolished. What remains is the New Tobacco Warehouse of 1811–14, also known as the Skin Floor because furs were stored there. The use of iron columns to support a timber roof was novel for a London warehouse. To reduce the number of columns, alternative roof trusses are supported on struts that fan like branches from a tree. All the warehouses at the London Docks had basement vaults for storing wine and spirits, and those at Tobacco Dock in Wapping Lane are still impressive for the way the angles of the capitals die into the shafts; however, the modern tinkering which has punched holes through and inserted partitions to make a second-rate Covent Garden with pirate ships is unforgivable.

The lessons learnt at St Katharine's Dock should have been salutary. Squeezed into a site of only 8 acres in 1825–8, its small scale prejudiced its subsequent development but should have made its conversion to a marina in the 1970s relatively easy. The engineer was Thomas Telford, who built two docks linked by a central entrance. The warehouses were designed by Philip Hardwick, whose innovation was to place his warehouses right on the dock

side so that goods could be unloaded directly into them. Those on the east dock were bombed, but his three west dock warehouses could have been saved. A cast-iron colonnade was recreated in facsimile at the base of the ill-proportioned World Trade Centre. Instead centre stage now goes to I Warehouse, now Ivory House, built in 1858–60 to the design of George Aitchison senior, with brick jack arches on wrought-iron plate girders.

182
King's Cross Gasholders
Goods Way, Camden

2/G1   Underground or British Rail to King's Cross or St Pancras

We are usually in too great a hurry to be somewhere else to look behind the massive engine sheds of King's Cross or St Pancras. The industrial hinterland of the King's Cross goods yard was anyway for years inaccessible and its architectural richness has only recently been discovered. Yet the Regent's Canal has always provided a public thoroughfare through the area and is still the best way to view the plethora of railway lines and quirky buildings, its tranquillity at odds with the trains gliding across the skyline. Here are some of the most unexpected and exciting views in London. Most dramatic of the buildings are five gasholders, three of which have an elaboration that speaks the classical language of architecture loudly, clearly and correctly. Once nothing was too mean for classical embellishment. Here the raw power of the Doric order is expressed in the simplest manner possible, with massive red triglyphs above the second of three superimposed orders.

The industrial nature of the area predates the two stations, originating with the Regent's Canal cut in 1812–20. The Imperial Gas Light and Coke Company established its works east of Pancras Road in 1824 on the site south of Goods Way where two holders still

Gwilt Stacks, West India Docks. EH

Gasholders, King's Cross. EH

183

Abbey Mills and Crossness Sewerage Pumping Stations

Abbey Mills, Abbey Lane, Newham

1/H4 Underground or British Rail to West Ham

Crossness, Eastern Way, Bexley

1/K4 British Rail to Belvedere

[B]

The opening of Crossness Outfall Works in 1865 and Abbey Mills in 1868 delivered London from engulfment in its own sewage. They were the culmination of a mammoth project by the Metropolitan Board of Works and its chief engineer, Joseph Bazalgette, and the basis of London's sewage system today.

London's drainage was originally provided by the streams that flowed into the Thames. Many were subsequently bricked in and diverted underground to become sewers. Attempts were made to force the discharge of offensive matter into cesspools instead, but these were swamped by the wider diffusion of the water closet after the Napoleonic Wars following improvements to the water supply, and there was no alternative but to permit discharge into the Thames. By 1850 it was an open sewer, typhoid was endemic and the spasmodic scourge of cholera was killing thousands, mostly those in the poorer areas whose drinking water came from the river.

In 1848 the General Board of Health was set up and London's various sewage commissions were amalgamated into a body which, seven years later, formed the core of the Metropolitan Board of Works. These bodies recognised the need for better sewers that would take the effluent down the Thames estuary, but Bazalgette's proposals were blocked by Parliament until in 1858 an Act allowed the Board of Works to raise a loan of £3 million.

Bazalgette's scheme was to construct five intercepting sewers at various levels

stand. In the 1860s it expanded to the west with three new holders, erected in 1861, 1864 and 1867 and replaced in the 1880s by the present telescoped set. Recently the holders have stored natural gas.

Other industrial premises followed the railway, adding to the character of the area whilst allowing the stations and gasholders to dominate. The chief goods carried by the railway were grain and agricultural produce, for which a six-storey granary was built at the same time as the station, facing a canal basin since filled in. In proved harder to wrest

coal from its traditional sea-borne route, so coal drops were provided to facilitate its transfer from trucks into merchants' wagons. One set was built at the same time as the granary and another was added to the west in 1856.

Proposals for the redevelopment of this complex area have been confounded at the time of writing by British Rail's uncertainly about the development of a rail link with the Channel Tunnel. It waits to be seen how much of Norman Foster's scheme for offices, housing and a new communications system around a central park will materialise.

parallel to the Thames, three to the north and two to the south. The most famous is that formed by embanking the Thames on its northern side, narrowing the river and forming Victoria Embankment and its western continuations. Sewage and rainwater were carried eastwards, largely by gravity. On the southern side the products were pumped up at Crossness, then settled in tanks and fed into the river, the tanks replaced by a more sophisticated sewage farm in 1878. On the north side the gravitational flow was interrupted by the River Lea, so the sewage was pumped up there and fed into a high landfall out-sewer over the marshes to Beckton.

Abbey Mills is the largest and most impressive of four pumping stations originally constructed. It was built to house eight beam engines, two in each of its cruciform arms and served by two flanking boiler rooms, each with its own chimney, now gone. The practicality of this plan is often overlooked amidst the richness of the decoration in which the building was enveloped. The engine house has a glazed central lantern and four minarets indicating staircases in the angles. Outside is a feast of polychromy in stone and brick with lavishly carved capitals, all in a vaguely Italian Gothic with Byzantine overtones. Inside is a cathedral in cast-iron. There is a central crossing of twelve fat and enriched columns, while even in the basement each spandrel, railing and floor grate is peppered with foliage answering the forms of the carved stone capitals and friezes along the walls. The beam engines were replaced in 1931–3 by more powerful electrically driven centrifugal pumps, together with gauges and indicator-boards of Wellsian massiveness. Subsidiary buildings erected to serve the Isle of Dogs, in 1891–4, and to deal with surplus rainwater, in 1910–14, are simpler but impressive internally because dug so deep.

Crossness is smaller, an oblong engine house served by a single boiler room, yet internally the iron framework is even more lavishly cast. What makes Crossness the more special is that its four beam engines, positioned in the four corners of the building, survive: they were made by James Watt and Son and each was capable of 125 horsepower. They have lain idle and rusting since the Second World War when a new pumping station was built alongside. A trust formed to preserve the building has now entered into protracted negotiations with the water authority.

184
St Olaf's House (Hay's Wharf Company Offices)
Tooley St, London Bridge, Southwark

2/K5   Underground or British Rail to London Bridge

Amidst the detritus of new construction along the Thames by London Bridge one building literally shines out. The shock of the clean lines and jazzy gilding of St Olaf's House must have been even greater when the building was completely surrounded by Victorian warehousing. Built in 1931 as the Hay's Wharf Company Offices, it is the principal office building of H S Goodhart-Rendel, landowner, musician and writer, whose historical essays, such as *English Architecture since the Regency*, have overshadowed his importance as an architect. His best work is a fusion of expressionist styling from the continent with fine craftsmanship that owes something to the work of Lethaby and Temple Moore.

Abbey Mills Pumping Station. GLRO

227

Hay's Wharf. River front. RIBA

Like the Daily Express Building, Hay's Wharf combines industrial premises with a company headquarters – this time for dock warehousing. It replaced St Olave's Church, built in 1740 by Henry Flitcroft and demolished between 1918 and 1928. The plan was dictated by the narrow site and the need for lorries to reach the riverside wharf. Instead of the lightwell usual in office buildings, the central range was narrowed to allow roadways to either side and raised on legs or *pilotis* (an early English use) to make for car parking underneath. The feature of the interiors is the obsession with decorative patterning, exemplified by the central staircase hall where the geometric stair-rail running through the building is complemented by stripy panelled walls, lift doors and terrazzo floors. The principal rooms are a common room and double-height board room for the company's directors, overlooking the river, the latter a striking combination of traditional scagliola with modernistic metal bands running over the walls and ceilings that house the light fittings.

These two rooms are denoted on the outside by little oriels that give

wonderful views, and by being framed within a sequence of reliefs that emphasise their importance from across the river. By Frank Dobson, the latter were originally highlighted with gold leaf. Similarly, the steel frame is stressed: the vertical casing is shaped to give the impression of being woven through the structure whilst the Portland stone cladding is stuck on like big tiles. The Tooley Street facade is simpler, the principal features being the angling of the walls inwards over the central windows to allow greater areas of glazing on this narrow street, and the lettering, no longer the original though in the same typeface.

Lecturing in 1931, Goodhart-Rendel effectively summed up the style of Hay's Wharf: 'the Five Orders are packed away in a cupboard – we are playing with new toys now, rather hard and cornery but sensible and strong.' The turrets on the Tooley Street elevation were to become a familiar Goodhart-Rendel motif, especially on the churches that form the main body of his work. Holy Trinity Dockhead nearby in Jamaica Street, built in 1951–60, affords an interesting comparison between his early and late work.

185
Daily Express Building
Fleet St, City of London

2/J4   Underground to Blackfriars

Until the 1980s national newspaper production seemed bogged down in Fleet Street – an anachronism prolonged by conservatism and bad labour relations, yet heir to a vital strand in the City's culture and history. A few years after News International's flight to Wapping in 1986, printers and journalists are no longer to be seen around Fleet Street. Money, the law and the hard-hearted offices that go with these pursuits have taken over the area. The last major industry left in the middle of London has departed.

Fleet Street itself was traditionally too valuable for printing to occupy its frontage. The little printing shops and

large newspaper works which grew from its bookshops and publishers hid away in narrow back streets. But for publicity reasons, a Fleet Street address and architectural front began in time to be valued. The first newspaper to grasp this was the *Daily Telegraph* which built on the north side in 1881–2. In 1929–31 new owners reconstructed the Telegraph building on an enlarged, American scale, busting open the scale of the street. Lord Beaverbrook's *Daily Express* responded a few yards further east in 1931–2 with a front almost as big but in a contrasting, snook-cocking style. Deserted now by their titles, these rival facades linger on to remind us of the pride and publicity-seeking of the inter-war newspaper barons.

The Daily Telegraph, overweeningly stone-faced and columnar, develops the Selfridges style of classicism – logically, since Thomas Tait, its architect, had just finished off Selfridges itself (pp. 212–13). The Express front would have been similar, had it not been for the ambition and functionalist persuasions of the engineer on the Telegraph project, Owen Williams. Because Fleet Street newspaper buildings sandwiched offices and heavy manufacturing together, there were often structural problems to sort out. At the Telegraph the new offices in front were distinct from existing printing works behind, so Williams's role was not critical. At the Express, where Williams was again retained, matters were more complex.

Since 1920 the brash Lord Beaverbrook had been buying up land on the east side of Shoe Lane, where the *Express* began, as part of his strategy to rival the *Daily Mail*. His architects, the newspaper specialists Ellis and Clarke, put up a small extension to house printing lines here in 1926–7. Then in 1930 Beaverbrook got a foothold on Fleet Street itself. The tricky brief was to extend the new lines south under a conspicuous office front, and to tuck in an unloading bay for newsprint. So Williams, whose flair for concrete construction was unequalled in Britain, took command. He objected to concealing his concrete frame behind lumpish stonework and pressed for something memorable and up-to-date.

Express moved south of the river in 1989, but Aitken House of the 1970s, abutting east of the headquarters building, is regrettably with us still. It deprived the original of its stylish, rounded end on this east flank and continues to detract from its completeness. In their post-newspaper incarnation, the Express front and lobby are just a shirtfront to a new office building behind.

186

Hoover Factory
Western Avenue and Bedford Avenue, Perivale, Ealing

1/D4   Underground to Perivale

Art deco in architecture was not a philosophically conceived style but a response to the new needs and new materials of a changing society. Its exemplary practitioners were not first-class architects like Goodhart-Rendel, but specialists in the design of new building types. Among these were the factory designers Wallis, Gilbert and Partners. The Hoover factory is the finest surviving example of their bizarre synthesis of art deco with Egyptian motifs – the two languages of flat patterning prevalent in the 1920s and early 1930s. No line is straight that could be battered, stepped or fluted. Complex concrete forms give weight to the front and form sharp arrises to the sides. By contrast, huge areas of metal windows curve round the corner staircases behind the supporting columns. The ensemble is given zest by narrow bands of vibrant colour: green for the windows, reds, oranges and blues for the tiles that converge above the central doorway in a fan of angled lines echoed in the jazzy metalwork of the doors and gates. The building shouts that this was a new age of technological sophistication.

The vacuum cleaner was invented in 1907 by an asthmatic caretaker in Ohio called Murray Spangler, who obtained financial backing from one W H Hoover. The Western Avenue was conceived as a new road to Oxford at around the same time but only reached Perivale in 1927.

Daily Express Building. GLRO

So the Daily Express acquired the first major Modern Movement front in London. But it was Bertram Gallannaugh, the new junior partner in Ellis and Clarke, not Owen Williams, who had the idea of clothing it with the slick black vitrolite which gives the Daily Express Building its distinctive image. He must have been looking at Raymond Hood's shiny-black Palladium House in Great Marlborough Street (p. 216).

The inside of the Daily Express had little but engineering interest. The exception was the lobby, handed over for Robert Atkinson to design. Ostentatiously visible from the street through sheets of tall plate glass, it was the last of the functioning newspaper lobbies, at which customers called to give in their small ads and collect the answers. The style, best beheld from the outside, is a tinselly 'Jazz Moderne', with exotic bronzed reliefs by Eric Aumonier on the side walls. Much of the original furniture has gone. Evelyn Waugh wrote a pungent parody of the Express lobby in *Scoop*. Mercifully, nothing like Waugh's 'chryselephantine effigy of Lord Copper in coronation robes' was attempted by Beaverbrook.

The vitrolite and glass curtain of the Williams and Gallannaugh front became the motif of later Express extensions. Most of them have vanished since the

In that year Percy Bilton began to develop the area with housing and new factory units that exploited the access provided by the railway and the new road. Companies like Hoover exploited the freedom offered by improving electrical power to site their factories away from the old manufacturing towns of the north, which declined as London boomed. Factories also spread along London's other new arterial roads, most famously on the Brentford stretch of the Great West Road. Many of these were also by Wallis, Gilbert and Partners. It was an architecture of facadism, advertising the products of a modern age: vacuum cleaners, tyres, chemicals, toothpaste, perfumes and aeronautical components.

The Hoover factory was designed in 1931 with Frederick Button, better known for the Stockwell Bus Garage (p. 245), as job-architect. Manufacturing began in 1932, although the domestic vacuum cleaner was not launched there until the main complex was completed in 1935. A canteen was added to the west in 1938–9, when the front block was raised a storey. The completed factory provided a logical assembly plant arranged on several levels: storage, casting and machining on the ground floor, assembly on the first, with tool shops on the second floor and model shops and laboratories for product development on the third. The offices were on the showfront facing Western Avenue, the battered and fluted facade suggesting the superiority of the office workers and directors over the blue-collar workers in the blocks to the rear.

Hoover closed its factory at Perivale in October 1981. What had once been cheap greenfield sites were now costly and incapable of expansion, and many other large factories in West London closed around the same time. This had two tragic results. It created an unemployment problem for skilled workers and caused the destruction of much of the Great West Road, including the bulldozing of Wallis, Gilbert's Firestone factory in August 1980. This loss prompted a wave of interest in art deco as a building style, which in debased form is now the idiom of many a vapid new office block in London.

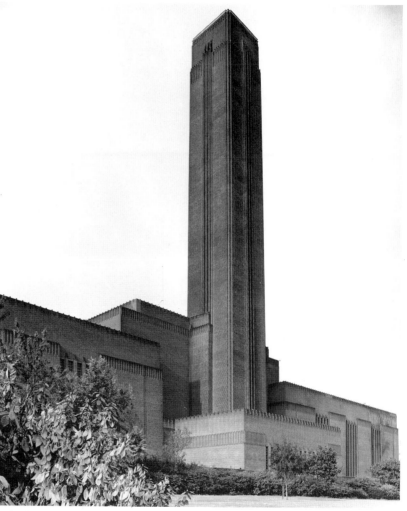

Bankside Power Station. EH

187
Bankside Power Station
Bankside, Southwark

2/J5   Underground or British Rail to Blackfriars or Waterloo

The generation of electric power in London was, until nationalisation in 1948, divided amongst a plethora of private companies and local authorities. In 1925 ten were amalgamated by Act of Parliament to form the London Power Company, and an Act in 1926 originated the national grid, fed by fewer but larger power stations. The first result of these Acts was Battersea Power Station, begun in 1929, where Sir Giles Scott provided an architectural veneer.

The London Power Company had a second riverside station, built for the London Electric Lighting Company in 1891 but bombed in the war. This was at Bankside, directly opposite St Paul's Cathedral. The County of London Plan, published in 1943, envisaged this area cleared of its traditional industries, but the London Power Company wanted a replacement power station. Scott had gained a reputation for dealing with awkward redevelopments on the Thames, having been the consulting architect not only for Battersea Power Station but also for Waterloo Bridge. He was recommended for Bankside by its engineers, Mott, Hay and Anderson. Unlike Battersea, Scott was involved in the design for Bankside from the first: whereas Battersea was a compromise and his Rye House station in Essex never got finished, Bankside was a complete masterpiece.

Had the scheme been delayed until nationalisation it might never have been built. However, in January 1947 Scott produced plans for a large brick power station with a chimney at either end. There was an outcry, and in June Lewis Silkin, Minister of Town and Country Planning, approved a revised design with a single tower on axis with St Paul's and a symmetrical massing much as was finally built. Silkin promised that sulphur fumes from the station would be dealt with in such as way that they would not endanger the leadwork of St Paul's. Bankside's tower was lower (at 325 ft) than the dome of St Paul's (370 ft) and was provided with a flue washing plant of cedar wood 'scrubbers' to its rear. The emission was to be a 'smokeless shimmer of vapour'. Ironically, if the chimney had been taller and the cleaning process less efficient, hot gasses would have shot up into the atmosphere; instead, super-cooled smoke drifted over the Thames straight at the leadwork of St Paul's. But so precarious is the future of Bankside that St Paul's looks set long to outlive it.

The first stage of the building, the tower and west wing, was finished in 1953 and the station was completed a little after Scott's death in 1960. The coup is its adoption of a single tower, or campanile. This is gently tapering with a slight entasis, and forms a cathedral-like composition with the high bulk of the turbine halls to either side and the taller washing plant behind. The result is a symmetrical facade that is a powerful play of vertical windows and brick mullions set against heavy horizontals that disguise subtle set-backs. The design is idiosyncratically Scott's: it owes much to early 20th-century Dutch architecture and something to Wright's work of the 1920s but no one else in Britain made himself such a master of

using brickwork as a module for exciting forms. The effect is chillingly simple, immensely powerful. Ancillary buildings such as offices are hidden at the sides, and storage and delivery facilities are tucked underneath the sheer blank wall to the rear.

Bankside ceased operations in about 1980, and its original nickname of 'Silkin's Folly' has in a sense been justified. Perhaps it should never have been built. But what was built was such a great piece of industrial architecture that we cannot allow it to be pulled down. And now that Battersea has been half-demolished, we can even less afford to lose Bankside.

188
Plant Construction PLC (Modern Art Glass)
Hailey Rd, Bexley

1/K5   British Rail to Belvedere

'A vivid dragonfly . . . on the empty swamp', Bridget Cherry graphically calls this colourful industrial hangar. Twenty years on there seems nothing out of the ordinary and more than a little hackneyed vulgarity about the outrageous blue walls and green ends of Modern Art Glass. But in 1972–3, when the concrete and brick housing of much-

planned and much-bruited Thamesmead was rising with laborious slowness on the dismal environment of Plumstead Marshes, the sudden apparition of Foster Associates' shed in its Eastern Industrial Area was a breath of fresh, cheap and quick air.

Industrial clients were always calling for architects to house them more simply. But before then nobody had thought to do what Norman Foster did here – just take an ordinary Portal frame for a shed, clad it in a standard corrugated metal, leave off eaves, glaze the ends and paint the thing bright blue. It was the blue which enraged the planners, who wanted politer grey. But after a battle Fosters won, and who shall say that Thamesmead needs more grey?

Inside, the space is divided laterally and visibly into offices above and production below. The glazed walls through which the division is seen were made by Modern Art Glass themselves, so the opportunity was taken to experiment with thin steel mullions and neoprene gaskets. Like the bald colours, the glazing looks familiar and self-evident now; but it was from this little building that the general look and broad glazed ends of Fosters' Sainsbury Centre for the Visual Arts at the University of East Anglia and a procession of smart industrial buildings of the 1970s and 1980s have descended. That Modern Art Glass looks commonplace now is a tribute to its enormous influence.

Modern Art Glass. FOSTER ASSOCIATES

16

Transport

Transport litters cities with an infrastructure which becomes more elaborate generation by generation. Primitive man made primitive paths by mere habitual use. In due course came roads and streets, whose upkeep has needed organisation and enforcement ever since Roman times. In London, provision for the making and maintaining of urban streets was central to the legislation that followed upon the Great Fire of 1666, and a major preoccupation of the ill-coordinated Georgian city. London's street development since, from the princely layout of Regent Street through the cheap but copious Victorian avenues of the Metropolitan Board of Works to the 'motorway box' of the 1960s, whose fragmentary execution no one laments, would make a fascinating study in urban engineering and design.

But roads in themselves do not create much that is strictly architectural. The first medium that does is water, or rather the interaction of road transport and water transport in the form of bridges. London owes its *raison d'être* to navigable water. Whole swathes of the historic city might be classified under the rubric of infrastructure for water transport – docks and warehouses most obviously, but also early markets, merchants' houses and Thames-side forts, palaces and villas as well. Potentates did not build next to the river because it was more amenable; often it stank, or made walls sodden with damp. They did so in order to get about more quickly. Mobility mattered to the rich, powerful and busy in the past, just as it does now.

To be at their architectural best, bridges require a certain structural logic and formality, at which the English rarely excel. London has had fine bridges of this kind, notably Robert Mylne's at Blackfriars and John Rennie's at Waterloo, both alas demolished. Such has been the toll of time and traffic that Richmond Bridge is the only survivor of London's close-arched, pre-Victorian

bridges. Albert Bridge and Tower Bridge, by contrast, are hearty reminders that the incorrigible English taste for picturesqueness insinuated itself even into river crossings with Old London Bridge and has endured in one form or another ever since. The gateway on the south side of the Blackwall Tunnel is another such manifestation. But taken as a whole, the Thames bridges are symptomatic of London's ungrateful inability to treat its magnificent river frontages with dignity.

Canals come next in the growth of London's transport. Such was the fury of railway development a few decades later that many have been all but obliterated, often by railway tracks along their line. The great exception is the Regent's Canal branch of the Grand Union Canal, still navigable. Its docks and basins in Maida Vale, Limehouse and King's Cross have suffered or are suffering the anaesthetic fate of becoming marinas with businessmen's housing all around, while the unique road-railway-canal interchange at Camden Lock is a shadow of its former self. At the top of Regent's Park, there is still the fine iron Macclesfield Bridge to admire (p. 111). A perambulation of the canal's towpaths, too, offers a key to the changing scene of the innermost northern suburbs.

Never has a city been so abused by railway-building as Victorian London. The sheer, unnecessary, unplanned extravagance of twelve separate main-line termini, not to mention lesser lines and stations, goods yards and elevated viaducts, created urban scars which have yet to heal. Worst affected because of its shape and because of the wantonness of the railway companies which rampaged over its surface was inner South London, where lines cross and re-cross in a wholly avoidable tangle. Such are the consequences, let governments be warned, of entrusting urban transport to private enterprise. Yet out of this chaos arose the familiar, magnificent monuments of the railway age that tempt us to forgive the perpetrators and

Leaving Arnos Grove. AP

233

Richmond Bridge. GLRO

to echo their canting talk about progress. Brunel's Paddington, Barlow's St Pancras and the western shed of Liverpool Street belong with the Palm House at Kew to the heroic moment when British iron architecture led the world. The heritage of early railway architecture is richer, too, than that of roads or canals. We represent this diversity with Barnes Station, little and rural, on the London and South Western Railway's burgeoning suburban network, and the unsmiling, industrial profile of the Roundhouse at Chalk Farm, where the London and Birmingham company serviced, turned and housed its early locomotives.

The 1860s was the worst decade of upheaval for London since the Great Fire, blitz-like in its building of railways, termini and roads to link them. Out of the experience, in an unplanned, empirical British way, came one lasting innovation: the underground railway. It took twenty years to become a 'system', and achieved unified control only in 1933. But it quickly became acknowledged as the single most essential element to modern transport in a great city. Much early underground architecture has been lost; Baker Street, over-restored, gives some sense of how the platforms used to be. With the era of electric traction and the deep-level tube

after 1890, the stations became more distinctive, with domes over the circular stairs on the early City and South London line, as at Kennington, and the faience-clad facades of the so-called 'Yerkes' tubes, built with American investment in the Edwardian years. It is lamentable that so many of these robust creations have now been needlessly defaced.

The golden epoch of the London underground system came between 1920 and 1940. These were the years when, through a series of compromises allowing partial public control, Lord Ashfield and his right-hand man, Frank Pick, gradually acquired for their

Underground Electric Railway Companies of London an effective monopoly of the capital's underground and bus systems. Unified image and striking design were critical to the Ashfield–Pick strategy. It was conferred by the cool but never desiccated modernism of Charles Holden and a variety of lesser designers around him. So striking was their achievement that Steen Eiler Rasmussen, looking for London's modern architecture in 1928 (five years before London Transport was formally created), said he could not find any – only the underground. Buses, tube trains, central offices at Broadway, stations, garages, depots, signs, advertisements and maps all felt the beneficial touch of unified design, and can still be enjoyed all over London; our selection just indicates a few of the best complete buildings. The policy continued on into the post-war years, as at Stockwell Bus Garage. It has broken down only in the past ten years, when a hotchpotch of piecemeal alterations has taken place. This is the more to be lamented because London has so few unifying and coordinating features to make it more comprehensible.

Finally, it is worth contemplating the injection of scale that the architecture of transport brings to London's landscape. Offices, flats and even churches can be small or large, according to the scale of human presumption, but many transport buildings have to be big. Bridges and tunnels must reach the full length from shore to shore, not omitting the necessary approaches; railway termini must accommodate rows of steam- or fume-belching locomotives and their carriages, and so be wide and high; depots must be long enough too for complete trains, garages lofty enough to house the fleets of double-decker buses upon which London still prides itself. The business of providing motive power, represented in our selection by the Greenwich Generating Station of London's lost electric tramways system, also requires a grand scale if turbines, boilers, chimneys are to operate with efficiency. Flying, too, creates huge buildings, of which Greater London's best example, inaccessible to most of us, is the former BOAC

maintenance hangar at Heathrow Airport of 1950–5, by Owen Williams. More than any other type of architecture, certainly more than tall offices or the 'point blocks' of housing, the architecture of urban transport offers that largeness of scale in context so essential to a sense of the sublime.

189
Richmond Bridge
Richmond

1/D6   Underground or British Rail to Richmond

London owes its existence not only to its port but also to its bridge. Until 1750 ferries were the only alternative to London Bridge as a means of crossing the Thames between Kingston and the sea. This ensured the City of London's trade monopoly as well as discouraging London's expansion. The opening of Westminster Bridge in 1750, built to the design of Charles Labelye, was the first challenge to the City's position. The City retaliated by commissioning Robert Mylne to build a bridge at Blackfriars, completed in 1768, that was far more sophisticated than Labelye's. An elegant design of nine elliptical spans forming a gentle curve, it served as a model for bridges into the next century: for John Rennie's Waterloo and London Bridges of 1811–17 and 1823–31 respectively, and for Richmond Bridge, built by James Paine and Kenton Couse in 1774–7. All the central London bridges have been rebuilt, the victims of increased traffic and erosion by strong tides and the chemical action of polluted water. But that at Richmond survives, widened in 1937.

Richmond Bridge was the brainchild of William Windham, the leaseholder of a ferry there. He first upset many local residents by proposing a cheap wooden bridge, in 1772, but then set up a committee of citizens to raise subscriptions and commission a design in Oxfordshire stone. The architects appointed had both built in Richmond for various members of the committee. James Paine is remembered as a country

house architect, although he built four bridges across the Thames late in his career; Kenton Couse was the architect of Holy Trinity, Clapham Common, and of Richmond workhouse. Surviving elevations are entirely in Paine's hand. In form it owes much to Mylne's work, though Paine had built very small elliptical-arched bridges in the grounds of his country houses from about 1755. The treatment of the arches is based on a design by Palladio of an 'ancient bridge' at Vicenza, though given cutwaters that are semi-circular above high-water level. The river was spanned in five arches, the central one 24 ft above low-water level. The resulting gradient was reduced in 1937 when the approaches were raised and the bridge widened on the upstream side in a careful copy of the original. An obelisk and pair of tollhouses were built at the Richmond end, the latter also removed in 1937.

190
Paddington Station
Praed St, Paddington, Westminster

2/B3   Underground to Paddington [C]

The best way to approach Paddington is in fact not by train, bus, underground or on foot, but by car or taxi. Ask your driver to come in via Bishop's Bridge Road, and he will swing round off the bridge on to a private road and make two tight little turns to align himself with the train shed. Suddenly you find yourself descending a ramp from roof level with the whole station laid out before you, to be deposited only too soon by one of the columns between Platforms 8 and 9. It is an exhilarating introduction to the spirit of Isambard Kingdom Brunel – and, indeed, of the Crystal Palace.

The Crystal Palace comes in because, as railway historian Robert Thorne has demonstrated, the relation between that long-lost building and Paddington Station is far from arbitrary. It was the prospect of the traffic anticipated by the Great Exhibition of 1851 that induced the Great Western Railway, late in the day, to plan an enlarged terminus at Paddington and, more revolutionary, a big railway hotel to put up visitors. Both station and hotel missed the deadline by miles, the station dragging on indeed till 1854. That meant that Brunel, engineer to the railway company and a member of the Great Exhibition building committee, and Fox, Henderson and Company, contractors for both the Crystal Palace and for the new station, had leisure to absorb the lessons of the immortal building in Hyde Park. Both parties were temperamentally prone to the 'can-do' philosophy of early Victorian engineering, and the time for reflection may have been no bad thing.

Not everyone was convinced that Paxton's colossal greenhouse was so marvellous. Monotony, despite the last-minute introduction of a cross transept, had been much complained of. That is why Brunel planned two cross transepts at Paddington, both fairly functionless, and why he pressed Matthew Digby Wyatt, another of the Great Exhibition design team, to come in with him as 'assistant for the ornamental details'. Precisely what Wyatt contributed we do not know. It is a good guess that the starlike piercing of the upper sections of the ribs, the Moorish leaf-ornament (bolted on, not integral with the rib structure) of their lower portions where they come down to meet the capitals, the dramatic, proto art nouveau flower patterns in the ends of the roofs (lost alas at the more visible western end), and the shape of the main capitals owe a lot to him. These elegant details give the lie to the old theory that functional structures look best without addition of ornament. No doubt the fetching detail of the stationmaster's balcony, which looks down on the station from above one of the transepts, is Digby Wyatt's as well.

Manifold changes and additions have been made to the station's structure. Brunel's original station – two 'aisles' with a wider and higher central 'nave' – was supplemented with an extra shed beyond the ramp and roadway in 1913. Within the older portion, the old circular cast-iron columns have given way to fussier polygonal steel supports.

Barnes Station. Road frontage. EH

The whole system of transverse ridge-and-furrow glazing in the roof, one of the main legacies of the Crystal Palace (and a Fox, Henderson speciality), has been supplanted too by the duller but more leak-proof arrangements above the ribs today. So even in the main sheds, we do not have quite what Brunel and Wyatt intended. What we do have, however, is enough to give Paddington one of the highest places in the roll-call of the world's early railway termini. British Rail has done its best to respect the colours Brunel chose for his ironwork, but of arrangements on the concourse it is better to be silent.

Blocking the back of the concourse is P C Hardwick's Great Western Hotel, the pioneer London railway hotel. It still has a fine, towered presence on Praed Street, but its interiors were gutted in the 1930s. Nor has its stuccoed exterior been treated as it deserved. By its presence right behind the train shed it set a tradition taken up at Charing Cross, Cannon Street, St Pancras, Liverpool Street and other British termini – never to the advantage of either station or hotel.

191
Barnes Station
Rocks Lane, Barnes, Richmond

1/E5   British Rail only

[C]

Travelling from Waterloo, you might be forgiven for never noticing this little station building, opened in 1846. Masked on one side by a monstrous road bridge, half-throttled by trees on the other, the train whisks away without your ever noticing what lurks behind the mishmash of canopies. But from the west, coming from Richmond and especially from Barnes Bridge, there is no excuse. Attenuated Tudor-Gothic stacks rise sentinel to either side of the station house they dwarf, and are given the full Hampton Court treatment of black diapering and angled cut-brick tops.

William Tite is today remembered as the designer of rather pompous classical public buildings. In fact no other reputable architect was so involved in the railway industry. Most of his larger stations were Italianate, like North Woolwich, built in 1847 as a grandiose terminal out of all proportion to the handful of trains it serves and now a museum. But the bulk of Tite's stations were for the London and South Western Railway (LSWR), which opened a line from Nine Elms, Battersea, to Woking in 1838. For their main line, extended to Southampton and Gosport in 1841, he remained wholeheartedly Italianate. But when the LSWR realised the potential of commuter traffic and built a branch line to Richmond in 1846, Tite went Tudor. Barnes is the only survivor of four country stations in the style. Tudor was hardly appropriate for Georgian Richmond, but it was well-suited to Windsor, whither the line was extended in 1851. There, hard by Wyatville's remodelled castle, Tite stretched the idiom to a grandeur appropriate to the royal patronage it was to receive. Barnes has been called a trial run for this piece of Victorian lavishness.

Nestling in its overgrown common, Barnes retains the feel of a country station. It is a clever composition, seemingly symmetrical, whose quirks are only revealed on closer scutiny. There are two parallel blocks, both of three bays. The picturesque composition is largely produced by shunting the range facing the tracks upline from that to the road, producing odd blind angles and half gables. What is a central door on the road frontage is therefore to one side on the other. The pretty lancet windows, some single, some paired, play similar games, with lots of stone-topped gables for good measure. Charming though the result is, it is not 'folksy', and never forsakes the toughness required of railway architecture.

192
The Roundhouse
Chalk Farm Rd, Camden

1/F4   Underground to Chalk Farm

Like a beached whale, the malm-brick rotunda of the Roundhouse lies looking for a use – a monumental relic of the

early railway age washed up on the side of the Chalk Farm Road. Buildings of what J M Richards named the 'functional tradition in industrial architecture' can be as hard to deal with as any others, once the specific function they were made for has altered.

The Roundhouse belongs to the second phase of London's railway development. The London and Birmingham Railway, planned by Robert Stephenson in the mid-1830s, was opened up to Chalk Farm on the capital's outskirts in 1837. Here the company had purchased 22 acres for a terminus and depot, close to the Regent's Canal so as to provide a link with the London docks – an interchange which has left many relics of Victorian road, railway and canal transport in the trendified vicinity of Camden Lock, including remnants of London's largest complex of industrial stabling. In the event the line was quickly taken on into Euston. So the Chalk Farm site developed haphazardly, with sheds, sidings and a marshalling yard. In 1846 there was an amalgamation, and the London and North-Western Railway Company came into being. Seeking to make better use of its assets, the new company ordered Stephenson to make a proper plan for what was to be called the Camden Goods Yard. The company's in-house engineer, Robert Dockray, and his assistant Mr Normanville did the work. A passenger-engine shed, coke

shed, a repairing shop and tank houses were constructed. Connected with the main goods sidings at the north-eastern extremity, Dockray placed the goods-engine house – the Roundhouse. It was built in 1846–7.

Most early British railway engine houses were rectangular. The idea of a circular shed is said to have been a French one. It simplified access and promoted order; locomotives could come in through a single modest entrance (at Chalk Farm on the west), turn on a central turntable and park in a series of radii with maintenance pits underneath. As there were roundhouses at Birmingham and Derby by the late 1830s, they cannot have taken long to catch on in England. So Dockray was following precedent. But the size of the shed, with a diameter of 160 ft and room for twenty-three engines behind the ring of circular cast-iron columns supporting the tent-like roof, seems to have been new. New too was the scale of provision for coke storage, clinker waste and even stabling beneath the engine pits.

Even so, the Roundhouse had an operating life of only about fifteen years. Rectangular sheds could be lengthened to accommodate more engines, but circular ones could not; what is more, the 40 ft diameter turntable proved too short for the longer locomotives of the 1860s, and the surrounding ring of columns precluded enlargement. But the building's proximity to road

The Roundhouse. GLRO

transport saved it from demolition. After a brief life as a goods shed it became an enormous storage depot for Gilbeys, the Camden Town distillery and drinks firm, who stopped up the engine entrance, slated over the original ring of rooflights above the columns, removed the tracks and in due course built wooden galleries all round reaching from the walls to the central circle of columns. In 1875 some 6,000 casks of port, sherry, brandy and whisky were 'laid up' here, reports drink historian Robert Thorne.

A warehouse the Roundhouse remained till 1963, when the playwright Arnold Wesker and others saw its possibilities for a trades-union-supported 'theatre in the round' – a phrase much in vogue at the time. After some false starts the building was loosely converted and reopened as a theatre (on a more commercial basis than Wesker had wanted) in 1968, while on ground to its south Richard Seifert and Partners designed a respectable small office block. The theatre survived precariously but with some *succès d'estime* till 1984. At the time of writing the great rotunda awaits an imaginative and rich user, preferably a railway enthusiast, to ensure its future.

193

St Pancras Station and Midland Grand Hotel
Euston Rd, Camden

2/G1   Also by underground or British Rail to King's Cross

[C]   station only

Where other London termini charge the soul with wanderlust, the height and drama of St Pancras's giant span and the magnificent sweep of the hotel across its front only exaggerate its under-use. As an advertisement for the delights of Derby, Sheffield and Nottingham, it goes well over the top.

But why go north when many of the region's best ingredients are here? The Butterley Company from Derbyshire – its name emblazoned on every third truss – supplied the ironwork, the fierce red bricks came from Nottingham, the

stone from Ancaster in Lincolnshire and the grey and red granite from Peterhead. The Midland Railway formerly covered much of northern Britain, and its London terminus reflected this. Moreover, the massive vaults under the train shed once stored Burton beer.

Comparisons are inevitably made with the adjacent Great Northern Station at King's Cross, completed by Lewis Cubitt in 1852. The Midland Railway Company shared King's Cross for five years, until in 1862 it was forced to petition for its own terminus. Begun in 1865, the station opened in 1868, the hotel in 1874. Like King's Cross the position of St Pancras was dictated by an edict forbidding railway companies from building south of the Euston Road. A shared problem, too, was the Regent's Canal immediately to the north. The Great Northern Company tunnelled under it; St Pancras gained some 17 ft over its rival because its tracks were raised on a bridge. Hence the space for the beer, between iron stanchions.

As its front to Euston Road shows,

King's Cross was built as two halves, one shed for arrivals and one for departures. St Pancras gave itself greater flexibility and visual dominance with a single span of 240 ft. The twenty-five main ribs are tied beneath the platforms by the joists that roof the basement vaults. Linked by purlins, these ribs are virtually self-supporting, leaving the side walls only the job of carrying the intermediate ribs and braces. This neat solution was designed by the engineers W H Barlow and R M Ordish, though construction historian Robert Thorne gives credit also to Sir John Alleyne, manager of the Butterley Iron Company, for its successful resolution. It was the world's widest-span train shed until eclipsed by Jersey City's Pennsylvania Station in 1888.

It is sacrilegious in the eyes of the ubiquitous Mr Thorne to divide the train shed from the hotel that shields it from the Euston Road. The latter is perhaps Sir Gilbert Scott's finest secular composition. Its success is that it is more than a screen, but a swish of

St Pancras Station by night. EH

Midland Grand Hotel. The rooftop. RCHME

lancets, flamboyant dormers and chimney pots stopped by a tower of municipal stature. Though, with the exception of King's Cross, termini hotels were generally placed across the front of their sheds as a visual landmark of corporate rivalry, nowhere else are the two elements linked so clearly, with the carriage drive to the station thrust through the hotel under a colonnaded vault. The hotel's own entrance was the *porte cochère* at its prow. Scott's public rooms follow the curve of the drive, with a coffee room on the ground floor and a dining hall on the first, reached by a grand staircase of two interfolding flights – the drama of 44 Berkeley Square on a massive scale and unashamedly dependent on cast-iron.

When, in the heady era of modernism, appreciation of Victorian architecture was at its lowest ebb, the shed was accepted for its engineering innovation whilst the hotel languished in under-use as offices. But Scott worked in harmony with Barlow, who admitted in 1870 to having pointed his giant arch not only to improve wind resistance but also to give it 'architectural effect'. The ticket hall, vaulted until the 1950s, is also Scott's. Yet despite the accolade of a Grade I listing awarded it in 1967, the hotel has been emptied of offices and left to slide into total dereliction.

194

Albert Bridge
Kensington and Chelsea/Wandsworth

1/F5   Underground to South Kensington, then bus

Albert Bridge looks as frail as Tower Bridge appears boisterous, its end towers graced with the slenderest of shafts and arches painted the most pastel of pinks and greens. Its elegance is enhanced at dusk, when strings of fairy lights add an ethereal shimmer to its steel chains.

This seeming frailty belies what is a *tour de force* of Victorian engineering, undertaken in 1870–3 under inopportune circumstances. The engineer was R M Ordish of St Pancras Station and Albert Hall fame; his international reputation, however, was based on a rigid suspension bridge built in Prague during the early 1860s whose form was repeated here. The iron piers sunk into the Thames were the largest cylindrical iron castings then made, produced at a foundry in Battersea and floated down the river. From their tops

were hung brackets to support the footways from beneath so that there was no need for a girder between them and the road as is usual in suspension bridges. The superstructure was necessarily kept cheap, and the original iron chains rapidly corroded, so that they had to be replaced with steel as early as 1885–7.

Battersea had been first linked to Chelsea by a wooden toll bridge in 1771–2, which by the 1860s was decrepit. In 1854 another toll bridge, predecessor of the present Chelsea Bridge, was erected to serve the fast-developing suburb, but even this was not thought enough as many houses remained unsold. Yet a Parliamentary Bill for Albert Bridge failed in 1863. Though ostensibly this was because of social-minded objections to another toll bridge, the likelier cause was opposition from the Battersea Bridge Company, which feared a loss of revenue. So the new Albert Bridge Company offered £3,000 a year in compensation to the Battersea shareholders and in 1864 secured the necessary Act. Then the Company discovered that the Metropolitan Board of Works was planning to embank the north side of the Thames to carry Joseph

Albert Bridge. GLRO

Bazalgette's sewage system, and had to wait until Parliament endorsed his proposals. Shares in the company, originally valued at £10, sank to 3d.

But in 1870 work on the bridge began, and two further Acts ensured its completion in 1873. The opening of a third toll bridge along the Battersea 'reach only stimulated the campaign to take the Thames crossings into public hands. In 1879, £170,000 compensation was shared between the Albert and Battersea Bridge Companies and the bridges were freed, passing into the care of the Metropolitan Board of Works.

195

Tower Bridge
Tower Hamlets/Southwark

2/L5   Underground to Tower Hill

Imagine two processional files of moored shipping, aligned with the central piers of the Tower Bridge and stretching with increasing density from Poplar and Wapping up the Thames into the Pool of London. Between them is a mere 200 ft of navigable fairway for big boats. Tugs, lighters and ferries ply tirelessly across the fairway from shore to shore. Traffic upon London Bridge and at its approaches is at a near standstill during the working day. Pedestrians toil to and from their labours across this most easterly of bridges in an endless straggle.

These were the conditions of river and cross-river traffic when Tower Bridge was constructed in 1886–94. Pressure for a major down-river crossing had been building up for half a century. But who was to undertake it – the City of London Corporation, responsible of old for Thames bridges, or the Metropolitan Board of Works, which had begun in the 1870s to take up the slack caused by the City's neglect of wider London interests? Though the Tower Bridge is just beyond its boundaries, it was the City that won. The site was selected in 1876. After private negotiation and public dispute as to the right form of bridge the City's Architect, Horace Jones, put forward the germ of the solution eventually adopted:

Tower Bridge. GLRO

a low-level bridge with lifting 'bascules' in the centre span, of a type common in the Low Countries but never before seen on a big scale in the British Isles. Hefty, historicising towers to hide the lifting machinery were present in the design from the first, originally detailed by Frank Brangwyn's father, then an assistant with Jones. The Tower of London was the obvious stimulus. But Jones, Brangwyn *père*, their successors and the City committee in charge saw in the great medieval fortress less something to respect or imitate precisely than a source of romantic

urban inspiration. The new bridge was to become 'the Water Gate of London', defining and defending the precinct of the City – the real and original Port of London – for the ships permitted to pass its august double drawbridge.

Horace Jones was not a great architect, and the engineer who worked with him and inherited the project after Jones's death in 1887, John Wolfe Barry (Sir Charles Barry's youngest son), was more concerned with the structure and mechanism of the bridge than in the detailing of its towers. In redesigning them, Barry's architectural assistant

George D Stevenson, a minor member of the prolific engineering clan of that name, seems mainly to have made them more reminiscent of his native Scotland – granite-clad, with rough-hewn masonry and off-white battlements in Portland stone. The persistent Scottish connection may owe something to the fact that the Tower Bridge and the Forth Railway Bridge are contemporary. All the steel came from Scotland, Sir William Arrol and Company of Glasgow, the contractors for the Forth Bridge, erected the skeleton and a firm from Paisley did much of the ornamental ironwork.

When the bridge was finished, a howl of protest rose from purist critics who thought it should have been of steelwork throughout, abjuring fancy dress. Had the towers been first-rate architecture, the outcry doubtless would have been more muted. Today, the Tower Bridge is too familiar to judge severely. Its conception, function and ornament have given innocent pleasure to millions. With that outcome, rare for any structure, the shades of Jones, Brangwyn, Barry and Stevenson may rest well pleased.

A visit to the engine room under the southern approaches is worthwhile. Here a display explains the hydraulic mechanism for lifting the leaves of the bridge – not converted to electricity till 1976 – and you can see the original great steam engines for pumping water into the towers' four accumulators, supplied by Sir W G Armstrong, Mitchell and Company, the great Newcastle hydraulics and armaments firm. The bridge was over-endowed with lifting power, mainly for fear of the strong winds which caused the Tay Bridge disaster of 1879 (again, the Scottish connection). After inspecting the engine room you can ascend to the high-level walkway, intended to avoid delaying the copious Victorian toing and froing of workers. Hence you can contemplate the power, the glory and the sheer muddle of modern London, look down on the lifeless river and reflect upon why it is that the Tower Bridge has rare commercial cause to operate its flawless engines any more.

196
Greenwich Generating Station
Old Woolwich Rd, Greenwich

1/H5   British Rail to Maze Hill

Greenwich is the cinderella of the big London power stations – not that something on its scale is truly inconspicuous. In modern generating terms, however, the station is a small one, and for some reason its claim to high status in the English 'functional tradition in industrial design' has been underplayed.

The station was built to create current for the London County Council's burgeoning electric tramway system. Under an Act of 1870, municipalities had the right to buy up private tramway lines. The LCC began doing so from 1898 in order to rationalise and electrify a hotchpotch of horse-tramways, particularly in South London, and to serve its projected network of outlying cottage estates. A central power plant was needed; Greenwich was chosen in 1901 because coal could be delivered straight from the

river and a horse-tram depot already occupied some of the site. A second LCC power station was supposed to follow when more tramways north of the river had been acquired.

The General Section of the LCC Architect's Department having set to work, the northern end of the double-naved station was built in 1902–6, the portion closer to Old Woolwich Road following on in 1906–10. Tradition ascribes an important role in the building's design to the young Vincent Harris, but this cannot be proved. The exterior is a masterly essay in the grandeur of plain stock brickwork. Stone is used sparingly, for the copings and the set-offs of the great flattened buttresses, which bespeak the austerities of the Edwardian school of urban Church Gothic. An unbroken string of 'monitor' lights runs along the outside length of either nave. It is a shame that the large extension at the northern end of the more visible, western flank was carried out in staring concrete, rather than in more appropriate brick.

The one thing that can be complained of is no fault of the architects – the station's setting, too close to the Royal Naval College and jammed up against the sweet but

Greenwich Generating Station. EH

battered almshouses of Trinity Hospital. In the event the position proved fateful for the building itself. After the northern pair of octagonal chimneys had been built to their full intended height of 250 ft, with crisply corbelled and machicolated tops, the Astronomer Royal complained that the smoke might interfere with his readings from the Observatory on Greenwich Hill. So the southern pair of chimneys was built without tops up to only 182 ft, to which level the northern pair was peremptorily lopped in 1972. To get a flavour of the original effect, you have to look at the miniature octagonal turret attached to the delightful custodian's house at the corner of Old Woolwich Road and Hoskins Street.

Originally the interior of the station was divided into coal-fired boilers in the eastern nave and engines, turbines and dynamos in the western one. The equipment was criticised at the time for being small and old-fashioned. The LCC's tramway system never expanded to the degree anticipated in Edwardian days, nor did the Council ever come near to controlling London's general electricity supply. In 1933 Greenwich was handed over to London Transport. In due course it became the back-up to the larger but architecturally cruder Lots Road Station, Fulham, for underground supply. A thorough renovation in 1969–72 left the eastern nave an empty but sublime internal vista, but entirely closed the western one from view. At the time of writing the building's future is most precarious.

197

55 Broadway
Westminster

2/F6   Underground to St James's Park

Charles Holden's 55 Broadway will puzzle the connoisseur of New York or Chicago architecture. It is inter-war London's response to that conundrum of 20th century urbanism – what Louis Sullivan called 'the tall office building artistically considered'. It takes as its

55 Broadway. BRITISH ARCHITECTURAL LIBRARY, RIBA

point of departure American debates about the form and the envelope of the high building, accepts the New York 1920s philosophy of set-back upper storeys to get good lighting all round, then blurs the result with a show of striking detail. The outcome is a building of rare thoughtfulness that falls something short of being a masterpiece. It is worth comparing with Senate House in Bloomsbury, Holden's later essay in the manner, where a simpler site led to a crisper but less sympathetic product.

55 Broadway, of 1927–9, comes early on in the distinguished list of buildings carried out by Adams, Holden and Pearson for the London underground network. At that date the network was still not unified. Holden's client was 'the Combine' – formally the Underground Electric Railway Companies of London – whose tough-minded boss, Lord Ashfield, and design-minded executive, Frank Pick, aspired to control London's whole transport system. Their offices, built over St James's Park Station, were part of that image-conscious campaign. They achieved their desire in 1933 when 55 Broadway became the headquarters of the London Passenger Transport Board, nominally public but in its day-to-day management under Ashfield and Pick's control. That is why the supple Holden was commissioned to design so many new stations in the 1930s. By that time his style had moved on to something like outright modernism.

The Broadway building, by contrast, belongs to a transitional phase of his work.

Tothill Street offers the best viewpoint. From here you see the building as Holden must have conceived it – a cruciform, Portland-stone wedge in the angle made by the two arms of Broadway. The perimeter is respected for a couple of storeys, above which the building line breaks back so as to give light and air to all the offices without the gloom of internal courts. Five floors go up like this, and then there are no fewer than five further set-backs up to the little roof garden, to conform with building regulations and minimise the eleven-storey bulk. An American architect of the 1920s would have managed these set-backs in a blocky, Babylonian sort of a way, but Holden's approach is more tentative. Corners are chamfered away and changes in plane made less decisive by a series of deep parapets. The temple form of the boardroom on top, too, is handled almost apologetically; here, Lutyens would have done better.

Where Holden, at heart an Arts and Crafts man, scores is in the refinement of his detailing. The street fronts, delicately bowed and endowed with simplified granite columns, are superb. Observe also the beauty of the lettering of the various inscriptions, the fine setting of the stonework and the slight recession of the tiers of metal windows and ventilation panels between them. Or there are the magnificent expressionist reliefs to dwell on – a first-class piece of architectural patronage on the part of the Combine, even if Holden had to badger his clients to accept them. At first-floor level are Night and Day, by Epstein; higher up, at a rather arbitrary point upon the parapets, are figures of the winds by six separate sculptors – Aumonier, Gerrard, Gill, Moore, Rabinovich and Wyon. Henry Moore's one panel is on the north side of the east wing; Gill's two on the east side of the north and south wings.

Till recent years one could walk through 55 Broadway, now London Regional Transport headquarters, along a broad corridor from one end to the other, past the office entrances, a proud display of chronometry and a map with blinking lights showing where trains were passing all around the underground system. This innocent public privilege has now been withdrawn. The visitor must glean what he or she can of Holden's interior detailing from the remaining travertine cladding and lighting arrangements in the St James's Park Station portion of the interior, at the north end.

198
Underground Stations

[C]

Corporate image began early on the London underground. Not at the first stations erected on the line from Paddington to Farringdon from 1863, of which little remains unaltered; nor among the stations associated with the first deep and electric line built in 1890 and extended to Clapham Common and King's Cross in 1900. But when the wily financier Charles Tyson Yerkes bought the District line in 1901 and began developing lines through the West End and northern suburbs, dozens of street corners were transformed with simple single-storey boxes, eyecatchingly clad in dark red tiles. Standardisation went with speed, for between 1903 and 1908 Leslie Green designed some fifty stations. The interiors were also fitted out with easy-cleaning tiles to standard patterns, usually green and white for the stairs and platforms, with names picked out in black at the ends, thick tiled surrounds to the ticket windows and a floral embellishment to the ironwork over lifts and entrances. All too few survive unsullied by 'improvements': **Mornington Crescent (1/F4)** and **Holloway Road (1/G3)**, both of 1907, are the best.

The round bulls-eye logo was adopted by Yerkes's 'combine', the Underground Electric Railways Company of London, from about 1909, when a solid red disc appeared behind station name-plates: Covent Garden and Caledonian Road hang on to examples. Edward Johnston's neat lettering followed in 1913. But it was in the 1920s and early 1930s that the company image was refined, under the guidance of Frank Pick, and extended over the Metropolitan line also after its acquisition in 1933. To Pick we owe the evolution of the logo, the topological map, and the employment of Charles Holden as architect from 1924. Holden's first major stations were at Piccadilly Circus, and for the extension of the Northern line south to Morden. Completed in 1926, every manner of planning around a street corner was attempted. **Clapham South (1/F6)**, reached through a little arcade of shops, is boldest because of its better materials. All are in essence neo-Georgian, spiced up with a Loosian hint of pre-Great War Vienna. The underground logo appears in two guises, in coloured glass over the entrances and, to either side, as the three-dimensional capital of an underground order.

Then in 1931 Holden accompanied Pick on a tour of Scandinavia and the Netherlands. The clean lines of Dudok's work for the municipality of Hilversum, and especially the town hall, were an inspiration. Such simple rationalism suited Pick's ideals, as well as being a natural architectural progression for Holden and his assistants. The first product of the trip was **Sudbury Town (1/D4)**, its booking hall a high brick box with a concrete roof and industrial metal windows. Variations can be found at either end of the Piccadilly line, sometimes with towers (Osterley and Boston Manor), with arched concrete sheds at the termini (Cockfosters and Uxbridge), and even where the design was entrusted to other architects: Uren at Rayners Lane and Welch, Cachemaille-Day and Lander at Park Royal.

A refinement to deal with entrances at awkward angles was to make the booking hall circular. **Arnos Grove (1/F2)**, completed in 1933, is a modern chapter house, its concrete roof radiating from a central sixteen-sided pillar around which is built the ticket office or passimeter. The shape cleverly masks the odd angle between the two street entrances and the offset exit to the platforms. It comes as a mordant intrusion at the end of a drab shopping parade. In a more impressive setting is **Southgate (1/F2)**. Low, with flying-saucer eaves, its circular form is just right for a busy road junction and is set off by a curved arcade of shops and bus station. Inside the pillar and roof forms are simpler, but as the platforms are here below ground, Holden could build a wide escalator hall. Here survive a line of bronze uplighters, once a feature of the system but removed almost everywhere else.

Balham Station. LONDON TRANSPORT MUSEUM

199

Stockwell Bus Garage
Lansdowne Way, Stockwell, Lambeth

1/G5   Underground to Stockwell

People tend to link London Transport's commitment to bold architecture with the immediate years after the London Passenger Transport Board was set up in 1933. But brave things had been done under the influence of Frank Pick before the Board was formed. After the Second World War, too, high standards of design continued to be upheld – standards not to be utterly abjured until the 1980s. Of the post-war phase of architectural excellence, the Stockwell Bus Garage is an outstanding example.

Among London Transport's post-war priorities, one of the most pressing was the phasing out of cumbrous trolley buses and trams and their replacement with RT buses. The new fleet needed garages of uninterrupted floor area and ample height and breadth, posing problems of roof-span which interested architects and engineers the world over at that time. In about 1950 garages at Loughton, Shepherds Bush, Stockwell and Thornton Heath were commissioned, each an experiment with a different type of structure. All but the Loughton garage were assigned to the architect Adie, Button and Partners, working with A E Beer, engineer. At Sulgrave Road, Shepherds Bush, they produced a handsome bow-spring-trussed shed; but their concrete-vaulted Stockwell, built between 1951 and 1954, is what catches the imagination.

Technically the Stockwell arches are nothing new; they belong to the tradition of shallow-concrete vaulting pioneered by German engineers in the inter-war period and taken up in post-war Britain, as at the Brynmawr Rubber Factory. The method of construction is quite conservative, with ribs in the form of hinged Portal frames dividing the 400 ft long parking space into nine top-lit bays. But the span of these bays, 194 ft as against a width of a mere 42 ft, and their gradual ascent from 16 ft at the side to 54 ft at the centre, give an uplifting, cathedral-like effect which a more daring form of construction might not have afforded. Great works of engineering always need scale for their appreciation. To see dozens of double-decker buses (200 can be housed here) dwarfed beneath the Stockwell arches is to savour an experience of the sublime unrepeatable elsewhere in South London.

Stockwell Bus Garage. AP

17

Commemorative

This section highlights the awkward subject of taste. Changing taste has dictated not only who or what should be commemorated in London's streets and open spaces, but also how. A history of outdoor sculpture, from Hubert Le Sueur's much-restored equestrian statue at the top of Whitehall to the recent memorials to Churchill and his generals in the open spaces around its foot, could be written here. What has changed less is the range of patronage that has sponsored so many memorials: the better-known monuments around Westminster and the West End erected by public subscription and royal or government patronage have tended to mask the munificence of civic bodies, societies and private individuals who have sponsored some of London's more unusual monuments.

How then, does the Monument, a memorial not to a person but to an event, fit in? Since in the seventeenth century few except the grandest burials were marked, such a preference should not surprise us. The Monument symbolises the tastes of the Restoration era for science and town planning, as well as, subsequently, its religious prejudices. Great columns make two brief appearances in British town planning: first in the late 17th century, as exemplified also by the obelisk at Seven Dials rebuilt in 1989, and more famously in the early 19th century. The sources for both were ultimately Roman but the later group differed crucially in being 'peopled', the London examples being those columns occupied by the Duke of York, erected in 1833–4 in Waterloo Place, and Lord Nelson, put atop his column in Trafalgar Square between 1839 and 1842.

At some point just before 1800 ideas of death and its commemoration changed. Public, non-sepulchral sculpture had hitherto largely been restricted to the benefactors of institutions and to monarchs, Queen Anne being especially fortunate in coinciding with an active period of house- and church-building, as well as the completion of St Paul's Cathedral. Neo-classicism meant the arrival of toga-clad figures (many of them politicians) on the streets, as sculpture forsook the landscape garden for the town. St Paul's Cathedral, populated from about 1790 with memorials, also boasts an impressive set, many the work of John Flaxman and John Bacon, father and son. Their stylisation may be compared with Alfred Stevens's impassioned memorial to Wellington in the cathedral, begun in 1857, a foretaste of how sculptural fashion was to change later in the 19th century.

Interest in the more functional paraphernalia of death grew at much the same time. Country estates had from the early 18th century often included mausolea as suitable adjuncts to the landscape, even if interment in them rarely followed. London had less scope for such monuments in its backyards, though John Soane's obsession with sarcophagi testifies as much as any column or sculpture to antiquarian interest in the language of entombment. Soane was architect of two successive mausolea to Noel Desenfans, the second of which is attached to the Dulwich Picture Gallery; and of one in the churchyard of Old St Pancras, where he and his wife are buried. These elaborate memorials may be contrasted with the luridly practical ideas of Jeremy Bentham whose monument is his own skeleton, dressed after dissection and placed in a cabinet behind the foyer of University College in Gower Street.

The cult of the personality took off in the 19th century. The first 'blue plaque' was erected to Lord Byron by the Royal Society of Arts in 1867, whilst Nelson, Wellington, Prince Albert and Charles Dickens were amongst many who inspired quantities of ephemeral memorabilia as well as more permanent public structures. That the taste of the 19th century so dominates London is due also to the closure of its earlier churchyards and burial grounds

Celebrations at the Shaftesbury Memorial.
RCHME

247

following an Act of 1851. This itself was a product of the period's increasing concern for the proprieties of a decent interment and a cult of the grave as well as concern for the sanitary state of London's overcrowded and badly managed churchyards and burial grounds. Tasteful commemoration led equally to public statues to the great and good, often erected by public subscription from 'a grateful nation', and to the attempted immortalisation of the middle classes in the commercial cemeteries that ringed London from the 1830s. The tribute could be a likeness or a symbolic representation. Prince Albert objected to a figure of him being erected in his lifetime, but after his death South Kensington nevertheless sprouted two: the monument of the Great Exhibition behind the Albert Hall, unveiled in 1863, and the shrine-like memorial in Kensington Gardens. Commemorative symbolism is best seen in the varied mausolea, animals and angels in commercial cemeteries such as Kensal Green, Brompton and Highgate, the gargantuan Egyptian mausoleum erected by Lord Kilmorey to his mistress in St Margaret's Road, Isleworth, and the curious fountain dedicated to the social reformer Lord Shaftesbury at Piccadilly, and better known as 'Eros'.

Public commemoration continued into this century, fuelled by the heroics of two world wars that caused likenesses of Edith Cavell, Winston Churchill and a tribe of generals to be erected. But from the late 19th century a desire to commemorate the commonality of man arose. This took two forms, one dedicated to personal heroics, the other to universal loss. G F Watts's only partially realised ambition was to pay tribute to the unsung heroes of the labouring classes who had paid the ultimate sacrifice in a moment of courage, recorded with sentimental detail on a series of plaques erected in Postman's Park. The earliest war to inspire general memorials to the fallen seems to have been the Crimean; a column in Broad Sanctuary to the ex-pupils of Westminster School is a rare example. The Boer War inspired more tributes, but it was the mass sacrifice of the First World War that produced a

return to bolder and more classical forms. Whilst war memorials in every suburb and village around London bear long lists of the fallen, those in central London have gained greater forcefulness by their anonymity. The best combine in their powerful classical simplicity a hallowing of the fallen with, albeit ambiguously, pacificist sensibilities. Many regiments have memorials there which are powerful displays of massively taut sculpture, such as the Guards' Memorial in Horse Guards Parade by H C Bradshaw and Gilbert Ledward, and Charles Jagger's Royal Artillery Memorial at Hyde Park Corner. But the national memorial to all the forces and the Merchant Navy is striking for its lack of any adornment and the brevity of its inscription. Its name, the Cenotaph, or empty tomb, sums up the concept of its universality.

200

The Monument
Fish Street Hill, City of London

2/K4   Underground to Monument [A]

Scaling the 311 steps to the balcony, it is hard now to address the Monument with more than schoolchild curiosity, or to grasp the sense of tragedy, pride and indeed anger that went into its erection. But the Monument (its simple, definitive title suggests there can be no others) is no joke; it was a solemn, loyal and Protestant commemoration of the most momentous event in London's history. It may also have been intended – this at least is curious – as an astronomical observatory.

The learned Latin panels that adorn the base, composed by the Master of St Paul's School and well worth reading (handy translations are affixed), give graphic statistics. In all, 13,200 houses, 436 acres, 400 streets, 89 churches and most of the City's public buildings were consumed by fire between 2 and 6 September 1666. In terms of property but not of mortality (which was slight, as the inscription notes), this made the Great Fire of London the most damaging

The Monument. GLRO

urban conflagration then known in history. While the ruins were yet smoking, we are told, Charles II made provision for the relief of the citizens, ordered Parliament to take steps for rebuilding London, established an annual service of intercession and ordered the Monument to be put up 'as a perpetual memorial to posterity'. So the idea was an immediate one. The original rebuilding Act of 1666 provided for 'a Colume or Pillar of Brase or Stone', no doubt already conceived on the scale of the colossal commemorative columns of ancient Rome, to be erected near the place where the fire started. The inscription was left to the City fathers; this, in due course, was to cause trouble.

The Monument went ahead in 1671–7 under the charge of the master-mason

Joshua Marshall. Its design was largely or in part delegated by Wren to his friend, fellow-scientist and cousin-by-marriage Robert Hooke, a clever, restless and difficult man for whom architecture was one of many sidelines. It is likely that Hooke, a keen astronomer, took special interest in the Monument because he hoped to put it to practical use. Its balcony, high above London's smoke, suggested a post from which Royal Society members might observe the planetary motions. Probably because Flamsteed's properly equipped observatory at Greenwich was built in 1675–6 (p. 172), there is no evidence it was so used.

Wren and Hooke first thought of surmounting the column with a phoenix, the obvious symbol of rebirth. Then Wren became worried that this might not look good from a distance and argued for a statue. But the King opted in 1675 for the peculiar flaming or bristling ball in gilt bronze, somewhat like a golden thistle, that tops the Monument today. At least we were spared flames emerging from the column itself, as adumbrated in an early design. The other main ornamental element is the vast, pedantic bas-relief on the westward-facing panel of the base. This is by C G Cibber and shows Charles II supported by a strong allegorical team (Science, Liberty, Nature, Architecture, etc.) coming to London's aid, while a withered-dugged Envy, chewing unpleasantly on entrails and breathing fumes, skulks in the sewers.

'The hand of God, a great wind and a very dry season' were found to be the causes of the fire by official enquiries in its immediate aftermath. This sufficed in the first instance, when citizens were rebuilding their lives and their houses. But in due course a scapegoat for the disaster had to be found. In the increasingly anti-Catholic climate of 1670s England, the Pope was good enough. So the simple-minded baker at whose house the fire had started was hanged as a Catholic agent on his own, confused confession, and extra words attributing the fire to 'Popish frenzy' were added to the north panel in 1681. This distasteful manifestation of civic paranoia was excised in 1830.

The Monument ought to have stood directly at the north end of London Bridge, to impress you with the tragedy of the fire and the triumph of reconstruction as you entered the City. In the event, by a typical English urban botch, it was consigned to one side of the main route of entry. Still, its position was striking enough before London Bridge was moved westwards in the 1830s. Its setting today is a shambles; the buildings that surround it in its little square pay it no respect at all. Nor, from the architectural viewpoint, can one be more positive about most of what can be seen today from the cage at its summit. Despite their religious bigotry, the City fathers of the 1660s and 1670s had a better grasp of how to replan and regulate commercial London than their counterparts 300 years later.

201
Dulwich Picture Gallery
College Rd, Dulwich, Southwark

1/G6   British Rail to West Dulwich
[A]

The paintings now displayed at Dulwich were intended for the national gallery of Poland. Sir Francis Bourgeois was an indifferent painter who, together with his benefactor Noel Desenfans, gained an international reputation as an art dealer. Their greatest coup was the commission in 1790 from King Stanislas of Poland, for whom they amassed a large body of mainly Dutch and Italian works of genuine and lasting quality. Then in 1795 Poland was partitioned and Stanislas abdicated, leaving the two dealers unpaid – but with the pictures. Bourgeois persuaded Desenfans to retain most of them, which were displayed at his house in Charlotte Street. At his death in 1807, Desenfans instructed Bourgeois to find an institution to put them on public display and John Soane erected a mausoleum to him at the rear of the Charlotte Street house, establishing the principle of benefactor and collection being commemorated together.

In December 1810 Bourgeois fell from a horse and had to act quickly to fulfil Desenfans's instructions before his death days later. The contact with Dulwich College, then an undistinguished charity on London's fringes, came through an actor friend, John Philip Kemble, and a College fellow, Robert Corry. Soane was the obvious choice for the new gallery, mausoleum and almshouses. He first attempted to link his buildings to the existing almshouses, opened in 1619, and produced several schemes for a new quadrangle. Lack of money prevented this, but the idea determined the placing of the gallery at right-angles to the old college. It was completed in 1814. The simple design and materials reflect a necessary cheapness, but despite accretions and near-destruction by bombing it is a *tour de force*.

Soane's sequence of five top-lit galleries owes much to country-house picture galleries, then fashionable. But the severity of his design was new: the groin-vaulted coves and top lanterns gave little relief. The lanterns were originally glazed only at the sides; after long debates about the dim light, their wooden tops were glazed in 1912–13 by E T Hall, who with his son Stanley added a range of galleries to the east in 1912–15 to accommodate further bequests of paintings. Another gallery, now the lavatories, was added by H S Goodhart-Rendel in 1937–8, so that the east side of the gallery owes nothing to Soane's hand. A competition for more facilities held in 1990 attracted a record 377 entries, most of which chose to treat the gallery as sacrosanct and instead develop Soane's courtyard idea. Whether the winning design, or any other solution, will ever be built is a matter of conjecture.

The west elevation is still Soane's. The composition is dominated by the projecting mausoleum with its idiosyncratic, segmental-topped lantern decorated with urns. The low ranges to either side were built as almshouses for six old ladies but converted to galleries and offices after 1884. The mausoleum is the most perfect space in the building,

as might be expected from Soane's interest in funerary monuments. The design closely follows his Charlotte Street design, a circular 'nave' with Doric columns (the only use of an order in the building) supporting the lantern and a chancel where the sarcophagi of Noel Desenfans and his wife and of Bourgeois were placed in niches. The mausoleum is right opposite the entrance, yet is distanced by the eerie yellow light oozing from the lantern. Nowhere is Soane's love of coloured glass put to more hallowing effect.

A smaller version of Dulwich's mausoleum is the tomb Soane erected to his wife in 1815, in Old St Pancras churchyard, north of the station. This more whimsical version, supported on fluted piers, is the closer model for Giles Gilbert Scott's red telephone box, first produced in 1924.

202

Kensal Green Cemetery
Harrow Rd, Kensington and Chelsea

1/E4   Underground to Ladbroke Grove or Kensal Green; British Rail to Kensal Green

[C]

The first of London's great cemeteries, Kensal Green is the only one still in private hands and something like its original condition. The discerning and affluent may still obtain a last resting place here, through the General Cemetery Company who have run it since its foundation in 1832. With its sweeping paths encircling a central Grecian chapel and clumps of dark trees, it is a landscape at once open and enclosed: a piece of the Mediterranean that has found a refuge on the borders of Victorian London and which offers inspiring views.

By 1800 London's churchyards and burial grounds were in a parlous condition, overcrowded and insanitary. Lack of space meant there was no

Dulwich Picture Gallery. The Mausoleum.
MARTIN CHARLES

Kensal Green Cemetery. The Anglican chapel. GLRO

chance of the dignified perpetual resting place the middle classes came increasingly to expect for their money. Images such as Gray's 'Elegy' had first sentimentalised death, where the dead were 'at rest', 'not forgotten' but visited as part of a family ritual. Yet overcrowding in the large cities meant that bodies were in practice exhumed within a few years and burnt, or rotted down with slaked lime, to make space for more; furthermore, in 1777 had occurred the first prosecution for body-snatching to supply the medical profession with material for dissection. Those who could avoid such horrors looked for a means to do so.

The huge suburban cemetery of Père Lachaise opened in Paris in 1804. It combined an aesthetic dignity for its clients with a handsome profit for its shareholders. Smaller versions subsequently founded in Norwich, Liverpool and Manchester particularly appealed to non-conformists, who were denied the privilege of interment in consecrated churchyards. In London, the barrister George Frederick Carden campaigned throughout 1820s for a

cemetery on similar lines in London, and in 1831 Sir John Dean Paul, a banker, purchased 54 acres at Kensal Green. The General Cemetery Company was founded the next year, with Paul as chairman and Carden as secretary.

A dispute then followed between the two as to whether the chapels and catacombs should be classical or Gothic in style. Classicism won. The architect was the company's surveyor, John Griffith, and it is his building that sets the tone for the place. Despite the attractions of burial in his catacombs, where lead coffins prevented decomposition, the ostentatious chose to erect mausolea. These, of a grandeur unsurpassed in London, reveal the architectural eclecticism of the 1840s and 1850s. Kensal Green scored a major coup with the arrival of two members of the Royal Family, in 1843 and 1848, who were given places of honour in front of the chapel. But more sumptuous are the memorials of self-made men upon prime sites close by: Ionic for John St John Long, a purveyor of dubious patent medicine, and Egyptian for Andrew Ducrow, a circus manager. Egos snubbed by social conventions in life could find everlasting retribution in death.

But it was for the respectable that Kensal Green found its lasting success. The high wall to Harrow Road offered security against common intrusion, even after an Act of 1832 made body-snatching no longer lucrative. Today two firms of stone masons judiciously sited by the main gates still do good business.

203

Highgate West Cemetery
Swain's Lane, Highgate, Camden

1/F3   Underground to Archway (nearest); or walk from Hampstead across the Heath (recommended)

[B]   guided tours most weekends

Highgate is the finest Victorian valhalla of them all. Early engravings show a smartness, and a symmetry in its upper section, smothered since by the plethora of monuments and vegetation that have sprung up everywhere. It is this envelopment, the confrontation between nature and the man-made held just about in balance, that appeals to the modern sense of the romantic. Credit is due to the Friends of Highgate Cemetery that it is still held so.

Highgate, opened in 1839, was the third of London's cemeteries and the most perfectly sited, ensconced on a quiet hillside in aesthetic and exclusive North London. It was one of two cemeteries promoted by the London Cemetery Company, the other being at Nunhead. Its location, its seclusion, its mixture of formal and informal layouts, made it an immediate success. Today access is largely by guided tour, which enforces the formality: you ascend the hill as if following a funeral cortège to the catacombs, and are led to the gates of Egyptian Avenue. Probably designed by the City architect J B Bunning, this grim tunnel flanked by bulbous columns is made to seem longer and more powerful by the trick of making the door at the top of the slope smaller than the

Highgate Cemetery. EH

entrance at the bottom. Beyond is the 'inner circle' of catacombs, a ring of stone portals cut into the hillside and topped by a cedar of Lebanon. The effect is of a circle of ghostly beach huts. The conceit is rumbled once you mount the stone steps to the side that lead to the terrace behind Highgate church, where the largest mausolea have settled themselves.

The landscapist David Ramsay made the rest of the layout less formal, a series of winding paths that form an intensely verdant and personal world after the

heart-thumping upper bit. The combination of formal centrepiece and surrounding meadow was repeated, less dramatically, at the City of London cemetery at Little Ilford some fifteen years later and at almost every municipal cemetery thereafter.

At Highgate the presence of so many personalities cannot be forgotten: from the well-remembered like the Rossetti family and Radclyffe Hall to the lion-tamers and sports manufacturers who would be forgotten but for their bizarre memorials. Characters worthy of greater renown include Tom Sayers, a champion prize-fighter and odd working-class intrusion who is commemorated by a model of his faithful mastiff, the chief mourner at his elaborate funeral. For that other popular champion, Karl Marx, you have to cross over Swain's Lane to the more bland East Cemetery and follow the crowds to a monolith of inhumane proportions by Lawrence Bradshaw, erected in 1954.

204

Albert Memorial
Kensington Gore, Westminster

2/B6   Underground to South Kensington

Prince Albert's early death from typhoid in 1861, coupled with the intense personal grief of Queen Victoria, elevated him to cult status. The Albert Memorial, unveiled in 1876 near the scene of the Great Exhibition, packages him as the universal man of the Victorian Renaissance. It encompasses all the sciences and arts of the day, from its cast-iron framework to its mosaic ornamentation, and every interest from the groups depicting the continents at its base to the crown of angels at its summit. It is a more sumptuous monument than any to an actual British monarch, a jewel that really belongs as a tabernacle in a cathedral.

Interested parties were in dispute soon after his death as to how Albert should be commemorated, with Henry Cole of the South Kensington Museum calling for a memorial college or hall and the Queen and her circle preferring a monument 'in the common sense'. Seven architects were invited to submit designs for the latter, of which only Sir Gilbert Scott belonged to the Gothic camp. Here was another source of tension, Scott's recent treatment over the Foreign Office competition (pp. 41–2) making him edgy and defensive. Scott claimed his design was derived from the Eleanor crosses erected in the 1290s to commemorate Edward I's consort, though the idea of a canopied statue is

closer to medieval German precedent and especially to Meickle Kemp's monument to Sir Walter Scott erected in Edinburgh in the 1840s.

The Albert Memorial stands out from the other buildings of South Kensington by its skeletal iron frame arranged with glass and mosaic like jewels. It is a lively contrast to the brick and terracotta that are the hallmark of the area. This may reflect Scott's desire to be independent of Cole; Cole it was, however, who persuaded Scott to raise the height of the fleche, the only major alteration from his original design and one he later regretted. Shortages of granite to clad the iron frame caused long delays, but more serious were disputes over the quality of the eight marble statuary groups, each commissioned from a different sculptor. They reveal the depths to which monumental heroic sculpture had descended by the 1860s. The biggest problem was the figure of

Albert himself, originally gilded: fortunately Carlo Marochetti, commissioned by the Queen, died before he could be dismissed. The figure was revised by J H Foley, who also carved 'Asia'.

Most successful was the work over which Scott had direct control, because he used artists who had worked with him before. The lead and copper-clad flèche bedecked with giant glass marbles and gilding was the work of Skidmore, a collaborator in many of Scott's churches. H H Armstead and J B Philip, who had worked at the Foreign Office, did the bronzes and carved the frieze of worthies along the plinth under Albert's feet. Scott was squeezed into the little knot of architects at a late date. The glass mosaics that today give the monument its brilliance were designed by J R Clayton of the stained glass firm Clayton and Bell. Seen as a whole the memorial is glorious. Mention should be

Albert Memorial: 'Asia'. GLRO

made too of the foundations, a spectacular forest of vaulted brick columns – 868 of them.

There were doubts at the time about the durability of the marble sculpture, and a giant glass case was suggested as a protection. Instead, it is the iron and leadwork that have failed, largely because of Scott's eccentric system of drains within the columns. A glass case has again been resisted, but the memorial is a massive conservation problem.

205

The Shaftesbury Memorial (Eros)
Piccadilly Circus, Westminster

2/F4   Underground to Piccadilly Circus

Only on close inspection does Eros reveal its dedication to Anthony Ashley Cooper, 7th Earl of Shaftesbury – the most pervasive of all Victorian philanthropists, who died in 1885. It seems odd that so serious a gentleman should have been rewarded by so lush a piece of sculpture, even if its innovation and quality are entirely fitting. It is the extreme example of a British public memorial sculpture that sought not to capture a physical likeness but the essence of its subject's work by a symbolic representation.

By the mid-19th century British sculptors seemed stifled by notions of classical purity and morality that denied any self-expression. The result was 'coat and trousers' statuary, or flaccid allegorical groups such as those around the Albert Memorial: sculpture that never tried to break free of its marble block. The movement towards a more impassioned realism combined with more personal symbolism was begun by Alfred Stevens, who produced the dynamic statuary groups on either side of the Wellington monument in St Paul's Cathedral before committing suicide in 1875 in despair at his lack of recognition, just as opinion began to shift in his favour. His ideals and

Shaftesbury Memorial. Nymph and dolphins. CI

teaching methods lived on in his followers, and by the 1880s were even recognised by such establishment figures as Joseph Edgar Boehm, Sculptor in Ordinary to the Queen.

It was Boehm who secured the Shaftesbury commission for his pupil, Alfred Gilbert, in 1886. They managed to convince a memorial committee of the symbolic representation insisted upon by Gilbert, but only by accepting that the monument be a fountain – to continue Shaftesbury's benevolence to his fellow man and beast even in death.

It was unveiled in 1893.

Gilbert conceived a series of shallow, octagonal basins linked by a writhing mass of shells, dolphins, helmeted water-babies and abstract forms. Its curves and cartouches are offset by the surmounting slender figure of Eros springing from a conch shell. Cast hollow in aluminium, the statue's only support is its solid left leg. Gilbert was outraged that the winged figure whose arrow or shaft has just left its bow should be thought a rebus of the name Shaftesbury, as is still often suggested.

He called it 'blindfolded Love sending forth indiscriminately, yet with purpose, his miracle of kindness'.

The design commissioned, the going got difficult. The first problem was the site. Shaftesbury Avenue, named in the Earl's honour, had just been cut and offered an appropriate location at each end of its Soho section. Cambridge Circus was a round, unencumbered space, but both Gilbert and the committee preferred the prestige of Piccadilly Circus, where only a small triangular plot was available close to a public lavatory. Always short of space, as roads have been widened and tube exits inserted, so Eros is shunted around the Circus in the vain hope of finding an appropriate spot for him.

The other problem is the total lack of any basin in which to catch the huge amount of water sent upwards, outwards and downwards by numerous jets. It seems there was a misunderstanding about the fountain's surrounds, which were confused by demands for a basin for dogs and an enclosing wall, removed in 1894. *The Times*, objecting also to the nude figure, called it 'a dripping, sickening mess' whilst subsequent alterations left Gilbert bitter and out of pocket. But on the few days when the fountain does work, Gilbert's aim that an 'imitation of foreign joyousness might find place in our cheerless London' seems achieved.

206

Postman's Park
Aldersgate, City of London

2/J6   Underground to St Pauls

G F Watts, the painter and sculptor, was consumed in his later years by a wish to commemorate his contemporaries. A huge series of paintings of his distinguished friends and acquaintances found their way to the National Portrait Gallery, which opened in 1896. For the unknowns he termed the 'heroes of everyday life' he conceived a national memorial as part of the celebrations of Queen Victoria's golden jubilee in 1887. As he claimed in a letter to *The Times* in

that year, 'the national prosperity of a nation is not an abiding possession, the deeds of the people are'.

No one took up his suggestion. But in 1900 Watts himself devised and paid for a monument in a corner of the former graveyard of St Botolph, Aldersgate. The structure was a simple shelter, 50 ft long, but its rear wall was to be lined with plaques to those who would otherwise be forgotten. Thirteen plaques were erected by Watts, another thirty by his widow, and five more followed in 1930. Only one has been added since. Whilst it is perhaps sad that Watts's scheme was not continued, its present form encapsulates the

Victorians' sentimentality and delight in the details of death. Its subjects seem to have been most susceptible to burning and drowning, and particularly careless of railway trains. The inscriptions are highly quotable, and that which commemorates Alfred Croft (see illustration) is a compelling example.

The garden was laid out in 1880, and extended by the incorporation of the graveyards of Christ Church, Newgate Street, in 1887 and St Leonard's, Foster Lane, in 1900. The name Postman's Park derives from its position immediately behind the City's General Post Office, for whose workers it became a lunchtime retreat.

Postman's Park. EH

207

The Cenotaph
Whitehall, Westminster

2/G5   Underground to Westminster or underground/British Rail to Charing Cross

Few architects are as closely associated with Edwardian grandiloquence as Edwin Lutyens. Yet the First World War, which saw not only the passing of a stylistic era but also a doubling of building costs, conversely gave him his best-known commission. The wish for a series of commemorative memorials seems to have begun around 1916, when Lutyens was appointed to the Imperial War Graves Commission. He is credited with the idea of a Great War Stone as a monolith of universal resonance, intended to stand on every battlefield in every continent. In June 1919 he was asked to design a temporary structure for a day of peace celebrations to be attended by foreign dignitaries the next month. Recalling the name jokingly given to a huge garden seat at Gertrude Jekyll's Munstead Wood, Lutyens hit on the idea of a cenotaph, or empty tomb, and produced a design within hours. It was chillingly simple, the Egyptian pylon used as a universal symbol of death that cut across all races and creeds. Lloyd George suggested the equally simple inscription: 'To the Glorious Dead'.

The Cenotaph caught the popular imagination. On 29 July Lutyens wrote to the First Commissioner of Works asking that a permanent version be erected in Portland stone on the site. He revised the design, invoking the most complicated mathematics to increase the effect of the pylon: the stepped plinth was gently tapered to an imaginary point a thousand feet in the sky, whilst the horizontals were made curves in a circle with a radius 900 feet below ground. A request for coloured marble flags to flank the long sides was refused, though the conventional

The Cenotaph. EH

flapping silk ones do indeed detract from the solemnity of the design. Lutyens succeeded in getting stone flags for his monuments in Northampton and at Etaples.

The Cenotaph was unveiled on Armistice Day, 11 November 1920, the same day as the tomb of the unknown soldier in Westminster Abbey was dedicated. Lutyens also designed a memorial for a committee of the Royal Artillery that was rejected as too similar to the Cenotaph. Instead the commission for a monument at Hyde Park Corner (unveiled in 1925) went to sculptor and former infantryman Charles Jagger, who expressed the same universal themes of endurance and sacrifice in a work of rugged monumental realism, particularly chilling in its brutal representation of a gun. Today we can admire the Cenotaph and Royal Artillery Memorial, in their different ways, as sculpture; it becomes increasingly difficult to conceive the loss of so many men.

208

Seven Dials Monument
Seven Dials, Camden

2/G4   Underground to Tottenham Court Road

The rebuilding in 1985–9 of the obelisk at Seven Dials reminds us that the Monument (pp. 248–9) was once part of a wider vogue for landmark columns in London. The original was erected here in 1693, following the first development of the area with houses. Covent Garden set the example for estates to be created around formal squares, where the better houses were placed, as Soho, Golden and Bloomsbury Squares testify. But Thomas Neale, master and worker of the Mint from 1678, secured only a small grant of land in Holborn with no room for a square. Instead he cut a road from St Giles to St Martin's Lane and converged other roads upon it, a meeting of seven in all. Edward Pierce, a stone mason, architect and associate of Wren, was commissioned to erect the obelisk to give the area its cachet. The

Seven Dials Monument. STEVEN PARKER

top of the column was given six faces, each bearing a sundial: the seventh dial was the shadow cast by the column itself. Seven Dials is smaller but earlier than Mansart's Place des Victoires in Paris, laid out with a central statue of Louis XIV in 1685. Seen from afar down the surrounding streets, the obelisk is more eye-catching than any statue.

In about 1773 the monument was removed from Seven Dials by the St Giles Vestry, perhaps because it had become a gathering place for prostitutes and other undesirables. In 1822 most of it was re-erected, with a new top, at Weybridge in Surrey, where it still stands. Seven Dials meanwhile slid down the social scale, its buildings refronted or rebuilt, especially at the corner sites. But the street pattern and something of the scale of the area remained, and the installation of a replica obelisk has restored to it an identity separate from that of Covent Garden.

A Note on Reading

The indispensable vade-mecum for the architectural traveller in London is 'Pevsner' – in other words, the London volumes of *The Buildings of England* (Penguin Books). This unique compendium of fact and criticism is the envy of the world. Originally Inner London was covered by Nikolaus Pevsner in one volume on the Cities of London and Westminster (1957, frequently revised) and another on the boroughs around the centre (1952); for outlying areas, one had to use the volumes on Middlesex (1951), Essex, (1954), Surrey (1962, revised 1971) and West Kent (1969). Now the series coverage of the metropolis is in process of complete recasting by Bridget Cherry. The Cities of London and Westminster volume has become *London 1* (most recent revision, 1973). *London 2: South* appeared in 1983. *London 3: North West* will appear in 1991, *London 4: North East* later in the decade.

For those seeking something more personal, vivid and impressionistic yet with a strong architectural focus, the best guides are *Nairn's London* (Penguin Books, 1988), a revision by Peter Gasson of Ian Nairn's *London* (1966); Ann Saunders, *The Art and Architecture of London* (Phaidon, 1988); and the two volumes of the Companion Guide series, *The Companion Guide to London* by David Piper (Collins, 1977) and *The Companion Guide to Outer London* by Simon Jenkins (Collins, 1981).

The official record of London's buildings is enshrined in the forty-two volumes (thus far) of *The Survey of London*, started by C R Ashbee in the 1890s. The scope of the volumes varies according to their date. Only a third of Inner London has so far been covered, but for those districts covered in the post-war years, notably Lambeth, Southwark, much of Westminster and the whole of Kensington, the *Survey* offers a wealth of minute historical and architectural detail, set off by beautiful measured drawings.

The London Encyclopaedia, edited by Ben Weinreb and Christopher Hibbert (Macmillan, 1983), has rapidly attained classic status for its compact and authoritative assemblage of facts and statistics. *The Book of London*, edited by Michael Leapman (Weidenfeld and Nicolson, 1989), treats much of the same material in essay form. For a single, readable book about London's history as a whole, Christopher Hibbert's *London: The Biography of a City* (Penguin, 1986) is the best of many efforts.

Among general books about London's architecture and planning, pride of place must still go to Steen Eiler Rasmussen's stimulating *London, The Unique City*, written in Danish, translated into English in 1934 and often reprinted, most recently by MIT Press (1982). Equally appealing but rather more dated are the manifold books by the sanguine Harold P Clunn, of which *The Face of London* (Phoenix House, 1951; revised edition Spring Books, 1970) is representative.

Studies of individual periods of London's architecture and planning are legion, but none surpasses Sir John Summerson's *Georgian London* (1945; most recent edition by Barrie and Jenkins, 1988), to which Dan Cruickshank and Peter Wyld's *London: The Art of Georgian Building* (Architectural Press, 1975) is an excellent supplement. For the medieval and Renaissance periods, John Schofield's *The Building of London from the Conquest to the Great Fire* (1984) is exemplary. The Victorian and Edwardian periods are best covered by Donald J Olsen's *The Growth of Victorian London* (Batsford, 1976); by Alastair Service's *London 1900* (1979); by Gavin Stamp and Colin Amery's *Victorian Buildings in London: 1837–1887* (Architectural Press, 1980); and by the enthralling collection of early photographs brought together by Gavin Stamp in *The Changing Metropolis* (Penguin, 1984).

There are no definitive books on 20th-century London, but the three Sidgwick and Jackson volumes arising out of a television series called *The Making of Modern London* (Gavin Weightman and Steve Humphries's *The Making of Modern London, 1815–1914*, 1983; the same authors' *The Making of Modern London, 1914–1939*,

1984; and Steve Humphries and John Taylor's *The Making of Modern London, 1945–1985*, 1986) offer an excellent stab at the subject. On the growth of Outer London and its architecture, T C Barker and Michael Robbins's two-volume *History of London Transport* (Allen & Unwin, 1975 and 1974 and Alan A Jackson's *Semi-Detached London* (Allen and Unwin, 1973) are always illuminating.

Index

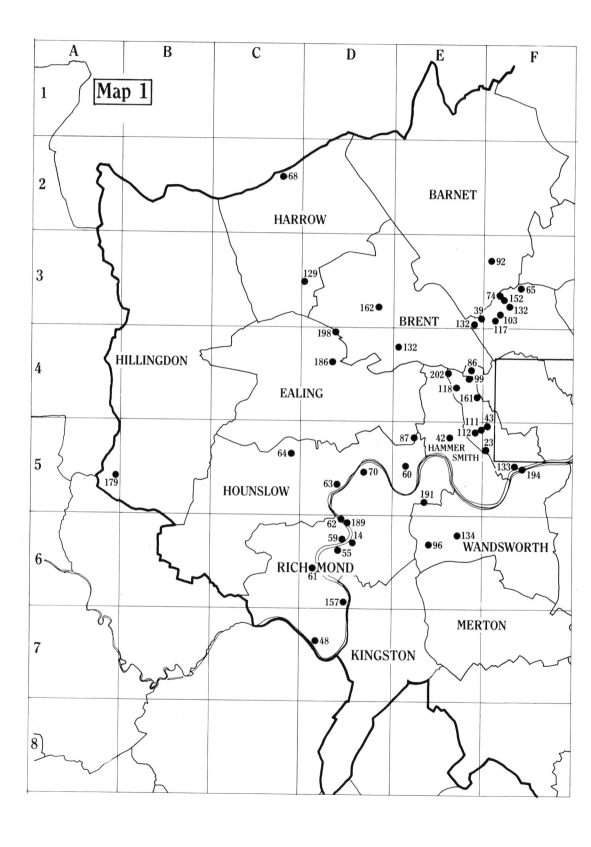

Map 1

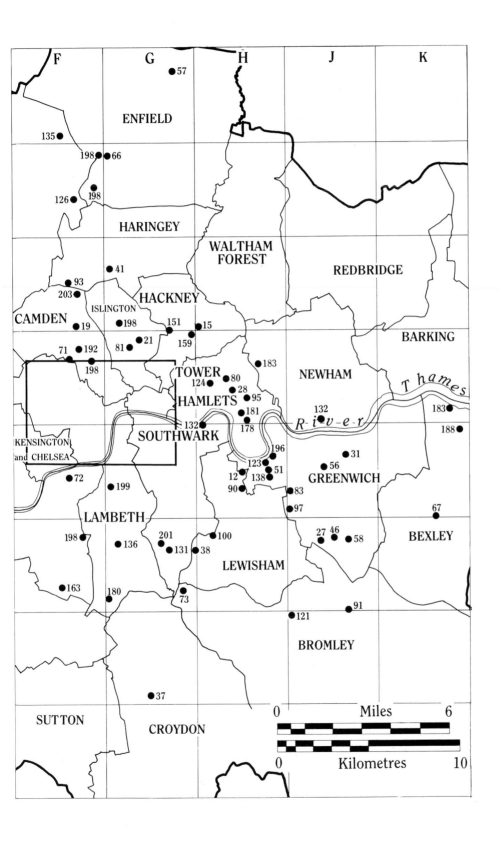

F G H J K

●57

ENFIELD

135●

198●●66

126● ●198

HARINGEY

WALTHAM
FOREST

REDBRIDGE

●41

93●
203●

HACKNEY

ISLINGTON

CAMDEN

●19 ●198 151● ●15

●192 ●21 159

71● ●81

198

BARKING

TOWER ●183

124● ●80

28 NEWHAM

95

HAMLETS 181● 132 183●

132● 178

SOUTHWARK R-i-v-e-r 188●

Thames

KENSINGTON
and CHELSEA

196●

123● ●31

72● 12 138 51 ●56

199● 90● GREENWICH

83● 67●

LAMBETH 97●

198● 201 ●100 27 46 BEXLEY

136● 131 38 ●58

LEWISHAM

163● 180●

73

●91

●121

BROMLEY

●37

SUTTON

CROYDON

0 Miles 6

0 Kilometres 10

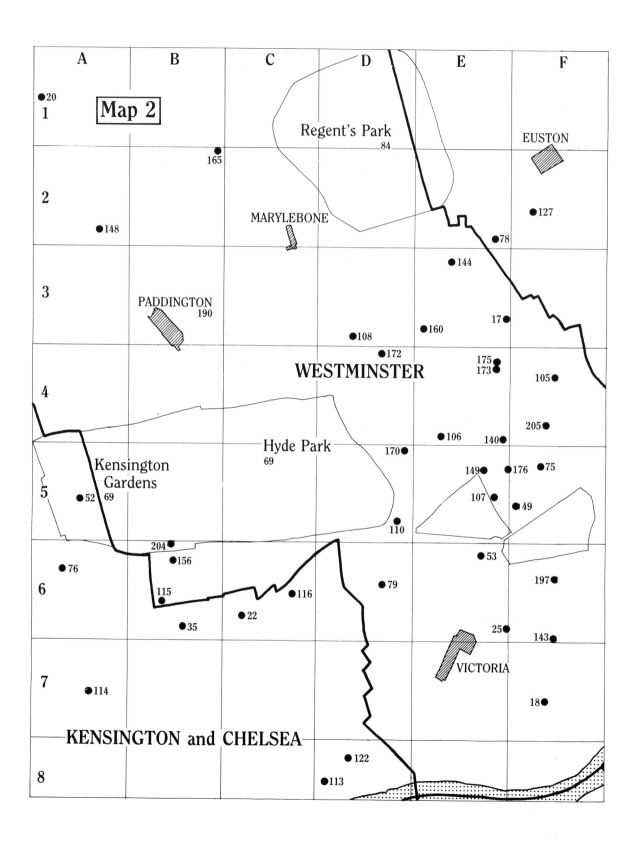

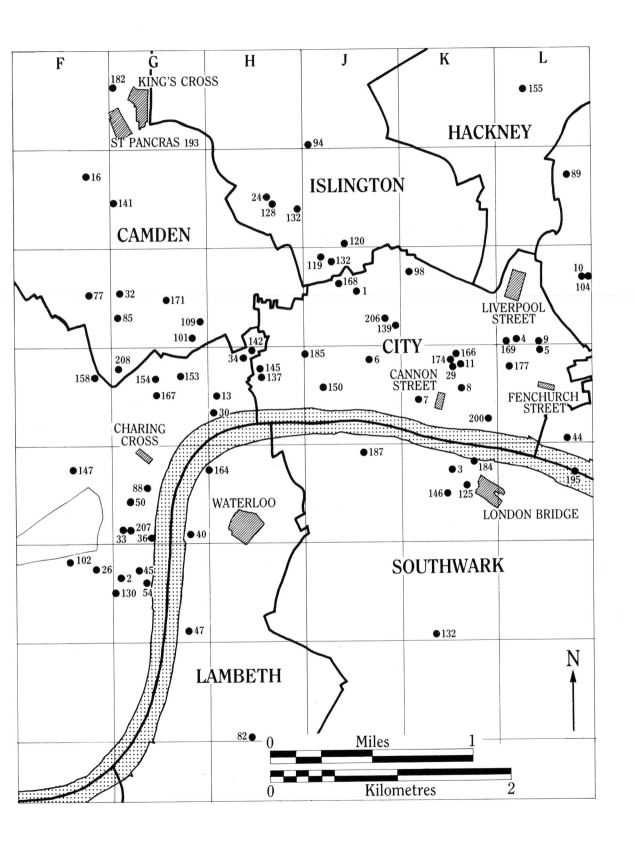

F   G   H   J   K   L

182 KING'S CROSS

155

ST PANCRAS 193

HACKNEY

16

141

24
128
132

89

ISLINGTON

CAMDEN

94

120

119 132

10
104

168

1

98

LIVERPOOL
STREET

77 32

171

206
139

85

109

101

CITY

4 9
169 5

142

185

6

174 166
11

177

34

208

145
137

CANNON
STREET

29

8

FENCHURCH
STREET

158

154 153

167

150

7

13

200

30

44

CHARING
CROSS

187

3 184

147

164

195

88

50

146 125

WATERLOO

LONDON BRIDGE

207
33 36

40

102

26

2 45

130 54

SOUTHWARK

47

132

N

LAMBETH

82

0   Miles   1

0   Kilometres   2